Writing Talk

Paragraphs and Short Essays

with Readings

Third Edition

Anthony C. Winkler

Jo Ray McCuen-Metherell

Glendale Community College

Upper Saddle River, New Jersey 07458

Library of Congress Cataloging-in-Publication Data

Winkler, Anthony C.
   Writing talk. Paragraphs and short eessays with readings / Anthony C.
Winkler, Jo Ray McCuen-Metherell. — 3rd ed.
      p.   cm.
   Includes index.
   ISBN 0-13-097886-8
   ISBN 0-13-045270-X
   1. English language—Paragraphs—Problems, exercises, etc.
2. English language—Rhetoric—Problems, exercises, etc.
3. English language—Grammar—Problems, exercises, etc.   4. Report
writing—Problems, exercises, etc.   5. College readers.   I. Title: Paragraphs
and short essays with readings.   II. McCuen-Metherell, Jo Ray.   III. Title.
PE1439.W55   2002
808′.0427—dc21   2002016990

Editor-in-Chief: Leah Jewell
Senior Acquisitions Editor: Craig Campanella
Editorial Assistant: Joan Polk
Production Liaison: Fran Russello
Prepress and Manufacturing Buyer: Ben Smith
Creative Design Director: Leslie Osher
Art Director: Ximena Tamvakopoulos
Cover and Interior Design: Wee Design group
Cover Image: Nicholas Wilton
Marketing Manager: Rachel Falk
Marketing Assistant: Christine Moody

This book was set in 11/13 New Century Schoolbook by
Publications Development Company of Texas and
was printed and bound by Courier Companies, Inc.
The cover was printed by Phoenix Color Corp.

10   9   8   7   6   5

ISBN 0-13-097886-8

Pearson Education LTD, *London*
Pearson Education of Australia PTY, Limited, *Sydney*
Pearson Education Singapore, Pte. Ltd
Pearson Education North Asia Ltd, *Hong Kong*
Pearson Education Canada, Ltd, *Toronto*
Pearson Educación de Mexico, S.A. de C.V.
Pearson Education—Japan, *Tokyo*
Pearson Education Malaysia, Pte. Ltd
Pearson Education, *Upper Saddle River, New Jersey*

Contents

PART 7   READINGS   531

Help for Your Reading   533

Narrating   536

Describing   545

Illustrating   556

Explaining a Process   565

Defining   571

Classifying   578

Comparing and Contrasting   584

Arguing   590

About the Authors

Anthony C. Winkler was born in Kingston, Jamaica, and educated at Mt. Alvernia Academy and Cornwall College in Montego Bay, Jamaica. In 1962, he came to the United States to attend school, and received an A.A. from Citrus College, and a B.A. and M.A. from California State University at Los Angeles.

For seven years, he taught as a part-time evening college instructor while working full time as a book representative first for Appleton Century Crofts, and then for Scott, Foresman.

Winkler began collaborating with Jo Ray McCuen in 1973, and became a fulltime freelance writer in 1976. He is the author of numerous textbooks, trade books (including Bob Marley: An Intimate Portrait by His Mother) and screenplays (including The Lunatic, based on his second novel). He lives in Atlanta with his wife and two children.

Jo Ray McCuen-Metherell was born in Belgium and grew up in Europe, coming to the United States for her college education. She received her B.A. from Pacific Union College and her M.A. and Ph.D. from the University of Southern California. While working on her doctorate, Jo Ray was hired to teach English at Glendale Community College, from which she retired in 1996.

A chance meeting in 1973 with Tony Winkler, who was a college textbook sales representative, led to a partnership that has produced fifteen coauthored textbooks used at colleges and universities across the country. "I have reached the place," says Jo Ray, "where I have difficulty remembering what I've said in what book."

Jo Ray has one son, David Cotton, a perinatologist at Wayne State University. When not revising her textbooks and writing new ones, Jo Ray enjoys traveling, reading, opera, snow skiing, and tennis.

Preface to the Third Edition

The third edition of *Writing Talk: Paragraphs and Short Essays with Readings,* like its predecessors, takes as its starting point the assumption that grammar for the native speaker is a *built-in skill,* not an added-on one, and that the best sense for grammar in the native speaker is the ear. People speak the language they hear spoken around them from birth. An English infant raised in a genteel drawing room will emerge from it speaking like an Englishman raised in a genteel drawing room. Transplant that same infant to an urban area like Brooklyn, and he will grow up to speak like someone raised in Brooklyn. We have never seen an exception to this observation. We learn to speak our mother tongue not from a book, but from using our ears.

As English teachers, we know that many of our students neither speak nor write what we have been trained to call "good grammar." Students use fragments; they punctuate badly; they misplace modifiers and garble sentences; they use the wrong case or tense; they speak and write slang. How can we say that a speaker's ear is the best sense of grammar when all around us we have evidence to the contrary?

The answer is simple: Much of the time these are not errors of bad grammar; instead, they are errors of inappropriate usage. If you are raised hearing *ain't* used everyday, you will grow using ain't in your speaking and writing. But because *ain't* is regarded as nonstandard and unacceptable usage in formal writing, it is our job as English teachers to wean students off that word when the circumstances demand the formality of standard English.

Usage variations aside, it is still a fact that all native speakers, as well as those who have spoken English for years, have within them an ear for grammar that students for whom English is a second language (ESL) do not share.

This assumption was thought by some to make previous editions of this book suitable only for native speakers and to exclude ESL students. But regardless of the differences between native speakers and ESL students, some school systems—many because of budgetary pressures—freely mix both populations in the same classroom, making no distinction between them. The upshot is that many teachers have asked us to include both groups, ESL students as well as native speakers. That is exactly what we have done in this third edition of *Writing Talk: Paragraphs and Short Essays with Readings.*

In coping with both audiences, we take a dual approach. We begin with a candid admission that ESL students and native speakers have different strengths. For the native speaker, the advantage is an ear that is finely attuned to the mother tongue. On the other hand, ESL students, who come to English as adults or near adults, often bring to the table a solid grounding in the grammatical basics of their adopted tongue. Gradually, as they progress in fluency, they will acquire what to the native speaker is a birthright, namely, an ear.

Until that happens, foreign speakers learning English often make mistakes in phrasing that would rarely, if ever, be made by a native speaker. For example, recently we overheard a foreign student say to another student who was about to take a test, "Have a good luck." This sentence is not ungrammatical; it is unidiomatic. But it is also the sort of sentence no native speaker would use. People say to one another, "good luck," all the time. But they never say, "Have a good luck."

On the other hand, a native speaker might write, "The men at the baseball park was talking throughout the game," confusing the prepositional phrase "at the baseball park" for the subject and making a classic subject verb agreement error. In short, both groups commonly make mistakes in English usage. But they make different mistakes.

With these differences in mind, we have adapted the pedagogy of this book to take into account many of the known difficulties that ESL students have with English as well as many of the common errors that all students make. Where appropriate, we issue an "ESL Advice" notice, alerting students that this particular usage is one that often troubles ESL students.

This dual approach is aimed at both audiences whose superficial differences cannot alter the fact that they have a common goal that this book can help them reach: namely, mastery of English.

There are occasions when, no matter what the background of the student, the ear is at odds with the formal rule and of no help whatsoever in deciding what is right and appropriate. A case in point is the infamous *between you and I*. Although used by a surprising array of prominent men and women in the media, this construction is incorrect. Yet the right form, *between you and me,* often sounds wrong. We flag such cases with a unique feature of the *Writing Talk* series, namely, an Ear Alert warning. We first explain the formal rule to both the ESL and the native student; we then show how its practice in everyday speech varies from the rule. Finally, the Ear Alert distinctive icon in the margin warns everyone that this is a point of grammar on which no one's ear can be fully trusted.

Writing Talk: Paragraphs and Short Essays with Readings is the second book in a series of two, and it has the following features:

- *Common Myths and Standard Written English.* We dispel some common and discouraging myths that students believe about writing. Writing is hard for everybody (no doubt rare exceptions exist, but we can't think of any offhand). We also know that the fumbling and revision that goes with writing is not a sign of ineptness, but a universal condition of the discipline. Many students do not understand how difficult writing is and tend to misinterpret the normal tedium of composing as a sign that they cannot write.
- *Paragraph Writing.* We break down the paragraph into its principal parts, discussing at length the topic sentence and supporting

details. We then discuss the importance of sticking to the point and linking sentences for coherence. A unique feature of this book, and one in keeping with its rationale, is its discussion of the paragraph and talking, where we show how a spoken paragraph differs from a written one and encourage students to use their "ear for language" to help their writing. The kind of advice we dispense is universal and applicable to everyone who wants to write English. In addition, for ESL students, we clarify potential problems either through an ESL Advice flag or in the textual explanation.

- *Rhetorical Strategies.* The discussion of rhetorical strategy is presented under three headings: "What Am I Trying to Do?" "How Can I Do it?" and "What Do I Need to Look Out For?" To counter the negative attitude that students sometimes have regarding the practicality of English writing assignments, every unit in this section begins with an example of how the particular rhetorical strategy might be used in a real example.

- *The Whole Essay.* Here we present the essay as a template, showing students exactly how an essay is written by breaking it down into three major parts—the introduction, the body, and the conclusion—with specific advice on the writing of each part, regardless of the topic.

- *The 20 Most Common Sentence Errors.* This section reviews the errors we've seen students make most frequently in their writing—from fragments and run-ons to unnecessary commas and misspelled words. Our explanation of grammar in this section of the book (1) emphasizes functional problems, not descriptive grammar; (2) uses minimal terminology; (3) gives short, pointed explanations with a light touch; (4) is followed by immediate practice; and (5) includes abundant exercises.

New to This Edition

This edition begins with a new first chapter, "The ESL Student and the Native Speaker," which outlines the differences between these two groups and presents a blueprint of how this book addresses their respective needs. All the well-known features that users of earlier editions particularly liked have been kept: Every chapter still has a *Talk-Write Assignment* that gives students practice in translating oral dialogue into its written formal equivalent. Each assignment presents a dialogue that might be overheard in an informal discussion and then asks students to write the equivalent in a more formal style. The new edition ends most chapters with the following four types of exercises:

- A *Unit Test* that tests mastery of the chapter. This is now a feature of virtually every unit.
- A *Unit Talk Write Assignment* that reinforces the difference between spoken and written language.
- A *Collaborative Writing Assignment* that gives students an opportunity to interact in group sessions and puts their ears to use in practicing the contents of the chapter.

- A *Unit Writing Assignment* that gives students a chance to apply the writing principles they have just learned.
- A *Photo Writing Assignment* that asks students to write on a topic suggested by a photograph.

We have made other changes and improvements as well. We have added more exercises throughout the book, but selectively, based on feedback from users. Instructors know the value of repetitive exercises as a learning technique—in this book we call them *practicings,* but also understand that exercises and drills walk a fine line between usefulness and tedium. Each chapter now has more numerous and varied exercises that reinforce every concept taught. We have tried to write exercises that are interesting to do and require a variety of responses. Every chapter now ends in a *Unit Test,* which asks students questions about the major concepts they have learned from the unit.

We have also changed our textual explanations, broadening them to take into account ESL students and their particular needs in learning English. Always, we've tried to be simpler and more direct, and where the opportunity presents itself, to add some humor to what might otherwise seem to the student to be a typically grim exposition of grammatical principles. Teaching grammar is a serious enterprise, but it does not deserve the graveyard sobriety of tone it is so often given.

The readings in this second book, *Writing Talk: Paragraphs and Short Essays with Readings,* unlike the first, are arranged rhetorically to give students authentic examples of how writers actually use the strategies. Grouped under the eight rhetorical strategies taught in the book—"Narrating," "Describing," "Illustrating," "Explaining a Process," "Defining," "Classifying," "Comparing and Contrasting," and "Arguing," the readings are, as before, multicultural and multiethnic. This section begins with an introduction, "Help for Your Reading," giving practical, nuts-and-bolts advice on the techniques of reading. The readings range from a funny process piece—"How I Was Bathed" by Sri Lankan writer Michael Ondaatje—to "Daddy Tucked the Blanket," a wrenching narration by an African-American writer who observed the painful unraveling of his parents' marriage. Three of these readings are new to this edition, each selected because of its appeal to this audience of students.

Each essay is prefaced by a headnote and followed by comprehension questions (Understanding What You Have Read) and thought-provoking questions (Thinking About What You Have Read). Finally, two Writing Assignments are included for each reading.

Throughout both books, we have tried to make our explanations simple and concise, to explain everything step-by-step, to provide exercises immediately after the introduction of any rule or principle, and to respect and encourage the student's innate "ear" for grammar while clearly explaining the underlying rule for those ESL students who are still struggling with the perplexities of idiomatic English. Instructors who use both books in sequence should note that there are no overlapping exercises between them, that each book, even in its coverage of the same topic, contains entirely different exercises. Students who work through the first book will therefore find the second one just as challenging.

Our thanks to Craig Campanella, senior acquisition editor at Prentice Hall, who oversaw this revision, and to the production and manufacturing staff at Prentice Hall.

We would also like to thank the following reviewers: Beverly Burch, Vincennes University; Joseph Booker, Palo Alto College; Toria Norman, Black Hawk College; Karen Jorgensen, Five Town College; John Panza, Cuyahoga Community College; and Kathleen Winter, Morehead State University.

Every writer needs an editor, and over the years it has been our good fortune to have assigned to us editors of sensitivity and insight, who have helped us every step of the way. In this edition, our good shepherd was Sylvia Weber, who stood diligent watch over everything we did and kept at bay the wolves of complacency and carelessness. She guided us in the revision with humor and thoroughness and was there to steady us at every misstep. We gratefully acknowledge her help. Because of her efforts, this new edition is a better book.

Anthony C. Winkler

Jo Ray McCuen-Metherell

Instructor's Teaching Package:

- **Instructor's Edition ~ ISBN 0-13-045270-X.** For the first time WRITING TALK has an Instructor's Edition. The IE contains in-text answers and to help instructors best prepare for class, and a 48-page built-in instructor's guide bound directly into the back of the Instructor's Edition. The Instructor's Guide provides sample syllabi, teaching tips, additional chapter-specific assignments, and selected answers to in-depth exercises from the text. Free to adoptors.
- **Test Bank ~ ISBN 0-13-045281-5.** The WRITING TALK: PARAGRAPHS AND SHORT ESSAYS 3E Test Bank provides additional chapter-specific tests for instructors. Available in print or downloadable format. Free to adoptors.

Student's Learning Package:

PH WORDS: An internet-based assessment tool like no other in the Basic Writing market, PH WORDS provides students with summary instruction and practice on each element of basic writing. PH WORDS includes over 100 learning modules covering the writing process, para-graph and essay development, and grammar. For each module, students have access to:

- **Watch** Screens, which provide an audio and animated summary of the content.
- **Recall** Questions, which test student's comprehension of the concept.
- **Apply** Questions, which test student's ability to identify the con-cepts in existing writing.
- **Write** Questions, which prompt students to demonstrate their knowledge of the concept in their own writing.

    This technology solution frees up class time by allowing stu-dents to work on their areas of weakness on their own. The soft-ware measures and tracks student's progress through the course with an easy to use management system. PH WORDS is available at a discount when packaged with the text. Contact your local Prentice Hall representative or visit www.prenhall.com/phwords for more information.

Student Answer Key ~ ISBN 0-13-045282-3. For the first time WRITING TALK will have a student answer key available. This answer key will provide answer to selected exercises in the text, and is available free when packaged to the textbook. Contact your local Prentice Hall representative for a package ISBN.

Companion Website ~ www.prenhall.com/winkler. The Compan-ion Website allows students to gain a richer perspective and a deeper understanding of the concepts and issues discussed in WRITING TALK: PARAGRAPHS AND SHORT ESSAYS 3E. This site is free to all students. Features of this site include:

- Chapter objectives that help students organize concepts.
- Online quizzes which include instant scoring and coaching.

- Essay questions that test students' critical thinking skills.
- Built-in routing that gives students the ability to forward essay responses and graded quizzes to their instructors.

The New American Webster Handy College Dictionary, Third Edition ~ ISBN 0-13-032870-7. Your students can receive a **free** *New American Webster Handy College Dictionary* packaged with their text when you adopt *WRITING TALK: PARAGRAPHS AND SHORT ESSAYS 3E*. This dictionary has over 1.5 million Signet copies in print and over 115,000 definitions, including current phrases, slang, and scientific terms. It offers more than 1,500 new words, with over 200 not found in any competing dictionary and features boxed inserts on etymologies and language. Ask your Prentice Hall sales representative package ISBN.

English: Evaluating Online Sources ~ ISBN 0-13-049620-0. This completely revised guide, available summer 2002, helps students develop the critical thinking skills needed to evaluate online sources critically. This supplement is available FREE when packaged with the text.

The Prentice Hall ESL Workbook ~ ISBN 0-13-092323-0: This 138-page workbook is designed for use with a developmental English textbook to improve English grammar skills. Divided into seven major units, this workbook provides thorough explanations and exercises in the most challenging grammar topics for non-native speakers. With over 80 exercise sets, this guide provides ample instruction and practice in: Nouns, Articles, Verbs, Modifiers, Pronouns, Prepositions, and Sentence Structures. The PH ESL WORKBOOK also contains: an annotated listing of key ESL internet sites for further study and practice, an answer key to all the exercises so students may study at their own pace, and a glossary for students to look up difficult words and phrases.

The Prentice Hall Grammar Workbook ~ ISBN 0-13-042188-X: This 21-chapter workbook will be a comprehensive source of instruction for students who need additional grammar, punctuation and mechanics instruction. Covering topics like subject-verb agreement, conjunctions, modifiers, capital letters, and vocabulary, each chapter provides ample explanation, examples, and exercise sets. The exercises contain enough variety to ensure student's mastery of each concept. Available to students stand alone or packaged with the text at a discount. Available Fall 2002.

The Prentice Hall TASP Writing Study Guide ~ ISBN 0-13-041585-5: Designed for students studying for the Texas Academic Skills Program test this guide prepares students for the TASP by familiarizing them with the elements of the test and giving them strategies for success. The authors provide practice exercises for each element of the writing and multiple choice portions of exam, and the guide ends with a full-length practice test with answer key so students can judge their own progress.

Ask your local Prentice Hall representative for information about ever-growing list of supplements for both instructors and students.

1

The ESL Student and the
Native Speaker

"Having an ear for the language means that you're usually able to tell when something doesn't sound right even though you can't say why."

Language typically consists of two main parts: sounds and rules. Its sounds are the way the language is spoken—its **pronunciation.** Its rules are its **grammar.** Of course, part of learning a language involves mastering the rules. But odd as it may seem, if you are a native speaker you already know, and correctly observe, many rules of the language simply because of the way it sounds. For example, do you see anything wrong with this sentence?

She will speaking with you be later.

You probably said that the verb "be" was out of place. The sentence should have read,

She will be speaking with you later.

This is just one example of a basic truth: You know more about your language than you think. For instance, did you realize that you know what the future progressive tense is? If you say you don't, you're wrong. The construction "she will be speaking" is in the future progressive tense. If you haven't spoken it today, you probably will later. It is a very complex tense, yet nearly every day you use it flawlessly as you do many other tenses. You do not need to know the formal definition of a preposition to correctly use one. Practically no native speaker would make this mistake:

I put book the table on.

1

It does not look right. But more important, it just does not sound right. Whether or not you know the formal rule that the preposition comes before the object it modifies, you still practice it. And you do that entirely by the way the construction sounds—strictly by ear.

Differences Between a Native and an ESL Student

We bring this up to help explain the difference that exists between a native speaker of English and the ESL (English as a Second Language) student. Both can learn to master English by using this book. But although both have the same goal—to learn to speak and write English well—they do not begin at the same place and therefore cannot learn English the same way. The main difference between them is this: The native speaker, from having heard English spoken since birth, has an ear for it. Having an ear for a language means that you're usually able to tell when something doesn't sound right even though you can't say why. Nearly all native speakers have this ability. It exists even if they mainly speak a dialect of the language. Most native speakers, for example, will automatically say "If I were you" without knowing the formal rule behind that expression. If an ESL student says, "If I were you," it is most likely because he or she has learned the formal rule of the subjunctive.

ESL students, in short, face different challenges than do native speakers. Indeed, the difficulties most ESL students have with learning English generally fall into these three broad categories: pronunciation, grammar, and idioms.

Pronunciation

Many words in English take on a different meaning depending on how they are pronounced. From experience, native speakers know, recognize, and use these differences almost instinctively. For example, place the emphasis on the first syllable of the word *present* and it means "a gift," as in "Thank you for that terrific birthday present," or a time period as in "There's no time like the present." However, place the emphasis on the second syllable of *present* and it means "to introduce," as in "Ladies and gentlemen, I would like to present the President of the United States." Another example is the word *invalid*. If spoken with an emphasis on the second syllable, this word means "legally flawed" as in the sentence, "Her check was invalid." But when the emphasis is on the first syllable, *invalid* means "a sick person."

Here are some other examples of meanings that depend purely on sound:

The lovely white <u>dove</u> flew from a branch just as I <u>dove</u> into the river.

Nancy was <u>close</u> to fainting, so the nurse asked that we <u>close</u> the door.

The <u>wind</u> was so powerful that the sailors could not <u>wind</u> the sails.

Many other examples of words that shift their meanings with sound can be found in English.

PRACTICING 1

Working in a small group, explain the difference in the meanings of the underlined words in the following sentences.

1. His parents expected him to <u>progress</u> in college and to receive a good <u>progress</u> report.

   _____

2. He was too <u>deliberate</u> to <u>deliberate</u> thoughtlessly.

   _____

3. They <u>project</u> the <u>project</u> to cost nearly a million dollars.

   _____

4. The <u>bass</u> opera singer went fishing for <u>bass</u> in the lake.

   _____

5. The <u>entrance</u> to the garden was decorated so as to <u>entrance</u> visitors.

   _____

6. They propose to <u>house</u> the visiting scouts in the headmaster's <u>house</u>.

   _____

7. With careful planning, they managed to <u>envelope</u> the plot in an <u>envelope</u> of secrecy.

   _____

8. He uses up all <u>proceeds</u> from the banquets and then <u>proceeds</u> to pack his clothes.

   _____

9. They agreed to <u>reject</u> every <u>reject</u> from last year's applying class.

   _____

10. The delegates <u>bow</u> to the princess who wears a pink <u>bow</u> around her waist.

    _____

Homonyms

Occasionally two words may sound alike but have different meanings. Such words are called **homonyms.** Here are some examples with the homonyms underlined.

> They're much too difficult for the students. Their homes are out of town. Place the book over there.

> Give the peach to your brother. He owns two motorcycles. I too love cats.

> You're about to win $300. Have you checked with your boss?

In the case of homonyms, however, the spelling always determines the meaning.

PRACTICING 2

Circle the correct homonym in parentheses.

1. Her classroom behavior landed her in the (principle's, principal's) office.

2. When Ani got married, her father proudly walked her down the (isle, aisle).

3. Some times it feels good to (bear, bare) your soul.

4. The (assent, ascent) to the top of Mount Everest was deadly.

5. We need another long (board, bored) to make a picnic table.

6. Is it true that (your, you're) favorite dessert is peanut butter pie?

7. That loud rock music is really testing my (patience, patients).

8. Don't let another selfish person (brake, break) your heart.

9. When did they return all of those gorgeous wedding (presents, presence)?

10. We (new, knew) him as Billy the Bully.

Context

Some words, though spelled and pronounced the same way, will still take on different meanings depending on the **context** in which they're used. Consider these examples:

The burglar was shot by the police.

After the sales meeting, my whole day was shot.

He gave me a shot of whiskey.

Most native speakers would immediately grasp from the context the different meanings of *shot* in these sentences. In the first example, *shot* means gunshot; in the second, it means ruined; in the third, it means measure or portion. Depending on how much or how little English they know, many ESL students would find these different meanings baffling.

Here are some other examples of words whose meanings change with context.

When he heard the news, he went into *shock.*
His freckled face was topped by a *shock* of red hair.

Let me just *lie* here on the green grass.
What that man just told you is a big *lie.*

In the first example, *shock* means a heavy blow of some kind; in the second, it means a thick mass. In its first use, *lie* means to be in a reclining position; in the second, it means an untruth.

PRACTICING 3

Working with a partner, define the underlined words whose meanings change with context.

1. Be careful when you <u>cross</u> the road./She has her own <u>cross</u> to bear.

_____

2. They were married one month after they were <u>engaged</u>./The two countries <u>engaged</u> in war.

_____

3. He played the clarinet in a brass <u>ensemble</u>./She wore a stunning velvet <u>ensemble</u>.

_____

4. She was carrying a <u>parcel</u>./He told the girls to <u>parcel</u> out the treats.

_____

5. He threatened to <u>beat</u> her up her if she did not give him the money./I love the <u>beat</u> of her latest record.

_____

6. Their <u>spirits</u> were broken by constant harassment./She said she never drank any hard <u>spirits</u>.

_____

7. They looked for a home that would be <u>safe</u> from earthquakes./Keep your gold coins in a <u>safe</u>.

_____

8. The geology lecture was <u>hard</u>./She said she adored <u>hard</u> candy.

_____

9. Her opinions are usually <u>objective</u>./Their <u>objective</u> is to complete the barn by winter.

_____

10. The landlord <u>left</u> in a huff./Turn <u>left</u> at the light.

_____

Grammar

English grammar is a difficult subject. Even professional grammarians often disagree about its rules, many of which sometimes seem ridiculous. The native speaker, who may know no more grammar than the ESL student, at least has the advantage of being able to recognize the usual and customary place for nouns and verbs in a sentence. It is the rare native speaker, for example, who would say, "I to the store now go," putting the verb in the wrong place. Likewise, native speakers are unlikely to make prepositional errors such as saying, "Peggy stayed her room," leaving out the preposition "in." Of course, native speakers do make grammatical errors. They're just likely to make errors of a different kind.

On the other hand, the proper use of prepositions and articles often baffles ESL students. An ESL student might say, "I must run to store," leaving out the "the," an error a native speaker is unlikely to make. Yet another difficulty often encountered by ESL students is in the use of pronouns. A pronoun is a word that takes the place of a noun. ESL students tend to omit pronouns as in the sentence, "The students shouted when won the football game," leaving out the pronoun "they." Another tendency that ESL students have is to use both a noun and a pronoun referring to the noun in the same sentence, as in "My boss she increased my hourly pay." The ear of most native speakers would immediately detect this error.

Many foreign students, especially those from countries like China, Japan, and Russia, where the grammar of the native language is totally different from English grammar, find it hard to write English correctly. We have had students complain in mournful tones, "I go over my writing again and again to make sure that I have corrected all grammar errors, but my teacher always finds more." Yet many millions of immigrants have arrived in America knowing absolutely no English and still mastered it sufficiently not only to survive, but to prosper.

In this book, we will teach English grammar while addressing the basic differences between the ESL student and native speaker. When we come across a usage that ESL students are known to have trouble with, we will issue an **ESL Advice** warning to be particularly careful. We will then follow up that warning with numerous drills. When the ear is an unreliable guide to a particular usage, we will issue an **Ear Alert,** warning the native speaker that the rule must be masteed.

Both populations should benefit from this dual approach. The native speaker, who has the ear but probably lacks a grounding in the formal rules, will benefit from the extra drills. On the other hand, the ESL student, who may lack the ear but is getting solid training in the formal rules, will gradually become familiar with ordinary idiomatic usage. In either case, the goal is the same: to learn to write and speak English better. And in both cases, whoever you are, if you apply yourself to this book, you will reach this goal.

PRACTICING 4

Using your ear or your grasp of the rules, correct the grammar of the following sentences. If the sentence is correctly written, mark a *C* beside it.

Example: _____ Soon I must go bed. (Soon I must go **to** bed.)

1. _____ When he was young, my father never go to school.

_____

2. _____ How can you believe such terrible lie?

_____

3. _____ Most Americans are proud of their many freedoms.

_____

4. _____ Last week I buyed a new car.

_____

5. _____ Mary should watch her wallet or it will be stealed.

_____

6. _____ Did you preregister at the Admissions Office?

_____

7. _____ By watching television, you can learn about many foreign country.

_____

8. _____ Which season of the year be your favorite?

_____

9. _____ Erica likes the pizza I baked.

_____

10. _____ When she shopping, she feels happy.

_____

Idioms

An **idiom** is a phrase or expression that means something different from what it seems to say. For example, the sentence "That guy is a fish out of water" does not mean the person being described actually resembles a beached tuna. It means, instead, that the person is in an uncomfortable position. Likewise, to say "I felt my heart leap into my mouth" does not mean that the speaker's heart suddenly became a jumper. Rather, it means that the speaker was terrified. Native speakers immediately get these meanings; ESL students may or may not, depending on their familiarity with such idioms.

To the ESL student, idioms can be a nightmare. The problem is that while there is sometimes a natural logic to an idiom, just as often there is not. For example, to say that someone is a "fifth wheel"—meaning unnecessary—immediately brings to mind an image of uselessness, which is exactly what a fifth wheel would be, giving a natural logic to that particular expression. But what does "kick the bucket"—which means die—have to do with dying? No doubt, there was once a logical connection between the two. But it has long been lost to most of us. What we are left with is an expression that is common in conversational English but means something totally different from what its individual words would suggest. That is the trademark of an idiom.

It is not only the colorful phrases of idioms that ESL students find troublesome. What is also hard for them is learning how words are customarily grouped to make up conversational expressions. For example, we heard a foreign student say to another who was about to take a test, "Have a good luck!" What the student meant was clear, and there was nothing ungrammatical about what she had said. It's just that no native speaker would ever phrase it that way. What a native speaker would've said was, "Good luck!" Another example: An ESL student wrote in an essay, "I altered my mind on this question," whereas a native speaker would write, "I changed my mind on this question." The phrase "altered my mind" is not technically wrong; however, it is unidiomatic.

Here is a letter written by a European travel agent to an American client:

> I have received your dated fax May 3. I communicate to you that we are in accord on the appointment for Friday, May 25. We request you contact us the same day to be at the hour that is convenient. The place of the appointment, if you believe it opportune, can be in our office. Receive a cordial greeting as we transmit our best wishes.
>
> Manuel Ortega

No word in this brief letter is misspelled, and the grammar is not wrong. Still, the letter sounds foreign because the writer has not mastered idiomatic English. Rewritten in everyday English, the letter might sound like this:

> I received your fax dated May 3 and wish to confirm our appointment on Friday, May 25. We ask that you contact us on that day to

arrange for a convenient meeting time. If you don't mind, we can meet in our office.

Cordially, sending our best wishes,

Manuel Ortega

Yet as difficult as it might be, with practice and exposure to conversational English, ESL students will gradually gain a mastery over the idioms of their adopted language.

PRACTICING 5

In the space provided, check the sentence that is in idiomatic English.

1. _____ (a). Once in a blue moon my sister writes me a letter.

   _____ (b). Once on the blue moon my sister writes me a letter.

2. _____ (a). All of us were terribly bored from the movie.

   _____ (b). All of us were terribly bored by the movie.

3. _____ (a). I wish you would get the lead out of your pants and finish the job.

   _____ (b). I wish you would take the lead from your clothes and finish the job.

4. _____ (a). She looks like the spit of her mother.

   _____ (b). She is the spitting image of her mother.

5. _____ (a). He hung off the phone in her ear.

   _____ (b). He hung up the phone in her ear.

6. _____ (a). My sister is forever on the go.

   _____ (b). My sister on the go is forever.

7. _____ (a). The essay he wrote is inferior to Martha's essay.

   _____ (b). The essay he wrote is inferior of Martha's essay.

8. _____ (a). No matter how educated, one should never talk down to other people.

   _____ (b). No matter how educated, one should never speak under other people.

9. _____ (a). Jim has never stopped living high on the hog.

   _____ (b). Jim has never stopped living on top of a hog.

10. _____ **(a).** I have awful hunger.

_____ **(b).** I am awfully hungry.

PRACTICING 6

In the lines provided, write the meanings of the following idiomatic sentences.

1. He washed his hands of the problem.

_____

2. What a rat he turned out to be!

_____

3. That accusing look of his gives me goose bumps.

_____

4. When she was sixteen, her stomach was flat as a pancake.

_____

5. Frankly, my economics teacher bores me to death.

_____

6. Let's bury the hatchet and revive our friendship.

_____

7. He warned us that he would drop a bombshell at the meeting.

_____

8. I could tell by looking at her that the lights were on, but nobody was home.

_____

9. She was simply drop dead gorgeous.

_____

10. She is as slow as molasses.

_____

11. At the crack of dawn they packed up their sleeping bags.

_____

12. So, what's the bottom line?

_____

13. She spends money as if it were water.

_____

 **Unit Test**

From each pair of sentences, check the sentence that is correct.

Example: ___✔___ **(a).** Native speakers often have an ear for correct language but often don't know the rules.

_____ **(b).** Non-native speakers usually have a better ear for correct English than do native speakers.

1. Having an ear for the language means that

_____ **(a).** you're usually able to tell when something doesn't sound right.

_____ **(b).** you have a talent for learning new languages.

2. _____ **(a).** Language typically consists of sounds and rules.

_____ **(b).** Languages are never based on grammar or pronunciation.

3. _____ **(a).** The native speaker does not need to learn correct grammar.

_____ **(b).** The ESL student often knows the rules of grammar better than does the native speaker.

4. _____ **(a).** Pronunciation is the way a word sounds.

_____ **(b).** Pronunciation is the way a word is spelled.

5. _____ **(a).** The word "wind" is always pronounced the same way in the United States.

_____ **(b).** The meaning of "wind" depends on how it is pronounced.

6. Homonyms are words that

_____ **(a).** sound alike but have different meanings.

_____ **(b).** originate from hymns.

7. _____ **(a).** Professors of grammar often disagree about grammar rules.

_____ **(b).** Professors of grammar show complete unity where grammar is concerned.

8. _____ **(a).** The sentence "I love to look at moon" is grammatically correct.

_____ **(b).** The sentence "I love to look at moon" is grammatically incorrect.

9. The statement "I don't give a fig" is

_____ **(a).** an exaggeration.

_____ **(b).** an idiom.

10. When your ear fails to give you the correct English,

_____ **(a).** you may receive help from extra drills.

_____ **(b).** assume that the rule is unimportant.

Unit Talk-Write Assignment

An ESL student (first student) and a native speaker (second student) have a talk about English. Correct any mistakes you find in any of the sentences. Rewrite any you think are too idiomatic to be understood by a foreign speaker familiar only with textbook English.

TALK

First student: I went to party last night.

Second student: I hit the books hard.

First student: I don't understand. You strike your books?

Second student: You're losing it, man. I didn't strike nothing. I hit the books.

First student: What am I losing? I said I went to party last night. You tell me you strike books.

WRITE

_____

_____

_____

_____

_____

_____

_____

_____

_____

_____

_____

_____

_____

_____

_____

_____

TALK

Second student: You're in over your head, man. I studied last night. That's what I meant by hitting the books. I studied prepositions. I was up to my armpits in prepositions.

First student: What do prepositions have to do with armpits?

Second student: I was drowning in them, is what I'm saying.

First student: You drown in prepositions?

Second student: Yes. I had prepositions coming out of my ear.

First student: Is it possible?

Second student: For the whole weekend, I did nothing but eat, sleep, and dream prepositions. They nearly drove me around the bend.

First student: What bend?

WRITE

_____
_____
_____
_____
_____
_____
_____
_____
_____
_____
_____
_____
_____
_____
_____
_____
_____
_____
_____
_____
_____
_____
_____
_____
_____

TALK

Second student: That's OK, man. Leave it alone. I've had it with prepositions.

First student: Had what?

Second student: I'm outta here, man!

First student: Wait! Don't you want to hear about party last night?

Second student: I don't have the time now, man. You can tell me later when I'm not tied up. Then you can go on until the cows come home.

First student: Cows? Do you have cows in home?

Second student: I'm hitting the road. I don't have time for this.

First student: You must be angry. You're hitting everything in sight.

WRITE

_____

_____

_____

_____

_____

_____

_____

_____

_____

_____

_____

_____

_____

_____

_____

_____

_____

_____

_____

_____

_____

_____

_____

_____

_____

_____

_____

_____

TALK

Second student: Later alligator!

First student: Alligator? Where?

WRITE

_____

_____

_____

_____

_____

_____

_____

_____

Unit Collaborative Assignment

Get together with three other students. Take turns having one student read the questions that follow aloud to the other three in the group. One by one, each of the three students should respond casually and spontaneously to the questions, perhaps even using idiomatic expressions. The one who has asked the question will write down the answers given. After all four questions have been answered, sit down with the group and rewrite the answers in formal English, avoiding idiomatic expressions that might be confusing to ESL students.

1. What is the best way we can conserve energy in our generation?

2. What is your opinion of people who believe in astrological signs?

3. What are the social values taught by the most popular television series today?

4. What living human being do you admire most and why?

5. What is your opinion of using embryos to do stem-cell research?

Unit Writing Assignment

Write a paragraph in which you use at least three colorful idioms; then, write the same paragraph using straightforward language void of idioms. Indicate which paragraph you prefer and why.

Photo Writing Assignment

In this photo, people from another country are observing a custom or ceremony that is not observed in the United States. How do you think this particular observance would strike the average American? Do we have any equivalent that would seem equally odd to people from another country? Make a list of the features of this particular ceremony that you find most exotic. Make every item in your list a complete sentence.

Myths About Writing

If you can talk English, you can learn to write it. Indeed, you already know more about writing than you think. However, if you are like most students, you probably believe some common and harmful myths about writing—our own students often do. Most likely, you use these myths to belittle your natural writing skills.

If a myth leads you to think that you write badly, for example, you'll try to avoid writing. Since practice makes perfect in writing as in nearly everything else, if you avoid writing, you won't get any better at it. To think you are naturally bad at writing is to plant a nagging critic inside your head who will scold every sentence you write. No one works well with constant scolding; everyone works better if encouraged. Human nature swims on "You can!" and drowns on "You can't!"

Let us begin then with a discussion of some myths about writing and how believing them can stunt your growth as a writer.

Myths About Writing

A myth is a popular but false belief. Among the many myths that students believe about writing are the following:

- I have nothing to write about.
- I can't write the way you're supposed to—with big words and long sentences.
- Writing is hard only for me.

- English teachers are too picky.
- I hate to write because I make too many mistakes.

We will take up these myths one by one.

I have nothing to write about.

Anyone who's not dead has something to write about. All of us have opinions that can be used as writing topics. The problem is that students often think that only stuffy, academic topics are suitable for college essays.

You can, however, write about many topics that are neither academic nor stuffy. You can write about an everyday event in your life, such as dating, or an idea that interests you. You can write about a friend, a hobby, your job. You can tell about an exciting experience, a favorite teacher, a kindly aunt, or a cruel uncle. One student we know wrote a funny essay about a goldfish. Another wrote a moving essay about burying a hamster. Everyone alive is interested in something; that *something* is what you can write about.

To see that you do have ideas worth writing about, do the following activity, which we call "Practicing." Chances are that everyone in your group will be able to come up with an idea suitable for a paragraph.

PRACTICING 1

Form a group of three or four students. Choose one topic from the list that follows. Everyone in the group should take turns talking about the same topic.

1. A teacher I really like (or dislike)

2. A movie that should have won an Oscar but didn't

3. My mother's (or father's, sister's, brother's) best trait

4. My least favorite relative

5. How I choose my close friends

I can't write the way you're supposed to—with big words and long sentences.

The first aim of any writer is to communicate. If using big words and long sentences will get a message across, a writer will use them. Ask yourself, though, how often do big words and long sentences help anyone communicate? The answer is, almost never. Writers therefore use big words and long sentences only when small words and short sentences will not do the job. Small words and short sentences often make the point as well, if not better, than big words and long sentences.

Furthermore, few people like reading big words clumped together in jaw-breaking sentences. Understanding such writing simply takes too much effort. Look at the following passages, for example. Which one do you think is better written and easier to understand?

The audience was lachrymose at the termination of the drama, especially expressing a predilection for the heroine's experienced reunification with her long-lost progeny.

The audience was tearful at the end of the play. They especially liked when the heroine was reunited with her long-lost children.

The first passage consists of big words in one python-long sentence; the second uses simple words and two straightforward sentences. The second passage, by being direct and clear, is better than the first because it is easier to read and understand.

Directness and clarity: These are desirable qualities of good writing, not big words and long sentences. This book will teach you to write clearly, directly, and always understandably.

PRACTICING 2

Get together in a small group. Each student should choose one topic from the list that follows and "talk a paragraph" about it. Be as clear and direct as you can. You might want to scribble down a few ideas in advance.

1. My most valued personal possession

2. How to get to the nearest fast-food restaurant

3. Where I live

4. A piece of good advice

5. A piece of bad advice

Writing is hard only for me.

"I hate to write, but I love having written." So said Eudora Welty, a famous American writer whose works are widely read. The fact is that writing is hard for almost everyone. There are some rare exceptions, but for most of us, writing is one of the most difficult tasks we do. It is easy to scribble a note to leave on the refrigerator: "Roy, did you pay the rent? The landlord called." It is equally easy to send a friend a quick e-mail message, "Kelly, see you at the ball game." But writing that requires us to frame a complex thought, explain it in detail, and back it up with facts and opinions gives everyone trouble.

That writing is hard for everyone is a pesky fact but one that does not have to get in a writer's way. Trouble, however, crops up if you begin to believe that you're the only one who finds writing hard. The raw truth is simply this: Writing is hard work for the great, the near great, the professional, the amateur, for your Aunt Susie, your Uncle Albert, for me, and for you. If you accept that writing is difficult, you will at least begin with a realistic outlook. Say to yourself, "Writing is hard." Now, having admitted that, you can simply roll up your sleeves and get to work.

PRACTICING 3

Try your hand at some "easy writing." Write a refrigerator note on each of the following topics. Address it to someone specific, your apartment-mate or someone in your family. Keep the message short and to the point.

1. You're going to be late. Say why.

_____

_____

2. A phone message you took for someone.

_____

_____

3. Ask a roommate or family member to leave you money on the kitchen table.

_____

_____

4. You're doing something with a friend and won't be home for dinner. Tell who and what.

_____

_____

5. Apologize for something (for example, being a grouch this morning).

_____

_____

English teachers are too picky.

Everyone who has had an English class, even English teachers themselves, have felt this way at one time or another. But it is the role of the English teacher to be your editor, and any editor who is not picky is useless. By picky, students usually mean that their teacher finds many "small" mistakes. But what may seem a small mistake to you may lead your reader to misunderstand you. Here is an example. A former student of ours has recently begun writing for a free neighborhood newspaper. One of her articles contained the following sentences:

> When it comes to gambling; the professional is no better than the amateur. It might even be said that the amateur has a better chance; by not knowing the real risk involved.

Did you spot the mistake in these sentences? It is in the use of semicolons. Obviously, we should have picked at her more vigorously about punctuation than we did. This mistake may seem trivial to you, but it is no small mistake. Writers who repeatedly make it will find themselves ridiculed by fellow-reporters or misunderstood and may even find the way to promotion blocked. This is not to say that using a semicolon properly is an earthshaking skill; it isn't. But even such a small misuse can embarrass you and harm an otherwise promising career since most professions require some amount of writing. As an old Chinese proverb says, "People do not fall over mountains; they trip over pebbles."

PRACTICING 4

Here is a chance to exercise your skill at being picky. Each of the sentences below contain an error that our students have called "picky." Find and correct the error. If you need help, ask your teacher!

1. We're having pecan pie for desert.

   _____

2. Between you and I, the band was awful.

   _____

3. She is the most hardest worker.

   _____

4. For a man of his size; he is very quick.

   _____

5. I'm majoring in biology, I want to be a veterinarian.

   _____

6. She moved to Florida. Which really surprised me.

   _____

7. For a person to get ahead, you must work hard.

   _____

8. A doctor know best.

   _____

9. A lawyer should respect his client's confidentiality.

   _____

10. That car is her's.

   _____

I hate to write because I make too many mistakes.

Everyone who writes or talks makes mistakes occasionally. We came across this sentence, for example, in a scholarly book about the Civil War Union General William Tecumseh Sherman:

> When victory was achieved, however, [the army should] stop the bloodshed and destruction immediately and help those in need irregardless of any oaths of allegiance.

Irregardless is not a standard word. If you check your dictionary, you'll see that the author should have written *regardless*.

In speech every one of us has, at one time or another, mispronounced a word, addressed someone by a wrong name, or misspoken a common phrase. Mistakes in speech are so common that many even have names. Here, for example, is a **spoonerism,** a mistake where a speaker mixes up the beginnings of words:

> Will someone please hick up my pat?

Of course, what the speaker meant was, *Will someone please pick up my hat?*

Yet even if you do make the occasional mistake, you also know a great deal more about language than you think. This knowledge—sometimes called an *ear* for the language—comes naturally from the thousands of hours you have spent listening to and speaking English. Using your ear for language can help you with your writing. If you are an ESL student, you will find yourself gradually acquiring an ear for the language as you learn more English. In the beginning, however, your best bet is to master the rules of grammar in small doses until you're able to practice them in your own speech and writing. (We recommend small doses because most students find grammar dry and boring.) Reading as much in English as you can will also help you become familiar with the ordinary usages of the language.

Of course, ESL student or native speaker, you do not know everything about the language. English is so complex that very few people do. Like the rest of us, you have your weaknesses. However, you also have your strengths, and they are considerable. This book can help you use what you do already know by ear about language. What you don't know, this book can teach you. And if you are an ESL student, this book will teach you grammar in the recommended small doses.

Let us begin with what you know. Take the following quiz. We think you will be pleasantly surprised to find out how much you already know about English. (ESL students should also take the quiz even if they have to rely more on the rules of English than on their ear.)

PRACTICING 5

Using your ear for the language, make a ✔ in the space beside any sentence you think is incorrect. If you think the sentence is correct, leave the space blank.

1. _____ I love to sailing.

2. _____ Jamaica is a beautiful island.

3. _____ Uncle never went Vietnam.

4. _____ Between you and me, I'm very tired.

5. _____ He have a twitch because he is nervously.

6. _____ She a good poem writes.

7. _____ What should we have for dinner?

8. _____ I gived the man a dollar.

9. _____ Stay sitted in your chair, please.

10. _____ Jim is a faster talker than me is.

Here are the correct sentences:

1. I love sailing. Or I love to sail. (Omit the *to* or change to *to sail.*)

2. Jamaica is a beautiful island. (Correct as written.)

3. Uncle never went to Vietnam. (Should be *went to,* not *went.*)

4. Between you and me, I'm very tired. (Correct as written.)

5. He has a twitch because he is nervous. (Should be *has*; no *-ly* needed after nervous.)

6. She writes a good poem. (Original misplaced the verb *writes.*)

7. What should we have for dinner? (Correct as written.)

8. I gave the man a dollar. (*Gived* is not a word.)

9. Stay seated in your chair, please. (*Sitted* is not a word.)

10. Jim is a faster talker than I am. (Not *me is.*)

To sum up, don't approach writing as if it were a kind of communication utterly different from the talking you normally do. See it first as a kind of talking—but on paper. Remember that if you can speak English, you can use your ear to become a better writer. Bear in mind, also, that writing well is difficult not only for you, but for everyone else.

IN A NUTSHELL

There are five common myths about writing:

- I have nothing to write about.

- I can't write the way you're supposed to—with big words and long sentences.

- Writing is hard only for me.

- English teachers are too picky.

- I hate to write because I make too many mistakes.

PRACTICING 6

State what you believe to be the three most serious difficulties you have with writing. State each in a separate sentence.

1. _____

2. _____

3. _____

PRACTICING 7

Form a small group of three or four classmates and discuss the difficulties you have with writing and what you might do about them.

Standard English

If you can speak English well, why do you sometimes have trouble writing it? The answer is simple. Writing is, for the most part, done in standard English, which is not the English we commonly speak. The exception is the ESL student, who typically begins by studying standard English from the very outset and becomes exposed to idioms later. Native speakers, on the other hand, usually come to standard English through the backdoor, after having been steeped in conversational idioms.

Standard English is English that is universally accepted by dictionaries and respected authorities. It is the universal English that all people who speak and understand English can use to communicate. Just as plumbing pipes have standardized sizes and fittings, standard English has a standard vocabulary—no slang or street-talk—and a standard grammar. Without standards, English would become so regional that a New Yorker might have a hard time communicating with a Californian. With standard English, however, all who speak the language can make themselves understood, at least on one level.

Consider, for example, these pairs of sentences:

Standard: You understand?
Nonstandard: You dig?

Standard: The game was exciting.
Nonstandard: The game rocked.

Standard: You're joking.
Nonstandard: You jiving.

Realistically, which sentence in each pair do you think, say, a native Russian who also speaks English would more likely understand? The nonstandard sentences would be understandable only to those who have an ear for nonstandard English.

Even if you speak mainly nonstandard English, you also have an ear for standard English. Every day you hear it in television newscasts and read it in magazines and newspapers. Most publications, including the supermarket tabloids with their alien three-headed babies and prowling bigfoots, are written in standard English. In fact, you are more likely to read this standard English headline in a tabloid,

Alien Spacecraft Sighted!

than this nonstandard one,

Alien Spacecraft in the Hood!

Your ear cannot help you, however, with some finer points of standard English. For instance,

"Let's keep this news between you and I."

This commonly used construction, which probably sounds right to your ear, is actually wrong. The *I* is technically wrong. The correct sentence should read,

"Let's keep this news between you and me."

Yet practically every day we hear people say *between you and I.* In standard English, that is wrong.

As we said before, when we think we see a situation where your ear for spoken language might trick you, we will warn you with an **Ear Alert** such as this one. Likewise, we will issue **ESL Advice** when we think the complexity of a rule needs to be clearly understood.

To sum up, use your ear for the language to help you with your writing although bear in mind that sometimes your ear can mislead. To become the best writer you can be, you must also learn certain ground rules for written work. You must learn the rules of capitalization and punctuation. You must learn how to use prepositions correctly (*between you and me* not *between you and I*), adverbs (*I speak quickly* not *I speak quick*), and verbs (*seated* not *sitted*). You must learn how to organize your thoughts into paragraphs and how to assemble your paragraphs into a clear essay.

In short, you must learn some grammar as well as some techniques for writing paragraphs and short essays. This book will not only teach you grammar, it will also teach you how to use the paragraph to make a point and how to knit paragraphs together into an essay.

The good news is this: As a speaker of English you are already ahead in the race to learn these skills. Indeed, many of the skills you need to be a good writer you already practice in your everyday talking. You know much more than you think!

IN A NUTSHELL

- Standard English is English that is universally accepted by dictionaries and respected authorities.

- Even if you speak nonstandard English, you still have an ear for standard English.

- Your ear for English can usually help you with your writing. When it can't, this book will warn you.

PRACTICING 8

For each of the following pairs of sentences, check the one written in standard English.

1. _____ **(a).** It ain't necessarily so.

   _____ **(b).** It isn't necessarily so.

2. _____ **(a).** You can't hang that one on me.

   _____ **(b).** You can't blame that on me.

3. _____ **(a).** Stop hound-dogging me about money.

   _____ **(b).** Stop pestering me about money.

4. _____ **(a).** He doesn't care about it.

   _____ **(b).** He don't give a rap about it.

5. _____ **(a).** I bought the coolest earrings.

   _____ **(b).** I bought some very pretty earrings.

6. _____ **(a).** She's preparing to go to the beach.

   _____ **(b).** She's fixing to go to the beach.

7. _____ **(a).** There's too much chin music at those meetings.

   _____ **(b).** There's too much talking at those meetings.

8. _____ **(a).** They spared no expense for the party.

    _____ **(b).** They went whole hog for the party.

9. _____ **(a).** I went to the seashore to relax.

    _____ **(b).** I went to the seashore to chill out.

10. _____ **(a).** I was, like, feeling real mellow.

    _____ **(b).** I was feeling very calm.

PRACTICING 9

Below is an e-mail message written in everyday informal language by one student to another. Underline the words or phrases that are informal or nonstandard English. Then rewrite the paragraph in standard English.

Hey, Marcy What a blast to hear from you! I just been down here kicking around in the new hood, chilling out every day, and having a ball. My Mom's been cool about everything She hasn't been on my back even once about school work. It just goes to show you that the old lady is not as over the hill as I had thought. As for friends, so far I've got zip, zero, zilch. My love life is equally exciting. I met a couple dudes in the cafeteria, but, I mean, like, guys always think they're so hot. It makes me want to puke.. This one guy I met, like, every second word out of his mouth was "I, I, I, I." I felt like saying, "gimme a break, will ya?" Well, whatever. So what's new by you?

_____

_____

_____

_____

_____

_____

_____

_____

_____

PRACTICING 10

On a separate sheet of paper write two paragraphs on one of the topics that follow. In the first paragraph, feel free to use non-standard English. In the second use only standard English.

1. A personal desire

2. Portrait of someone I really admire

3. A time when I was lucky

4. A time when I was unlucky

5. Something that makes me laugh just thinking about it

Unit Test

In the blank provided, check the statement that most accurately represents the truth about writing.

Example: _____ **(a).** If a myth leads you to think you can't write, you'll simply try harder.

✔ **(b).** If a myth leads you to think you can't write, you'll avoid writing.

1. ✗ **(a).** To think you are bad at writing, helps you to write carefully.

   √ **(b).** To think you are bad at writing, is to feel constantly scolded when you write.

2. √ **(a).** A myth is a belief that is popular but false.

   √ **(b).** A myth is a religious truth.

3. √ **(a).** To be a good writer, you don't necessarily need to write about stuffy topics.

   _____ **(b).** While in college, you must write only about intellectual ideas.

4. _____ **(a).** Writing with big words and long sentences tells your audience you can write well.

   √ **(b).** Directness and clarity are what good writers aim for.

5. √ **(a).** Writing is difficult for almost everyone.

   ✗ **(b.)** A talented writer is one for whom writing is easy.

6. _____ **(a).** Writing a note to stick on the refrigerator requires complex thought.

   √ **(b).** Good writing requires hard work.

7. _____ **(a).** If you write well, you will make no mistakes.

__✓__ **(b).** Your ear for language can help you write.

8. __✓__ **(a).** Standard English is English that is universally accepted by authorities.

_____ **(b).** Standard English is not acceptable to dictionaries.

9. _____ **(a).** The expression "between you and I" is standard English.

__✓__ **(b).** The expression "between you and I" is not standard English.

10. __✗__ **(a).** *Irregardless* is a standard English word.

__✓__ **(b).** *Irregardless* is not a standard English word.

Unit Talk-Write Assignment

In this Talk Write exercise and the ones to follow, you are asked to convert a spoken paragraph into a more structured written one. The exercise is designed to apply your speech skills to your writing. To do the exercise, turn the spoken sentences into standard written English.

This particular assignment presents one student's comments during a class discussion about personality. Here is what the student actually said in response to the question, "What is the most interesting part of your personality?" Rewrite the casual spoken speech into standard English in the lines provided.

Spoken Paragraph

Actually, I'm sort of a funny guy, I guess. Mom always called me the clown of the family. Come to think of it, kids in grade school used to—I just think they did—look to me for monkey tricks—like giving smart alecky answers to questions asked by teachers. Some times I'd cross my eyes, bare my teeth, and stick out my tongue—just to look geeky, you know. The kids always laughed. I mean, I still play that role. Trouble is, I don't always feel like being funny. Some times I just want to tell everyone to bug off and leave me alone, but when you've gotten the reputation of goofy Joe, you kinda feel obligated, you know. It's like, you know, they're expecting you to make 'em laugh. Even you guys in this class put pressure on me, you know. The other day our psych teacher asked us to define *pessimist*. She probably expected some high-falutin answer from our textbook assignment, but I couldn't resist being the class joker by waving my hand high above my head as if I had the perfect answer. "Yes, Fred?" The teacher asked—and, of course, all heads jerked around as if to say, "O.K., goofball, say something funny ..." With triumph I belted out my dad's saying, "A pessimist is a guy who looks both ways when crossing a one-way street." Naturally, the class giggled, and some looked at the ceiling as if to say, "There goes that nut case." What can I tell you? I'm a total joker.

Written Paragraph

_____

_____

_____

_____

_____

_____

_____

_____

_____

_____

_____

_____

_____

_____

_____

_____

Unit Collaborative Assignment

Get together with a classmate and describe to him or her a time when you lacked self-confidence. Have the classmate ask you questions about the circumstances involved and how you felt. Then reverse roles and ask your partner about a situation in which he or she lacked self-confidence. Use your discussion to write a paragraph in standard written English. Your partner's description and answers to your questions may help you with your own writing.

Unit Writing Assignment

Write a paragraph about a time when you got something you wanted and found it wasn't as desirable as you thought. Use standard English. Here is how one student accomplished the assignment:

I always thought it would be wonderful to be in charge of our household. But when this opportunity actually came my way, the task proved extremely hard. For eight months while I was in high school, while my mother toured Iran, I was completely in charge of my dad's household. I was the woman of the house. I became a master of finding the right kinds of detergents and bathroom cleaners. I clipped supermarket coupons to get special discounts. I found a little Armenian market where I could buy fresh vegetables at modest prices. I even discovered that with the right amount of club soda I could get out any stain from our carpet. At three o'clock in the afternoon, when I came home from school, I would put away my books and put on my apron. Cookbooks no longer scared me because I learned to follow their instructions and make scalloped potatoes, stuffed grape leaves, and lamb kabobs. My dream had come true: I was in charge of my house. But I was not happy. First of all, I had no time for studying. Then too, as soon as my mother had left, my father began to brood and to keep himself away from me and my sister. He would leave at eight in the morning and come back at eight at night. I did my best to cook his favorite foods, hoping that it would cheer him up, but he continued to be sad. Then, one early September morning I received a surprising phone call from my mother. She said she would be home a month earlier. "Hooray!" I thought. At last I can lead a normal teenage life again—with Mother in charge of the household.

Photo Writing Assignment

The following photo depicts a place where young people "hang out." First, in a small group of classmates, discuss favorite gathering places. Then write a description of a place where you and your friends hang out regularly. State why the place is popular and what about it appeals to you. Compare your gathering place to the one in the photo. Use only standard English.

3

Purpose and Audience

"Purpose is why you are writing. The audience for your writing is the person for whom you write it."

We write for different reasons, in different ways, and with different tools. Some of us sit at a desk and write with a computer. Others curl up in a chair with a legal pad and scribble away with a pencil. Some of us outline what we want to say before we begin, while others discover their ideas as they write. Our reasons for writing likewise vary. They can range from a letter applying for a job, to a report on U.S. history, to a personal note jotted in a birthday card.

Yet all writing has at least two things in common: *purpose* and *audience*.

Purpose

Purpose is *why* you are writing. Knowing the purpose of an assignment can actually help you with its writing. However, you'll get no help from thinking that your purpose for writing an essay is to get a grade. A newspaper reporter writes for money—but imagining a paycheck as the purpose for a story about a local bus strike will not tell the reporter how to write it.

On the other hand, the reporter who understands that the purpose of a story is to *inform* the public about the local bus strike knows exactly what to do: *inform*. State the facts. Give background information. Stick to the point; don't make jokes, just tell the story behind the strike. *Why* you write, in short, will always affect *how* you write. To know your purpose is to understand not only *what you must do* but, equally important, *what you must not do*.

Basically, all writing serves one of three purposes:

1. To entertain
2. To inform
3. To persuade

Writing to entertain

Writing to entertain is fun to do because it is writing at its most informal and lighthearted. Your main purpose is to amuse your reader. You do not have to be faithful to logic or facts. You do not have to do any research. You can exaggerate, twist situations, and use colorful language.

Students are often hesitant to use *I* in their college writing, and this hesitation is well-founded. In a research paper, for example, many teachers prefer that students not use *I*. In writing to entertain, however, the *I* is not only welcome, it is unavoidable. How could you tell the story of your funny summer vacation, for example, without calling yourself *I*? After all it happened to you, not to *one* or to *nobody.* Writing meant to entertain, therefore, is often told by an *I*, as it should be.

Here is an example from a very funny writer, Mark Twain. His purpose is to entertain an audience of young people by giving them tips on how to live a moral life.

> Always obey your parents, when they are present. This is the best policy in the long run, because if you don't they will make you. Most parents think they know better than you do, and you can generally make more by humoring that superstition than you can by acting on your own better judgment.
>
> *Mark Twain, "Advice to Youth."*

Here is another example, from a student paper, about visiting the dentist:

> Most dentists have been taught in school to put their trembling patients at ease by talking to them. My dentist is a pro at this. He waits until my mouth is packed to the brim with cotton and dry from the saliva suction tube. When I am helplessly pinned to the chair, he will ask a heavy question such as, "So, you're taking philosophy in school? What's your take on Plato's 'Myth of the Cave?' " As I try to answer, he'll say, "Open wider and turn toward me," with the result that I can't get a word out. If I do manage to blubber an opinion and he disagrees with me, he immediately starts drilling below the gum line until I take it all back.

PRACTICING 1

For each of the following pairs of topics, check the one whose primary purpose is more likely to entertain.

1. _____ **(a).** Being completely broke is a great way to keep your roommate from borrowing your money.

   _____ **(b).** Bird-watching is an educational hobby.

2. _____ **(a).** The homeless problem in the United States is getting worse.

   _____ **(b).** I love to help out hypocrites—just to listen to their extravagant praise.

3. _____ **(a).** Medical research is offering new hope for AIDS patients.

   _____ **(b).** The most effective labor-saving device on the market is a spouse with lots of money.

4. _____ **(a).** Usually, progress means exchanging one nuisance for the other. Consider garbage disposals.

   _____ **(b).** I believe strongly that NASA should send more humans into space.

5. _____ **(a).** Marriage is a great institution, but I'm not ready for an institution yet.

   _____ **(b).** Banking is a sensible career choice.

PRACTICING 2

Write a letter to your best friend relating something that happened to you. Your purpose is to entertain.

Writing to inform

"Just the facts, ma'am." Years ago a renowned television cop made that statement popular. It neatly sums up what should be your aim when you write to inform: to give the facts.

When you write to inform, your aim is usually to explain something to your reader. You might define the meaning of a little-known term. You might describe what bacteria look like under a microscope. You might compare running to power walking. You might explain the stages of a process: First you do this, then you do that. In all cases, though, you remain mainly serious while trying to be as clear and understandable as possible. Here is an example of informative writing.

In the United States, we seem to awaken to social problems in stages: In the case of family violence, awareness of child abuse increased during the 1960s, spousal abuse was the issue of the

1970s, and abuse of the elderly was publicly acknowledged in the 1980s. Abuse of older people takes many forms, from passive neglect to active torment, and includes verbal, emotional, financial and physical harm. Most elderly people suffer from none of these things; but research suggests that some 1 million elderly people (3 percent of the total) suffer serious maltreatment each year, and three times as many sustain abuse at some point.

John J. Macionis, Sociology, Prentice Hall, 1999.

The writer focuses on an emerging social problem—abuse of the elderly.

Here is another example, this one from a student paper about *ki,* a martial arts concept:

How can a man in a threatening situation jump higher or run faster than he thought possible? How can another lie on broken glass with a 150 lb. concrete slab on his chest while enduring the blows of a sledgehammer and not be harmed? The answer, known to those advanced in the martial arts, is a phenomenon called *ki*— an invisible force present in all living things that can be developed by anyone. *Ki* consists of four powers that are classified as *lightness* (*kyung ki*), *heaviness* (*hung ki*), *hardness* (*chul ki*), and *numbness* (*ma ki*). With proper training and discipline, anyone can attain these powers and use them to perform extraordinary feats of strength and athleticism.

This writer is informing us about a martial arts concept by defining it. Later in this book you will learn to use definition in your writing.

PRACTICING 3

Both paragraphs that follow try to inform, but one does a better job than the other. Read both paragraphs and decide which one is better. Then, in the space provided, state the reasons for your choice.

A.

Cable TV offerings have become really ridiculous. There are too many choices. A viewer can have many, many choices. There's something for everyone. There's something for the sports fan and something for the cook. The gardener has a special program, and children have many choices. If you are history buff, there's a program for you, and if you love music, there are music programs, too. For the weather enthusiast, there are live radar displays of local weather. Yet in spite of all these choices, you still hear people say, "there's nothing on TV."

B.

Cable TV offerings have become ridiculous. One local cable company in my area offers 160 channels in its regular subscription. There are programs for gardeners, history buffs, sports fans, cooks, and just about anyone else with a special interest. Premium subscribers can choose another dozen or so channels offering nonstop movies, and even these are specialized. There are channels called Classic Movies, Romance Classics, Independent Film Classics, True Stories, and Science Fiction. The Cartoon Network shows nonstop children's cartoons. One station, called Animal Planet, screens nothing but wildlife shows. In addition, there are 30 stations devoted to playing music of all types, from classical to rap. Yet with all these choices, people still complain, "there's nothing on TV."

_____

_____

_____

_____

_____

_____

_____

_____

_____

_____

_____

PRACTICING 4

Check the topics which follow that would make good informative paragraphs.

1. _____ Guide-dog training is a complicated process.

2. _____ Grafting plants is not as simple as it might look.

3. _____ My Aunt Trudi reminds me of a horse.

4. _____ The popularity of golf in the United States is soaring.

5. _____ Finches are the largest family of birds and include several distinctive types.

6. _____ There are several ways to improve your neighborhood watch program.

7. _____ Three kinds of students annoy me: Vapid Vivian, Stupid Steve, and Holy Herbie.

8. _____ My brother is a rat.

9. _____ Let me tell you about my operation.

10. _____ Harry Truman accomplished four major goals while he was president.

Writing to persuade

Your primary aim in writing to persuade is to win over your reader to your point of view. You wish either to change your readers' minds or to prod them into taking some action. You do so by stating the facts, making logical arguments, and quoting the supporting views of experts. Often, you present the opposing viewpoint to spell out its inconsistencies or weaknesses. You always aim for a logical presentation of your case.

Here is an example of a paragraph written to persuade:

Extremists within the animal-rights movement take the position that animals have rights equal to or greater than those of humans. It follows from this that even if humans might benefit from animal research, the cost to animals is too high. It is ironic that despite this moral position, the same organizations condone—and indeed sponsor—activities that appear to violate the basic rights of animals to live and reproduce. Each year 10,000,000 dogs are destroyed by public pounds, animal shelters, and humane societies. Many of these programs are supported and even operated by animal-protectionist groups. Surely there is a strong contradiction when those who profess to believe in animal rights deny animals their right to life. A similar situation exists with regards to programs for pet sterilization, programs that deny animals the right to breed and bear offspring and are sponsored in many cases by antivivisectionists and animal-rights groups. Evidently, animal-rights advocates sometimes recognize and subscribe to the position that animals do not have the same rights as humans. However, their public posture leaves little room for examining these subtleties or applying similar standards to animal research.

Frederick A. King, "Animals in Research:
The Case for Experimentation."

This writer is trying to persuade us that animals should be used in medical research. His argument attacks those who disagree and points out inconsistencies in their views.

Here is an example of a student paragraph written to persuade:

If you're like many people, you've probably passed by runners, seen the look of agony and pain on their faces, and said to yourself, "I'd rather die." Runners do not look happy, but walkers do, and walking is every bit as good for you as running. Walking reduces the risk factors for heart disease and stroke as much as running. Walking also produces the same healthy cellular changes as running does, with the same beneficial effects upon the heart and the lungs. Moreover, walking helps prevent diabetes, strengthens bones, and improves the immune system. Best of all, you do not have to walk until you're ready to drop like runners often do. In fact, walking for 20 to 30 minutes a day has been shown to have a highly beneficial effect on a person's overall health. This was recently proved again in a study conducted by the National Institutes of Health. Next time you come home worn out at the end of the day, don't just slump in a chair and watch TV. Get out and walk. Not only will it be good for you, it'll make you feel better.

This student presents the advantages of walking with straightforward logic. She is serious, but not stuffy as she tries to persuade others to her point of view.

IN A NUTSHELL

- The three broad purposes for writing are to entertain, to inform, and to persuade.
- Knowing the purpose of your essay tells you what to do as well as what not to do.

PRACTICING 5

Some students live in dorms while attending college. Others choose off-campus apartments, while still others live at home. Which do you prefer? List three reasons you would use to persuade someone to your opinion.

1. _____

_____

_____

2. _____

_____

_____

3. _____

_____

_____

PRACTICING 6

Compose an argument either for or against your present study habits. If you think your study habits are sufficient for your workload, make a case for that. If you think your study habits need to be improved, argue for that.

Audience

The **audience** for your writing is the reader, *the person for whom you are writing*. Most writing is aimed at a specific audience—an individual or a specific group of readers.

If you are a native speaker or a non-native speaker who knows English well, you already know more about audience than you think. For example, you know that you can talk to your roommate using language you would not utter to your grandmother. Indeed, so sophisticated is your sense of language and audience that you can tell about a social situation just from a line of casual talk. Take the following quiz to test your intuitive sense of how language is used for a specific audience. We shall use as an example the everyday greeting, "Hey girl, what's going on?"

PRACTICING 7

From the following greeting, "Hey girl, what's going on?" draw some conclusions about the people and social situation involved.

1. Who do you think the person being greeted is most likely to be of the choices below?

   (a). An elderly relative.

   (b). A professor.

   (c). A dean at the greeter's college.

   (d). A person of similar age as the greeter.

2. How old do you think the greeter is?

   (a). Over 50.

   (b). A teenager or other young person.

   (c). Over 60.

   (d). At least 80.

3. What is the likely sex of the person being greeted?

   (a). Male.

   (b). Female.

   (c). Could be either male or female.

4. What is the likely relationship between the greeter and the person being greeted?

(a). They're strangers.

(b). They're enemies.

(c). One is the boss of the other.

(d). They are friends.

The answers we had in mind are (d), (b), and (b) and (d).

You know that you'd most likely greet only someone close to your own age so informally, not a professor, dean, or elderly relative. You know that a young person would most likely use this particular greeting, and that "girl" is a popular term among young female friends today. You also know that the tone of the greeting is one you would use not with a stranger, but a friend. On the other hand, depending on how much of an ear for idiomatic American English they have, ESL students might find this quiz more challenging.

In sum, we spontaneously choose appropriate language with surprising sophistication during our daily talking. If we make mistakes, people tend to overlook them during the give-and-take of conversation. Writing is not so forgiving of mistakes. You can still use your intuitive understanding of audience when you write, but you must use this sense more carefully, taking the time to edit your work until it fits its audience.

The instructor as audience

Whenever you write anything, you always should ask yourself, "Who will read this?" Naturally, in your present circumstance, the expected answer is, your instructor. Yet your instructor is only your symbolic audience. That is, your instructor stands for someone else.

In the classroom your instructor is, first, an editor who will suggest ways to improve your writing. Your instructor also has a second role—to stand for the educated reader. This is the reader for whom most of us write in the everyday world of work and business—someone who is educated but not an expert on our topic.

Asking questions about your audience

After you ask the question, "Who will read this?" you must ask yourself two more questions: "What does my audience know about this topic?" "What does my audience need to know for me to achieve my purpose?" The answers to these two questions will tell you what information you must provide and what you can safely leave out.

For example, if you are a sailor writing to another sailor, you can use common sailing terms and know you will be understood. Here, for example, is one sailor writing to another about upwind sailing:

> To head upwind, block in the mainsail as tight as you can while
> easing the tiller in the direction of the heel until the mainsail gives

signs of luffing. Do not head up any higher or you'll find yourself in the irons. Once you've reached the luff line, fall off five points to weather until the sail is drawing fully without further signs of luffing. That is your tack.

This description would puzzle anyone but a seasoned sailor. For the average educated reader, therefore, your explanation might be given this way:

> A sailboat can sail with the wind behind it, with the wind coming from the side, or with the wind blowing off the bow (the front). This last course is known as "upwind sailing." To sail upwind, take in the mainsail as tight as you can while easing the tiller (the steering stick) in the direction of the heel (the tilt of the boat) until the mainsail begins to sag and flap where it is joined to the mast. This is known as luffing. Do not head up any higher or you'll find your sails flapping wildly and your boat at a standstill in the water. This condition is known as being "in the irons" and can pose a danger to the boat on a blustery day. Once the sails have begun to luff, slowly pull the tiller away from the direction of the heel until the sail is drawing fully and showing no signs of luffing. The boat should be heeling and driving ahead. You are now sailing upwind.

The writer now defines all the terms. Although a fellow sailor will know the meaning of *bow, tiller, luffing, in the irons,* and *heeling,* these terms would stump the average educated reader who's never been on a sailboat. Yet someone with a general knowledge can be expected to know the meaning of *mast* and *mainsail* so the writer doesn't define these terms. This is what writers do—they adapt their work to their audience.

Similarly, if you are writing an essay about how to tune a car for a reader who can't tell a fender from a bumper, you know right away that not only must you explain the process, you must also name and explain basic parts. You must say, these are the sparkplugs. You can find them here. This is what they look like. This is what they do. Here is why they must be changed when you tune the car.

If your reader knows the difference between a fender and a sparkplug, you can start your explanation at a higher level and skip the basics. In either case you know which information to include and which to omit by asking the two basic audience questions: "What does my audience know about this topic?" "What do they need to know for me to achieve my purpose?"

IN A NUTSHELL

- Your audience is the person or group for whom you are writing.

- The two questions you should ask about audience are, "What does my audience know about this topic?" "What does my audience need to know for me to achieve my purpose?"

PRACTICING 8

The following writing assignment is aimed at three different audiences. What details about your family life would you focus on for each audience?

1. Describe your family life for a cousin who is planning to spend the summer with you.

_____

_____

_____

2. Describe your family life to a college admissions officer.

_____

_____

_____

3. Describe your family life for a student living in China.

_____

_____

_____

PRACTICING 9

Fill in the spaces as indicated.

1. Write an appropriate greeting for a distinguished professor you meet in the cafeteria.

_____

2. In the same cafeteria you leave the professor and sit down with a friend. Write an appropriate greeting for him or her.

_____

3. A student you've seen around and would like to know better sits at your table and makes eye contact. Write down how you greet him or her.

_____

Unit Test

Circle "T" if the statement is true; circle "F" if it is false.

1. T   F   Knowing *why* you write can help your writing.

2. T   F   The main purpose of writing in college should be to get a good grade.

3. T   F   Basically, all writing serves one of the following three purposes: 1) to entertain, 2) to impress, and 3) to inform.

4. T   F   When writing to entertain, you can exaggerate, twist situations, and use colorful language.

5. T   F   When you write to inform, you are usually trying to explain something to your audience.

6. T   F   When you write anything, you always should ask yourself "Who will read this?"

7. T   F   It doesn't matter what your audience knows or doesn't know about your topic.

8. T   F   Knowing your audience let's you decide what information to provide and what to leave out.

9. T   F   When you write in class, you need to address the lowest reader.

10. T   F   Spoken mistakes are forgiven more easily than written ones.

Unit Talk-Write Assignment

We spend much of our talking time trying to persuade, and we use different techniques, depending on our audience. Sometimes we make an emotional argument, sometimes a logical one. What we say is often not what we would write in a more formal written argument.

The *Talk* section below presents a spoken paragraph that is persuasive. A student is talking to her apartment-mate about a city council proposal to tag all cats, just as dogs have to be tagged. Cindy, the speaker, is heatedly against the proposal and decides to write her council representative. Your assignment is to rewrite Cindy's spoken paragraph into standard English. Consider the different audience and the reasons she presents. Add whatever you think is necessary to improve her argument.

Spoken Paragraph

Obviously our City Council has no clue about cats. What a bunch of bozos. Really. I can't believe real people would come up with a moronic idea like that. Cats aren't like dogs. I mean, can you imagine a cat wearing a license tag around the neck? My Siamese cat, Rama, would have a conniption fit if you tried to tie anything around her neck. I'm not kidding. She would claw and spit and scratch like a crazy witch before being dissed by a tag. "Just like a stupid dog," she would sniff to herself. Can't be on a leash, either. Doesn't everybody know that cats are boss when it comes to being completely independent? You can't wow them; you can't push them around; you can't threaten them; and you can't tag them. No way, Jose! They live in their own world where they reign like kings and queens. Forget this tag stuff. I'll bet you any amount of money that the dummy politicians who came up with this stinker don't own a cat or they'd know better. Cats have to be allowed to stalk, hunt, chase, and track—day or night—whenever they feel like it and without some crummy necklace bothering their necks. I'm telling you, keep tags away from cats.

Written Paragraph

Unit Collaborative Assignment

Working with a friend or classmate, choose one of the topics that follow and decide what kind of paragraph you would like to write—a paragraph to entertain, inform, or persuade.

1. A favorite outdoor activity

2. The benefits of fairy tales

3. A popular television sitcom

4. A sport I enjoy

5. What I would like to do with my life

Now talk with your partner about the details you might use and how you would go about developing the paragraph for an average educated reader. Now switch places with your partner, who should do the same as you did.

Unit Writing Assignment

On a separate sheet of paper develop the topic you discussed in the Unit Collaborative Assignment into a paragraph. Before you begin, write down your purpose and audience. Then stick to your purpose and write with your audience in mind.

Photo Writing Assignment

The following picture shows concert-goers enjoying a live performance at a rock concert. Choose a specific person—an elderly relative, a roommate, a teacher—and write to persuade him or her that rock concerts are fun, boring, or whatever else you think about them. Is there any evidence in the photo to support your argument?

4

Gathering Ideas

Writing is always hardest at the beginning when the page is blank. We start to write, find the going slow, and imagine our secret fears about our inability to write confirmed.

The truth is that for nearly everyone, writing is hard and slow work; the only solution to the slow start is to get started quickly. Once the words are flowing, self-doubt will give way to the practical business of writing.

In their working habits writers tend to resemble baseball pitchers. For both *warming up* is essential. Pitchers throw practice balls to flex their arms; writers warm up their writing skills by scribbling words on the page. Indeed, the longer you sit and write, the better you will gradually find yourself getting at it.

There are several things you can do to start yourself writing:

- Talking writing
- Freewriting
- Brainstorming
- Clustering

All these activities will help you warm up, get ideas, and arrive at a suitable writing topic.

Talking Writing

One of the simplest ways of getting ideas is to talk aloud about your topic to a friend, yourself, your cat, or even a chair (better not to do this in public, however!). The idea is to use talking to inspire thinking. Most of us feel better after we talk over our troubles with a friend. Similarly, discussing your topic with a friend will give you a clearer picture of what you want to write.

The talking we have in mind is not hit-or-miss gabbing, but talking aimed specifically at your topic. Begin by opening a notebook so you can jot down any ideas or suggestions that you get during the talking. If you have a friend to share your thoughts with, start by simply stating your topic. No one can predict what will happen next, but here is an idea of what might possibly follow.

You: I've got a paragraph to write.

Friend: What about?

You: Someone I admire.

Friend: So who are you going to write on?

You: I don't know. Maybe Sandy, a girl I work with. She is someone special.

Friend: What's so special about her?

You: She's so down-to-earth. When she walks into a room, she always says hello to everyone. She always tries to say something cheerful or positive.

Friend: Oh, yeah? What's she look like?

You: She always looks great. The other day she walked in with a black sweater. She was a knockout.

Friend: I hate her already.

You: No, you'd like her. She's always nicely dressed. It isn't often that I see her wearing the same outfit twice. She has black hair, and never a strand out of place.

Friend: Where's she from?

You: California. But she lived for years in London. She has this British accent that makes her sound so cool on the phone. But she's not snobby. Just nice and straightforward.

Friend: That's good.

You: And when you're talking to her, she always looks right at you and really listens. It doesn't matter if you are the janitor or the President of the United States. I definitely admire her.

Talking can help you come up with the kinds of details your reader will be interested in. Notice, for example, that in this exchange the friend asks where Sandy is from, which leads to interesting information that might be included in the paragraph. Talking can also help you decide what your purpose is and how you need to approach the topic for your particular audience. It is even possible to talk out a topic sentence that you can refine later. The point is to use talking to start yourself thinking about the topic and to get ideas about it.

Talking to yourself or a friend about your writing topic can help you find things to say about it.

PRACTICING 1

Your teacher has asked you to write a paragraph about one change that you would like to see at your college and why. Choose a friend and talk out the assignment. Jot down notes.

PRACTICING 2

Write the paragraph you talked about in Practicing 1.

_____

_____

_____

_____

_____

_____

_____

_____

_____

_____

Freewriting

A good warm-up exercise for the writer is freewriting. To **freewrite,** you write about a topic for a timed period of about ten minutes. Forget about grammar, spelling, and punctuation. Just sit and write freely. If you have nothing to say, write, "I have nothing to say," until you do say something. The result of such freewriting will be sense mixed with nonsense, but gradually you'll find yourself warming up to the topic.

Here is an example of student freewriting:

> How I spend my free-time? Most of the time, I don't have none. Between school and work, I hardly have time for anything else. I don't know what else to say. What can I say? When I have a day off, I like to fix cars, I like taking them a part. If I thought I could get a good job in a garage without going to school, I would. But today, even the garages want someone with at least a junior college degree. I don't know what else to say. If I had any free time, I wouldn't spend it, I would save it. But I never have any. I get up around six. Then I feed the dog and the cat, make myself coffee, and read the paper. At least, I read the funnies. Sometimes the sports page. Then I go to work for most of the morning. In the afternoon I go to school, and try to make heads and tails of English. Usually I have to write essays such as this one about topics that have nothing to do with cars. Then I go home and play with the dog and the cat and watch TV and do my homework and try to write essays like this one, which is supposed to be about how I spend my free time, which I never have any of.

Notice that the paragraph contains several grammatical errors, which is fine in freewriting. For example, the writer says, "most of the time, I don't have none," which is a double negative. He says about cars, "I like taking them a part" when what he really means is, "I like taking them apart." What other errors do you find? Errors are normal and expected in freewriting. The idea is not to write perfectly, but simply to think out loud on paper. As a result of this freewriting session, the student decided to write his essay on the topic, "Not having any free time." The freewriting session did its job: It generated an idea for an essay.

Your own attempts at freewriting should be similarly loose. Don't try to correct your mistakes, control your writing, or muzzle your thoughts. Freewriting should be as free and uncontrolled as a pitcher's warm-up tosses. The goal in both cases is the same: to warm up.

IN A NUTSHELL

You can warm up to a topic by freewiting about it.

PRACTICING 3

Freewrite for five or ten minutes on whatever topics come to mind. Then read what you wrote and answer the following questions to determine whether freewriting focused your thinking. Did you write more on one topic than others? Were any of the topics related to each other?

PRACTICING 4

Freewrite for five or ten minutes on one of the following topics.

1. A job I once had

2. What I like to cook

3. A favorite singer

4. Dreams

5. A movie I think is overrated (or underrated)

PRACTICING 5

Write a paragraph based on one of your freewriting sessions (Practicing 3 or 4).

_____

_____

_____

_____

_____

_____

_____

_____

_____

_____

_____

_____

Brainstorming

The aim of freewriting is just to get you writing. Once you're warmed up and are ready to write, however, you need to focus on finding ideas to put down on paper. One especially good technique for finding ideas is brainstorming.

Brainstorming is an exercise in thinking. You simply list every thought that pops into your head about a particular topic. Don't try to write in sentences. Don't worry about logic or whether your ideas are good or bad. Just jot down your thoughts. You can always sort them out later.

Brainstorming produces a random list of ideas, as you can see from this student's list on the topic "things I like":

apple pie

riding my mountain bike

dressing up

fancy restaurants

watching my little sister eat

teasing my brother

popsicles

caramel apples

popcorn

walking

birdwatching

Uncle Fred

quiet

alone

peaceful

saw a blue heron once

fabulous

lifted off like some spirit

huge wing span

slow, beating wings

breathtaking

bird watching is actually fun

When you are finished brainstorming, you look over the ideas scribbled on the page to find out what you really think about the topic. Odd as it may seem, many writers learn what they really think about a topic only when they try writing about it.

For example, this student remembered the excitement he felt when he saw a rare blue heron in the park last summer. He decided to write a paragraph on that one thrilling moment in his hobby of bird-watching, which he'd learned from his uncle. That experience became the focus of his paragraph. Brainstorming will often give you this kind of new slant on your topic.

IN A NUTSHELL

Brainstorming is a warm-up technique of freely jotting down ideas about a topic.

PRACTICING 6

Brainstorm by yourself on one of the following topics.

1. Why your room is important to you

2. Showing love

3. A hobby or special interest

4. Planning a surprise party

5. Your favorite sport

PRACTICING 7

Brainstorm in a group session on one of the following topics.

1. How to become more organized

2. What makes a good boss

3. What makes a good employee

4. What makes a good parent

5. How to eat well on a tight budget

PRACTICING 8

Write a paragraph on one of the topics that you brainstormed on in either Practicing 6 or Practicing 7.

Clustering

Clustering is thinking with the help of a diagram. As with brainstorming, you don't worry about grammar or wording. You simply think about your subject, jotting down your ideas in a diagram.

The aim of clustering is to narrow a broad subject down to a manageable topic. Let us say that your assigned subject is the Internet. Even though you may have used it many times, you still find that subject impossibly broad and can think of nothing meaty to say beyond the usual generalities. So you decide to do a cluster on the subject of the Internet.

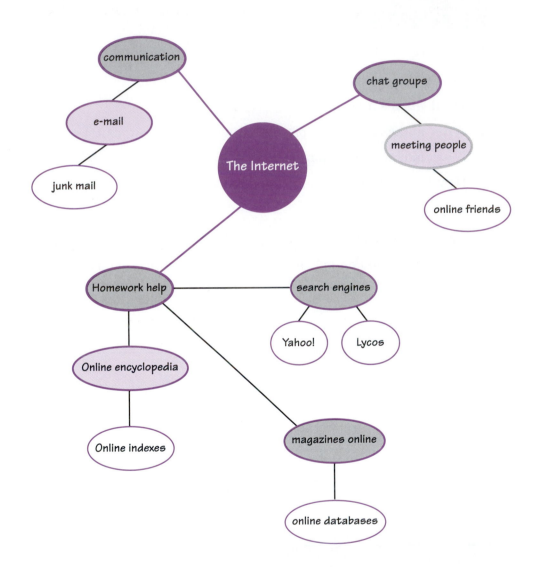

You begin by writing down your general subject, the Internet, and drawing a circle around it. You ask yourself what parts of the Internet you are familiar with, and you come up with four: communications, chat groups, homework help, and search engines. You draw spokes from the central big circle so that each of these parts is enclosed in a smaller circle. These are the first divisions of your subject, the Internet. Then you try to break down each part further. In this particular case, the student focused on the homework help that is offered through the Internet. She broke down homework help into those features she found most useful—online encyclopedias, databases, and indexes. Now she had a topic she could sink her teeth into, homework help offered on the Internet, and was able to draw on her own experiences as a source of examples.

IN A NUTSHELL

Clustering is using a diagram to think about your topic.

PRACTICING 9

Do a cluster on one of the topics that follow.

1. Neighbors

2. Exercise

3. Music

4. College sports

5. High school teachers

PRACTICING 10

Examine your cluster diagram from Practicing 9 for a manageable topic about which you have lots to say and write a paragraph about it.

_____

_____

_____

_____

_____

_____

_____

_____

_____

Journal Writing

As we have mentioned earlier, the skill of writing is like a muscle: The more you use it, the stronger it gets. If you never write, your writing muscle will shrivel up. One way to keep the writing muscle exercised is to keep a daily journal.

The **journal** is a notebook in which you pour out your heart about everything and nothing. Because a journal is private, you can write anything you like in it. Getting in the daily practice of expressing your deepest self on paper can help you to get used to writing.

You can use your journal as a source of ideas for writing topics. You can add to it anything that interests you: cartoons, magazine clippings, newspaper articles, quotations, notes from friends, and so on. Here are some sample entries from a student's journal:

8/16/01—Sometimes the news is so depressing. Now we're worried about suicide bombings like are happening in West Jerusalem, where a fanatic with a bomb strapped to his body, blew up a pizzaria, killing 16 people and injuring scores of bystanders. Then it happened again, this time on a Sunday, wounding 20 people. Some people are saying that it could happen here. There's almost no way to prevent fanatics who are willing to give up their lives from blowing themselves up in crowded places. Meanwhile, the economy is still in a nosedive. Yesterday my neighbor, who's a computer programmer and thought he was safe, got laid off from a job he'd had for five years. You just never can tell these days who is safe and who isn't.

8/17/01—Today was a stinky day. My alarm clock didn't go off, and I was late for my 8:00 psych class. The professor gave me a dirty look, and when I tried to explain to him after class that my alarm clock wasn't working, he said he didn't care. Well, if he doesn't care, I don't care either. Then John, who I usually eat lunch with, was in a stinky mood over some stupid girl. I told him not to take it out on me, that my day was hard enough already. Later, I found out at my job that the new fry cook quit, which meant I had to work a double shift and close up. When I got home it was late, and I found that my cat had eaten a bird and left the feathers and bones all over the living room floor. Maybe a bird will eat her one day. I'm in a bad mood. Then there's this whole business about the suicide bombings in the air, too. As if I didn't have enough to worry about.

8/21/01—I heard a poem today on the radio that I really like. It's short:

Whether the weather be cool

or the weather be hot,

we'll weather the weather

whether we like it or not.

I wonder who wrote it?

8/24/01—Today I got a raise at work. It's only 50 cents an hour, but I can sure use it. My boss said I've been doing a good job and deserve it. She said she wished she could give me more, which I thought was very sweet. Maybe one day I'll be able to get a better car.

Here are a few suggestions for keeping a journal:

1. *Write regularly.* Keep your journal regularly, even if you have nothing special to say. If you get in the habit of writing regularly, you'll find something to say about even a boring day.

2. *Don't worry about grammar or spelling.* Write from your heart. Don't edit your entries, and don't think you have to be in a cheery mood. ESL students should similarly ignore grammar and usage problems. Use your journal to get your feelings off your chest. Just write about anything that's on your mind.

3. *Keep your journal handy at all times.* Keep your journal with you so you can pick it up whenever you get the urge to write. Some people like a small spiral notebook, while others prefer a regular class notebook. The choice is yours. Use whatever notebook you prefer—small, big, spiral, or bound. Some students have even used exam *blue books* as journals.

4. *Date your entries.* Dating your journal entries will help you remember when you made them. You'll have fun looking back at specific events that happened during the year. You'll also be able to watch your writing skills grow over the passing months and years.

IN A NUTSHELL

Keeping a daily journal can help exercise your writing muscle.

PRACTICING 11

To get a feel of what it's like to keep a journal, write a brief journal entry on what you did this morning.

_____

_____

_____

_____

_____

_____

_____

_____

PRACTICING 12

From the journal entry that follows, written during the Civil War by a 16-year-old Southern girl just out of school, extract an idea that could be used for writing a paragraph. Use the space below to write.

Charleston, June 20, 1863. It is too delightful to be at home! In spite of the war everyone is so bright and cheerful, and the men are so charming and look so nice in their uniforms. We see a great many of them, and I have been to a most delightful dance in Fort Sumter. The night was lovely and we went out in rowing boats. It was a strange scene, cannon balls piled in every direction, sentinels pacing the ramparts, and within the casements pretty, well-dressed women, and handsome well-bred men dancing, as though unconscious that we were actually under the guns of a blockading fleet. It was my first party, and the strange charm of the situation wove a spell around me; every man seemed a hero—not only a possible but an actual hero! One looks at a man oh so differently when you think he may be killed tomorrow! Men whom up to this time I have thought dull and commonplace that night seemed charming. . . .

From the diary of Esther Alden

_____

_____

_____

_____

_____

_____

_____

_____

_____

Unit Test

In the blank provided, write the word that most accurately completes the thought of the sentence.

1. The skill of writing is like a _____ ; the more you use it, the stronger it gets.

2. The _____ you write, the better you get at it.

3. Talking writing means to _____ aloud about your topic.

4. Use a _____ to jot down any thoughts you get during your talking writing session.

5. In freewriting you forget about _____ errors.

6. The aim of freewriting is to get you to _____ .

7. In brainstorming, you list every _____ that comes to you about your topic.

8. Brainstorming will produce a random _____ of ideas.

9. The beauty of clustering is that it _____ a broad subject.

10. A good way to improve your writing is to write a _____ in which you pour out your private thoughts.

Unit Talk-Write Assignment

A good way to get ideas on a subject is to talk with friends and class-mates. Below is the transcript of a conversation among four students who were assigned to write a paragraph about television sitcoms.

Use the space provided below to turn this four-way conversation into a paragraph that either supports or opposes the view that sitcoms benefit society. You may use the ideas reflected in the four-way conversation as if they were your own. You may also want to add your own ideas.

Conversation

Dexter: I think sitcoms are a stupid waste of time. I'd much rather watch the history channel.

Sonik: I disagree completely. A good sitcom is like an extended family.

Armineh: Sonik is right. My friends and I discussed every *Dharma and Greg* episode. They think it's hilarious to have a free-spirited yoga teacher married to a conventional, Harvard trained lawyer. The combination is hysterical! All of my friends love rehashing the episodes. It keeps us close—we know something special—we're insiders—like belonging to a private club.

Sonik: I agree. I feel as if I know everyone on that show personally, like they are a part of my life. I really feel bad when they're not getting along.

Dexter: You've got to be kidding. How can you take a TV show seriously? The show is hot air, about nothing. The characters stand for nothing. Nothing important ever happens—nothing—just silly stuff. It's worse than a soap opera.

Bryan: Now M*A*S*H—I've seen re-reruns of that show—that was a sitcom worth tuning in on. You could learn about the Korean war, about petty human jealousies, about true friendship, about how military big shots can make your life miserable.

Bryan: Have you guys every seen re-runs of *All in the Family?* My dad loved that show.

Sonik: What was it about?

Bryan: About a middle-aged guy who was really politically conservative, and everything his liberal son-in-law said or did drove him crazy. He called him "Meathead." The old guy was really stupid, but you got sucked into watching him and even liking him.

Armineh: What do you mean?

Bryan: Well, he said stupid stuff, but then he'd always try to do the decent thing.

Dexter: If I want opinions about politics, I'll watch the news.

Armineh: Wasn't the main character Archie Bunker? And didn't he become a household word for stupid conservatism?

Bryan: Yeah.

Dexter: You're all talking about how popular these shows are. But people get addicted, and that's bad. My sister lives for Monday night and *Ally McBeal.* When I was in the hospital, she left early so she could get home in time to see it.

Sonik: Oh, come on. It's comforting to know that anything can pull together a whole country, even a TV show.

Dexter: Well, I don't think sitcoms contribute anything worthwhile to our society.

Bryan: I think anything that gives people a common experience is good.

Written Paragraph

_____

_____

_____

_____

_____

_____

_____

_____

_____

_____

_____

_____

_____

_____

_____

_____

 # Unit Collaborative Assignment

Pair up with another student. Choose one of the topics that follow and talk out a paragraph. Take notes on your ideas.

1. A serious problem that exists in your community

2. Raising responsible children

3. An obsession of yours or of a friend

4. How country music has changed

5. The problem with being too in love

Unit Writing Assignment

From the notes you took in the Unit Talking Assignment, write a paragraph.

Photo Writing Assignment

Study the following photo. Use talking, freewriting, brainstorming, clustering, or journal keeping to develop ideas for writing a paragraph. Then write the paragraph.

5

The Topic Sentence of a Paragraph

Before the invention of the printing press, writing was done on long rolls of paper called *scrolls*. The writing itself appeared as a solid, unbroken block of print. To help readers follow the writing, *scribes,* those workers who hand-copied the scrolls, would make a small mark in the margin of the manuscript wherever a new idea appeared. This mark was known as a *paragraphus*. From that word comes the word *paragraph*.

Today, instead of making a mark in the margin, we indent five spaces to signal the beginning of a new paragraph. In other words the idea behind the paragraph has remained unchanged through the centuries. A paragraph is still a group of sentences discussing a single idea. And the focus of all its sentences on a single idea—not the indentation or blocklike shape—is still the defining feature of a paragraph.

Here are two examples. Which of these is the better paragraph?

A.

Alzheimer's disease is a dreadful disease that hits many of the elderly at an alarming rate, including my grandmother. Grandmother soon forgot her identity, her relatives, and her past. For five years she lived with us at home. Sometimes, Grandmother would insist that the house next door was her house and that she wanted to go there. One afternoon, she asked me who "the lovely lady" was visiting her. I had to tell her that it was her own sister. "Oh, how nice," she exclaimed, without a glimmer of recognition. Her condition worsened as the months passed until she lost complete control of most bodily functions. After much inner turmoil my parents decided that it would be in everyone's best interest if Grandmother went to an extended care facility. Today my grandmother just lies in bed, staring at the ceiling. We visit her and hold her hand and wonder why her "golden years" have to be so horrible.

B.

"The cows don't care how smart you are, and General Motors doesn't require a degree." That's what a counselor told me at Juniper High in Michigan. Being book-smart, artistic, and cultured were not admirable qualities in this community, where most people went into farming or into factory work. One of my best friends became a farmer. In fact, he's been very successful. He has a big dairy, and he sells most of his milk to the Miller Cheese Factory. In the fall of 1995 I entered Southwest Institute, where I enjoyed the courses in art and literature. When I studied van Gogh's paintings, I wished I could paint like him. My teacher became a sort of guru for our whole class. He was a model teacher—always prepared, very fair, and very interesting. He really helped us gain insight into our own inner selves.

The first paragraph focuses its every sentence on one single point, namely that Alzheimer's is a dreadful disease. The second paragraph has no unifying topic to hold together its sentences. Separately, they are good sentences, but jointly they go nowhere. Paragraph A is a paragraph, whereas Paragraph B is a block of sentences.

The lesson the examples teach is this: Just because a block of print is indented, it is not a paragraph unless it functions like one. To be a paragraph, all the sentences must focus on and add to the same single point.

IN A NUTSHELL

A block of print is a paragraph only if all the sentences are focused on the same topic.

PRACTICING 1

The block of writing that follows contains some good ideas, but it is not a paragraph. Delete all details that are off the topic.

My dog Fazzi is a kick. I found him one late afternoon about two years ago, hovering behind a fence, sick and scared. He has taught me what it means to love unconditionally. I can truthfully say that no one has given me more pure joy in life than this little mutt. He rarely makes demands. All he seems to want to do is give affection and receive it. His loyalty is so fierce that he would attack Godzilla to defend me. I wish human beings would learn certain character traits from dogs. Society might be improved if it could be more like dogs. Too many people today just live the "gimme, gimme" life of greed and ambition. In fact, most politicians, businesspeople, and professionals just want to climb the social ladder and make money. Little Fazzi couldn't care less about ambition and power. He's happy just walking with me or riding in my car when I have to run an errand. People who don't have dogs miss a great opportunity for genuine friendship.

Talking and the Paragraph

Although the paragraph is an invention of writing, for the most part we also talk paragraphs. For example, here is a "spoken" paragraph:

> My new apartment is very convenient. It's close to everything. The bus passes right in front of the building. Right across the street is a mini-grocery store that is always open. Next to that is a shopping plaza that has a laundromat, supermarket, drugstore, and Radio Shack. The campus is only a mile away. I can easily walk to my classes. Also, my best friends live only a half-mile away.

How is this description a "spoken paragraph"? First, it discusses a single point—that the speaker's new apartment is convenient. Second, every sentence adds another detail about that single point.

Of course, we do not always talk in paragraphs. Sometimes, we exchange rat-a-tat single sentences. Other times, we talk in scatter-shot fashion, hopping from one topic to another like a bumble bee in a garden. But if you listen carefully, you'll also find many instances of talk all around you that sound remarkably like paragraphs.

PRACTICING 2

Get together with a classmate and take turns talking paragraphs on one of the following statements. Remember to stick to the point. Tell your partner if he or she strays from the subject.

1. I really get stressed out during final exams.

2. I can't stand (or I love) vegetables.

3. My parents treat me like a little kid.

4. I wish my girlfriend (or boyfriend) weren't so demanding.

5. I like (or I hate) cooking.

The Topic Sentence

The **topic sentence** of a paragraph is a single sentence that sums up what the paragraph is about. The topic sentence is like a road sign telling your reader where your paragraph is heading. If your topic sentence is *Baseball is a boring sport,* your reader knows what's ahead: a discussion of why baseball is boring. It makes sense to put this road sign before, rather than after, the discussion. Typically, then, the topic sentence comes first in a paragraph.

Not every sentence, however, can be a topic sentence. Indeed, some sentences simply won't work as topic sentences. The ideal topic sentence should do the following:

- Make a single point
- Make a discussible point
- Not be too narrow
- Not be too broad

The topic sentence should make a single point.

How many times has someone come up to you and said, "I want to tell you about my girlfriend and my new car"? Hardly ever. We usually don't mix two topics in a single breath. It is far more likely that you will hear first about the girlfriend and then about the new car.

Yet students will often write topic sentences that propose to take up two topics in one paragraph. Here are some examples:

Two topics:	My neighborhood is beautiful, and it has the best bakery in town.
One topic:	My neighborhood is beautiful.

or

My neighborhood has the best bakery in town.

Two topics:	The best time to form good habits is when you're young, and bad habits have a way of staying with you as you get older.
One topic:	The best time to form good habits is when you're young.

or

You should get rid of bad habits while you're young.

Two topics:	My best friend helped me get over my fear of computers, which really helped me write essays for English composition.

One topic: My best friend helped me get over my fear of computers in one easy lesson.

or

A computer is a wonderful tool for writing English class essays.

The paragraph that tries to take up two topics at once is doomed to be confused. It is hard to keep two topics straight in a spoken paragraph; it is even harder to do in the written one. Read your topic sentence aloud to be sure that it commits you to discuss a single topic. If it does not, rewrite it.

PRACTICING 3

Place an *S* in the blanks provided for each sentence that makes a single point. Leave the others blank.

1. _____ Your vocabulary can be improved if you force yourself to use new words, but a good vocabulary alone will not guarantee good writing.

2. _____ If you want to get along with people, learn which battles to fight and which ones to ignore.

3. _____ It's important to buy the right shoes for mountain hiking, and you should maintain good health so that you can make it up steep inclines.

4. _____ My brother lacks consideration for the other members of our family.

5. _____ His optimistic attitude makes my 80-year-old grandfather one of the most popular people in our neighborhood.

The topic sentence should make a discussible point.

To be discussible, your topic sentence should give you something to say. It should state your opinion, point of view, or feelings on the topic. Consider this sentence:

Yesterday I went to a baseball game.

If this were a line of talk, your listener would probably reply, "Oh? What game did you see?" The conversation would pick up from there and could lead to a friendly chat about sports.

Writing, however, is not a dialogue. Rather, it is a monologue. There's no one to ask, "Oh? What game did you see?" Your topic sentence must therefore do the work of asking for you. Indeed, the ideal topic sentence not only says, "Oh?" it also says, "Prove it!" Here is an example:

Baseball is a boring sport.

"Oh? Prove it!" which you then do:

> Baseball is a boring sport. For example, yesterday I went to a baseball game. It lasted nearly three hours. During that time there was one home run and three singles hit over nine innings. The rest of the time the game consisted of "strike one, strike two, strike three," or, "ground ball to the shortstop, a throw to first, and he's out." For some innings—six to be exact—almost nothing happened. The sun was hot, the seats were hard, and the hot dogs were gummy. I spent $25 to get sunburned, eat bad food, and see a dull game with no athletic feats whatsoever.

One way to check whether or not you have a suitable topic sentence is to apply the "Oh? Prove it!" test. The topic sentence that passes this basic test will at least give you a discussible topic.

PRACTICING 4

Turn the following dead-end topic sentences into discussible ones.

Example: Harriet wore a brown suit to the bridal shower.
            Harriet always wears understated clothes.

1. The other day Laurie used a cussword.

_____

_____

2. Banana cream pie is high in calories.

_____

_____

3. Mr. Wang makes jokes in our algebra class.

_____

_____

4. I like my new computer.

_____

_____

5. Sometimes we get carry-out for dinner.

_____

_____

The topic sentence should not be too narrow.

If your topic sentence is too narrow, you will have a hard time finding anything interesting to add to it. Here are some examples:

Too narrow:	Dallas parking meters have a parking limit of 30 minutes.
Discussible:	The parking in our city should be improved in order to increase business.
Too narrow:	There are always a lot of dishes after a party.
Discussible:	Doing the dishes with my roommate after a party can be as much fun as the party itself.
Too narrow:	The international student center contains 20 foreign flags.
Discussible:	The international student center serves our F-1 Visa students well.

An overly narrow topic sentence is seldom discussible without strenuous effort. It will often flunk the "Oh? Prove it!" test. Even if it can pass that test, its narrowness is still likely to make it boring to the general reader. The best course for the beginning writer is the middle ground: the topic sentence that is discussible and not overly narrow.

PRACTICING 5

Rewrite the following narrow topic sentences into discussible ones.

Example:	My basketball team wears old-fashioned yellow shorts.
Discussible:	Basketball uniforms should be modernized to keep up with new styles.

1. My car needs a tune-up.

_____

_____

2. My sister works at McDonald's.

_____

_____

3. Every morning I read my horoscope in the newspaper.

_____

_____

4. We have 300 Vietnamese students and 250 Korean students on our campus.

_____

_____

5. A television soap opera writer earns as much as $250,000 a year.

_____

_____

The topic sentence should not be too broad.

The opposite of a too-narrow topic sentence is the topic sentence that is too broad. The broad topic sentence proposes too big a topic for a paragraph. It is so general that the writer will struggle to find anything specific to say about it. Here are some examples:

Too broad:	Golf has a long history.
Discussible:	Tiger Woods is my favorite golfer.
Too broad:	The U.S. family has changed over the past 100 years.
Discussible:	My mother did a great job as a single parent.
Too broad:	A good education is the basis of a good life.
Discussible:	You have to know standard English to get a good job.

Each of the too-broad topics could fill a book, but they cannot be covered in a paragraph unless the writer is very skilled. Use your common sense. Ask yourself whether you could talk an intelligent paragraph—not an essay, but a single paragraph—on the topic. If you can't, you can't write one about it, either.

IN A NUTSHELL

The topic sentence of a paragraph should make a single discussible point. A good topic sentence is neither too narrow nor too broad.

PRACTICING 6

Rewrite each of the following broad topic sentences so it presents a single discussible point.

Example: The history of skyscraper architecture is a colorful one.

Discussible: Skyscrapers were built in New York in the mid-nineteenth century.

1. Sports build character.

_____

_____

2. People in the United States love to go on diets.

_____

_____

3. Music is an important part of life.

_____

_____

4. If you don't have your health, you don't have anything.

_____

_____

5. Computers run our lives today.

_____

_____

 **Unit Test**

From the four possible answers, check the one that best completes the thought of the sentence.

Example: Before the invention of the printing press, writing was done on

_____ **(a).** leaves from trees

 (b). scrolls

_____ **(c).** pieces of pottery

_____ **(d).** cave walls

1. Today, to indicate a paragraph, we

_____ **(a).** skip a line.

_____ **(b).** write in bold.

_____ **(c).** indent five spaces.

_____ **(d).** use the paragraph sign.

2. A block of writing is a paragraph only if

_____ **(a).** all of the sentences focus on the same topic.

_____ **(b).** the writer uses correct grammar throughout the paragraph.

_____ **(c).** the writer doesn't use more than three major ideas in the paragraph.

_____ **(d).** the writer indicates a thorough knowledge of his or her topic.

3. In making a single point, which of the following statements would work best as a topic sentence?

_____ **(a).** Some scientists believe that our universe will end by being burned up.

_____ **(b).** Our universe used to harbor dinosaurs, and it is now expanding.

_____ **(c).** Some scientists believe that the universe started with a big explosion and that we are living in an era of anti-gravity, but this view is disputed.

_____ **(d).** Do you believe that humans will be around forever and that ancient Greece was a wonderful civilization?

4. To be discussible, your topic sentence should

_____ **(a).** be on a topic that everyone likes.

_____ **(b).** state your opinion, point of view, or feelings on the topic

_____ **(c).** be short and clear.

_____ **(d).** reflect your educational background.

5. "Bill sang 'It Had to Be You' at my sister's engagement party" is _NOT_ a good topic sentence because it is:

_____ **(a).** too personal.

_____ **(b).** an utterly boring topic.

_____ **(c).** referring to an old song.

_____ **(d).** too narrow.

6. If your topic sentence is too narrow, you will have a hard time

_____ **(a).** making it humorous.

_____ **(b).** writing an essay that will earn you a top grade.

_____ **(c).** finding anything interesting to add to it.

_____ **(d).** pleasing your audience.

7. The broad topic sentence proposes

_____ **(a).** too big a topic for a paragraph.

_____ **(b).** several unrelated ideas.

_____ **(c).** an idea that broadens your mind.

_____ **(d).** a sentence that contains several subordinate clauses.

8. A good topic sentence should

_____ **(a).** be shocking so as to catch the reader's attention.

_____ **(b).** sound as if you were speaking to your reader.

_____ **(c).** be neither too narrow nor too broad.

_____ **(d).** make you feel enthusiastic about your topic.

9. Which of the following is *NOT* a requirement for the ideal topic sentence:

_____ **(a).** Make a single point.

_____ **(b).** Make a discussible point.

_____ **(c).** Make a point that is neither too narrow nor too broad.

_____ **(d).** Make an unforgettable point.

10. Although the paragraph is an invention of writing, we also

_____ **(a).** sing in paragraphs.

_____ **(b).** dream in paragraphs.

_____ **(c).** talk in paragraphs.

_____ **(d).** do crossword puzzles in paragraphs.

Unit Talk-Write Assignment

The following conversation in the student lounge took place between two students. The topic was drinking water—a subject covered in a television special report one student had seen the night before. From the discussion, extract a discussible topic sentence and develop it into a paragraph written in standard English and supported by appropriate ideas and details. You may use any sentences and ideas found in the discussion as well as add your own. Write your paragraph on the lines provided.

Conversation

Francine: Cool. You like Evian water, too.

Chuck: This is my last bottle. I'm going on the wagon.

Francine: Gee, you sound like you're addicted.

Chuck: Yeah, I know, but didn't you watch Channel 4 last night when they reported on bottled water?

Francine: Nah, I was too busy doing homework. What'd they say?

Chuck: They reported on some lab tests done on bottled water—you know, Evian, Naya, Sahara, Arrowhead, Alpwater, Crystal Geyser, and others I can't remember.

Francine: So?

Chuck: Well, it was awesome. They found that these so-called designer waters had just about the same level of purity as tap water. Can you believe that?

Francine: You're kidding? How can that be?

Chuck: I don't know, but that's what the lab tests showed. Maybe microbes accumulate while the water sits on shelves, or maybe tap water just isn't that dirty.

Francine: Well, I don't care. I'll pay a few pennies more; the taste is worth it.

Chuck: It's more like bucks more.

Written Paragraph

_____

_____

_____

_____

_____

_____

_____

_____

_____

_____

Unit Collaborative Assignment

A. All of the following sentences could be written in a paragraph, but they are missing a topic sentence. Read them aloud to a partner, who should then supply a topic sentence for you to write below. Working together, make the topic sentence clear and discussible.

1. Benjamin Franklin invented the lightning rod, bifocals, and other practical items.
2. He was apprenticed to a printer and became a successful editor.
3. He became the U.S. ambassador to France.
4. He started the first lending library.
5. He helped draft the Declaration of Independence.
6. He was a member of the 1787 Convention that produced the U.S. Constitution.

Topic sentence: _____

_____

B. Now have your partner read you the following sentences, and then you try to supply an appropriate topic sentence.

1. The curtains are grimy and torn.
2. The posters on the wall are old and falling off the wall.
3. Mark's bed is unmade.
4. Dirty dishes and coffee mugs litter Mark's desk.
5. Clothes are flung over chairs and even on the floor.
6. Candy wrappers lie all over the stained carpet.

Topic sentence: _____

_____

Unit Writing Assignment

Choose one of the numbered topics listed below and write a paragraph about it. Be sure to do the following:

- Decide on a purpose—to entertain, inform, or persuade.
- Take your audience into account.

■ Gather ideas by talking, freewriting, brainstorming, clustering, or journal writing.

■ Write a topic sentence that makes a single discussible point.

■ Check that all the sentences in your paragraph are about that single point.

1. High salaries paid to sports stars

2. A valuable lesson you learned in high school

3. Your opinion of sex and violence in movies

4. Your favorite restaurant

5. Why college students drink

Photo Writing Assignment

Study the following picture of people at a garage sale. Write your opinion about why these kinds of neighborhood events are so popular today. Begin with a discussible, single-point topic sentence.

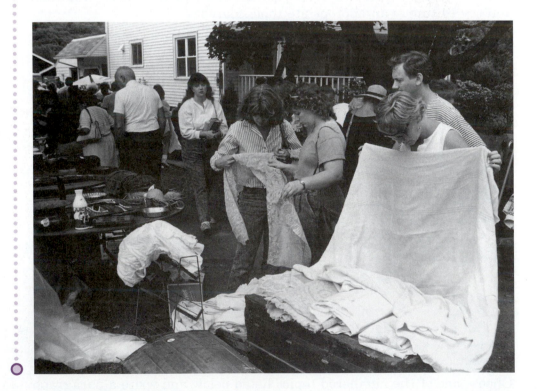

6

Adding Details

"What kinds of supporting details do paragraph writers most often use?
That depends on the topic sentence."

A typical paragraph consists of two main parts: a topic sentence and supporting details. The topic sentence is the sentence—usually the opening one—that states the main point of the paragraph. Supporting details are sentences that back up this main point with specifics. Here is a typical paragraph with the topic sentence underlined:

For all its popularity, satellite dish television is still riddled with drawbacks. The first drawback is the most serious. Most satellite dish television systems do not pick up local channels. If you want to watch the local news or local programming, you have to have a separate antenna. The second drawback is the expense. Satellite dish television can be quite expensive. In addition to installation charges, you also have to pay monthly subscription rates to a service provider. These charges can easily add up to a substantial monthly fee. The third drawback may seem odd, but it is nevertheless real. Satellite dish television systems offer too many program choices. Depending on the system you have and the server you subscribe to, a satellite dish system can offer in excess of 200 programs. Just navigating the maze of programming choices is a challenge and a headache. Finally, a satellite dish is not suitable for every home site. In fact, a lot of homes cannot use satellite dishes because of surrounding hills.

Supporting Details

What kinds of supporting details should writers use in a paragraph? That depends on the topic sentence. A good topic sentence suggests the kinds of details needed for its support. Basically, there are five kinds of supporting details:

- Examples
- Facts
- Testimony
- Reason and logic
- Personal observation

We'll cover each type of supporting detail separately.

Examples

An **example** is a part used to represent the whole. You say that working at Joe's Diner is hard. Someone asks, "What do you mean by hard?" For example, you say, employees must work 12-hour shifts without a break. Working long hours without a break is one small part of why working at Joe's Diner is hard.

The example is an effective supporting detail that is used as often by writers as by speakers. Here is an example from a student essay on the usefulness of the Internet:

> There's a lot of useful information available on the Internet. For example, I needed to find the words of the national anthem of Trinidad. I went to Yahoo!, entered "national anthem" in the search box, and was directed to a site called the World National Anthem Database. There I found the entire text of the national anthem for Trinidad. Another time, my mother wanted to find the exchange rate for Singapore dollars to send some money to a relative. Again, this information was readily found on the Internet, merely by going to a search engine and typing "foreign currency rates." It took all of two minutes to find what I was looking for. Indeed, almost anything you need to know can be found on the Internet. Here's another example: Not too long ago, I was doing a paper on old television shows and needed information on the sitcom "The Farmer's Daughter." I found an entire Web page devoted to the star, Inger Stevens. It contained all that I was looking for. Before the Internet, I would have had to go to the library and manually dig through reference books. What would have taken me a half a day to find, I found on the Internet in the matter of minutes.

To use examples, all you have to do is introduce them with a suitable phrase such as *for example, for instance, take the case of,* and then spell out the example you have in mind. Naturally, any example you use should support your point. For instance, Joe's Diner may have a wonderful employee training program but mentioning that won't support your point that *working at Joe's Diner is hard.*

PRACTICING 1

Write two appropriate examples that support the following topic sentences.

1. Topic sentence: The sound in movie theaters today is deafening.

First example: _____

_____

Second example: _____

_____

2. Topic sentence: There are some advantages to owning an ordinary wristwatch with a minute hand.

First example: _____

_____

Second example: _____

_____

3. Topic sentence: Telling lies can ruin a friendship.

First example: _____

_____

Second example: _____

_____

Facts

A **fact** is a statement that is accepted or can be verified. Anyone who is curious can look up the statement in a proper source and verify its truth. For instance, the fact that George Washington was born on February 22, 1732, can be confirmed by checking the encyclopedia or any biography of our first president. Some facts are simply accepted by everyone because they have never been proven untrue. That sooner or later all humans die is one such fact.

The opposite of a fact is an opinion. Unlike a fact, an **opinion** is a personal belief that cannot be proved either true or false. Here are some examples of facts and opinions:

Accepted fact: The sun rises in the east.
Verifiable fact: Toni Morrison wrote *The Bluest Eye.*
Opinion: Toni Morrison's best book is *The Bluest Eye.*

That the sun rises in the east is a universally accepted fact, and every morning nature again confirms its truth. Anyone can look up who wrote *The Bluest Eye,* and every book consulted will give the same answer: Toni Morrison wrote it. However, it is not universally accepted that *The Bluest Eye* is Morrison's best book. Some readers will argue that *Song of Solomon* is her best, whereas others will make that claim just as strongly for *Sula*. The third statement is therefore an opinion because it is not universally accepted like the first nor verifiable like the second.

Here is a paragraph that supports its topic sentence with facts:

> <u>The prices of computers have come down dramatically</u>. Just a little over a year ago I bought a 233 MHz computer with 32 megabytes of RAM, a CD-ROM drive, and a 14-inch monitor. I paid a little over $1800 for it. Today in the newspaper, that same system, with the same amount of memory and same size monitor, was advertised for $199. To make matters worse, my system was a clone—meaning an off-brand that was assembled locally. The $199 system was a known national brand backed up by a good warranty. But when it comes to buying a computer, it's no use waiting. Prices are always coming down.

Properly cited, facts add believability to a paragraph. Of course, you must always be sure that your facts are indeed facts and not opinions. Ask yourself, can a reader look up this statement and confirm its truth? If not, the statement is an opinion, not a fact.

Unfortunately, facts do not grow on trees. Seldom do writers have at their fingertips all the facts they need to write about a particular topic. Most of the time, they have to dig them up before they can do the writing. Digging up facts may involve interviewing particular people or even conducting a mini-survey. Some assignments may require you to interview certain professors or even your fellow students.

Generally, the best place for finding facts is the library. Encyclopedias there are literally brimming with helpful facts on nearly every topic. Moreover, many libraries are staffed by friendly librarians who can help you find facts on almost anything. All you have to do is ask. In addition to the books and magazines available in your local library, another vast storehouse of facts on virtually any topic is the Internet. To search the Internet, you merely go to a search engine such as *google.com* and type in your topic. Many libraries provide Internet hookups through their local computer systems. Ask your librarian what's available in your own local library.

PRACTICING 2

Fill in the blank beside each statement with an *F* if it states a fact or an *O* if it states an opinion.

1. _____ Winter is the most dismal time of the year.

2. _____ From the outside, the White House is an attractive building.

3. _____ The U.S. soldiers who served in the Vietnam War have not been appreciated enough.

4. ＿＿＿ English is the national language of Jamaica.

5. ＿＿＿ The Civil War ended on April 9, 1865.

6. ＿＿＿ Many critics say *Plan 9 from Outer Space* by Ed Wood is the worst movie ever made.

7. ＿＿＿ The first jigsaw puzzle was made in 1762.

8. ＿＿＿ Crossword puzzles are challenging to do.

9. ＿＿＿ Over the years, many comic strips sound stale.

10. ＿＿＿ English should be made the national language of the United States.

PRACTICING 3

Support the following topic sentences with at least three facts. You may need to interview or survey classmates or visit your library or log on to the Internet.

1. **Topic sentence:** Foreign students are a large and important part of my college campus. *Or,* There are few foreign students in my school.

First fact: ＿＿＿＿＿＿＿＿＿＿＿＿＿＿＿＿＿＿

＿＿＿＿＿＿＿＿＿＿＿＿＿＿＿＿＿＿＿＿＿＿＿

Second fact: ＿＿＿＿＿＿＿＿＿＿＿＿＿＿＿＿

＿＿＿＿＿＿＿＿＿＿＿＿＿＿＿＿＿＿＿＿＿＿＿

Third fact: ＿＿＿＿＿＿＿＿＿＿＿＿＿＿＿＿＿

＿＿＿＿＿＿＿＿＿＿＿＿＿＿＿＿＿＿＿＿＿＿＿

2. **Topic sentence:** The school cafeteria serves a nutritious menu at reasonable prices. *Or,* The school cafeteria serves bad food at high prices.

First fact: ＿＿＿＿＿＿＿＿＿＿＿＿＿＿＿＿＿＿

＿＿＿＿＿＿＿＿＿＿＿＿＿＿＿＿＿＿＿＿＿＿＿

Second fact: ＿＿＿＿＿＿＿＿＿＿＿＿＿＿＿＿

＿＿＿＿＿＿＿＿＿＿＿＿＿＿＿＿＿＿＿＿＿＿＿

Third fact: ＿＿＿＿＿＿＿＿＿＿＿＿＿＿＿＿＿

＿＿＿＿＿＿＿＿＿＿＿＿＿＿＿＿＿＿＿＿＿＿＿

3. Topic sentence: Riding a motorcycle can be dangerous and expensive.

First fact: _____

_____

Second fact: _____

_____

Third fact: _____

_____

Testimony

Testimony is expert opinion that backs up your topic sentence. The expert may be someone who is recognized in the field or who has had personal experience with your topic. Of course, getting the testimony you need may require you to do research or interview the right people. Here is a paragraph that has both kinds of testimony—the personal experience and expert opinion. The topic sentence is underlined.

When it comes to swimming in an unfamiliar place, it is always wise to look before you leap. I found out that truth one day when I dove into an unfamiliar river and hit the bottom. Fortunately, I was only dazed, not seriously hurt. My friend, Brenda, who is a park ranger, says that almost every week she is called to the scene of a diving accident. She says the accidents are usually caused by reckless diving into unfamiliar water. Only last year she pulled a young boy out of the Chattahoochee River, who had dived and hit his head against a rock. He'd never swum in that stretch of the river before and was showing off to his friends. Although he broke his neck, he was lucky because he regained the use of his legs after physical therapy. "Two summers ago, another boy did the same thing in the same stretch of river and is now confined to a wheelchair for the rest of his life," Brenda said. "When it comes to a strange stretch of water, never dive without knowing the depth and first checking for submerged rocks and trees," Brenda advises.

As testimony, the writer first cites his own experience, and then quotes the expert opinion of his friend, Brenda.

PRACTICING 4

Cite at least two opinions as testimony supporting the following topic sentences.

1. Topic sentence: Students who study invariably get better grades than students who don't.

First opinion: _____

_____

Second opinion: _____

_____

2. Topic sentence: Speed reading techniques do not help in understanding poetry.

First opinion: _____

_____

Second opinion: _____

_____

3. Topic sentence: Living in a college dorm can be stressful.

First opinion: _____

_____

Second opinion: _____

_____

Reasons

Some topic sentences are best supported by **reasons**—explanations based on common sense, good judgment, clear thinking, and logic. This kind of support is most commonly used when a writer is trying to persuade the reader to change an opinion.

In the following paragraph reason is used to support the writer's argument that a constitutional amendment against flag burning should not be passed:

A constitutional amendment outlawing flag burning is a bad idea and should not be passed. To most Americans, flag burning is a repugnant gesture. I myself do not believe in flag burning and would never burn the American flag. Yet common sense tells us, and a 1989 Supreme Court decision agrees, that burning the flag is a form of political speech protected by the First Amendment. As a matter of fact, according to flag etiquette, the proper way to dispose of an old flag is to burn it. What we should respect and honor, above all else, are the principles of freedom enshrined in the Bill of Rights.

That, in part, is what the American flag stands for—the right to protest, even if the protest is unpopular, as protest frequently is. It makes no sense to desecrate what the flag stands for—freedom— in a misguided attempt to protect it.

Not every topic sentence can be supported by reason. However, for those topic sentences that can be—and your common sense should be the judge—reason and logic can be highly effective support.

PRACTICING 5

Use reasoning or logic to support one of the following topic sentences.

1.   Topic sentence: Imprisonment without the possibility of parole is cruel and unusual punishment.

_____

_____

_____

_____

_____

2.   Topic sentence: For certain inhuman crimes, imprisonment without the possibility of parole is just punishment.

_____

_____

_____

_____

_____

Personal observation

Some topics are strictly personal and must be supported mainly by your own **personal observation.** That old standby topic, "How you spent your summer vacation," is a classic example of a personal topic. Unless he or she vacationed with you, no librarian can help you find support for it. You must draw entirely on your own personal observations for support.

Personal observation includes descriptive details and examples. Here is an example of the use of both descriptive details and examples in a paragraph:

About a year ago I tried water skiing and hated it. Getting up on the skis was a battle to begin with, and once I got up, I found the ride frightening. I found myself stung by spray from passing boats, bumped by waves, and occasionally flattened by the wake of a passing boat. Falling was no joke. It hurts. Being slammed against the water when you're traveling over twenty miles an hour might look good in a television commercial, but in real-life it's painful. I fell three times. Once I thought I'd dislocated my shoulder. The second time I got water in my ear, and it took more than a week for it to come out. The third time I was almost knocked unconscious. That's when I decided water skiing was not for me.

The details this writer uses are not available in any library, but come solely from memory. Similarly, paragraphs written on such topics as a favorite place, a special friend, or the first day on a new job must be supported by such personal observations.

IN A NUTSHELL

The supporting details of a paragraph typically consist of examples, facts, testimony, reasons, and personal observations.

PRACTICING 6

Develop a topic sentence on one of the following subjects and write a paragraph about it, supporting the topic sentence with personal observations.

1. The best summer vacation I ever had

2. A family celebration

3. An encounter with prejudice

4. The first time I fell in love

5. A spectacular act of nature I once witnessed

Unit Test

Underline the words in parentheses that best complete the meaning of the sentence.

Example: The kinds of details a writer should include in a paragraph (are dictated by the writer's attitude on the subject/<u>depend on the topic sentence</u>).

1. A typical paragraph consists of two main parts: (the topic sentence and supporting details/five spaces of indentation and one topic sentence).

2. If you use an example, it (should be brief and vivid/should support your point).

3. A fact is a statement that (can be verified/is specific and concrete).

4. "Maine is a state in the United States" qualifies as (a myth/ a fact).

5. Testimony can back up your topic sentence if it is by (a famous person/an expert in the field).

6. Reasons are (decisions made by parents and teachers/ explanations based on logic).

7. Reason and logic (are always deceptive/can be effective) in supporting your topic sentence.

8. Because some topics are personal, they can be supported only (by your own observation/by the testimony of personal friends).

9. Personal observations come from (books in the library/one's own memory).

10. A good topic sentence (will suggest the details that should be used/cannot tell the writer what details to use).

Unit Talk-Write Assignment

In both talking and writing, we often use examples, facts, testimony, reason and logic, and personal observation to support our ideas. You can see this in the following example. Students in an English class were asked to talk to a classmate about the topic "useful inventions of the past twenty years" using at least two kinds of these supporting details. Here is what one student did. Using this paragraph as your source, write a paragraph in standard English on the lines that follow. Begin with a topic sentence, and use at least two kinds of supporting details.

Spoken Paragraph

I'm getting mixed up here because I can't member when the computer was invented. It would have my vote. Let's see . . . hmm . . . I think it was invented earlier than twenty years ago, so I guess that won't count. What was invented in the last twenty years—a useful invention? . . . hmm. I know there're lots of things, but it's hard to come up with something right off the bat . . . Oh, I got it! I love my strawberry toothbrush! My toothbrush tastes and smells like strawberries. It's a product that was invented by a woman who lives in Southern California right next-door to my family. Her company is called Plak-smacker, Inc. She also invented dentists' rubber gloves that smell like different fruit, but my dentist doesn't use these gloves, so I haven't smelled them. Anyway, they're probably more for little kids. But I think they are so cool. The newspaper said she started her company 11 years ago and now it's worth ten million dollars. Wow! I mean, why can't I think up something like a neat-smelling toothbrush? It's such a simple idea . . . man, it's almost stupid it's so simple. But, I suppose just having the idea ain't enough. You have to figure out how to make it, how to advertise it, and how to distribute it. But, man, you'd be independent with that kind of business. You'd be your own boss. I'd sure like that. So, anybody here want to start a business with me?

Written Paragraph

_____

_____

_____

_____

_____

_____

_____

_____

_____

_____

_____

_____

Unit Collaborative Assignment

Get together with two or three students in the class and talk out a paragraph on each of the following topic sentences. Discuss what types of supporting details the topic sentence requires and suggest some specific details that could be used.

1. Bicycle riding is good exercise.

2. It is hard to write without using "I."

3. Alcoholism is a disease, not a choice.

4. Doctors often keep their patients waiting too long.

5. Car phones are dangerous.

6. Television shows often give an unrealistic view of life.

7. The movement to rid the language of sexism has gone too far.

8. The movement to rid the language of sexism needs to go further.

9. Exercise is the best thing you can do for your health.

10. Polygamous marriages should be permitted for people over 75.

Unit Writing Assignment

Devise a discussible topic sentence on one of the topics listed below. Then develop a paragraph by supporting it with appropriate examples, facts, testimony, reason and logic, or personal details.

1. A boring event

2. Career moves

3. Tests as a predictor of success

4. Living with an older relative

5. The computer as an aid to education

6. What I would do if I won the lottery

7. Dealing with a phobia

8. The best way to meet people

9. Morality in politics

10. Going to the theater

Follow these steps:

- Choose the topic.

- Warm up by freewriting.

- Gather ideas by brainstorming.

- Narrow the subject to a manageable topic by clustering.

If you aren't happy with your topic at this point, put away what you've done, choose another topic, and repeat the listed steps.

Check your topic sentence by asking the questions that follow.

- Is it discussible, or is it too dry and narrow?

- What kinds of supporting details does it need?

Now complete your paragraph.

Photo Writing Assignment

The following photo shows a politician campaigning for office. Write about why candidates appear in public during a political campaign, even in the age of TV, radio, and the Internet. Begin with a discussible topic sentence, then support it with appropriate details.

7

Sticking to the Point and Linking Sentences

"The sentences of a true paragraph always function to make a common point. They are like horses pulling a cart in the same direction."

A paragraph has structure: It consists of lines of print, it is usually rectangular, and its first line is indented five spaces. A paragraph also has function: All the sentences are about a single point. If its sentences do not function this way, then the block of print cannot be called a paragraph.

Basically, here is what a paragraph does. First, it makes a point in the topic sentence. Second, it sticks to that point. Third, it tries to prove the point with details. Finally, all its sentences are linked together so that it is easy to follow the train of thought.

To write a solid paragraph, you should therefore do the following:

- Begin with a discussible point.

- Stick to the point.

- Prove the point; don't merely repeat it.

- Link your sentences to make your ideas easy to follow.

Unit 5 talked about the importance of making the point of a paragraph discussible; Unit 6 discussed how to prove your point by adding details. In this unit we will focus on how to stick to the point and how to link the sentences of your paragraphs.

Stick to the Point

A block of print on the page is not necessarily a paragraph just because it looks like one. Consider this example:

> Coach Burns is the opposite of what a coach should be. The clock in the kitchen is broken. The *Type A personality* is always nervous about something. Sailing is my favorite hobby. My mother saves everything—money, string, even rubber bands. This winter was unusually cold.

Although this block of print looks like a paragraph because its first sentence is indented, it isn't really one. Its sentences do not function like the sentences of a paragraph: Namely, they do not make a common point. Rather, each sentence is like a horse galloping in a direction different from the others. The sentences of a true paragraph, on the other hand, always function to make a common point. They are like horses pulling a cart in the same direction.

If you begin to write a paragraph about fairy tales, discuss only fairy tales—nothing else. Save all your other thoughts for another paragraph. Here is an example of a paragraph that drifts from the point:

> A fairy tale is a story about someone who faces difficulties but overcomes them. The lovely Cinderella is forced to stay home and clean the fire place while her mean stepsisters go to the royal ball. Sleeping Beauty is poisoned by her envious stepmother and falls into a deathlike sleep. As far as I'm concerned, fairy tales are silly. The kinds of stories I like are murder mysteries. I love Sherlock Holmes. He is the best fictional detective ever created. On a dull, rainy day, I love to sit home and read murder mysteries. In a sense, fairy tales reflect life as a challenge to succeed despite overwhelming odds. But fairy tales always have happy endings: Goodness is rewarded whereas evil is punished. In the end, Cinderella marries the handsome prince, and Sleeping Beauty is awakened by her lover's kiss. Of course, real life doesn't always have happy endings. Fairy tales are the ideal and represent life with hope.

It is easy to spot the annoying drift in the above paragraph. Here is the paragraph without it:

> A fairy tale is a story about a someone who faces difficulties but overcomes them. The lovely Cinderella is forced to stay home and clean the fire place while her mean stepsisters go to the royal ball. Sleeping Beauty is poisoned by her envious stepmother and falls into a deathlike sleep. As far as I'm concerned, fairy tales are silly. Yet in a sense, fairy tales reflect life as a challenge to succeed despite overwhelming odds. But fairy tales always have happy endings that teach moral lessons: Goodness is rewarded whereas evil is punished. Cinderella marries the handsome prince, and Sleeping Beauty is awakened by her lover's kiss. Of course, real life doesn't

always have happy endings. Fairy tales are the ideal and represent life with hope.

When the writer sticks to the point, the resulting paragraph is always sharper, crisper, and easier to read.

PRACTICING 1

Cross out the sentences that stray from the point in the paragraph below. The topic sentence is underlined.

If you're nervous about flying, here are a few tips to help you overcome your anxiety. First, before your trip, avoid coffee and candy or sweets. Caffeine and sugar raise your blood sugar level and will just make you more nervous. Second, take along something to do: A good book or some magazines or music tapes can take your mind a million miles away. On my last plane trip, I read the best book. I can't remember the title, but it was about a girl growing up and how she just eats and eats to smother the pain in her life. Some parts were very funny, but other parts were so sad. Sometimes it made me laugh; sometimes it made me cry. Another good way to avoid anxiety when you're flying is to practice deep-breathing. Put your head back, close your eyes, and breathe deeply. Inhale through your nose; exhale through your mouth. Fourth, try systematic muscle relaxation. Again, close your eyes and loosely fold your hands in your lap. Tense your toes, count to five, and relax them. Then do the same with your calves. Go all the way up your body to your jaw—tensing, counting, and relaxing. You can also do this exercise in other situations when you're tense or feel physical or emotional stress. You can do muscle relaxation and deep breathing exercises in just about any setting; you don't need to go to a gym. Don't expect to get over a fear of flying in one trip, but if you regularly practice these techniques, you'll soon be taking off and landing like a bird.

Prove the Point; Don't Merely Repeat It

Proving a point is not the same as repeating it. When you prove a point, you add something new to it—an example, a fact, a reason, an expert's opinion. Look at this paragraph, for example:

A sensible diet is an important part of keeping healthy. But many people just don't eat well. They are content to gobble on the run, paying no attention to what they eat. Gobbling down food without regard to what you're eating is unhealthy. You should always ensure that the diet you eat is good for you. How can you expect to avoid illnesses if you pay no attention to your eating habits? Truly, poor diets lead to poor health.

The paragraph adds nothing to the underlined topic sentence, but merely repeats the idea in different words. Here, on the other hand, is a paragraph that adds supporting details to the same topic sentence:

    <u>A sensible diet is an important part of keeping healthy.</u> By "sensible diet," I mean eating the following foods on a daily basis: whole grains, fresh vegetables and fruit; low-fat or nonfat dairy products; small portions of chicken, fish and occasionally red meat; and 4 to 5 servings of nuts and seeds per week. Whole grain breads and pastas supply necessary fiber. Vegetables and fruits are also good sources of fiber as well as vitamins and minerals. Some vegetables, such as broccoli and cabbage, even have cancer-fighting agents. Nonfat dairy products add calcium to the diet. Fish, chicken, and beef are important for protein. Nuts and seeds are good sources of fiber and unsaturated or "good" fat. Following such a diet seems a sensible and easy way to feel energetic and safeguard your health.

The writer moves quickly from the assertion that a sensible diet is healthy to explaining exactly which foods are healthy and why.

IN A NUTSHELL

To write a solid paragraph, you should do the following:

- Begin with a discussible point.
- Stick to the point.
- Prove the point; don't merely repeat it.

PRACTICING 2

The following topic sentence is followed by a number of details. Mark a plus (+) beside the statements you think add something specific to the topic sentence and a minus (−) beside those that merely repeat it.

Topic sentence: <u>The prices of new cars are coming down for several reasons.</u>

1. _____ Rather than going up, new car prices have been coming down.

2. _____ The U.S. dollar has been strengthening against the Japanese yen, allowing Japanese car manufacturers to lower their prices without sacrificing profit.

3. _____ My dad, who sells new cars, says now is the time to buy—when prices are low.

4. _____ Many analysts project that U.S. sales of cars and light trucks will fall in 2003 by nearly one million units. Less demand means lower prices.

5. _____ The return of leased cars to the market contributes greatly to lower demand for new cars.

6. _____ Some sticker prices have fallen as much as eight percent.

7. _____ Sports utility vehicles, compact cars, luxury cars—they all cost less today.

8. _____ To increase sales, many manufactures have not only lowered sticker prices, they've also increased their rebates.

9. _____ If you've been trying to decide between a new and a used car, bear in mind that new car prices are down.

10. _____ Because of lower demand, many new car dealers are willing to sell their vehicles for only 3 to 4 percent over dealer costs.

Link the Sentences

A paragraph is a block of print with all its sentences on the same topic. Consider this example:

> Coaching a youth soccer team may look like fun, but it's actually hard work. You have to teach the children which goal to score on and which one to defend. I line them up with their backs toward the goal they are to defend. I point to the goal they are facing and tell them that that is their target. You have to teach them how to dribble. You have to teach them the stutter steps that soccer players use when they run with the ball. They trip and stumble. They get the hang of it. You have to teach them how to shoot a goal. They kick the ball with their toes, not their insteps. They do drills. They learn how to make the basic soccer shot. You have to teach them how to make a soccer tackle. It takes a while. They get the idea that they should go for the ball, not for the opponent's foot. They thoroughly enjoy the game, especially the running up and down the field, which exhausts them but leaves them feeling good.

By our definition, the above is definitely a paragraph, but it is not a good one. The writing is choppy, and the writer's train of thought is hard to follow. Helpful links between its sentences are missing. Here is the same paragraph rewritten to add sentence links. The words that function as links are underlined:

> Coaching a youth soccer team may look like fun, but it's actually hard work. The first thing you have to teach the children is which goal to score on and which one to defend. I do that with a simple exercise. I line them up with their backs toward the goal they are to defend. Then I point to the goal they are facing and tell them that that is their target. The second thing you have to teach them is how to dribble. You have to teach them the stutter steps that soccer players use when they run with the ball. Usually, at first they trip and stumble, but then they get the hang of it. The third thing you have to teach them is how to shoot. At first, they kick the ball with their

toes, not their insteps. <u>But usually after a few</u> drills and a few practice shots, they learn how to make the basic soccer shot. <u>Finally,</u> you have to teach them how to make a soccer tackle. It takes a while, <u>but again, after a few drills,</u> they get the idea that they should go for the ball, not for the opponent's foot. <u>When they finally get it together,</u> they thoroughly enjoy the game, especially the running up and down the field, which exhausts them and leaves them feeling good.

Now we can easily follow the writer's thinking. The words *first thing, second thing, third thing,* and *finally* specify what the writer has to teach young children who play soccer and in what order. What was formerly an unemphatic series of steps is now expressed in a commonsense sequence. The transition sentence, "I do that with a simple exercise," and the transition phrase, "when they finally get it together," also help make the writing smooth, not choppy, by bridging the gap between ideas.

A paragraph whose sentences are properly linked is said to have **coherence.** The word *coherence* comes from *cohere,* which means "to stick together," "to be united." Simply putting down one sentence after another in sequence on the page is not enough to make them coherent. It is usually necessary to somehow link them by grammar or by theme. To link the sentences of a paragraph, writers use the following techniques:

- Transition words and phrases
- Repeated key words and pronouns
- Similar sentence patterns

Transition words and phrases

A *transition* is a word or phrase that links the sentences of a paragraph together. In the following paragraph, the transitions are underlined:

> A simple but nutritious meal you can prepare is Jamaican stew peas. Moreover, it can be prepared in advance. Begin by soaking the peas overnight—actually, kidney beans but Jamaicans call them "peas"—until they soften somewhat and swell. <u>The next morning,</u> put the peas in a big pot with a ham bone that has just enough meat left on it to add flavor to the dish. Cover the peas and ham bone with water. Then add half a green pepper. Usually the best pepper to use is a Scotch Bonnet, which is found in the produce section of most big supermarkets. <u>However,</u> be sure to take the seeds out before you put the pepper in the pot. <u>Remember, also,</u> to leave out the salt; the ham bone adds enough salt. <u>Next,</u> add a sprig of fresh thyme. <u>Now,</u> partly cover the pot and allow the dish to stew down. Gradually, the mixture will turn brown and thicken. This can take anywhere from 5 to 7 hours. <u>All you have to do then</u> is serve the stew peas hot over rice for a delicious and unusual main dish that will stick to the ribs.

The writer makes it easy to follow the directions by linking the sentences with transitional words—*you begin, the next morning, however, remember, also, after that,* and *all you have to do then*. Here are some other common words and phrases used to link sentences:

Common transitional words or phrases

after all	but	however	in spite of	plus
also	finally	in addition	moreover	therefore
and	for example	in contrast	nevertheless	what's more
as a consequence	for instance	in fact	next	

PRACTICING 3

Link the following sentences to make it easy for the reader to follow the train of thought.

Example: He knew that no one could blame him for being late. It was not his fault that his car broke down.

Answer: He knew that no one could blame him for being late. <u>After all,</u> it was not his fault that his car broke down.

1. It rained and stormed the whole night long. We enjoyed ourselves.

_____

_____

_____

2. I love my English class. I like grammar.

_____

_____

_____

3. First I stopped at an ATM. I went to the bookstore.

_____

_____

_____

4. Chang skipped breakfast that morning. She skipped lunch.

_____

_____

_____

5. We stood in line for hours. The box office opened.

_____

_____

_____

6. I have three goals. I want to get my diploma. I want to find a job in Seattle. I want to go to Australia.

_____

_____

_____

7. He's very organized. He's the most organized person I know.

_____

_____

_____

8. I had a lot to do this morning. I still found time to study.

_____

_____

_____

9. My mother paid me a surprise visit. I couldn't go out on a date.

_____

_____

_____

10. My sister Jane is tall and skinny. My sister Elizabeth is short and muscular.

_____

_____

_____

Repeating key words and pronouns

Another way to link the sentences of a paragraph is to repeat key words and pronouns. **Pronouns** are words that take the place of nouns, such as *he* for *Uncle Bertie* or *it* for *the book*. Here is an example (the topic sentence is also underlined):

My uncle Bertie is an avid fisherman. He has caught more fish than anyone I know. When he sets out on a fishing trip, it's like he is going on an expedition. He generally packs at least two tackle boxes full of fishing equipment. One time I went trout fishing with him in the mountains of Reno, and we spent the night camping at the trout stream. He showed me how to tie a fly and how to cast in the whirlpools where trout like to hide. He taught me so well that I caught five trout. Uncle Bertie is not only a great fisherman, he's a great teacher, too. His love for fishing is catching.

The sentences of this paragraph are tightly linked by the repetition of the key words *Uncle Bertie, fishing, fisherman, trout* and the pronouns *he* and *him*.

PRACTICING 4

Read the following paragraph to understand what is happening. Then write the appropriate key words or pronouns in each blank.

Mary decided her dog, whose name is François, needed a bath. _____ grabbed the doggy shampoo, and then _____ grabbed _____ as _____ was trotting past. Before _____ knew what was happening, _____ dunked _____ in a basin filled with water. _____ put up a fight, but _____ was no match for _____ . First _____ wriggled furiously, but _____ held _____ firmly and refused to let go. Then, _____ began an unearthly howling, but it had no effect whatsoever on _____ . In fact, _____ began howling too as if _____ were playing a game. Suddenly, _____ gave a huge leap and nearly bounded out of the basin. But _____ was ready for this tactic, which _____ had tried during previous baths. No matter how _____ struggled, _____ could not escape _____ grip. Eventually, the poor dog surrendered, and _____ scrubbed _____ until _____ was the cleanest _____ on the block.

Similar sentence patterns

This linking technique simply means that similar ideas are expressed in similar words. For example, you could use the same sentence patterns to compare people, places, things, or ideas, as the writer does below (the topic sentence is also underlined):

My Aunt Rosa and my Uncle Harry are so much alike that it's almost scary. Aunt Rosa worries constantly and about everything. Uncle Harry also worries about everything. When Aunt Rosa goes on an airplane trip, she always buys millions of dollars worth of flight insurance. When Uncle Harry goes on an airplane trip, even a short one, he always makes sure that his will is up-to-date. If Aunt Rosa is driving to the neighborhood grocery store, she always gets dressed in her best clothes so she will look good if she's killed in an accident. If Uncle Harry is driving to the convenience store, he likewise always dresses up in his best clothes for the same reason.

<u>Should a black cat cross</u> Aunt Rosa's path, she'll turn around and come right back home. <u>Should a black cat cross</u> Uncle Harry's path, he'll go to bed for the rest of the day. Both, however, have a sense of humor about the way they are. <u>Aunt Rosa laughs</u> at Uncle Harry and tells him he's foolish. <u>Uncle Harry, in turn, laughs</u> at Aunt Rosa. Yet both of them are unable to see how much alike they are.

Notice the definite pattern used in this paragraph to compare Aunt Rosa to Uncle Harry. For each point the writer first talks about Aunt Rosa and then Uncle Harry, using the same sentence pattern. This technique makes the ideas in a paragraph easy to follow.

IN A NUTSHELL

Help your reader follow your train of thought by:

- Using transitions.
- Repeating key words and pronouns.
- Using similar sentence patterns.

PRACTICING 5

In the following passages underline the repeated sentence patterns.

Example: Emotion <u>has taught people</u> to reason; reason <u>has taught people</u> the importance of emotion.

1. Exercising is a habit; not exercising is also a habit.

2. I hate opera almost as much as I hate ballet.

3. In the 1960s, it was rock and roll; in the 1970s, it was disco; and in the 1980s, it was hard rock.

4. Are we here to talk or are we here to work?

5. Love is ennobling; hate is demeaning.

6. I have many a dream. I also have many a nightmare.

7. To feed a man for a day, give him a fish. To feed a man for a lifetime, teach him to fish.

8. I clean the basement every spring, and I clean the garage every fall.

9. The food we like to eat as adults is the food we liked to eat as children.

10. At out first meeting, we fell in love. At our second meeting, we fell out of love.

Unit Test

Mark the sentence in each pair that agrees more closely with this unit.

Example: _____ **(a).** Sentences are like horses pulling a cart in different directions.

✔ **(b).** Sentences are like horses pulling a cart in the same direction.

1. _____ **(a).** A paragraph has both structure and function.

_____ **(b).** A paragraph has no special function, but it does have structure.

2. _____ **(a).** It is desirable to have a paragraph stray from its main point.

_____ **(b).** A paragraph must stick to its main point.

3. _____ **(a).** If your point is that chocolate makes you happy, then stick to that point.

_____ **(b).** If your point is that chocolate makes you happy, then contrast it with broccoli, which you hate.

4. _____ **(a).** When you prove a point, you just repeat it until it sinks into your reader's mind.

_____ **(b).** When you prove a point, you add something to it.

5. _____ **(a).** Several ways to prove your point are to use an example, a fact, a reason, or an expert opinion.

_____ **(b).** Your point is best proved by restating it in different words.

6. _____ **(a).** If all of the sentences of a paragraph are on the same topic, the paragraph will be a good one.

_____ **(b).** Having all of the sentences in a paragraph focus on the same topic does not guarantee that the paragraph will be a good one.

7. _____ **(a).** A paragraph that is choppy or hard to follow is probably the result of having no links between sentences.

_____ **(b).** If your writing seems choppy, use longer words.

8. _____ **(a).** Links between sentences are often called "transitions."

_____ **(b).** Links between sentences are often called "verbals."

9. _____ **(a).** One way to link sentences properly is to delete key words.

_____ **(b).** One way to link sentences properly is to repeat key words.

10. _____ **(a).** Using similar sentence patterns means that all ideas must be expressed in the same word order.

_____ **(b).** Using similar sentence patterns means that similar ideas are expressed in dissimilar words.

Unit Talk-Write Assignment

When we talk, we do not always take the time to **make a point, stick to the point, prove the point,** and **link sentences so that they make sense**—the main lessons of this chapter. However, in the passion of an argument, we generally make a point, stick to it, and try to prove it. Here is an example, a paragraph spoken by a student who thinks dog owners ought to train their pets properly. Her grammar is not always correct, nor are her sentences perfectly linked, but she does stick to her point and try to prove it. Your job is to turn this spoken paragraph into one that obeys all the rules in this chapter (boldfaced above) and is written in standard English. Feel free to add more or better supporting details that prove the point. Use the space provided below.

Spoken Paragraph

I get so ticked at people who just let their dogs run wild. It's so disgusting how many dog owners don't train their dogs to behave right. Really, it is. They must think that dogs will just outgrow their bad habits—puff! Magic!. Now that's just doggone stupid—oops, excuse the pun. Dogs don't know nothing about manners if you don't teach them. They're like children. They'll chew furniture, jump on strangers, bark when you leave the house, poop all over the place, and generally cause gross problems. Getting a dog is like having a child. You've got to be responsible. You can't just let a dog run wild cause once its growed up, you won't be able to control it. If you're too lazy to teach your dog, then take him to obedience school, where dog trainers will do the job for you. What I'm trying to say is that owning a dog means more than just providing food, water, and shelter, for Pete's sake. A good dog has to show respect for people. Our neighbor's dog terrifies me. Every time he sees me or anyone else, he growls and puts out his front paws in a weird way; then he tries to attack me even when he is on a leash. Our neighbor keeps his yard nice and his lawn mowed, and that's O.K., but he sure hasn't trained his mutt.

Written Paragraph

Unit Collaborative Assignment

Pair up with a classmate. One person should read the following paragraph aloud. Discuss how the paragraph can be improved according to what you have learned in this unit. Check the following:

- Does it have a discussible topic sentence?

- Does it stick to the point?

- Does it prove the point, or merely repeat it?

- Are all the sentences linked so the reader can easily follow the train of thought?

Then, you and your partner should work together to correct the paragraph. The topic sentence is underlined. Do all the sentences stick to the point? Are there enough details to prove the point? Are the sentences smoothly linked?

My grades would improve if I just learned to manage my time better. I could do some of my homework immediately after class. I have at least one free period after every class. I usually just goof around. I love hanging out with my friends. We go to the student union. We watch television together. We get something to eat. We look for girls to talk to. In the afternoons that I don't have to work, I could do homework. I don't. I read the sports pages. During the baseball season. I like to read the box scores for each game. Since I used to be a pitcher in high school, I especially like to read the stats on the pitchers. Greg Maddux is my favorite pitcher. He has the best ERA of any working baseball pitcher today. He's sure to get into the baseball Hall of Fame even if he never pitches another game. I don't know why I don't spend more time on my homework. My grades would improve. The only thing I can think of is that I should learn to manage my time better.

Unit Writing Assignment

Choose one of the numbered writing topics listed below. On a separate sheet develop a strong paragraph, observing the following guidelines:

- Begin with a discussible topic sentence.

- Support the topic sentence with appropriate examples, reasons, or personal observations.

- Stick to your point.

- Link your sentences smoothly.

You may want to first gather ideas by talking, freewriting, brainstorming, clustering, or journal writing.

1. Why you chose the college you did.

2. A time when you felt loved and appreciated.

3. A funny experience on the job.

4. What you like to do for exercise.

5. Expensive shoes.

Photo Writing Assignment

Examine this picture of two couples enjoying a meal in a restaurant. Do you like to dine out? Write a paragraph about your favorite restaurant. Make sure that your writing has a discussible topic sentence, is supported by appropriate evidence, sticks to the point, and contains smoothly linked sentences.

8

Narrating

*"The most frightening day of my life was when
I blew out to sea in a small rowboat."*

You are a careful driver, but one day as you sit at a stoplight minding your own business, someone rear-ends you and drives away. Fortunately, an alert pedestrian gets the hit-and-run driver's license plate, which you turn over to the police. You call your insurance agent, who asks you to write a paragraph telling how the accident happened. She says doing so might prevent an increase in your premium. This is what you write:

> The rear-end accident I was involved in last Saturday, April 6, 2002, was not my fault. I was stopped at a red light at the corner of Chamblee Road and Harts Mill, waiting for the light to change. I glanced in my rearview mirror and noticed a pickup approaching very fast from behind. Before I could react, the pickup was on top of me. At the last second, the driver swerved to avoid me, but still clipped my right rear fender. Then he ran the red light and sped away. Fortunately, a woman who lives in the neighborhood, Ms. Smith, was out walking her dog and got the pickup's license plate number, which I turned over to the police. I am a careful driver who pays all premiums promptly. I hope this accident, which was not my fault, doesn't increase my premium.

Without even knowing it, you have written a narration.

What Am I Trying to Do?

Tell a story: That is your assignment. It may be a make-believe story—fiction—or something that actually happened to you—a personal recollection. Telling a story of any kind requires you to use the strategy called **narration.**

Here is an example of a paragraph developed by narration:

> <u>The most frightening day of my life was when I blew out to sea in a small rowboat.</u> My father had warned me not to row out, saying that it was too windy, and I would have trouble controlling the boat. But I was 13 and knew it all. So I set out in the sound off Hilton Head Island and soon I was out in deep sea. Two dolphins swam up to the boat and began playing. I became so fascinated with them that I lost track of where I was and how hard the wind was blowing. By the time I looked around, I had drifted to the mouth of the sound. I ran out the oars and began pulling, but it was no use in that wind. The boat was being blown out to the Atlantic. I screamed. I waved at passing boats. But no one heard or saw me. Soon I was in dark blue water and bouncing in a strong sea. Suddenly, I saw a motorboat slicing through the whitecaps, heading for me. It was Dad. He threw me a rope and towed me to shore. He never said a word. He didn't have to. I had learned my lesson.

This is a typical narration. It has a beginning, middle, and end. It occurs in time and makes a point.

Any assignment that asks you to recollect an incident, relate a memory, or tell a story is asking for a narration. Of all the strategies for writing, narration is probably the one you use most in daily talk. We all tell stories during the course of our waking hours, whether brief little incidents that happened to us or longer, more involved episodes. We may tell those stories off-the-cuff and without any conscious eye to technique, but a story is a story, whether it is written or told orally. In sum, you know how to do a narration because you have a lot of experience with talking the form.

The aim of most narratives is to entertain. Long before radio or television, people got together and told stories. Some narratives, however, aim to inform or even persuade. The rowboat story, for example, preaches a valuable lesson: We should heed the advice of those who are more experienced. If we don't, we put ourselves at risk and may pay a high price.

IN A NUTSHELL

- Narration is the strategy of storytelling.
- Most narratives are written to entertain, but they may also inform or persuade.

PRACTICING 1

In the blanks provided check the sentences that would best be developed by narration.

1. _____ Something dreadful happened to me on the afternoon of my graduation from Freemont High School.

2. _____ Thousands of criminal shootings each year prove that no one except police officers or military personnel should be allowed to carry guns.

3. _____ Martha's career has taken some interesting twists and turns.

4. _____ Let me tell you about how I risked my life when I flew in a private plane.

5. _____ I thought my first fishing trip would be my last.

6. _____ Donations of body organs are increasing annually.

7. _____ It is easy to learn to play the piano if you follow these four tips.

8. _____ The day of my parents' divorce was one of the most difficult of my life.

9. _____ Rats live in many neighborhoods where ivy grows abundantly.

10. _____ It was time to say goodbye to my family.

How Can I Do It?

Even though you've told hundreds of stories in your everyday chats, you probably have done so without consciously thinking of any technique. On the other hand, in *writing* a story it is best to start off with a definite idea of what to do. These are the steps you should take:

1. Compose your topic sentence.

2. Organize your story in time.

3. Use enough details.

Compose your topic sentence.

An old Chinese proverb says that a journey of one mile or 5,000 miles begins the same way: with a single step. To write a narration, this first step should be to compose a topic sentence.

The topic sentence is the point of a narrative. It is a single sentence that tells what your story is about. A story without a topic sentence is pointless. Here is an example:

We would pretend to be making mud pies. Sometimes, we would splatter each other in a game of war. One day we imagined that we were pigs and flopped down on our backs in a mud puddle. Then we had a contest to see who could make the most convincing oink. My mother came home, caught us wallowing, and threw a fit. She said that we had gotten our clothes filthy and would have to wash them ourselves. And then she made us do it, too!

What is this all about, we wonder? We can't tell because, without a topic sentence, the story has no main point. Notice how much the paragraph is improved when we add a topic sentence:

<u>When I was 11, my cousin and I discovered how much fun it was to play in mud.</u> We would pretend to be making mud pies. Sometimes we would splatter each other in a game of war. One day we imagined that we were pigs and flopped down on our backs in a mud puddle. Then we had a contest to see who could make the most convincing oink. My mother came home, caught us wallowing, and threw a fit. She said that we had gotten our clothes filthy and would have to wash them ourselves. And then she made us do it, too!

A pointless story is not interesting or funny. Yet it is easy to fix. Simply express the point—whatever it is—in a topic sentence. Note, however, that some topic sentences are more interesting than others. You should word your topic sentence in a way that arouses your reader's interest. A dull topic sentence does not make someone want to read on. An interesting topic sentence has the opposite effect. It pulls the reader in. Here are some examples:

Dull: Once I almost got lost at sea.

Interesting: The most frightening day of my life was when I blew out to sea in a small rowboat.

Dull: My first kiss happened when I was 13.

Interesting: I'll never forget that thrilling moment when I was 13 and experienced my first kiss.

Read aloud your topic sentence, asking yourself whether it would make you want to read on or run out and see a movie.

PRACTICING 2

Rewrite the topic sentences below to make them more interesting. You can use your imagination to make up the details.

1. We almost missed our plane.

_____

_____

2. An interesting thing happened last Saturday.

_____

_____

3. My latest run-in with a family member bothered me.

_____

_____

4. Some things take courage.

_____

_____

5. From personal observation I know that drugs can ruin lives.

_____

_____

Organize your story in time.

Narration or storytelling is based on chronology for the simple reason that life, as well as stories, always takes place in time. Some of the time sequences used by storytellers are complicated, involving **flashbacks,** for example, which means beginning a story in the present and then going back to the past before returning to the present. The person telling the story might be an adult who sees a tree, which brings back memories of a childhood swing that dangled from the branch of a favorite oak tree. The story will then flashback to the narrator's childhood experiences with the swing.

Other stories, however, are quite straightforward and use a simple pattern: First this happened, then that, with one episode logically following another in a time sequence. Here is an example:

> My most memorable experience from elementary school happened in Ms. Higgins' geography class. She gave us a pop quiz that I hadn't studied for. When I saw the ten questions, I knew I was dead. I didn't know a single answer. I decided to guess. So I sat there at my desk, pencil in hand, and took a stab at giving my answers: A, or B, or C, or D. The next day Ms. Higgins returned our papers with a big orange smiley face drawn on mine. That meant only one thing—I'd gotten the highest mark in the class. And I had. I'd guessed nine of the ten correctly. Later, Ms. Higgins said to me that this just went to prove what I could do if I would only study!

This narrative takes place in time, as do all narratives, and the writer uses transitions to move the story along—*when, so, the next day,* and *later.* Without these transitions, the story loses its sense of episodes occurring in time. Here it is with the transitions omitted:

My most memorable experience from elementary school happened in Ms. Higgins' geography class. She gave us a pop quiz that I hadn't studied for. I saw the ten questions. I knew I was dead. I didn't know a single answer. I decided to guess. I sat there at my desk, pencil in hand, and took a stab at giving my answers: A, or B, or C, or D. Ms. Higgins returned our papers with a big orange smiley face drawn on mine. That meant only one thing—I'd gotten the highest mark in the class. And I had. I'd guessed nine of the ten correctly. Ms. Higgins said to me that this just went to prove what I could do if I would only study!

Some common time transitions are:

afterward	later	when	immediately
shortly afterward	soon	while	suddenly
the next day (or night)	before	then	now

When you write your own stories, use suitable transitions to link the episodes together in an understandable time order.

PRACTICING 3

The sentences that follow, from a paragraph describing the beginning of a student's day, are jumbled in their time sequence. Using your common sense, arrange the sentences in the most emphatic time order.

(1) For the six years he has been my favorite pet, I hadn't wanted to have him neutered for the same reason that I wouldn't want to be neutered. (2) The vet explained that Thumper would be less territorial if he were neutered. (3) This morning when I woke up, my cat, Thumper, was licking my face. (4) But this macho behavior that was always getting him involved in cat fights had to stop. (5) And so the deed was done for another $35. (6) It cost me $100 that I couldn't afford. (7) I hope it works. (8) I got dressed in a hurry and rushed him to the vet, where he was given seven stitches. (9) I decided it was time to neuter Thumper. (10) At first I thought he was hungry and wanted to be fed, but then I realized he was bleeding from a gash on his ear. (11) I don't know who was winning all those fights, but I know that my wallet was losing. (12) I made a decision then that I had been putting off.

_____

_____

_____

_____

_____

_____

_____

_____

_____

_____

_____

PRACTICING 4

Supply the missing transitions in the following sentences. Try to vary the transitions you use.

1. For six days, he worked steadily, but made little progress. _____ he gave up and went home.

2. The whole room broke into loud noise. Some people were singing; others were praying; and yet others were shouting. _____ it was dead still.

3. That morning, we parted in great anger. _____ he called me on the telephone and apologized for being so immature.

4. Life in Samoa begins at dawn when the cock crows. _____ mothers wake up to feed their babies, children drowsily roll out of their beds, and men get ready for early fishing.

5. I arrive at the airport and begin the aircraft check while my instructor waits. The check takes about 15 minutes, and I wish it were over. _____ my instructor and I climb into the cockpit.

Find enough details.

The details of your story will most likely come from your personal observations. Vivid details add to any story. To give you an idea of how important details are, here is the rowboat story with its details omitted:

> Once I almost got lost at sea. I was in a rowboat, which my father told me not to take out, but I did. Before I realized what was happening, I had drifted far from shore. But then my father came in a motorboat and got me.

Without details, the story is dull and bare. All kinds of questions are left unanswered. When did this happen? Where? Why didn't you notice that you were drifting out to sea? How did your father find you?

Details flesh out the drama of your story and give your reader a sense of "being there." They add believability and realism. Your reader will be swept along with your narrative if its details are convincing.

IN A NUTSHELL

To write a narrative, do the following:

- Compose your topic sentence.
- Organize your story in time.
- Use enough details.

PRACTICING 5

The following paragraphs are vague and empty because they lack details. Rewrite them, using details that make the narrative livelier.

1.

My uncle told me about something that happened to him. While on a business trip, he decided to buy gifts for his wife and daughter. He strolled around, looking into shop windows for ideas. He was getting tired so he decided to have a cup of coffee and rest. The man sitting next to him looked somehow familiar. Gradually my uncle recognized that the man was his college roommate, whom he had not seen for 20 years.

_____

_____

_____

_____

_____

_____

_____

_____

2.

My first day in Math 101 was bad. The teacher's name was Mr. Goodman. At the stroke of 10:00 A.M., he called the roll, handed us a syllabus, and announced that usually 40 percent of the class dropped out because it was too difficult. I was concerned because I needed this class to graduate. I looked around and noticed that all the students looked worried. But I studied hard, and I got an A.

_____

_____

_____

_____

_____

_____

3.

Today my bird died. I had gone to work as usual. When I returned home, I opened the bird cage to let her out. I could tell something was wrong. I put her back in the cage, placed a warm towel under her, and tried to get her to drink some water. She wouldn't move. I went to the kitchen, and by the time I returned, she had died.

_____

_____

_____

_____

_____

_____

_____

_____

PRACTICING 6

Choose one of the following topics and write four episodes that make up the narrative. Use a transition to link each episode.

1. Recalling a severe or unjust punishment

2. Meeting an unusual person

3. Making peace after an argument

4. A funny adventure

5. How I survived an earthquake, a flood, a fire, a car crash, or some other disaster

Episode 1: _____

_____

Transition: _____

_____

Episode 2: _____

_____

Transition: _____

_____

Episode 3: _____

_____

Transition: _____

_____

Episode 4: _____

_____

Transition: _____

_____

What Do I Need to Look Out For?

Narratives are usually easy and fun to write. Nevertheless, here are three tips to help anyone write better narratives:

- Stick to one time frame.
- Pace the story.
- Stay in character.

Stick to one time frame.

Whenever you tell a story, you must choose one time frame and stick with it. If you are recalling an incident that happened in the past, you must begin in the past and end in the past. If you are telling the story in the present tense, you must stay in the present. You should not, say, switch midway, as in this sentence:

Shifting:　　I ran into the house and say to Jim, "Where have you been?"

Here is the sentence rewritten entirely in the past, and then entirely in the present. Either one is fine, as long as you are consistent.

Consistent:　　I ran into the house and said to Jim, "Where have you been?"

Consistent:　　I run into the house and say to Jim, "Where have you been?"

Hopscotching from past to present while telling a story is a common error. Here is an example:

> My cousin Lisa has proved once again that she is a perfect slob. Yesterday, at the First Presbyterian Church service where everyone dresses up, Lisa appears in an oversized sweatshirt, worn over bright red tights with a large hole in the left knee. Young and old members alike look away—anywhere but at Lisa—so they would not reveal their shock. But Lisa sits in her pew, quietly chewing gum as if she were a saint.

The story is easier to follow when the writer stays in one time frame, as in the corrected version that follows:

> My cousin Lisa has proved once again that she is a perfect slob. Yesterday, at the First Presbyterian Church service where everyone dresses up, Lisa appeared in an oversized sweatshirt, worn over bright red tights with a large hole in the left knee. Young and old members alike looked away—anywhere but at Lisa—so they would not reveal their shock. But Lisa sat in her pew, quietly chewing gum as if she were a saint.

PRACTICING 7

Correct the following paragraph so that it remains in one time frame—the past.

Last Wednesday I cleaned out my mother's garage, which made me feel proud of myself. It is spring vacation and I am home for the week. Each time I drive into the garage, I think to myself, "I really should help clean out this mess," but I let the first two days go by without acting on these better instincts. Mom did not say a word; in fact, she just washes all of my clothes, bakes me my favorite peanut butter cookies, and lets me use her car to go visit my friends. When I arrived home past midnight, she did not scold me or complain. She probably thinks that because I am a college student I am mature enough to keep whatever hours I choose. But midweek, my conscience just won't let me continue to take and not give. I announced, "Mom, today I am going to clean out the garage because it's too hard a job for you." Well, my mother was so grateful, she almost had tears in her eyes. To tell you the truth, once I was finished, I couldn't remember any job that had given me more satisfaction.

Pace the story.

Pacing the story means including the most important episodes and details. Although providing some of the details makes a story more interesting, good storytelling does not include every little detail. Narrating is not the same as keeping a diary in which you note every event in a day. Instead, a good narration is paced to include only the events and details that are important to moving the story forward.

Let us assume, for instance, that you have been asked to narrate an experience with crowds. Here's one student's first draft:

The only experience I've ever had with a crowd occurred at a rock concert where I was nearly crushed. As I waited for the concert to start, I was worried about how I would get home. My friend and I were wondering if we should take the bus or the train. My friend, whose name is Hazel, was saying that the bus might be slower but since everyone would probably want to take the train, we might be better off on the bus. We were deep into this discussion when a loud G-flat rang throughout the arena, and the concert got underway. About six songs into the concert, the mass hysteria began. The crowd began surging toward the stage, carrying me along like a riptide, separating me from Hazel and shoving me against the apron of the stage. The sweaty, pressing bodies of the audience crushed against me. I couldn't breathe. Somehow, I managed to escape, and the next thing I knew I was being swept to the side of the theater. There I saw Hazel, terror in her eyes. We wriggled along the wall until we reached an exit door. Frightened and bruised, we decided to leave, even though we could hear the concert in full, blaring swing. We didn't take the bus as we had decided we would. Instead, we took the train because it wasn't at all crowded.

This narrative is not well paced because it bogs down in unnecessary details about whether the narrator and her friend would take the bus or the train home. When the student was asked why she included these details, her answer was, "Because that's what happened."

But putting in everything that actually happened, especially if it has nothing to do with the point of your story, is a mistake. Notice how much the story is improved once its pacing is tightened:

The only experience I've ever had with a crowd occurred at a rock concert where my friend Hazel and I were nearly crushed. With the playing of a loud G-flat, the concert got underway. About six songs into the concert, the mass hysteria began. The crowd began surging toward the stage, carrying me along like a riptide, separating me from Hazel and shoving me against the apron of the stage. The sweaty, pressing bodies of the audience crushed against me. I couldn't breathe. Somehow, I managed to escape, and the next thing I knew, I was being swept to the side of the theater. There I saw Hazel, terror in her eyes. We wriggled along the wall until we reached an exit door. Frightened and bruised, we decided to leave, even though we could hear the concert in full, blaring swing.

Remember, pace your story. Skip over boring details that are beside the point. Focus only on what matters to the point you are making.

PRACTICING 8

Imagine that your assignment is to write a narrative paragraph with the following topic sentence: *My roommate, Buto, from West Nigeria, taught me a lesson about the dangers of stereotyping.* Read through the twelve details; then, go back and, in the blanks provided check the details that would slow down the pace of the narrative and make it boring. Now write the paragraph, using the topic sentence provided and the details that advance the narrative. Turn the details into complete sentences, and connect them with linking expressions where needed.

1. _____ My first meeting with Buto.

2. _____ My feelings about dorm life.

3. _____ How I stereotyped Buto as unsophisticated because he was from Africa.

4. _____ My reaction to other foreign students in our dorm.

5. _____ What happened when I was asked to join a fraternity.

6. _____ The first time I saw Buto working on a laptop computer.

7. _____ How I overcame my own computer phobia.

8. _____ Buto setting up a database for a large travel agency.

9. _____ Observing that he seemed to click on varied icons with enormous speed.

10. _____ A description of every computer command Buto gave.

11. _____ Learning later that because of his brilliance, Buto had received a $10,000 grant to study computer science at my university.

12. _____ My decision never again to prejudge an individual.

_____

_____

_____

_____

_____

_____

_____

_____

_____

Stay in character.

Many narratives are told from the first-person viewpoint, that is, I. Using this viewpoint often requires us to assume a certain voice. Whatever voice you begin with is the one you must use throughout the story, or its believability will suffer. Here is a narrative in the first person that uses the voice of a young child:

> When I was six years old, one of my Texas relatives tweaked my nose and told me that I had a "cute potato nose." I remember looking up at this towering woman and telling her, "No, I don't, and you

have a fat bottom." My mother, who was standing close by, looked at me in shocked horror, exclaiming, "Now, Marcie, that's no way to speak to Aunt Dorothy." I wondered, <u>"Why not? This woman has humiliated me by castigating my nose. She has hurt my ego, and she deserves to have me retaliate; it's only just."</u>

The underlined passage is a lapse in point of view because a six-year-old child would not use words like *humiliated, castigating, retaliate,* or even know the meaning of *ego.* A rewrite follows.

When I was six years old, one of my Texas relatives tweaked my nose and told me that I had a "cute potato nose." I remember looking up at this towering woman and telling her, "No, I don't, and you have a fat bottom." My mother, who was standing close by, looked at me in shocked horror, exclaiming, "Now, Marcie, that's no way to speak to Aunt Dorothy." I wondered, <u>"Why not? She hates my nose. I hate her fat bottom."</u>

The decision about which voice to use is largely a matter of common sense. Whichever voice you do use, you must stick with that voice (and character) throughout.

IN A NUTSHELL

When you write a narrative, be sure to stick to one time frame, pace the story, and stay in character.

PRACTICING 9

The following narration has an inconsistent voice. It is supposed to be written from the point of view of a dignified elderly woman. Cross out and rewrite the paragraph as necessary to keep the voice consistent.

Last Friday, I dented the passenger side door of my 1980 Buick. Gee whiz, what a bummer! I was sure ticked when I realized what had happened. I had reason to be seriously concerned because I am 78 years old and wondered whether the state would renew my license. Unfortunately, three months earlier I had slammed into a car as I was backing out of a parking space in front of Target's. Wow! When it rains it pours! It made me nuts. Alas, we "senior citizens," as society labels us, are treated as if we were a terrible

Unit Talk-Write Assignment

If you think that nothing worth writing about ever happens to you, you're wrong. If you have a topic sentence, pace your story, and include vivid details, the most ordinary experience can be made interesting, funny, or even suspenseful. Here is one student's spoken story of a frightening experience. Read the account carefully, and then turn it into a well-developed narrative, paced properly, supported by vivid details, and with a clear sense of an adult looking back on a childhood experience. Use the blanks provided.

Spoken Paragraph

When I was eight years old, I thought I was going to drown. Water is such a scary thing anyway. Even as I stand here remembering the experience, I feel a shiver go through my body. Man, it was such a . . . I mean, I'll never forget it. Moments like that stay glued to your brain for sure. Let's see, how did it all start? Oh yeah, my home town had a municipal swimming pool that created waves for five minutes every hour on the hour. I can't remember exactly how they did it, but it involved a machine that forced air out through an iron grid with bars about 1 inch apart. We loved going to this pool and would beg our parents for the $1.00 entrance fee. My brother, my little sister, and me would go every Saturday. We'd have so much fun. "Come on, let's dive the waves!" we'd scream as soon as it was wave time. Then we'd jump in the water, shoving each other, laughing, and spitting water in the air like fountains. We would dive under the surface and make faces at each other under water. Man, we had fun. One afternoon, I decided to swim under water to the end of the pool to see how the air was pushed through the grid. Whoa, what a bum idea! I was practically out of breath when I reached the grid. But in order to hang on and look inside, I grabbed the iron bars with my hands as well as one foot. Remember that all the time I'm under water. For some weird reason, my right big toe got stuck between two bars. I couldn't pull it out. I yanked, I tried to turn my toe sideways where it was thinner, but I couldn't move it. I started panicking and swallowing water. I figured I had had it. Finito! One thing I know, my whole life didn't pass before me as people say it does. I just felt scared, big time. In total desperation I yanked at my toe one more time, practically breaking the bone and scraping off the skin. Miracle! I was loose. I floated to the top. Then—get this—my brother yells, "Hey, Marty, let's play Blind Man's Bluff." "Yeah, Marty, come on," says my sister. These clowns never even noticed I was gone—and here I'd almost drowned!

Written Paragraph

_____

_____

_____

_____

_____

_____

_____

_____

_____

_____

_____

_____

_____

_____

_____

_____

Unit Collaborative Assignment

Choose a partner and take turns narrating to each other a humorous or embarrassing incident. Try to keep your partner interested in your story by practicing the lessons in this unit—use enough details, stay in one time frame, pace your story, and keep a consistent voice. The purpose of this exercise is to prepare you to write a good narration.

Unit Writing Assignment

Select one of the two following assignments:

    1. Narrate an event that helped you mature. Start with a topic sentence that gets your reader's attention. Pace your story to emphasize important actions and gloss over less important ones. If your event occurred during childhood, maintain a child's point of view throughout. Also, stay in the same time frame—the past. When you have completed your narration, read it aloud to someone whose opinion you value but do not fear. See what effect the narration has. If you are not satisfied, pace yourself better or add more vivid details.

    2. Write a paragraph describing the last time you quarreled with someone important to you. Arrange the main episodes in the most effective order and use transitions. Practice the other tips given in this unit.

Photo Writing Assignment

Study the following photo. Then use your imagination to tell a story about the picture. Keep in mind these rules: (1) watch your pacing and do not get bogged down in details that are off the point of the story; (2) maintain chronological order; (3) use a consistent time frame; and (4) use a consistent voice.

Describing

"What I saw was life on the edge of decay."

Picture this: You work in maintenance for an apartment complex. A renter has filed a complaint about a neighbor's messy patio. Your boss sends you to inspect the patio and write a report of what you see. You pay a visit to the apartment, look around, and write the following paragraph:

> The patio of apartment 14B is dirty and unsanitary. From the street you can see old tires and the rusty frame of a bicycle. When you get closer, you can see debris of various kinds—cans, empty soda bottles, and clothes. Stacks of old newspapers create a fire hazard. A rotten odor wafts up from the rubbish and over the entire backyard. The patio is clearly a filthy mess.

You have just written a description.

What Am I Trying to Do?

A **description** is a word picture. When you write a description, you try to portray a scene as you see, hear, taste, smell, and feel it, using nothing but words. Writing a good description requires close and careful observation with all your senses—sight, sound, taste, smell, and touch. Here is an example of one student's description:

> Rainbows add to the fairy-tale atmosphere of Hawaii. Warm showers are part of each day's weather. Lasting from five to ten minutes,

131

these pleasant showers are followed by beautiful rainbows. The rainbows on the island of Maui are particularly beautiful because Maui is mostly mountainous and filled with lush, green vegetation and brilliantly colored flowers. Driving through the mountains of Maui, you can suddenly spy a fully arched rainbow in the mist of a waterfall, with its orange, violet, and green bands bleeding into each other. Framing the picture is a shiny jungle of blooming vines and trees. The sight could be entitled "Rainbow Magic." It is absolutely breathtaking.

We use descriptions all the time in the business and academic worlds, in both writing and talk. Indeed, next to narration, description is probably the strategy we most use in our everyday chatting. You may have to describe for an insurance adjuster the damage a storm did to your property. Lab reports describe how cells look under a microscope. Eyewitnesses describe fleeing felony suspects. We write descriptions of missing pets and post the notices on lightposts. Indeed, description is quite possibly the most commonly used way to develop paragraphs.

IN A NUTSHELL

Description is a word picture.

PRACTICING 1

In the spaces provided check the topics that require a description.

1. _____ The techniques of safe driving
2. _____ A portrait of your mother
3. _____ What your room at home looks like
4. _____ The long-term effects of eating poorly
5. _____ Why good manners are important
6. _____ Typical student excuses for not doing homework
7. _____ Your new sofa
8. _____ How to deal with a grumpy boss
9. _____ What a typical gang member wears
10. _____ Your favorite scenic view

How Can I Do It?

To write a description, follow these three steps:

1. Decide on a dominant impression.
2. Use vivid supporting details.
3. Organize the details.

Decide on a dominant impression.

To write a vivid description, zoom in on a dominant impression. The **dominant impression** is the one feature that most stands out about what you are describing. It will become the topic sentence of your descriptive paragraph and guide you in selecting supporting details.

For example, let's say that you are describing a really nasty slum. You begin by asking yourself, "What feature of the slum most stands out?" Then you make that feature your topic sentence. Here is an example:

> <u>Cabbagetown is a hellish part of town where life is in a process of decay.</u> Its streets and dingy alleys are blanketed with a smelly humidity. Glancing at the wall to my left, I notice an ancient advertisement, rotting under years of dirt and dust. It reads, "Taylor's Drugstore—Coca-Cola 5 cents." An ugly, huge iron door dangles off its hinges under the Coca-Cola sign. Streams of water leak down the wall from the rusted roof gutters, like long fingers trying to claw the cement floor. Not far from where I stand is a soggy pile of wrappers, milk cartons, toilet paper, and rotting food. Next to my foot lies a faded, yellowish wrapper from a Mallow Cup. I jump instinctively when I hear a strange rustling noise, and see a grinning rat carrying a rotten apple core across the cracked concrete. A sudden mental slap reminds me of where I am. I turn and hurry away from this black hole of decay.

In deciding on a dominant impression, use your common sense: Pick the feature that most stands out about what you are describing. For example, a hummingbird generally appears to the naked eye as a whirring, fidgety blur. If you use "whirring, fidgety blur" as your dominant impression, writing the description will be fairly straightforward. You have lots of details to draw on. On the other hand, if you select as a dominant impression the brief glimpse you had of a hummingbird at rest, writing that description will be hard to do. Because hummingbirds are always moving and seldom still, it is far easier to find details to describe one that is whirring and fidgety than one that is at rest.

ESL Advice!

Don't be afraid to write about your homeland. American readers often find descriptions of foreign places very appealing. Moreover, you would be writing about something you know well, which is always easier to do than to tackle an unfamiliar subject.

In other words if you choose as your dominant impression a rare rather than a dominant feature, you make your job harder. An elephant can be described in terms of its delicateness rather than its massive bulk, but it is not easy to do. The feature that most stands out about a scene, person, animal, or object is always easier to support with details than the one that is rare and seldom seen.

IN A NUTSHELL

Use as a topic sentence the most dominant feature of what you are describing.

PRACTICING 2

Supply a dominant impression that might work for each of the following.

1. A baby lying in a crib

_____

2. Your local supermarket

_____

3. An elderly neighbor or relative

_____

4. The front of the main building of your college

_____

5. A particular musical instrument

_____

Use vivid supporting details.

The details of a good description come from your personal observations. They consist of what you see, smell, hear, taste, and feel. The trick in writing descriptive details is to be concrete, so your reader can see the picture you're creating. Here are some examples:

Vague: He was a big man.
Concrete: He was six feet five inches tall, weighed 250 pounds, and was bursting with muscles.

Vague: I bought a blue rug.
Concrete: I bought a deep blue rug with flecks of beige and a wide maroon border.

Vague: The restaurant was noisy.
Concrete: The restaurant was so noisy that we could barely talk above the blaring jukebox and clattering dishes.

Rich sensory details give your description believability and realism. To write with rich details means to use specifics. You name the colors and describe the sounds and odors, using language that is as exact as possible. Don't be satisfied with the dim picture. Brighten it by being specific and detailed.

Here is a description of a person that lacks specific sensory details:

> My political science teacher takes looking natural to an extreme. She doesn't wear makeup and dresses very casually. Professor Lola Bloodgood is what I call a granola woman.

Here is the same paragraph with specifics and sensory details added:

> My political science teacher takes looking natural to an extreme. She wears her stringy blond hair straight down to her shoulders, without even bothering to tie it back. Although her skin is pale, she wouldn't dream of using a light shade of blush on her cheekbones or a soft pink lipstick. She prefers khaki pants and gray sweatshirts to more attractive outfits. Whether it's cold or hot, she wears leather sandals, so she always looks as if she's going camping rather than giving a lecture in a college classroom. What can I tell you? Professor Lola Bloodgood is what I call a granola woman.

PRACTICING 3

Imagine that you are going to meet someone for the first time today. Write a description of yourself that will enable your new acquaintance to recognize you.

_____

_____

_____

_____

_____

_____

_____

_____

_____

_____

Comparisons

Comparisons can add sparkle to descriptions. Two such types of comparisons are the simile and the metaphor. The **simile** is a comparison that uses *like* or *as*. A **metaphor** is a comparison drawn without the use of *like* or *as*. Here are some examples:

Simile: He was <u>like a raging bull</u> when he saw the smashed fender.

He was <u>as angry as a raging bull</u> when he saw the smashed fender.

Metaphor: He <u>was a raging bull</u> when he saw the smashed fender.

Simile: He <u>cooed like a dove</u> when he first saw his newborn daughter.

Metaphor: He <u>was a cooing dove</u> when he first saw his newborn daughter.

Similes and metaphors add color to descriptions by creating images—pictures that spring to mind. We can well imagine the anger of a bull thundering with rage. Here are some other examples:

Simile: The ballerina leaped into the air and landed as delicately <u>as a butterfly</u>.

Metaphor: The ballerina <u>was a delicate butterfly</u>.

Simile: He ran the race <u>like a gazelle</u>.

Metaphor: He <u>was a gazelle</u> running the race.

Although similes and metaphors add color to a description, they should be used sparingly. They are like pepper in a stew: The trick is to add enough for flavor, but not too much to burn the tongue.

IN A NUTSHELL

- The supporting details of your description should back up your dominant impression.
- Use similes and metaphors in your descriptions.

PRACTICING 4

In the blanks provided indicate whether the comparison in each of the following sentences is a simile or a metaphor. Use *S* for simile and *M* for metaphor.

1. _____ I was as tired as the 1000-year-old man.

2. _____ Her eyes were two burning black coals.

3. _____ His heart beat like a drum.

4. _____ He was as stingy as old Scrooge himself.

5. _____ What an angel she turned out to be!

6. ____ He looked like a great big shaggy dog.

7. ____ My dorm monitor is all heart.

8. ____ She stood as still as a statue.

9. ____ The coffee was like hot lava flowing down my throat.

10. ____ She is my alarm clock.

PRACTICING 5

Try your hand at making an interesting comparison about each of the following subjects. Write in complete sentences, and tell whether you have written a simile or a metaphor.

Example: People crowding onto a bus

People crowded onto the bus like pigs trying to get to a mud hole on a hot day.

Simile or metaphor? *Simile*

1. A pizza with everything on it

_____

_____

Simile or metaphor? _____

2. Someone dressed up for a fancy party

_____

_____

Simile or metaphor? _____

3. The taste of chocolate fudge pie (or another favorite food)

_____

_____

Simile or metaphor? _____

4. Standing in a line for a long time

_____

_____

Simile or metaphor? _____

5. A soft breeze blowing across your face

_____

_____

Simile or metaphor? _____

Organize the details.

Most descriptions lend themselves naturally to spatial organization—that is, moving from top to bottom or from bottom to top, from left to right or from right to left. However you organize your description, you should make this spatial movement consistent. For example, if you are describing a person from head to toe, don't go from the head to the midriff, and then shoot back up to the head. Instead, choose one direction for the movement of your description and stick to it. Here is a description that moves from top to bottom:

> My favorite possession is a handcarved wooden fox, given to me by one of my closest friends. His ears stand straight up as if on the alert for guests. He holds his head high, proud of his position in life. In his two front paws, he carries a little round crystal candleholder containing a burgundy candle. The fox is painted a dark burgundy, and he stands on his hind legs as if offering to light my way through the darkness. His tail trails along the ground, and he looks as if, any minute, he could set down the candle and start dancing a waltz. He's an elegant fox, and I never get tired of studying him.

There is a built-in logic to using spatial organization for a description: After all, you are physically present in one place and your eye travels along a path like a camera. It doesn't hop erratically from here to there. Moreover, moving slowly and in a predictable path in your description makes it easier for your reader to follow. You might describe a cave from its entrance to its back wall. A boat may be described from bow (front) to stern (back). A tree may be described from its roots to its crown or its crown to its roots. If you look again at the descriptions that begin this unit, you will notice that they use the same kind of deliberate movement.

Spatial order works for most descriptions, but not all. If, for example, you want to describe how you feel when you see your latest love, you'd probably just use a lot of comparisons—similes and metaphors—rather than a spatial organization. For most descriptions, though, spatial organization works fine.

IN A NUTSHELL

Use a spatial organization for most of your descriptions.

PRACTICING 6

In the spaces provided tell how you would move through a description for each of the following topics.

1. An unusual-looking person with whom you are acquainted

_____

2. A workplace

_____

3. The inside of an interesting room

_____

4. A view seen from some height

_____

5. Your car, or a car you'd like to own

_____

PRACTICING 7

Write a one-paragraph description of someone you personally know and admire. Begin with a dominant impression expressed in your topic sentence. Use sensory details and perhaps a simile or metaphor. Organize the details to make it easy for your reader to follow your description.

_____

_____

_____

_____

_____

_____

_____

_____

_____

_____

PRACTICING 8

Write a paragraph developing one of the following dominant impressions.

1. It was a dreary late afternoon by the lake.

2. The living room was a shambles after the party.

3. It was the most beautiful wedding dress I'd ever seen.

4. The motorcycle stood at the curb, gleaming in the sun.

5. The closet couldn't hold one more thing.

_____

_____

_____

_____

_____

_____

_____

_____

_____

_____

What Do I Need to Look Out For?

Many descriptions rely too heavily on only the visual sense; however, we have five senses. We also hear, taste, smell, and touch. So if, for example, you want to describe your beloved Persian cat, don't mention only her dazzling white fur and proud stride. Talk also about how soft her fur is (touch), her motorboat purr when she's content (sound), or even her fish breath after eating (smell). At the same time be sure you select only those details that support your dominant impression. Here is a student example:

> Uncle Jack, who is normally a handsome, athletic man, looks pitiful. About three weeks ago, as he was driving along the freeway on his Harley Davidson, he was sideswiped by a truck. Down he went on the pavement, shattering his right foot into 16 pieces. Now he uses a walker, and you hear him before you even see him. Click, click, click goes his walker, accompanying his winded "huh . . . huh . . . huh." Every move he makes is painful. His hair is uncombed, and his face is pale. His eyes have no gleam in them. His jogging suit hangs on his thin frame—a frame that used to be hefty and muscular. In the past Uncle Jack always smelled like Allspice, his

favorite aftershave lotion, but now he smells like someone who hasn't taken a shower for a week. It is hard to reconcile this frail, rumpled little man with the dapper uncle I had admired all of my life. He seems so much smaller.

IN A NUTSHELL

Use all your senses—not just vision—in your descriptions.

PRACTICING 9

In the following paragraph underline the descriptive words and phrases. Above each, write the sense that is appealed to.

I was 21 years old when I saw my first Thanksgiving table. As a foreign student, I had been invited to have Thanksgiving dinner with an American family. The table was truly a cornucopia of bright colors, savory aromas, and delectable looking dishes. It was spread with a linen tablecloth that felt smooth and cool as expensive silk. Each place setting was decorated with lovely yellow chrysanthemums from my hostess's garden. The flowers, picked earlier that day, perfumed the air of the dining room and seem to soak to the fabric of the upholstered furniture with their fragrance. From the kitchen wafted smells of sweet potatoes and roasted turkey. Against this tranquil setting came the crunch of a football game on television, the patter of talk from the adults, and the squeals of the children who sensed the excitement of the season without really understanding its meaning. I myself didn't understand what we were celebrating until I remembered that beneath all the food, decorations, and chatter we had all come together for one simple reason: to give thanks.

PRACTICING 10

Write a one-sentence dominant impression of each of the following places. Then choose one of the topics and write a descriptive paragraph about what you **hear, smell, taste, touch,** as well as what you **see.**

1. Your favorite restaurant _____

_____

2. Your best friend's house or apartment _____

_____

3. An amusement park ride _____

_____

4. An auto body shop _____

_____

5. A dentist's office _____

_____

Unit Test

From the four answers given, check the one that most correctly completes the sentence.

Example: A description can be called a

   _____ **(a).** List of details

   _____ **(b).** Prescription for how to write

   ✔ **(c).** Word picture

   _____ **(d).** Paragraph full of colorful adjectives

1. When you write a description, you

   _____ **(a).** Portray a scene as you see, hear, taste, smell, and feel it.

   _____ **(b).** Write exactly how you feel about what you see.

   _____ **(c).** Compare one place with another.

   _____ **(d).** Want to make sure that you don't exaggerate what you see.

2. Which of the following words is NOT a sensory organ?

_____ **(a).** Your nose

_____ **(b).** Your ears

_____ **(c).** Your tongue

_____ **(d).** Your hair

3. We use description

_____ **(a).** Only when we talk

_____ **(b).** Only when we write

_____ **(c).** Both when we talk or write

_____ **(d).** Both when we hear or touch

4. Which of the following topics most likely requires a description?

_____ **(a).** Reasons why babies cry during the night

_____ **(b).** Arguing against taking dietary supplements

_____ **(c).** How to grow large roses

_____ **(d).** What an old house in your neighborhood looks like

5. The *dominant impression* of a scene is

_____ **(a).** The one feature that stands out most

_____ **(b).** The most frightening detail

_____ **(c).** One that you want to forget

_____ **(d).** What you like most about a scene

6. Which of the following phrases involves a simile?

_____ **(a).** Her teeth were like little pearls.

_____ **(b).** His heart was on fire for his beloved.

_____ **(c).** The world is a field of battle.

_____ **(d).** I do not like my roommate.

7. Which of the following phrases involves a metaphor?

_____ **(a).** He is always having accidents.

_____ **(b).** Most people are kind and compassionate.

_____ **(c).** Neutral men are the devil's wings.

_____ **(d).** The longing for peace and contentment is in every human being.

8. Both similes and metaphors are based on

_____ **(a).** Exaggerations

_____ **(b).** Unique definitions

_____ **(c).** Story telling

_____ **(d).** Comparisons

9. Most descriptions are best organized by

_____ **(a).** Going from top to bottom, or bottom to top, or side to side

_____ **(b).** Going from the biggest to the smallest item

_____ **(c).** Moving from bright, colorful objects to dull, lusterless ones

_____ **(d).** Moving from the unknown to the known

10. When writing a description, you need to

_____ **(a).** Be sure always to describe only beautiful things.

_____ **(b).** Describe only persons you know well.

_____ **(c).** Use all your senses—not just your eyes.

_____ **(d).** Focus on what is least obvious about the scene.

Unit Talk-Write Assignment

The students in an English composition class were preparing to complete a writing assignment to describe a familiar person, animal, place, or thing from memory. First, pairs of students talked about their descriptions to work out a dominant impression and supporting details. One student, Maggie, decided that it would be easier to describe something offbeat, different, or even ugly than something perfectly normal and routine. So she did a description of "Sir George," a stuffed animal in the living room of her home. Her description is a good start but needs polishing. After you have read it, use the blanks provided to write an improved version—beginning with a dominant impression that is supported by vivid details.

Spoken Paragraph

One of my favorite things is "Sir George," a stuffed, life-size Chinese pug who stands near the fireplace in our living room. I guess my mom fell in love with him at a flea market in Arizona. He is made of dark greenish-gray velvet. His ears stick up like two little triangles. He has goldish eyes—I mean the color of that stuff people wear as jewelry—oh yeah, amber. And the pupils are black and huge. His eyes are surrounded by bulging wrinkles. His nose looks like a black prune, wrinkled and stuck right above his shut mouth. Around his fat neck the person who made this dog placed a leather band studded with big brass tacks. Now, to give Sir George the aristocratic bearing he deserves, a small silk Persian carpet covers his back. The design is typically Persian—sort of mythology, I think. It has gold and royal purple fringes. "What a dude!" as my dad has said. The blanket has a hole for his stubby little tail to stick through. Officially, Sir George is a footstool, but no one ever has the nerve to use him that way. He just stands by our fire place, staring into space—a miniature monster—no, not really, just a fierce aristocrat.

Written Paragraph

_____

_____

_____

_____

_____

_____

_____

_____

_____

Unit Collaborative Assignment

Get together in small groups of three or four and brainstorm about how you would describe a favorite building on campus. Talk in particular about the dominant impression that could be used in the description and the supporting details you could draw on to back it up.

Unit Writing Assignment

Write a description of the building discussed by your group in the Unit Collaborative Assignment above. Use what you have learned in this chapter about writing good descriptions. Organize your description with a suitable spatial order.

Photo Writing Assignment

Study the child in the following picture. Use a dominant impression in a topic sentence. Choose vivid details that support your dominant impression.

10

Illustrating

"My cat, Tabby, is a snobby eater. For example, she refuses to eat anything but roast duck and fresh trout."

You have a job selling a new miracle furniture polish at flea markets, but lately you've been getting some bad feedback about the product. It doesn't work. Worse yet, it actually ruins the finish on wood. You are bombarded by complaints, and many angry customers prove its worthlessness by bringing Polaroid pictures of their damaged furniture. You tell your boss, but she's disbelieving. She finally asks you to write a brief report about the customer complaints. Here is what you write:

> Brand X, our new furniture polish, not only does not work, it leaves furniture looking streaked and dull. In some cases, Brand X has even taken off the finish. We have many complaints from our customers. For example, Ms. Phillips of Lithonia applied our polish to a table inherited from her grandmother. She said it left the table looking as streaked as if it had been left out in the rain. Three customers from Richfield came to complain, and one from Morton Grove even brought Polaroid pictures showing how her furniture was left streaked and dull from Brand X. Finally, Mr. Prentiss of Stone Mountain may need to have a chair refinished because of the damage Brand X did to its veneer. These are just a few of the complaints I've received in the past weeks.

What you've done in your report is develop a paragraph by examples.

What Am I Trying to Do?

To support a topic sentence with **examples** means to give some instances or cases that illustrate your point. For example, you say that Janet is a good friend. Then you add that once when you badly needed help with a paper you were writing, Janet came over and worked with you through the night. Giving such help is an example of why you think that Janet is a good friend.

Illustrating with examples is as natural as breathing. Every day in our ordinary conversations we use such expressions as *for instance, for example,* and *just to show you.* We constantly give examples to back up what we're saying. Often, in everyday talk we even give examples without introducing them. Here is an example we overheard:

> I hate shopping at the mall because it's so big it takes too long to find what you want. [For example] Yesterday it took me almost two hours to find a store that carries the kind of sunglasses I was looking for.

Although the speaker didn't say *for example,* she clearly meant the incident about hunting for sunglasses to serve as an example. Examples are important because they keep us from making wild generalizations.

Examples also serve as supporting details. Without examples, a statement will often seem thin and unconvincing. Here, for example, is a topic sentence that desperately needs the support of examples:

> <u>Everything bores my friend Merrilee</u>. Nothing seems to interest or excite her. She begins the day convinced that it will be dull and that nothing interesting will happen. This attitude, of course, requires no energy from her. She can just give in to it and let it overcome her. Sometimes, I wonder what would happen if an earthquake hit. Would that raise Merrilee's blood pressure?

Something is obviously missing, for the writer repeats herself without proving her point. Each sentence merely parrots the one before.

Here is the same paragraph with its main point supported by examples:

> <u>Everything bores my friend Merrilee</u>. Nothing seems to interest or excite her. <u>For instance</u>, last week a group of us decided to rent a conversion van and go camping in Yosemite over spring break. The more we planned our adventure, the more thrilled we got. But when we asked Merrilee to join us, she just shrugged her shoulders and said, "That sounds pretty pointless to me." <u>On another occasion</u>, I wanted Merilee to teach me how to make a decorative wreath out of twigs and dried flowers because she is very talented in arts and crafts. At first she agreed, but before I could even collect the materials, she decided that making wreaths sounded like a lot of work for nothing. <u>On still another occasion</u>, when I was completely heartbroken after watching one of my favorite soap operas, Merrilee looked at me with scorn and commented, "That was so dull; I fell asleep watching it." Sometimes, I wonder what would happen if an

earthquake hit. Would that raise Merrilee's blood pressure or would she just yawn and say, "So what?"

What makes the second paragraph better than the first is its use of examples. They convince us of the writer's topic sentence, *Everything bores my friend Merrilee.*

IN A NUTSHELL

An example serves to illustrate a general statement.

PRACTICING 1

List three examples that would appropriately illustrate each of the following topic sentences.

1. I am definitely an indoor (or outdoor) person.

   (a). _____

   (b). _____

   (c). _____

2. My roommate (or family member) is annoying (or pleasant) to live with.

   (a). _____

   (b). _____

   (c). _____

3. Personal service is being replaced by technology.

   (a). _____

   (b). _____

   (c). _____

4. Old age has its privileges.

   (a). _____

   (b). _____

   (c). _____

5. People treat the homeless in a variety of ways.

   (a). _____

   (b). _____

   (c). _____

How Can I Do It?

You can use examples effectively in your writing if you follow these tips:

- Introduce the examples.
- Use strong examples that fit.
- Give enough examples.

Introduce the examples.

It is always a good idea to introduce an example with a simple *for example, for instance,* or similar phrase. This lead-in mentally prepares the reader for what is to come. If you are giving several examples in a row, introducing each one will also help your reader keep them straight and follow your train of thought. Here is a paragraph with lead-ins missing:

> <u>This year, I am trying hard to practice good study skills</u>. After every lecture, I go over my notes and make a list of questions about anything I didn't understand. When I do reading assignments, I highlight key ideas and answer the review questions. I start studying for tests early, instead of cramming at the last minute. My efforts seem to be paying off. I got all As and Bs on my midterms.

Notice how much clearer the paragraph is when appropriate lead-ins are used:

> <u>This year, I am trying hard to practice good study skills.</u> <u>For example</u>, after every lecture, I go over my notes and make a list of questions about anything I didn't understand. <u>Also</u>, when I do reading assignments, I highlight key ideas and answer the review questions. <u>Perhaps most important of all</u>, I start studying for tests early, instead of cramming at the last minute. My efforts seem to be paying off. I got all As and Bs on my midterms.

ESL Advice!

Don't leave out the indefinite article "an" in the much used phrase "here is an example."

Here are common phrases used to introduce examples:

for example	for instance	another example
another instance	on another occasion	once
another time	that is	namely
in particular	specifically	first, second, etc.
finally		

PRACTICING 2

For each of the following topic sentences supply at least three examples. Underline the introductory phrase used for each.

Example: This was the most relaxing vacation I've ever had.

Answers: **(a).** <u>For one thing</u>, I didn't set my alarm clock, so I just woke up whenever I felt like it.

(b). <u>Also</u>, I didn't do anything but sit on the beach and read.

(c). <u>Finally</u>, I didn't tell my boss where I was going, so I couldn't get any phone calls about work.

1. It takes planning if you want to avoid junk food and eat right.

(a). _____

(b). _____

(c). _____

2. _____ is one of the funniest people I know.

(a). _____

(b). _____

(c). _____

3. I am amazed at how badly some children are allowed to behave in public.

(a). _____

(b). _____

(c). _____

4. A good restaurant server should be available but not pushy.

(a). _____

(b). _____

(c). _____

5. Some slang is colorful and enhances the English language.

(a). _____

(b). _____

(c). _____

Choose strong examples that fit.

Your examples should both fit your point and clearly prove it. To do both, examples have to be strong. If your point is that your friend is stingy, you must give strong examples of that stinginess. For example, this would be a weak example of your friend's stinginess:

> My friend Bob is very stingy. For example, I asked him to lend me $1000 and he said no, even though he could easily afford it.

Refusing to lend someone $1000 is hardly an example of stinginess. Here is a stronger example:

> My friend Bob is very stingy. For example, he refuses to go to any birthday parties because he might have to buy presents.

Here is another weak example, this time of your hometown's friendliness:

> My home town is a very friendly place. For example, many people say good morning back if you greet them first.

A stronger example would be people going out of their way to say good morning instead of just responding. Here is a stronger example:

> My home town is a very friendly place. For example, one day my mother got a flat tire on Main Street, and five people stopped and offered to help her change it.

Here are some more weak and strong examples:

Topic sentence:	My Uncle Bob is a great cook.
Weak example:	For example, he makes good chili.
Strong example:	For example, his chili is so good that people have offered him money for the recipe.
Weak example:	For example, he often cooks the Thanksgiving dinner for the family.
Strong example:	For example, his Thanksgiving feast last year was so delicious that for months afterward it was the talk of the family.

PRACTICING 3

List three strong examples for each topic sentence.

1. **Topic sentence:** Some movies are a waste of time.

   (a). _____

   (b). _____

   (c). _____

2. **Topic sentence:** I have some bad habits I would like to overcome.

   (a). _____

   (b). _____

   (c). _____

3. **Topic sentence:** People are becoming more polite.

   (a). _____

   (b). _____

   (c). _____

4. **Topic sentence:** Little things matter, sometimes the most.

   (a). _____

   (b). _____

   (c). _____

5. **Topic sentence:** _____ is a very _____ person.

   (a). _____

   (b). _____

   (c). _____

Give enough examples.

Always give enough examples to support your point. How many are enough is largely a matter of common sense. If you are making a small point, one or two examples may be enough. Here is an example:

> My boyfriend sometimes spends money foolishly. For example, last week he sent me a huge bouquet of flowers that cost him $50. It was his way of apologizing. Another time he bought front-row tickets to a show that was in town. That set him back $75, which was half of what he earned that week in his part-time job.

To support a small point about her boyfriend's foolish spending, the writer cited two cases—which were enough.

Here is a bigger point that requires more support:

> <u>My school, a community college of 13,000 students, is always being sued</u>. For example, this year alone, three students filed formal grievances against teachers for what I consider silly reasons. The first was a returning student who had been caught red-handed cheating on an exam. He screamed and yelled that he was innocent and filed a formal grievance accusing the teacher of abusive treatment. Another student decided that her accounting teacher should be fired because she thought he lacked patience. That particular teacher had consistently received outstanding student reviews, yet this angry student blamed him for her own poor performance. A third student decided that his dance teacher was deliberately humiliating him in front of the class because he could not get the movements as quickly as the other students and was holding up the class. All three cases were either dismissed by the Judiciary Board or settled between student and teacher.

Sometimes, however, one extended example may be enough to support a topic sentence. An **extended example** is an example developed in some detail. Here is an example:

> <u>Sometimes no matter how carefully you drive, you can still have an accident through no fault of your own</u>. For example, last month I had just moved off at a green light and was going no more than ten miles an hour, when a car traveling in the opposite direction suddenly crossed the center line and headed straight for me. I honked and tried to get out of the way, but the car bore down on me like a heat-seeking missile. It raked the side of my car, jumped the curb, and crashed into a wall. Angry and scared, I jumped out and ran over to the driver. When I got there, I found a young man behind the steering wheel in convulsions. It turned out that three months before, he'd had a brain tumor removed and now suffered occasional blackouts since then. When he came to, he was very apologetic and admitted that he shouldn't have been driving. I was no longer angry, however. I figured it was just one of those days.

IN A NUTSHELL

When using examples, do the following:

- Introduce the example.
- Use examples that fit.
- Use strong examples.
- Use enough examples.

PRACTICING 4

Reread the paragraph on the bad furniture polish on page 147. How many examples does it give? Could any of these examples have been omitted? If so, which ones and why? What is the purpose of the last line, "These are just a few of the complaints I've received in the past weeks"?

_____

_____

_____

_____

PRACTICING 5

Pick one of the topic sentences below and develop it into a paragraph with one extended example.

1. If you believe in yourself, you can do anything.

2. Rules are often annoying, but sometimes they can protect you.

3. Once in my life I had a serious case of hero worship.

4. It's better to act than just complain.

5. Sometimes when you least expect it, something wonderful will happen.

What Do I Need to Look Out For?

Writers often make the mistake of saying *for example* and then merely repeating the topic sentence in different words. This is a false example. A true example does not simply repeat the topic sentence, but supports it with a specific instance. An example of a false example follows.

> My cousin Boris is a generous man. For example, he is always being helpful and kind.

In spite of the lead-in, this is not an example. *Generous, helpful,* and *kind* all mean the same thing. The writer has not given a specific instance of cousin Boris's generosity. Here is a true example:

> My cousin Boris is a generous man. For example, when he learned that the house of an elderly couple in our neighborhood had been spray-painted by vandals, cousin Boris organized some neighborhood volunteers to repaint it.

Here are two more examples:

False example:	My cousin Boris is a generous man. For example, he has a soft heart.
True example:	My cousin Boris is a generous man. For example, every year he spends one week of his vacation working with a group that builds houses for the homeless.
False example:	My cousin Boris is a generous man. For example, he feels sorry for the sick.
True example:	My cousin Boris is a generous man. For example, he takes part in nearly every charity walk there is, such as the Cancer Walk, the AIDS Walk, and the Annual Walk for Diabetes.

Always be sure your example is more specific than the point it is meant to support.

IN A NUTSHELL

The example must always be more specific than the point it supports.

PRACTICING 6

Check the true example in each case, the one that is clearly more specific than the point it supports.

1. Appearances can be deceiving. For instance,

_____ **(a).** Mrs. Parker lives in a big house on the lake, but she can't pay her telephone bill.

_____ **(b).** you can't know a person's real circumstances just by looking at them.

2. Learning something new can be really exciting. For instance,

_____ **(a).** classes make you feel good because they are full of interesting information.

_____ **(b).** there is great satisfaction in understanding a new poem or discovering how sociology applies to everyday life.

3. Not following directions in a welding class can be disastrous. For instance,

_____ **(a).** most activities connected with welding are dangerous.

_____ **(b).** if you do not light your torch correctly, you can set yourself on fire.

4. Children have such lively imaginations. For example,

_____ **(a).** they make up imaginary friends and talk to them.

_____ **(b).** they fantasize a great deal and make up things.

5. You can save a lot of money at the grocery store by using coupons. For example,

_____ **(a).** clipping newspaper coupons can result in big savings.

_____ **(b).** tuna fish was on sale and with a coupon, I got another 25 cents off.

Unit Test

Write a *T* when the statement is true; *F* if it is false.

1. _____ You should never consider illustrating a point by using examples.

2. _____ The following passage uses an example to illustrate its point: "The sky was filled with huge billowy clouds. These clouds are called cumulus clouds."

3. _____ "For instance," and "for example," are typical phrases used to introduce an example.

4. _____ In everyday talk, we often give examples without introducing them.

5. _____ All of the examples that follow support the point that: Most of life's major decisions have long-term effects: For instance, choosing a profession can lead to personal self-fulfillment or personal emptiness. Choosing a life partner can make one happy or miserable. Moreover, happiness and fulfillment are difficult to define.

6. _____ In using examples, you must make sure that each example fits the point you are making.

7. _____ When using examples, the rule is to use at least three examples for each point.

8. _____ An extended example is an example developed in detail.

9. _____ A good writing policy is to write "for example," and then just repeat the topic sentence in different words.

10. _____ Always make sure that your example is more specific than the point it supports.

Unit Talk-Write Assignment

What follows below is a three-way conversation among students discussing people who lie because of a poor self-image. After studying the passage, assemble the examples into a paragraph, written in standard English. Come up with a topic sentence that the examples support. Introduce each example, and leave out any that is irrelevant.

Conversation

Ben: I'll tell you an example that happened in my own family. When my sister was in the sixth grade, we had just moved from Iran to the United States. She felt so strange and unwanted in her class that she announced one day that she was the great granddaughter of the Shah of Iran. She came up with a bunch of baloney about how she was brought up in a palace, had her own personal maid, and took ballet lessons from a famous Russian teacher. She even described her bed, covered with pink satin and beautiful dolls. At first her story worked, and the other kids in the class stuck around her like she was a princess. But the teachers didn't buy her story and called my parents. Poor kid. If she had felt good about herself, I don't think she would've done that.

Rita: I'm telling you, people who make up stories about their backgrounds are everywhere. I read where some guy who owned the *Phoenix Gazette*—can't remember his name—something like Bully or Mully—no, I think it was Tully. Anyway, this guy grew up a nerd—you know, reading all the while his older brother was one of these super athlete types. The brother eventually became a Marine lieutenant and was killed in an air collision. Now get this—this nerd made up an entire war record for himself. Pretended he had been in combat flights, had earned every kind of medal. All of this totally made up—not a bit of truth in it. He lived these lies for 30 years until one day, the military found him out. Then, his whole lie fell in on him. He was ruined.

Jean: Well, I have to admit that I like to fantasize. I admit it. But I'll bet lots of you do the same thing. I'll sit on a bench at the mall, watching handsome guys pass by, and I'll pretend the most handsome one wishes he could meet me. At other times, I'll daydream that I'm dating someone like Taye Diggs or Will Smith. Don't laugh. I'm convinced we all fantasize that way. It makes life more exciting.

Ben: Wait a minute; day dreaming is different from lying. I'll tell you about lying. My cousin tells everyone he graduated from college with a degree in journalism. But he didn't. He flunked out his senior year. I guess he felt so bad about flunking out that he thought he could build up an image by lying. I don't know why he doesn't just go back to school and finish.

Written Paragraph

_____

_____

_____

_____

_____

_____

_____

_____

_____

_____

_____

_____

_____

_____

_____

Unit Collaborative Assignment

Get together with a partner and discuss good teachers you've had in other classes. You and your partner should then each decide on your favorite teacher. Next, each of you should talk out a topic sentence that sums up what made your teacher so good. Then you should both give examples to support your topic sentences.

Unit Writing Assignment

Develop a paragraph on the topic of good teachers, using as material the ideas in the above Unit Collaborative Assignment. Be sure to introduce your examples, make them strong, and cite enough of them to support your point adequately. Also be sure you are not merely repeating the topic sentence but are instead using true examples.

Photo Writing Assignment

The following photo shows someone in a ridiculous situation. Use the photo as a basis for writing a paragraph illustrating the following topic sentence: A sense of humor can help you through embarrassing incidents. You may give a single extended example or several examples.

11

Explaining a Process

"Four simple exercises can help you warm up before exercising vigorously."

You work as a fry cook in a restaurant. It is your job to stand at the grill and cook hundreds of eggs in specially maintained egg frying pans. Because of the high turnover among grill cooks, the egg pans are often improperly maintained and become sticky. The chef asks you, the most experienced cook, to write and post directions detailing how the egg pans should be maintained. This is what you write:

To keep the egg pans in good condition, all cooks should follow these steps: First, never allow metal utensils to come in contact with the cooking surface. Always use plastic, rubber, or wooden spoons or spatulas on the pans, since even the slightest contact with metal can pit the cooking surface and cause the pans to stick. Second, never stack egg pans on top of each other, for the same reason given above. Third, never wash the pans in water. Instead, wipe them with a clean towel. The high temperatures at which the pans are used make them sterile. Fourth, always begin and end a shift by wiping the pans with a thin coating of cooking oil. This creates a protective barrier that keeps the pans slick so they never become sticky. Finally, if you notice a pan sticking, throw it away immediately and bring in a new one. Once a pan begins to stick, it will never be completely slick again. It will cause problems for other cooks during the rush hour. Let's follow these simple directions and make life easier for all of us.

What you have just written is a *process* paragraph.

What Am I Trying to Do?

A **process** is any task that is done step by step. Learning how to write is a process; so is making beef stew. Getting ready for work or school is as much a process as shaving, tying shoelaces, or warming up the car. Indeed, nearly every waking hour of our lives finds us involved in one process or another.

Process paragraphs are usually one of these three types:

1. How to do something (giving instructions)

2. How something works (giving information)

3. How something happened (giving the history)

Here is an example of the first and most common kind of process writing—giving directions on how to do something:

> Getting your house ready for winter can be a chore but can also be done in some easy steps. First, check the caulking on your windows and doors. Pay particular attention to the gap between the bottom of the door and the threshold. Even a small spacing between these two will result in a colder room. Next, do the same for your windows. Make sure that there is a good seal all around the window. If there isn't, go to the hardware store and invest in some caulking tape. Once you've made sure that the doors and windows are not leaking cold air, it is time to check your furnace. Don't make the mistake of waiting until you need the heat to check your furnace. Try it when you don't need the heat so that if anything is wrong you'll know about it under nonemergency conditions. Finally, if your home is equipped with a clothes dryer, try venting the air inside the house. The exhaust from a clothes dryer is actually moist, warm air that can help keep you cozy rather than being wasted outside. Once you have done these things, you're ready for winter.

Here is an example of the second kind of process paragraph—one that explains how something works:

> My computer printer is very easy to use. In fact, if anything is wrong, it tells you exactly how to fix the problem. All you need to do is look at the status panel at the top. It has three amber lights that indicate problems. First, there is the "error" light. When lit, it indicates a problem such as a paper jam, empty toner cartridge, or open printer cover. Second, there is the "tray 1" light. When it is lit, the main paper tray is empty and must have paper added before the printer can function. Third, there is the "tray 2" light. When it is lit, paper must be added to the number 2 tray. If none of these lights is on and the printer still isn't working, I check my printer manual. I also check to be sure that the printer is plugged in!

The third kind of process paragraph—how something happened—is shown next:

My sister loves to tell how a funny series of coincidental meetings led her to marry Jeff. Sally met Jeff when she substituted—very reluctantly—for someone on my bowling team who was sick. (Sally would rather have her fingernails pulled out than bowl.) The funny thing was that Jeff was also a reluctant substitute for someone who was out sick from his brother's team. A couple of days later, Sally got a flat tire on the freeway, and who do you think pulled up in a police cruiser to see if he could help? Right. It was Jeff, who just happened that day to be on patrol. Then, not even a week later, Sally was in the laundromat, where she has been going every Monday night for years because it's the least busy night, and who walks in—Jeff. That night Jeff and Sally decided they'd better start dating rather than trust to keep meeting by luck. Ten years later, they're still happily married.

Explaining a process is a very practical matter and something we do often, even daily. We tell a stranger how to get to Main Street. Our biology teacher explains how cells divide. The new sales manager explains how sales projections were met. In everyday life, the academic and business world, we are constantly giving instructions, explaining how something works, or relating how something happened. Knowing how to write a good process paragraph is a useful and practical skill.

IN A NUTSHELL

The process paragraph is any step-by-step explanation. It includes the following:

- How to do something.
- How something works.
- How something happened.

PRACTICING 1

In the blanks provided indicate what kind of process the assignment calls for. Use *A* for how to do something, *B* for how something works, and *C* for how something happened.

Example: __A__ How to use a telephone credit card

1. _____ How to build a bookcase

2. _____ Five swimming exercises you can do to develop a strong back

3. _____ The steps involved in preparing to sky dive

4. _____ How the Food and Drug Administration works

5. _____ What led up to World War II

6. ____ How to make a good cup of coffee

7. ____ What to do when you see an accident

8. ____ How Abraham Lincoln was assassinated

9. ____ How cold germs spread

10. ____ How to be a good date

How Can I Do It?

Basically, a good process explanation covers every step of a process and leaves nothing out. Writing it involves these three steps:

1. Clearly state your purpose at the beginning.

2. Cover the steps in logical order.

3. Use transitions to guide your reader.

Clearly state your purpose at the beginning.

You've learned that the topic sentence—the single sentence that sums up what the paragraph is about—usually comes first, but can come last. However, in the process paragraph the topic sentence must come first. Explaining a process without first telling the reader what you are explaining is like giving someone directions without saying to where. Here is an example of a process paragraph without a topic sentence at the beginning:

> Begin by mixing one cup of margarine or butter with one cup of brown sugar. Beat the mixture until it is pasty. Add half a cup of granulated sugar. Beat in one egg, one teaspoon of vanilla, and mix well. Stir in three cups of oatmeal, one cup of raisins, one and a half cups of all-purpose flour, one teaspoon of baking soda, and one teaspoon of cinnamon. Mix everything together until the ingredients are well blended. Drop spaced tablespoons of the mixture on a greased cookie sheet and bake at 350 degrees for approximately 10 minutes. The result will be delectable and delicious.

Yes, but what are you making? The topic sentence tells us:

> <u>Oatmeal and raisin cookies are very easy to make</u>. Begin by mixing one cup of margarine or butter with one cup of brown sugar. Beat the mixture together until it is pasty. Add a half a cup of granulated sugar. Beat in one egg, one teaspoon of vanilla, and mix well. Stir in three cups of oatmeal, one cup of raisins, one and a half cups of all-purpose flour, one teaspoon of baking soda, and one teaspoon of cinnamon. Mix everything together until the ingredients are well blended. Drop spaced tablespoons of the mixture on a greased cookie sheet and bake at 350 degrees for approximately 10 minutes. The result will be delectable and delicious.

In the topic sentence tell your audience exactly what process you plan to explain. Just be straightforward and clear. Here are some examples of topic sentences for process paragraphs:

Balancing a checkbook consists of five major steps.
Planting a garden is easy if the soil is properly prepared.
Line dancing is easier to learn than it looks.
My father built our house over many stages.

PRACTICING 2

Write a topic sentence for each of the processes listed.

1. How to get better grades in college

_____

2. How exercise helps with weight reduction

_____

3. How you found your job (or the last job you had)

_____

PRACTICING 3

Write a paragraph on one of the topic sentences you composed for Practicing 2.

_____

_____

_____

_____

_____

_____

_____

_____

_____

_____

Cover the steps in logical order.

Most processes have a built-in logic to their sequence of steps. Often, it is a logic based on a fixed chronological order. First you do this, next you do that. If, for example, you are making a cake, before you prepare the icing you should first mix the batter and bake it (or you'll have nothing to ice). If you are changing a tire, before you jack up the car you must first remove the spare from the tire-well in the trunk (removing the tire from the trunk of a jacked up car may cause the car to fall off the jack). Other processes may have no obvious sequence but, instead, require you to invent your own steps. For example, there's no obvious sequence that explains how to discipline a child, how to boost self-confidence, or how to break the habit of watching too much TV. You have to come up with your own list of steps and arrange them in logical order of your own invention. You may choose to proceed from the least important to the most important step. You may go from the simplest to the most complex step. Regardless of your topic, you must list the steps of any process in the order in which they most logically occur. Do not hop around as this writer does:

> You can relax in five simple steps. Don't think of anything, especially not events that have angered you during the day. Sit and try to empty your mind of all thoughts. Next, relax your muscles by clenching and unclenching your fist 20 times. Don't clench too hard—just hard enough to be purposeful. Before you do this, stand and stretch your arms as high as you can. Stop stretching and slowly lower your arms. Stretch and lower ten times. As you sit quietly, lightly breathe in and out. Concentrate only on your breathing. Your chair should be comfortable and away from unpleasant distractions. Finally, close your eyes and imagine something relaxing, such as passing clouds, the ebb and flow of the ocean, or a flowing river. Hold this view in mind for several minutes. By the time you finish the fifth step, you should feel much calmer than you felt at the start of this exercise.

Did you have trouble following these directions? They jump around a lot. A process explanation should never jump around; it should march from start to finish like a well-trained soldier. Here is an improvement:

> You can relax in five simple steps. First, find a comfortable chair, away from unpleasant distractions. Sit and try to empty your mind of all thoughts. Don't think of anything, especially not events that have angered you during the day. Second, stand and stretch your arms as high as you can. Stop stretching and slowly lower your arms. Stretch and lower ten times. Next, sit down again and relax your muscles by clenching and unclenching your fist 20 times. Don't clench too hard—just hard enough to be purposeful. Step four is to sit quietly and lightly breathe in and out. Concentrate only on your breathing. Finally, close your eyes and imagine something relaxing, such as passing clouds, the ebb and flow of the ocean, or a flowing river. Hold this view in mind for several minutes. By the time you

finish the fifth step, you should feel much calmer than you felt at the start of this exercise.

One way to avoid hopping about is to jot down and number the steps you intend to explain before you actually begin writing. Process assignments are generally easier to write if you work out the steps in advance.

PRACTICING 4

The following paragraph presents a process in a jumbled order. Put the steps of the process in logical order by rearranging the sentences. Delete any sentences that are unnecessary to the process.

If you have roses growing in your yard, you can, with little effort, create a lovely bouquet of flowers for the center of your breakfast table. According to my grandmother, here's what you do: First, choose a glass pitcher approximately eight inches high and five inches wide, filling it three fourths full with fresh water. My grandmother kept fresh flowers in vases throughout her house. She loved to grow flowers. Arrange your roses in the pitcher, placing the longest rose in the center and the shorter roses surrounding the longest. If necessary, trim away some of the lower leaves on the rose stems so as not to create a bottleneck at the top of the pitcher. Drop an ice cube in the water to perk up the flowers. Pick up a pair of scissors or a plant clipper from your utensil drawer. You are now ready to go into your yard, where you will gather six to eight roses still in full bloom by cutting their stems at varying lengths, but no higher than twelve inches. By the way, put on some garden gloves to save your hands from being pricked by rose thorns. (Remember always to cut above a knot and to slant your cut.) You don't need to be a horticulturist with formal flower arrangement training to create this charming centerpiece or one like it to decorate your table for as long as your roses bloom.

_____

_____

_____

_____

PRACTICING 5

Choose one of the following processes and list the steps from start to finish. Review your list, numbering the steps in a logical sequence to confirm or correct the order.

1. How to throw a birthday party for a friend

2. How an automatic washing machine works

3. How to study for a major exam

4. How you or someone you know got over a failed love relationship

5. How to live on a limited income

_____

_____

_____

_____

_____

_____

_____

_____

_____

_____

Use transitions to guide your reader.

All processes consist of steps that follow one after another. First comes *this,* then comes *that.* You can help your reader follow even a complicated sequence if you use transitions. The transitions most often used are *first, second, third, next, then,* and *finally.* Transitions help your reader in two ways. First, they clearly label each separate step. Second, they connect the steps in logical order. Here is a paragraph with effective transitions:

When I revise my writing, I find it useful to follow a specific set of steps. *First,* I read the entire piece all the way through without making any corrections. *Next,* I read it aloud just to hear how it would sound to a reader. *After that,* I take a pencil and delete any phrase or word that doesn't sound right. I take out or otherwise correct the bigger elements first—the sentence that may not fit or the phrase that is awkward, penciling in between the lines a replacement. *Next,* I tackle the individual words, hunting for better choices and penciling them in when I find them. *After* I have done all that I can do, I read the piece aloud again, making changes as I go along. I continue this process until I'm satisfied with the writing.

Here are other transitions you can use in a process paragraph:

first	second, third	when
at first	the second, third step	while
afterward	when you have finished that step	meanwhile
after that	before	during
then	at the same time	finally
next	later	last of all

ESL Advice!

Be particularly careful not to omit the transitions between steps.

IN A NUTSHELL

Writing a process involves three steps:

- Clearly state your purpose in the beginning.
- Cover the steps in logical order.
- Use transitions to guide your reader.

PRACTICING 6

Use your notes from Practicing 5 to write a process paragraph. Be sure to use helpful transitions.

_____

_____

_____

_____

What Do I Need to Look Out For?

To explain a process clearly, keep the following tips in mind:

- Know the process.
- Don't leave out any critical steps.
- Remember your audience.

Know the process.

You cannot write about a process that you yourself don't thoroughly understand. The first step for writing a successful process paragraph is therefore simple: Know the process well. If you want to explain how to mulch a lawn, you should thoroughly understand the steps involved before attempting to explain it. If you want to write about how a vacuum cleaner works, you should master the details before you do any writing. The same advice applies if you want to explain how an accident happened—get the facts before you write a word.

PRACTICING 7

List five processes that you know thoroughly. They can be any of the three types of processes—how to do something, how something works, or how something happened. List all the critical steps for one of the processes you've selected.

1. _____

2. _____

3. _____

4. _____

5. _____

Don't leave out any critical steps.

This mistake—leaving out a critical step—is especially likely when we're explaining a process we know well. We think that a certain step is so obvious that it needn't be mentioned. What is obvious to you, however, may not be so obvious to your reader.

Here, for example, is a process paragraph about changing a tire that omits an important step:

> <u>Changing a flat tire is a lot simpler than it looks</u>. First, locate the jack and lug tools in the trunk. Second, jack up the car. Before the car wheels are completely off the ground, partly loosen the lugs. Third, with the wheels off the ground, remove the lugs and tire. Place the spare tire on the hub of the axle, lining up all the holes. Fourth, replace the lugs and hand-tighten. Fifth, lower the car and finish tightening the lugs with the lug tool. You're ready to travel again. Remember not to drive long on the temporary spare and never over 45 mph. Instead, drive to the nearest gas station and have your regular tire repaired.

Can you spot the omission in this common process? It is this: Before attempting to change a tire, always put the car in park, turn off the motor, and set the hand-brake. Otherwise, the car could roll off the jack and crush the tire changer.

PRACTICING 8

Choose one of these familiar processes and list the major steps in the process. Do not leave out a crucial step.

1. Preparing for a job interview

2. Washing your car

3. Curing a cold

4. Dealing with a bully

5. Preparing a healthy breakfast

_____

_____

_____

_____

_____

_____

_____

_____

Remember your audience.

A process that is easy for you to understand may be hard for someone else. For instance, an experienced angler knows how to handle a catfish to avoid the barbel—the spine on its back—that's poisonous. Those who've never fished for catfish before are unlikely to even know what a barbel is—to say nothing of its poisonous nature. The point is that you have to adjust your level of explanation to what your audience can be expected to know and not know.

Here, for instance, is a technical explanation of how a sphygmomanometer works:

> When the cuff of the sphygmomanometer is wrapped around the upper arm and fully inflated, it becomes a tourniquet, cutting off all blood flow. As the nurse then slowly releases an air valve, blood flow returns to the arm, generating Korotkoff sounds. The reading at this point, when the Korotkoff sound is first heard, is the <u>systolic</u> pressure. As the cuff continues to deflate, the sounds become fainter and fainter until they disappear altogether. The point of disappearance is the <u>diastolic</u> pressure, the pressure when the heart is at rest.

This explanation may be clear to a medical professional, but to the rest of us, who don't even know what a sphygmomanometer is, it is mystifying. Here is how you might explain this same process to someone with no medical training:

> A <u>sphygmomanometer</u> is a device for measuring blood pressure. It consists of an inflatable cuff and a measuring gauge that gives a digital reading. A sphygmomanometer measures a person's blood pressure by inflating the cuff around the upper arm until the blood flow is completely cut off. Air is then gradually released from the cuff. At the first sound of blood flowing again, the gauge registers the rate of flow. This is the <u>systolic</u> pressure. As the cuff continues to deflate, the gauge registers when the sound of flowing blood disappears altogether. That is the <u>diastolic</u> pressure. It is the lower of the two numbers and represents the rate of blood flow when the heart is at rest.

The point is to tailor your explanations to what your readers are likely to know and what they are likely not to know.

IN A NUTSHELL

When writing a process, you should do the following:

- Know the process.
- Don't leave out any critical steps.
- Remember your audience.

PRACTICING 9

Write a paragraph explaining one of the following processes to a classmate. Indicate who your audience will be—whether your classmates or some other group—and adjust your explanation accordingly.

1. Folding a piece of paper into a sailboat or a hat

2. Applying makeup

3. Warming up before exercising

4. Winterizing a car

5. Barbecuing chicken

_____

_____

_____

_____

_____

_____

_____

_____

_____

_____

 ## Unit Test

Use the blank provided to complete the sentence so that it agrees with this chapter on how to explain a process.

Example: A process is any task that is done <u>step by step</u>.

1. How to ride a bicycle, how a lightbulb works, and what steps led to the Civil War all involve explaining a _____ .

2. When you give directions, you are telling how _____ .

3. When you give the history of an event, you are telling how _____ .

4. Indicating how something works is the process of giving _____ .

5. When you start your process paragraph, state _____ clearly.

6. The steps of most processes have a built-in logic which you should _____ .

7. "First," "second," "third," are useful transitions to _____ your reader.

8. Before you explain any process, be sure that you _____ it well.

9. In explaining a process, don't leave out a critical _____ .

10. Adjust your level of explanation to what your _____ can be expected to know.

Unit Talk-Write Assignment

Students were asked to explain any how-to-do process with which they were familiar. Jennifer decided to tell the class how to have a successful garage sale. Here are her informal spoken comments. In the space provided, rewrite what she says into a paragraph that follows the guidelines in this unit. In other words, state your purpose, present your steps in a logical order with transitions between steps, include all necessary steps, and keep your audience in mind.

Spoken Paragraph

Last weekend I helped my mom with her garage sale. We made about two hundred bucks, but I think we could've made more if we'd been better organized and had done things a little differently. If I were to make suggestions for a successful garage sale, here's what I would include—sort of in random order: First of all, have enough stuff to sell. When people see only a few items, like some clothes, a bicycle, a toilet seat, and thinly scattered junk on the lawn, they aren't going to park to take a better look. Also, make your items look good. Wash and iron the clothes. Clean and polish anything that needs it. Who do you think wants to buy a toaster filled with bread crumbs or a pot lined with scum? Display your things properly. Don't just have them laying on the ground where people have to stoop down to see them. Use card tables for objects and racks for clothing. If you don't own card tables, at least use some strong cardboard boxes from your local grocery store. Let's see what else can I say? Hmmm. Oh yes, don't forget to price all items. Experienced garage sale givers have told me that people like to see price tags—even if it's just a sign saying "All items in this box 50 cents." Just remember that people who go to garage sales are usually penny pinchers and are looking for a deal. Give it to them. By the way, get up real early on the day of the sale so that you're ready by 9:00 A.M. when the shoppers arrive. Saturday is the best day for your sale because people aren't at work and they're out doing errands and stuff. Give everyone a warm welcome. Don't make them feel like you're doing them a favor. Smile and answer their questions in a friendly way, no matter how stupid they are. I can't think of anything else, so that's it. Good luck!

Written Paragraph

_____

_____

_____

_____

_____

_____

_____

_____

_____

_____

_____

_____

_____

 ## Unit Collaborative Assignment

Pair up with a classmate to whom you explain the steps involved in one of the following processes. Only describe the steps; do not demonstrate them. (You might want to jot down the steps on a piece of scratch paper before you begin.)

1. Tying a tie

2. Scrambling eggs

3. Improving your golf swing (or some other sport skill)

4. Packing for a weekend at a beach

5. Videotaping a movie that's on in the middle of the night

When you're finished, ask your classmate to critique your explanation.

- Did you state the process at the beginning?
- Did you include all the steps in their logical order?
- Did you use transitions?
- Did you tailor your explanation to your partner's level of expertise?

○ Then reverse roles and repeat the exercise with a different topic.

Unit Writing Assignment

Choose one of the following options and write a process paragraph.

1. Write a how-to-process paragraph on one of the Unit Collaborative Assignments.

2. Write a how-it-works process paragraph on one of the following topics:

   (a). How local rent regulations work where you live.

   (b). How fast car chases help the popularity of a movie

   (c). How drug use ruined a rock band

   (d). How recycling newspapers helps the ecology

   (e). How a famous person lost his or her popularity

3. Write a how-it-happened process paragraph on one of the following topics:

   (a). How someone you know climbed the success ladder

   (b). How you broke up with a girlfriend or boyfriend

   (c). How you perfected your skills in something

   (d). How you or someone you know accomplished a task in the face of obstacles

   (e). How parents can make children feel unnecessarily guilty (or vice versa)

Photo Writing Assignment

The following photo shows a process involving several steps. Detail each step for an audience that can't see the picture. Begin by stating the process in a topic sentence. Arrange the steps in logical order, and link them with strong transitions.

12

Defining a Term

"An entrepreneur is a person who takes on the risk of
starting a new business."

Your neighborhood is under pressure. Ugly mini-malls and apartment buildings are springing up everywhere around it, like weeds. One particular fast-food chain wants to build practically in your backyard. Your mother protests that a proper buffer is not being maintained. The builder insists that it is.

Angry, your mother asks you to go to City Hall and research the city's definition of *buffer* so she can write a letter to the developer. After doing some reading, this is what you write:

> A <u>buffer</u>, as defined in city zoning, is a strip of land that separates two properties used for different purposes, especially for business and for private residence. To qualify as a buffer, the strip of land must be at least 50 feet wide. It must also run the entire length of the boundary between the two properties. If possible, the buffer should contain mature landscaping so that the two properties are screened from each other. Otherwise, a fence should be built. The design of the fence must be agreed on by the adjoining landowners. Anything other than what is described here is not a buffer according to the city code.

You have just written a definition.

What Am I Trying to Do?

A **definition** is any writing that tries to pin down the meaning of a word. Definitions are usually necessary because a word is either unclear or technical, or its meaning is in dispute.

Here are two examples of words defined in passing because the writer thought they might be unclear to a particular audience:

> He <u>endorses</u>, or <u>supports</u>, Bob Miller for class president.

Endorses is defined in passing.

> They needed a <u>dolly</u> to move that couch. (A <u>dolly</u> is a platform on wheels used to move heavy objects.) It is not expensive to rent one.

Dolly is defined in parentheses because its meaning, which some readers might not know, is of secondary importance.

Here is an example of a technical word that is defined. The definition is given immediately and not in parenthesis because the term is important to the discussion, and most people won't know its meaning.

> Many reptiles, unlike mammals, are ecdytic. <u>Ecdysis</u> refers to periodically shedding skin, as snakes cast off their outer skin. Ecdysis is important because . . .

Sometimes a definition requires an entire paragraph, especially for words whose meanings are likely to differ among various people:

> <u>Patriotism</u> means love or support of country. A <u>patriot</u> is one who feels patriotism. But patriotism is probably the most abused word in our language. Some define patriotism in the way the well-known bumper sticker does, "My country, right or wrong," which seems to mean that to be patriotic is to support anything your country does. But this is a false patriotism. Just as it is bad parenting to put up with everything your child does, it is false patriotism to support everything your country does. The real patriot, the person who truly shows a love of country, will support his or her country when it is right but speak up when it is wrong.

When should you define a word? Often this is a judgment call. Some words are so complex that their meanings cannot be taken for granted but must be defined. Others are so clear to the world at large that defining them is unnecessary.

Here are four guidelines to help you decide on whether or not a definition is necessary:

1.   Define any word likely to be unknown to your audience. Your common sense must help you here. Some words you can simply assume your readers know.

> To hang a door properly, you need a hammer, a screwdriver, and a plumb bob. A <u>plumb bob</u> is a lead weight attached to a line that is used to determine perpendicularity. To hang the door, begin by . . .

Notice that the writer defines *plumb bob* but not *hammer* or *screwdriver*. Most people know what a hammer and screwdriver are; few, however, know what a plumb bob is, so the writer defines it.

2.   Define all technical words and terms when you are writing for a general audience. While a biology professor will readily know the meaning of *ecdysis,* a general audience will not. Here is another example:

Erythromycin is a drug used for treating bacterial infections.

3.   Define slang and specialized terms when you write for a general audience.

The Dallas Cowboys often use a nickel defense. In football the nickel defense consists of five defensive backs who protect against the pass.

4.   Define any word that doesn't have the same meaning for everyone. Most people, for example, agree on the meaning of *toaster* or *car engine.* But not everyone agrees on the meaning of *courage, loyalty,* or *success.* Such words have to be defined.

Faith is a word that has many meanings. In this essay, faith is used to mean a belief that rests more on spiritual outlook than on facts.

IN A NUTSHELL

- A definition tells what a word means.

- Define any word your audience might not know, especially technical words, slang, and specialized words. Also define words that are not likely to have the same meaning for everyone.

PRACTICING 1

Circle the word in the following pairs that you think would need defining in an essay.

1. cockroach, crackpot

2. fast (referring to speed), fast (diet)

3. arson, fire

4. battery (for your car), battery (as in physical assault)

5. bummed out, upset

6. vacation, sabbatical

7. streptokinase, blood

8. sole (the fish), soul

9. gross, disgusting

10. experiment, replica plating

How Can I Do It?

In defining a word, writers generally use one or a combination of these strategies:

- Synonym
- Formal definition
- Example
- Saying what the word is not
- Origin of the word

Use a synonym.

A **synonym** is a word with more or less the same meaning as another word. To cite a synonym is to use the meaning of one word to pinpoint the meaning of another. *Hope,* for example, may be defined by its synonyms—*expectation, optimism, prospect.* Synonyms are found in general dictionaries as well as in specialized synonym dictionaries. Here is an example of a definition with synonyms:

> Reputation is the name or standing a person has in a community. To have a good reputation means to be held in high esteem by people who know you or have heard about you. A reputation is a person's name. Reputation means more or less the same as character, position, standing, regard, and name. If your reputation is good, people show you respect when they meet you. If your reputation is bad, people are cautious when they meet you because they've heard bad things about you and don't know what to expect.

Note that synonyms by themselves only narrow meaning (reputation = name, standing) but do not pinpoint it. Therefore, it is often a good idea, after you give the synonym, to add some further explanation, as the writer above does.

> ### ESL Advice!
>
> Be sure that the synonyms you cite refer to the intended meaning of the word you're defining and not to another meaning. *Dash,* for example, means *style,* but it also means *to splash. Bespatter* may therefore be cited as a synonym of the second meaning, but not of the first.

Many handy sources of synonyms exist. One is a regular dictionary. For instance, our dictionary offers the following synonyms for the word *terror:* "horror," "panic," "fright." Another is a thesaurus, a book of synonyms and antonyms (words that mean the opposite). Word processing programs that come with a built-in thesaurus are a third. Often, the synonym found in a thesaurus will add clarity to the writer's original word. One student, for example, writing an essay on the *monsoons* of his native India, was afraid that some of his readers would not know that "*monsoon*" meant "wet season." Synonyms listed in a thesaurus included "downpour," "deluge," "torrent," and "storm," all of which make the meaning of *monsoon* unmistakably clear.

IN A NUTSHELL

The synonym of a word can be used to narrow or further pinpoint its meaning.

PRACTICING 2

Using synonyms, write a one-sentence definition of the following words. You may consult a dictionary or thesaurus.

1. anticipation

_____

_____

2. deteriorate

_____

_____

3. frantic

_____

_____

4. chivalrous

_____

_____

5. autobiography

_____

_____

6. roughneck

_____

_____

7. felony

_____

_____

8. indigestion

_____

_____

9. confidential

_____

_____

10. dawdle

_____

_____

Give a formal definition.

A formal definition first states what group the word belongs to and then shows how it differs from other words in that same group. The following chart shows what we mean:

WORD	GROUP	DIFFERENCE
pizza	is a food	consisting of a crust usually topped with a spiced mixture of tomato and cheese
buffer	is a strip of land	that separates two properties
penance	is an act	that shows sorrow for doing wrong
to rescue	is an act	of freeing from danger
measles	is a disease	characterized by red spots on the skin
Detroit	is a city	in Michigan

Notice that in each case the definition is a two-step process. First, the term is placed in a general group. Second, its differences from other members in that group are specified. So, _pizza_ is a _food,_ but it is different from other foods by having a _crust and toppings._ A _buffer_ is a _strip of land,_ specifically one that _separates two properties._ Likewise, _measles_ is a _disease,_ but one _characterized by red spots on the skin._ Dictionaries always give such formal definitions.

To give a formal definition, proceed this way: First, state the group to which the word belongs; second, tell how the word differs from others in the group. Formal definitions, in other words, always have two parts.

Anxiety is <u>a psychological disorder</u> that <u>is characterized by irrational fears</u>.

Love is <u>an emotion</u> of <u>passionate affection for someone or something</u>.

A neighbor is <u>a person</u> who <u>lives near another</u>.

The three words—*anxiety, love,* and *neighbor*—are first identified as belonging to the groups, *psychological disorder, emotion,* and *person.* Then we're told how each word differs from others in that group.

Note that in a formal definition, for the sake of clarity and smoothness, wherever possible it is better to begin your definition with wording similar to the wording of the term you're defining. For instance, the following opening of a definition is awkward: "A *litterbug* is "to strew garbage in public areas." *Litterbug* is a noun while *strew* is a verb. It is better and smoother to define the word using a noun, "A *litterbug* is *a person* who strews garbage in public areas."

IN A NUTSHELL

A formal definition first places the word in a group, then shows how it differs from others in that group.

PRACTICING 3

Using the chart that follows, choose ten words that you know well and formally define them as we did on page 184.

	WORD	GROUP	DIFFERENCE
1.			
2.			
3.			
4.			
5.			
6.			
7.			

WORD	GROUP	DIFFERENCE
8. _____		
9. _____		
10. _____		

PRACTICING 4

Give a formal definition for each of the following words. Give your definition in a complete sentence that specifies two parts—the group the word belongs to and how it differs from other words in that group. Also be sure that your definition begins with the same wording of speech as the term being defined. Write a complete sentence.

Example: daisy

A daisy is a flower with many white petals and a yellow center.

1. doorbell

_____

2. century

_____

3. giggle

_____

4. yogurt

_____

5. tuxedo

_____

Give an example.

A well-chosen example can add meaning to a word. Here are some examples:

Laconic means "concise" or "brief." For instance, a trial lawyer whose opening argument is very short and to the point, without wasting a word, would be considered laconic.

Goldbricking is slang for avoiding work by coming up with excuses. For example, you're goldbricking if you say you can't work because your allergies are acting up when there's nothing really wrong with you.

An illuminating story or anecdote about a word or term can also shed light on its meaning. An example follows.

> My tennis partner is a prude. Now the term prude is applied to people who are overly concerned about being proper or modest. That's Jenny for you. She will not play mixed doubles in shorts or a tennis skirt because she says men always look at her in a "certain way" when she does. Last Friday, my brother and his buddy wanted to play a couple of sets, and Jenny was happy to join in, but she wore a jogging suit even though it was in the nineties. I think that is being prudish.

IN A NUTSHELL

Giving an example or telling a story can add to the meaning of a word.

PRACTICING 5

Define the following terms by using a synonym or giving a formal definition. Then further clarify their meanings by giving an example or telling a story.

1. rude

_____

_____

_____

_____

2. loyalty

_____

_____

_____

_____

3. admonish

_____

_____

_____

_____

4. hero

_____

_____

_____

_____

5. limber

_____

_____

_____

_____

_____

Say what the word is not.

Many words are close in meaning without being exact synonyms. _Love_ and _infatuation_ are examples: Their meanings are close, but not the same. _Frugality_ and _miserliness, pride_ and _arrogance_ are also close, but still different. Sometimes the best way to define a word is to show how its meaning slightly differs from another word whose own meaning is close. Here is an example:

> Jealousy is a feeling of fear at the possibility of losing a loved one. Jealousy usually comes into play in a love triangle, where two people are competing for the affections of a third. Jealousy differs from envy in that jealousy is being possessive of what you think is (or should rightly be) yours, such as a husband being jealous of his wife or a wife of her husband. Envy is wanting what someone else has, such as a person envying another's good looks or success or wealth.

IN A NUTSHELL

Some words may best be defined by saying what the word is not.

PRACTICING 6

Define each of the following terms by stating what it is _not_, namely the similar word in parentheses.

Example: Cheap (frugal)

A person who is cheap tries to get away without paying his or her fair share. A cheap person is not the same as a frugal person. A frugal person tries to save on purchases by getting the best bargain but is still prepared to pay his or her fair share.

1. casual (sloppy)

_____

_____

_____

_____

2. annoyed (angry)

_____

_____

_____

_____

3. accidental (careless)

_____

_____

_____

_____

4. funny (silly)

_____

_____

_____

_____

5. confident (cocky)

_____

_____

_____

_____

PRACTICING 7

Expand the definitions below by giving an example or anecdote, or saying what the term is not.

Example: Fairness is the virtue of treating everyone equally. For instance, a teacher with a reputation for fairness does not give A's to a student just because that student is likable. The teacher gives the grade that is deserved.

1. *Guilt* is the responsibility for having done something wrong.

_____

_____

_____

2. *Greed* is a strong desire for more than one needs.

_____

_____

_____

3. To feel *defeated* means to feel crushed and beaten.

_____

_____

_____

4. A *genuine* person is honest and frank.

_____

_____

_____

5. To *ooze* is to flow or leak out slowly.

_____

_____

_____

Give the origin of the word.

It can be useful in defining a word to say what it originally meant. This tactic, however, will work only for words whose origins add to their present meanings. Here is an example:

Sarcasm comes from the Greek word <u>sarkasmós</u> meaning "to tear flesh." Today, sarcasm means "harsh or bitter derision" and is an especially cruel tone that one uses in criticism. The person who is sarcastic tries to wound—to tear flesh. Sarcasm is not gentle.

Not every word has an origin that can help with its present meaning. *Buffer,* for example, does not. Neither does *father.* However, as long as you're looking up a word in the dictionary, you might as well check to see if its origin can help you define its present meaning.

IN A NUTSHELL

Occasionally, the origin of a word will help add to its present meaning.

PRACTICING 8

Give the origins of the following words. Use a good dictionary for this assignment. If there is more than one origin given, use the oldest.

1. banshee _____

2. danger _____

3. egad _____

4. game _____

5. IOU _____

6. magazine _____

7. mesmerism _____

8. origin _____

9. permanent _____

10. seduce _____

PRACTICING 9

Choose one of the words in Practicing 8 and define it in a short paragraph. Use its origin in your definition and any other way of defining that you've learned.

PRACTICING 10

Choose one of the terms that follow and write a paragraph defining it. Begin with a formal definition, and then use any of the strategies explained in this unit.

1. gourmet
2. failure
3. mischief
4. debate (verb)
5. sob (verb)

What Do I Need to Look Out For?

Two common problems can occur in defining. Your definition can be circular, or it can be incomplete.

Circular definitions

A definition is circular if it simply repeats the word without adding substantially to its meaning. An example of a circular definition follows.

> <u>Middle-aged</u> refers to the period in the <u>middle years</u> of a person's life. When a person is <u>middle-aged</u>, he or she is <u>between young and old</u>, not one or the other.

This definition is circular because it adds nothing to *middle-aged* except the obvious meaning already contained in the words *middle of life*. In short, the writer does not define the word, but merely repeats it. Here is a better definition:

> <u>Middle-aged</u> refers to the period in the middle years of human life. It is not a fixed but a variable period. Long ago, when humans lived an average of 35 years, middle-aged was, strictly speaking, anywhere between 15 and 25. But with the human life span now 78.8 years for women and 72 years for men, middle-aged is now usually defined as the years between 45 and 65. The term, middle-aged, however, does not just refer to a period of time, but more accurately to a life condition. Middle-aged people go through certain physiological and psychological changes. Their metabolism slows down; sexual energy and appetite decrease. Some men and women go through a period of self-examination and doubt known as the "mid-life crisis." Middle-aged, in sum, describes the transition that all people go through as they move from youth to old age.

PRACTICING 11

In the blanks preceding each of the following sentences, write *C* if the definition is circular. Leave the blank empty if the definition is not circular. Then correct and rewrite the five circular definitions in the lines provided.

1. _____ A *mask* is a cover for the face used as a disguise.

2. _____ *Stressed* is what people feel when they have too much stress in their lives.

3. _____ *Pepper* is a pungent product from the fruit of an East Indian plant used as a seasoning spice.

4. _____ A *servant* is one who serves.

5. _____ *Dissing* is an act of dissing someone.

6. _____ A *subhead* is one head lower than a main head in an outline.

7. _____ *Team spirit* refers to the team's spirits, whether they're high or low.

8. _____ The *capitol* is the building in which a state legislative body meets.

9. _____ A *barbarian* is a person who does barbaric things.

10. _____ A *monk* is a man who is a member of a religious order and lives in a monastery.

Use the following lines to correct and rewrite the circular definitions:

_____

_____

_____

_____

_____

_____

_____

_____

_____

_____

Incomplete definitions

The second problem to look out for in writing definitions is the **incomplete definition**—the definition that doesn't say enough. In particular, the incomplete definition doesn't spell out the meaning of the word in the ways we've described in this chapter. Here are some examples:

A <u>migraine headache</u> is a severe headache.

The definition below is more complete, but still lacking:

A <u>migraine headache</u> is a severe headache characterized by nausea, vomiting, and an extreme sensitivity to light. It can last for as long as a day.

As migraine sufferers will tell you, this definition still hardly does justice to their awful condition. Here is a better definition that is complete:

A <u>migraine headache</u> is a severe headache that is characterized by nausea, vomiting, and extreme sensitivity to light. No one knows for sure what causes the migraine or how to prevent one. But migraine sufferers are often so stricken when an attack occurs that they can do nothing more than go to bed. A migraine often lasts from several hours to a day or longer. When my Aunt Ida has a migraine, she can do nothing more than draw the shades in her bedroom and go to bed, where she'll stay for 24 hours, retching and feeling as if she will die. Not even the newest medications help her migraines. The only solution is isolation and bed rest.

Both errors—being circular and being incomplete—can usually be caught if you reread your work. Indeed, the best way to catch both problems is to read your work aloud, either to yourself or to another person, pretending to know nothing about the topic. Ask if you really answer the question, "What is it?" If you have doubts, rewrite the definition until you are satisfied that it fully defines your word or term.

PRACTICING 12

Half of the following definitions are incomplete. Identify the incomplete definitions by marking them *I*. Then rewrite them in the lines that follow. Use a dictionary, if you like.

1. _____ Coffee is a beverage.

2. _____ Acrylics are a type of paint that dry fast and can be mixed with water.

3. _____ A magician is an entertainer.

4. _____ A chauffeur is a person employed to drive a private car.

5. _____ Sautéing refers to cooking food fast in a shallow frying pan.

6. _____ The cuticle is part of your nails.

7. _____ A sergeant is a military officer.

8. _____ Tweezers are small metal instruments used for plucking or handling small objects.

9. _____ A hot dog is a type of fast food.

10. _____ Glucose is a type of sugar used by the cells for energy.

Now rewrite the incomplete definitions, making them clear and complete.

_____

_____

_____

_____

_____

_____

_____

_____

_____

_____

IN A NUTSHELL

Avoid definitions that are circular or incomplete.

PRACTICING 13

Read the following paragraph, then underline and label the techniques used to make the meaning of the word clear: *S* (synonyms), *N* (saying what the word is not), *E* (example), or *O* (giving the origin of the word).

Normal—a word all of us use—means "typical" or "standard."

It comes from the Latin *normal,* meaning "a rule or pattern." *Normal*

indicates some kind of balance, either physical or mental. For exam-

ple, we say the "normal" body temperature is 98.6°F because tests show that that is the typical temperature of a well person. We also say that it is "normal" for a teenager to be rebellious because we know from developmental psychology that during the teen years many adolescents try to assert their independence. *Normal* is not the same as *average*. An "average student" is one who receives average grades. But that same student could be abnormal in some other way, say, for example, in being very tall. Someone who falls within the standards of what is expected is considered "normal." We refer to "normal" height, weight, and curiosity, meaning that these all fall within the range of the expected.

Unit Test

From the answers offered, choose the *ONE* that does *NOT* apply.

Example: A definition is writing that

    _____ **(a).** tries to pin down the meaning of a term.

    ✔ **(b).** specifies how to use a word within a limited context.

    _____ **(c).** helps the reader to understand a word.

    _____ **(d).** states a precise interpretation of a term

  1. Definitions are necessary because words are often

    _____ **(a).** ambiguous.

    _____ **(b).** unclear.

    _____ **(c).** too specialized.

    _____ **(d).** interpreted falsely.

  2. "to nullify," "to abolish," "to cancel," or "to revoke"

    _____ **(a).** are synonyms.

    _____ **(b).** have the same meaning.

    _____ **(c).** have totally different meanings.

    _____ **(d).** can be used interchangeably.

3. The following cases require a definition:

    _____ **(a).** when the word is understood by most people.

    _____ **(b).** when the word is obscure and not known.

    _____ **(c).** when the word might be known to a specialized audience only.

    _____ **(d).** when the word could have a double meaning.

4. The following words are most likely to require definition:

    _____ **(a).** honor

    _____ **(b).** truth

    _____ **(c).** harlequin

    _____ **(d).** broom

5. A formal definition

    _____ **(a).** states the general group to which the term belongs.

    _____ **(b).** uses the word to describe a scene.

    _____ **(c).** shows how the word differs from others in its group.

    _____ **(d).** is a two-step process.

6. The following groups of words are synonyms:

    _____ **(a).** harden, toughen, strengthen

    _____ **(b).** job, task, occupation

    _____ **(c).** hide, conceal, display

    _____ **(d).** waste, squander, spend

7. Sometimes a word is best defined by

    _____ **(a).** stating what the word is not.

    _____ **(b).** classifying it grammatically.

    _____ **(c).** defining the word and showing how its meaning differs slightly from another word.

    _____ **(d).** using it in several different contexts.

8. When defining a word, it helps to

    _____ **(a).** cite its origin

    _____ **(b).** make up a story about it

    _____ **(c).** use it the way it was used in Colonial times.

    _____ **(d).** check to see if Shakespeare ever used it.

9. A circular definition

    _____ **(a).** always helps define a term.

    _____ **(b).** adds nothing to the meaning of a term.

    _____ **(c).** simply repeats the term to be defined.

    _____ **(d).** goes in a complete circle.

10. A definition that doesn't say enough does

_____ **(a).** an incomplete job.

_____ **(b).** a complete job.

_____ **(c).** no justice to the word.

_____ **(d).** a bad job and needs to be rewritten.

Unit Talk-Write Assignment

Your assignment is to write a definition of a word. After much thought, you choose the word _asteroid._ You look up the word in your _American Heritage Dictionary,_ and then you talk a paragraph to your reflection in the mirror, hoping the exercise will increase your fluency—and it does. Here is your monologue:

Spoken Paragraph

My dictionary tells me that an asteroid is a small celestial body that orbits around the sun. Most asteroids are found between Mars and Jupiter. They are much smaller than planets. At most, about 700 miles in diameter. They are very irregular in shape. Don't think anyone knows where they came from. Actually, I already knew that because I've always been interested in planets and space. I'm a real _Star Wars_ addict. But I'm not nearly as interested in the definition of asteroid as I am in the idea that one could hit Earth. NASA has decided that any news of an asteroid heading toward Earth will be kept secret because it would upset too many people. Well, I should say so. I'd just as soon not know if the end of the world is near. The thing is, asteroids move at incredible speeds, like comets, and a large one moving toward us at a humongous speed would simply create another big bang—except there wouldn't be anyone left to read about it. It's really best not to think about such a disaster. I think I have more or less explained what an asteroid is. At least I tried.

Your spoken paragraph is a good start toward developing a clear definition of asteroid. Now, use this paragraph as the groundwork for a more polished version. Be sure to make your definition complete and avoid giving circular definitions. Check your dictionary to see if there is an interesting origin of the word to include.

Written Paragraph

 ## Unit Collaborative Assignment

Choose a partner. Give your partner a word that you know well and ask him or her to define it. Write down your partner's definition. Then exchange places and define a word given by your partner. Collaborate on the definitions until both of you agree that the meanings of the defined words are clear.

Unit Writing Assignment

Write a definition of one of the words that you worked on in the above Unit Collaborative Assignment. Use any of the strategies for defining that you learned in the unit: synonyms, formal definitions, examples, saying what the word is not, and the origin of the word.

Photo Writing Assignment

Use the following photo as the inspiration for defining *friendship*. Start with a formal definition, and then use synonyms or any of the other techniques taught in this unit, including saying what the word is not, giving an example, or relating an anecdote that illuminates its meaning. Make sure that your definition is not circular or incomplete.

13

Classifying

Your school is being visited by a group of computer students from Japan, and you have been asked to head up a committee to welcome the visitors and show them around campus. You tell the student government president that you need various types of students to help out. The president asks you to e-mail her about the kinds of volunteers you need. You send the following message:

> The host committee for our Japanese visitors should be made up of three types of students, each with a special talent. To begin with, we need students who are fluent in both Japanese and English. They will serve mainly as translators. We also need some good organizers with sunny personalities to schedule the activities of the visitors, arrange their sleeping accommodations, and generally make them feel welcome. Third, we need computer science students who are willing to share their expertise with our visitors and show them around the computer lab. With these three types of students on our committee, I'm convinced our visitors will enjoy their stay with us.

You have just written a paragraph that classifies.

What Am I Trying to Do?

To **classify** means to sort out into types. If you say—"I've had four kinds of jobs," or "I have three kinds of friends"—whether you know it or not, you're classifying. Here is an example of a paragraph written to classify:

> <u>I have three kinds of friends in my life: close friends, just friends, and acquaintances</u>. The first type, my close friends, are people I have known most of my life who love and accept me for myself. George is the best example of this kind of friend. We've known each other since first grade. I trust George and can tell him my deepest feelings. My second type of friend, "just friends," are people I like and do things with. Missing, however, is the feeling of trust I share with George. We're friends, but "just friends," not "close friends." Finally, I have friends who are just "acquaintances." These are people I occasionally see at parties or sit next to in class. We chat and are friendly with one another if we happen to meet. But that's as far as we go. We don't plan things together. My life is richer for these three types of friends, for they provide me with a healthy variety of company.

This is a typical classification paragraph. In it the writer is trying to sort her friends into personal categories.

Her classification, however, may be called an **informal classification:** The categories are made up; they do not already exist. A **formal classification** is classification based on categories that already exist and are not personally invented. For example, vehicles can be classified by manufacturers according to body types such as *two-door, four-door, convertible, van,* and *sports utility vehicle* (SUV). Medicine uses categories such as *internists* (general doctors for adults), *pediatricians* (general doctors for children), *cardiologists* (specialists in the heart), and *neurologists* (specialists in the brain and nervous system), to name a few of the better-known types. History courses are similarly classified into such types as *History of South America* or *History of the Renaissance.*

Imagine, for a moment, what life would be like if we were incapable of classifying. Every object or experience would strike us as utterly unique. The world we live in would soon overwhelm us with its sheer variety. Nothing would be like anything else; everything would be spectacularly different. We'd scream with discovery at the sight of a cat. Two blocks later, we'd scream just as loudly at the sight of another cat, for we would have no concept of the second cat being the same kind of animal as the first. Its uniqueness is all we would see. We'd soon be blubbering with the shock of too much novelty. In short, classification—both formal and informal—is useful because it helps us simplify the world.

PRACTICING 1

Check the topics that should be developed by classification.

1. _____ Types of houses

2. _____ Why good work habits are important

3. _____ Kinds of popular part-time jobs

4. _____ Organizing your time

5. _____ How to find information on the Internet

6. _____ Comparing Disneyland and Disneyworld

7. _____ Categorizing legal drugs

8. _____ Dividing mall shoppers into types

9. _____ The need for job retraining in large companies

10. _____ Kinds of freedom we should cherish

How Can I Do It?

Here are four tips to help you write a good classification:

1. State your purpose.

2. Use a single principle.

3. Be complete.

4. Use transitions to present your classification in a logical order.

State your purpose.

Classification is an exercise in thinking. It requires you to think logically in categories and types. Your teacher might ask you to informally classify your hobbies, relatives, or friends, or to formally classify the types of literature. All such assignments are intended to sharpen your ability to think in categories and types.

The most useful way to begin any classifying paragraph, whether formal or informal, is to state what you're going to do. Here is an example of a paragraph where the writer hides her purpose:

> Many of my boyfriends don't like to spend money. Jack is the exception. Jack never takes me anywhere without paying for both of us. If he doesn't have the money, he doesn't ask me out, but waits until he has earned it. Jack is very old-fashioned in that way. Peter always makes it clear that we're going Dutch. If I tell him I can't afford it, we don't go out. He's very modern in that way. Tony is what you would call a moocher. He wants me to pay for everything. And sometimes, if I can afford to, I do and like it because paying makes

me feel in charge. Of the three, I prefer Jack if I'm broke, but don't mind either Peter or Tony when I can afford them.

This paragraph classifies the writer's boyfriends but doesn't plainly state the purpose. Here is a sharper and crisper version because it openly lists specific kinds of boyfriends. Generally, if you use a word like *kinds, types,* or *sorts* in your topic sentence, you're probably doing a good job of stating your purpose.

> <u>I have three kinds of boyfriends: those who are willing to pay my way on dates, those who are willing to pay only their own way, and those who expect me to pay everything</u>. Jack is the first kind of boyfriend. He never takes me anywhere without paying for both of us. If he doesn't have the money, he doesn't ask me out, but waits until he has earned it. Jack is very old-fashioned in that way. Peter is the second type. When he asks me out, he always makes it clear that we're going Dutch. If I tell him I can't afford it, we don't go out. He's very modern in that way. The third type of boyfriend can be summed up in Tony. He's what you would call a moocher. He wants me to pay for everything. And sometimes, if I can afford to, I do and like it because paying makes me feel in charge. Of the three types, I prefer Jack if I'm broke, but don't mind either Peter or Tony when I can afford them.

Always be straightforward about your purpose in your topic sentence. Your reader will thank you.

Use a single principle.

All classification must be made according to some ordering principle—the measure or yardstick you use for your sorting. For example, if you use *height* as the ordering principle for sorting your friends, you might come up with the categories of *tall friends, medium-height friends,* and *short friends.* Such a classification, however, would be silly and hardly useful. The trick is therefore to find an ordering principle that yields significant categories. For example, the student who classified her friends on page 202 used degrees of closeness as her ordering principle. This gave her the categories of *close friends, just friends,* and *acquaintances.* These categories are significant because they tell how people relate to each other at different levels of intimacy.

How you classify something depends on your ordering principle. For example, you might choose to classify cars by body styles—*two-door, four-door, convertible, van,* and *SUV.* You might also choose to classify cars by size—*subcompacts, compacts, intermediates,* and *full size.* If you choose price as your ordering principle, you might classify cars into *economy, medium-priced,* and *luxury.* The point is to choose the single ordering principle that best suits your purpose. Once you have chosen an ordering principle, you must stick with it.

If you do not use a single ordering principle, you might end up with an illogical topic sentence like this one:

There are five main types of car manufactured today: <u>subcompacts</u>, <u>compacts</u>, <u>intermediates</u>, <u>full size</u>, and <u>luxury</u>.

Here the writer is actually using two ordering principles: size and price. Size yields the categories *subcompacts, compacts, intermediates,* and *large*; price yields the category *luxury*. This is an illogical division since a full size or even a compact car can also be luxurious.

Sometimes this kind of mixed classification occurs in an otherwise well-written paragraph, such as this one:

My recreation consists of three types of activities: indoor activities, outdoor activities, and sports. For indoor activities, I really enjoy playing pool, especially eight-ball, and bowling. Sometimes I also like to play ping-pong. My favorite outdoor activities are playing softball on my company team, golf, and jogging. The sports I especially enjoy are pool, softball, bowling, golf, and jogging. These types of activities help me get over a dull and boring day of working.

Do you see the problem with this paragraph? It is that *sports* can be an indoor activity (pool, bowling, ping-pong, for example) or an outdoor activity (softball, tennis, football, for example). The groups are illogical, and the writer ends up being repetitious.

Here's how the student rewrote the paragraph after finding a more logical ordering principle for his recreational activities:

<u>My recreation consists of three types of activities: sports I play with a team, sports I do by myself, and sports that I love to watch on television</u>. My favorite team sport is softball. I play on my company's team, usually as a pitcher, and enjoy the fellowship that comes from the competition. The company also has a ping-pong team that I'm on, and sometimes I also practice with the company tag-football team. The sport I do by myself and really love, when I can afford it, is golf. I like to go to the driving range alone and hit practice balls. I like to play by myself so if I do badly, I won't feel embarrassed. I also like to run alone and try to get out at least three times a week. On weekends, especially if the weather is bad, I like to watch college basketball games and NFL football games on television. I'm also an Atlanta Braves fan and watch all their televised games. Without sports, I think I would be bored, and my life would be dull.

In any classification, you must choose a single, logical principle for ordering items into types and stick to it.

PRACTICING 2

For each of the following topics, cross out the one type that doesn't fit. In the spaces provided, identify the organizing principle of the related four items as well as the principle behind the one that doesn't fit.

Example: Pies

    (a). Fruit pies

    (a). Cream pies

    (c). ~~Homemade pies~~

    (d). Meat pies

Why: Pies a, b, and d are categorized by filling; c is categorized by where it is made.

1. Places to live

    (a). Apartment

    (b). Single-family home

    (c). Condominium

    (d). Downtown

    (e). Two-family home

Why: _____

2. Radio stations

    (a). Oldies

    (b). All-news

    (c). All-talk

    (d). Country and western

    (e). FM

Why: _____

3. Milk

    (a). Skim

    (b). Two percent

    (c). Chocolate

    (d). Whole milk

Why: _____

4. Movies

   (a). PG

   (b). PG-13

   (c). R

   (d). Documentary

   (e). G

Why: _____

5. Transportation

   (a). Cars

   (b). Ambulances

   (c). Trains

   (d). Planes

   (e). Buses

Why: _____

PRACTICING 3

Classify each of the following topics into at least three types. Then state your principle for classifying.

Example: Types of cars

   (a). Expensive cars

   (b). Medium-priced cars

   (c). Economy cars

Principle of classification: price

1. Types of desserts

   (a). _____

   (b). _____

   (c). _____

Principle of classification: _____

2. Types of athletes

   (a). _____

   (b). _____

   (c). _____

Principle of classification: _____

3. Types of television programs

(a). _____

(b). _____

(c). _____

Principle of classification: _____

4. Types of restaurants

(a). _____

(b). _____

(c). _____

Principle of classification: _____

5. Types of music

(a). _____

(b). _____

(c). _____

Principle of classification: _____

PRACTICING 4

Write a paragraph on one of the topics from Practicing 3.

Be complete.

If you are classifying a subject whose parts are well known, be sure to include them all. An example of a glaring omission follows.

> The military services available to young people are the Army, Navy, and Air Force.

This division omits the Marines and the Coast Guard. Here is another example:

> There are seven parts of speech: nouns, verbs, adjectives, adverbs, prepositions, conjunctions, and interjections.

In fact, there are eight parts of speech. The writer has omitted pronouns, and we are left wondering why.

You don't have to worry about completeness in a personal classification of your own invention. For instance, no one can seriously challenge this classification:

> High school students come in four primary types: nerds, jocks, party animals, and brains.

Obviously, this is a personal classification based on opinion.

However, in a formal classification, omitting a known category is a glaring mistake. Here is an example:

> There are three types of marital status: married, divorced, and widowed. I've been two of the three and know what each feels like. I was married for three years. The first year was happy, but the next two were terrible. My wife and I fought constantly. Finally, we agreed to give up and get a divorce. I've been divorced now for two years and can't say I really like it. I feel like I failed at something that might have worked if I had tried harder. I'll probably never know what it feels like to be widowed because it's unlikely I'll ever get married again. Being married was the best of the three marital statuses; too bad it was so short for me.

This classification is incomplete: *single* is one of the marital statuses and should be mentioned.

In sum, if your classification is formal rather than personal, be careful not to leave out any categories.

PRACTICING 5

In the blanks provided, list the category that was omitted from each of the following classifications.

1. College teachers: instructors, assistant professor, associate professor, _____

2. Students: freshman, sophomore, junior, _____

3. Student accommodations: dorm, rented room, apartment, _____

4. Furniture: living room, dining room, kitchen, _____

5. Baseball infield positions: first base, second base, third base, _____

Use transitions to present your classification in a logical order.

All good writing uses transitions generously, and the classifying paragraph or essay is no exception. Any paragraph or essay that jumps between different categories or groups—as classifications do—will need transitions. Such commonsense phrases as "this first category is . . ." or "this second category, on the other hand . . ." are the kinds of transitions we have in mind. Without such transitions, a reader might find the jumps in a classification difficult to follow. Here is an example, from a paragraph that gives an informal classification of casino gamblers.

When I used to live in Las Vegas, I worked as a night janitor in a casino and found that there were three kinds of late-night gamblers. First, there was the insomniac gambler. This person, generally a woman, had difficulty sleeping and used gambling as a way of exhausting herself. She would sit at the nickel slot machine and pull the handle until she was ready to drop. Then she would go to bed. The second type of late-night gambler was the adventurer. Las Vegas was like a drug to that person, who would hop from game to game and get a buzz from playing. With that person, the drug was adrenaline, and the excitement of being in a brightly lit casino was reason enough to continue playing until the wee hours of the morning. Finally, the third type of late-night gambler was the one who had dreams of being a professional. This person would think of himself or herself as working and would take the game being played very seriously. Of all the three types, this was the one that I felt sorriest for, because by then I had learned that no matter what type of gambler you are, you can't beat the casinos.

Notice that this writer uses transitions such as "First, there was," "The second type of late-night gambler was," and "Finally, the third type of late-night gambler was" to classify the kinds of gamblers he observed while working nights in a casino. This use of transitions is not peculiar to classification but is a part of any good writing.

PRACTICING 6

Choose one of the topics that follow and divide it into categories, types, or kinds by following a logical order. In the space provided, state the logical order you used. Be sure you use appropriate transitions between the groups or types.

Example:

> **Topic:**   Fanaticism
>
> **1.** The most dangerous kind of fanaticism is the religious kind.
>
> **2.** The next most dangerous kind of fanaticism is the political kind.
>
> **3.** The least dangerous fanaticism is the economic kind.
>
> **Logical order used:** From most dangerous to least dangerous.

1. Types of mail you receive

2. Three breeds of dogs

3. House chores

4. Marriages

5. Telephone calls

PRACTICING 7

Develop the topic you used in Practicing 6 into a full paragraph. Be sure to use appropriate transitions between the types or groups.

What Do I Need to Look Out For?

Classifying means sorting items into either informal types, based on your own observations, or into formal categories. The errors usually made in classifying, as you might expect, are therefore errors of sorting. When you classify, be sure to do the following:

- Include at least three categories.
- Do not overlap categories.

Include at least three categories

Generally, a classification is made up of at least three categories. For example, it makes little sense to say:

> The people in my life fall into two categories: friends and not friends.

Similarly, a vehicle is either a car or not a car, a fruit either an orange or not an orange. Neither observation says much about either cars or fruit. Another problem occurs when you use less than three categories: You end up comparing or describing, not classifying. For instance, if you write, "I like to listen to two kinds of musical instruments—the guitar and the piano," you will most likely end up comparing the two instruments, not classifying them. This topic sentence, however, with its three categories, is clearly a classification:

> The people in my life fall into three categories: family, friends, and acquaintances.

Make sure that your own classifications contain at least three categories.

PRACTICING 8

List at least three categories for each of the following items.

1. vacations

    (a). ⎯⎯⎯⎯⎯⎯⎯

    (b). ⎯⎯⎯⎯⎯⎯⎯

    (c). ⎯⎯⎯⎯⎯⎯⎯

2. stress

    (a). ⎯⎯⎯⎯⎯⎯⎯

    (b). ⎯⎯⎯⎯⎯⎯⎯

    (c). ⎯⎯⎯⎯⎯⎯⎯

3. communication

    (a). ⎯⎯⎯⎯⎯⎯⎯

    (b). ⎯⎯⎯⎯⎯⎯⎯

    (c). ⎯⎯⎯⎯⎯⎯⎯

4. home appliances

    (a). ⎯⎯⎯⎯⎯⎯⎯

    (b). ⎯⎯⎯⎯⎯⎯⎯

    (c). ⎯⎯⎯⎯⎯⎯⎯

5. indoor entertainment

    (a). ⎯⎯⎯⎯⎯⎯⎯

    (b). ⎯⎯⎯⎯⎯⎯⎯

    (c). ⎯⎯⎯⎯⎯⎯⎯

Do not overlap categories.

As we said, if you do not stick to a single ordering principle, you will produce a classification with overlapping categories. The overlapping category is such a major error of classifications that it deserves a second mention. Consider, for example, this topic sentence:

> Movies can be categorized as drama, comedy, science fiction, and children's film.

The problem here is that a children's film can be a drama, a comedy, or science fiction. In other words, the categories are overlapping.
   Here is another example:

> I am a person with four basic moods: good mood, bad mood, bored mood, and morning mood.

Morning mood doesn't fit, since the writer could be in a good, bad, or bored mood in the morning. Good mood, bad mood, and bored mood are types based on how the writer feels. *Morning mood* is a type based on time of day. This mistake is the same as classifying living creatures as no-legged, two-legged, four-legged, and camels.

The primary thing you need to look out for, then, is illogical thinking about types. Be sure that you select a single principle for a classification so it yields types rather than overlapping categories. Watch out for a topic sentence like this:

My typical day has four parts: school, work, play, and night.

IN A NUTSHELL

When classifying, be sure to do the following:

- Include at least three categories.
- Do not overlap categories.

PRACTICING 9

Circle the overlapping category in each of the following classifications. Explain why the category is overlapping or doesn't fit by identifying the two different organizing principles.

1. Magazines: news, gossip, inexpensive, fashion, sports

_____

2. Main dishes: beef, pork, chicken, stew, fish

_____

3. Books: hardbacks, novels, spiral bound, paperbacks

_____

4. Drinkable liquids: sodas, water, sport drinks, Gatorade

_____

5. Gasoline: high-octane, unleaded, Mobil, low-octane

_____

Unit Test

From the replies given, check the one that most correctly answers the question asked.

Example: What are you trying to do when you classify?

_____ **(a).** List items in alphabetical order.

_____ **(b).** Deal with items in the order of their importance.

✔ **(c).** Sort out something into its types.

_____ **(d).** Explain the class system in the United States.

1. Which of the following topic sentences would best be developed as a classification?

_____ **(a).** The Honda company claims to be passionate about every engine it builds.

✓ **(b).** Amusement park rides can be divided into four different types.

_____ **(c).** Playing Monopoly is a good way to learn about handling money.

_____ **(d).** Akika and Beverly are two opposite types of students.

2. Which of the following topics could be developed as a classification?

✓ **(a).** Three types of critters that might bother you while camping.

_____ **(b).** The two most difficult mountain peaks ever climbed.

_____ **(c).** The steps involved in resolving labor disputes.

_____ **(d).** The best subway system for large cities.

3. Which of the following rules will *NOT* help you write a good classification?

_____ **(a).** Use a single principle.

_____ **(b).** Be complete.

✓ **(c).** State your purpose.

_____ **(d).** Write with passion.

4. Which item in the following classification of historical American Indians does not fit?

_____ **(a).** Plain Indians

_____ **(b).** Warrior Indians

✓ **(c).** New Delhi Indians

_____ **(d).** Pueblo Indians

5. Which item does not belong in the following classification of ways to pay for purchases?

_____ **(a).** Cash

_____ **(b).** Credit cards

_____ **(c).** Checks

___✓___ **(d).** IOU's

6. When you are classifying a subject whose parts are well known, what should you be sure to do?

_____ **(a).** Repeat each part.

_____ **(b).** Include all parts.

_____ **(c).** Define each part.

_____ **(d).** Use good transitions.

7. What is the best way to begin a classification paragraph?

_____ **(a).** Start with the last item.

___✓___ **(b).** Use an intriguing anecdote to catch your reader's attention.

_____ **(c).** Don't state what you are going to do.

_____ **(d).** Never use the word "type."

8. What are the most common errors made in writing a classification?

_____ **(a).** Errors in spelling.

___✓___ **(b).** Errors in sorting.

_____ **(c).** Errors in style.

_____ **(d).** Errors in point of view.

9. Why should you include at least three categories when doing a classification?

_____ **(a).** Because the number three is a complete number.

_____ **(b).** Because then you can have a well-developed essay.

_____ **(c).** Because most teachers require a minimum of three paragraphs from their students.

___✓___ **(d).** Because fewer than three categories ends up being a comparison or description.

10. What is the error in the topic sentence that follows: "Magazines can be divided into four types—intellectual, sensational, practical, and expensive"?

_____ **(a).** Lack of purpose.

___✓__ **(b).** Not enough categories.

___✓__ **(c).** Overlapping categories.

_____ **(d).** Illogical classification principle.

Unit Talk-Write Assignment

Following is a conversation among students about ugly neckties. Study it and then turn the ideas into a paragraph based on classification. Begin with a topic sentence that clearly states the ways ties can be ugly. Be careful not to overlap categories. Use the lines that follow for your paragraph.

Conversation

Dave: It's sort of hard to say what makes a tie ugly, but I sure know one when I see it.

Melissa: I'll tell you one way ties are ugly—when they're made of weird material. Have you ever seen a tie made of wool? It looks as if it's been hand-crocheted. I mean, the knot is so thick it looks like some malignant tumor growing on the guy's neck.

Andrew: I agree. Ties should be made of smooth material—but not polyester or acrylic because they look cheap. I like ties made out of natural fabrics—like cotton.

Kiki: What about the designs on ties? I saw a tie with a picture of the Mona Lisa on it. To me that's dissing a world famous artist.

Melissa: I saw a tie once that had huge broccoli, cabbage heads, and bananas printed all over it! I wanted to barf!

Kiki: Let's not even mention ties that are sexually stupid. I mean, showing parts of women's anatomy or Santa Claus and Mrs. Claus—well, I won't say more. How gross.

Dave: Yeah—I know. But ties can be ugly even if they're made of natural material and they don't have any design at all on them. I'm talking about color. My grandmother once gave me a tie that was puke green.

Melissa: Yeah—nothing like a prune purple tie! And some of the designer ties are worst of all—combining orange bubbles with hot pink squares or dark brown stripes with neon blue rectangles.

Andrew: Hey—what's wrong with orange parrots and lavender fish? Just kidding. I have to say there's nothing like an elegant silk tie with simple stripes or squares in subdued but rich colors—you know, the kind of tie my Grandpa wears.

Written Paragraph

_____

_____

_____

_____

_____

_____

_____

_____

_____

Unit Collaborative Assignment

Working with a classmate, take turns finding personal categories for the following topics. Be sure you have at least three categories and that they do not overlap.

1. Roommates
2. People in a grocery checkout line
3. Sports fans
4. People you often see in a library
5. Blind dates

Unit Writing Assignment

Write a classification paragraph on one of the topics you discussed in the above Unit Collaborative Assignment.

Photo Writing Assignment

The following picture shows an aerial view of a neighborhood that could be categorized according to several different principles. For example, if it were categorized by type of building, it would be considered residential rather than commercial or mixed. Select an organizing principle for categorizing neighborhoods. Write a paragraph describing three to five categories of neighborhoods, including the category illustrated by the neighborhood in the picture.

14

Comparing and Contrasting

"Professor Chang's class is more fun than Professor Blythe's."

Which job should you take for the summer? That is what you're wondering. You have two offers and are weighing both. You talk to friends and get so much advice that you're confused. Finally, your English teacher suggests that you write down the pros and cons of each job. You do so and come up with this:

> Both jobs—parking valet and grocery checker—have advantages as well as disadvantages. Both would give me good experience dealing with different kinds of people. Otherwise, though, each has pluses and minuses. The hours are very different. The valet job is night work, from 7 P.M. to 1 A.M. every night, including Fridays and Saturdays. The grocery checker position is strictly day work, from 9 A.M. to 5 P.M., weekdays and an occasional Saturday. If I take the valet job, I'll have no nightlife at all. The two also have very different working conditions. The valet job is an outdoor job. I will get a lot of exercise running to and from the cars. On the other hand, the grocery checker's job is indoors. I'll stand on my feet all day, with little physical activity. Finally, the jobs differ in pay. The valet job pays strictly on tips. The checker's job, on the other hand, pays a steady $5.25 per hour, with no tips. Which one do I want? I guess I should take the checker's job. I need to earn some sure money, and I don't look forward to a job that makes it hard for me to hang out with my friends.

You have just written a comparison and contrast.

What Am I Trying to Do?

A **comparison** shows similarities; a **contrast** highlights differences. Often, the two go hand in hand. In the job comparison, for example, the writer notes some similarities between the two jobs—the experience each offers as well as the chance to meet new people—before covering their differences.

We use comparison/contrast daily to make decisions and choices. You compare and contrast reviews and opinions about movies before deciding whether to see the one about a bank robbery or the one that tells a passionate love story. You buy a Honda because you think it is better made than other cars. You select one history class over another because, after comparing the instructors, you like one better. Every day we use comparison/contrast to make big and little decisions, from deciding whether to take a certain job or whether or not to buy bananas. Indeed, of all the strategies you will learn, comparison/contrast is the most useful in helping to make daily choices.

Comparison/contrast paragraphs and essays usually focus on the similarities and differences between two things. But two is not necessarily a sacred number for such writing. It is possible, for example, to compare and contrast three or even four items. But it is not typical. Likewise, while it is true that contrasts are usually drawn between items that are naturally opposite, comparison-contrasts have also been written about things that are only slightly different. Whether or not such attempts are successful depends heavily on the skill of the writer. The same, however, is true of writing of any type.

IN A NUTSHELL

- To compare is to show similarities.
- To contrast is to show differences.

PRACTICING 1

In the spaces provided, check the assignments that call for development by comparison or contrast.

1. _____ The beauty of the Blue Ridge Mountains

2. _____ How early rock and roll and the rock and roll of the 1970s differ

3. _____ The defensive lines of two college football teams

4. _____ How to change a car tire

5. _____ Why patience pays off

6. _____ The benefits of living in the city rather than the suburbs

7. ____ How fast-food chains differ from diners

8. ____ The meaning of *poltergeist*

9. ____ How blue-collar workers differ from white-collar workers

10. ____ Women's basketball then and now

How Can I Do It?

You already have experience with comparisons and contrasts. They are a part of your daily conversations and life. You might not, however, have as much experience with writing them. Here are some tips to help you write sharp comparison/contrasts:

- Compare things that have something in common.
- State your purpose in the topic sentence.
- Choose a pattern of comparing/contrasting and stick to it.
- Use comparing or contrasting transitions.

Compare things that have something in common.

No doubt you've heard the saying that "you can't compare apples and oranges." Of course, it is nonsense. If you are buying fruit, you not only can, you should compare apples and oranges. Some things, however, are like apples and oranges in the old saying: They simply cannot be compared because they have nothing in common. So, a man may be compared to a woman because both are human beings, but a woman cannot be compared to a pin nor a man to a bicycle. Man, woman, pin, and bicycle simply do not have enough in common for a serious comparison. The same is true of a football and a chrysanthemum, or a candy bar and a lawnmower: They are simply too different to be compared seriously.

To write a serious comparison, begin with items that have enough in common to be compared. Common sense will help you make that decision. Here, for example, is an attempted comparison between a dog and stamp collecting that falls apart:

> My dog and my hobby of stamp collecting are similar in many ways and different in others. My dog spends a lot of his time roaming the woods behind our house. He likes to chase squirrels and bark at them. My hobby, stamp collecting, is also a lonesome hobby. I spend a lot of time doing it alone in my room. My dog is very energetic for he is a young dog and likes to play. Stamp collecting as a hobby, however, needs no energy. I just sit down and arrange stamps in my book. Then I look at them for their appearance. Finally, my dog usually comes when I call him. Of course, my stamp book is dead and cannot come when I call it. But I still like to take it outside, sit under a tree, and look at my stamps.

This student is trying to compare things that have nothing in common: a dog and stamp collecting.

With some refocusing, however, this comparison could work. The paragraph could be rewritten to compare two things the writer likes to do, play with his dog and collect stamps. In such a comparison the emphasis is no longer on dissimilar things—a living creature and a hobby—but on things that have something in common, namely, the writer's two favorite pastimes. Here is the rewritten paragraph:

> <u>My two pastimes, playing with my dog and collecting stamps, offer me similar as well as different pleasures</u>. When I play with my dog, I get to enjoy the outdoors. We roam the woods behind my house together, sometimes staying out for hours. I get good exercise chasing after my dog and racing him through the woods. Whereas stamp collecting gives me no exercise, it does allow me to roam in a different sense. I can look at stamps from different countries and imagine what it is like to live in them. Playing with my dog takes my mind off school and the pressures of making good grades. Stamp collecting also takes my mind off my troubles and makes me forget whatever is worrying me. But when it comes to being affectionate, nothing can beat my dog. He gives me more love and affection than a hundred stamp albums.

Notice that with the emphasis now on pastimes, the comparison works. The writer is no longer trying to make comparisons between a dog and a stamp album, but is instead focusing on two things he likes to do: play with his dog and collect stamps.

PRACTICING 2

Check those pairs that follow that *can* be the subject of a comparison/contrast essay. Then state what those pairs have in common.

1. _____ A bird and chewing gum

_____

2. _____ Lions and tigers

_____

3. _____ Pot roast and fish stew

_____

4. _____ Private elementary schools and public elementary schools

_____

5. _____ Your home and a bus station

_____

6. _____ A big chain supermarket and a corner convenience store

_____

7. _____ A used-car lot and a pretty garden

_____

8. _____ Two teachers

_____

9. _____ Swimming and sleeping

_____

10. _____ Rhinestone buttons and lizards

_____

State your purpose in the topic sentence.

If you are comparing/contrasting, you should plainly say so in the topic sentence. Stating your intent to compare and contrast in the topic sentence is a good focusing device for both you and your readers. For your readers, declaring your purpose in the topic sentence tells them what to expect. For you, stating your purpose at the very beginning will help keep you on track. Here is an example of a paragraph that hides its intent:

> I take both English classes and math classes at school. In math the method you use to solve a problem is as important as the answer. But the answer is either right or wrong, and there's no arguing about it. In English, the question of right or wrong is not that clear-cut. A poem, for example, may have one meaning to one reader and a different one to another. If you can show how you arrived at the meaning of a poem, as long as your interpretation is not ridiculous and far-fetched, you are at least partly right. In math, two plus two is always four, and there is no other possible interpretation of that result. In math, we pay attention only to the problem we are working on, and the discussion is only about that. In English, we often discuss social issues and other topics that we write about.

This is a little vague because we have no idea what the writer is trying to do. Notice how much easier the paragraph is to read and follow if the purpose is given in the topic sentence:

> <u>English classes and math classes are similar in some ways but different in others</u>. Both are taught by the same methods—lecture, class discussion, and homework. But they differ in other ways. I take both English classes and math classes at school. In math the method you use to solve a problem is as important as the answer. But the answer is either right or wrong, and there's no arguing about it. In English, the question of right or wrong is not that clear-cut. A

poem, for example, may have one meaning to one reader, and a different one to another. If you can show how you arrived at the meaning of a poem, as long as your interpretation is not ridiculous and far-fetched, you are at least partly right. In math, two plus two is always four, and there is no other possible interpretation of that result. In math, we also pay attention only to the problem we are working on, and the discussion is only about that. In English, we often discuss social issues and other topics that we write about. Both classes are very interesting, but I prefer English.

PRACTICING 3

Write a topic sentence that clearly announces a comparison/contrast paragraph for each of these topics.

Example: Running versus jogging

Running and jogging may seem identical to someone unfamiliar with these activities, but they have differences.

1. Your taste in movies versus the taste of someone else.

_____

_____

2. A vegetable you love versus a vegetable you hate.

_____

_____

3. Two people you know well who differ sharply.

_____

_____

4. Getting carry-out versus eating in a restaurant.

_____

_____

5. A class you love versus one you hate.

_____

_____

PRACTICING 4

Choose one of the topic sentences from Practicing 3 and write a comparison/contrast paragraph. After the topic sentence, discuss similarities and then differences.

Choose a pattern of comparing/contrasting and stick to it.

Comparison/contrasts may be written in one of two possible patterns. In **pattern A** you cover the items being compared/contrasted within a single paragraph. In **pattern B** you cover the same points in two separate paragraphs, one for item A, the second for item B. In either case your comparison/contrast should be done point by point.

Here is an example of what we mean by comparing point by point. Let us say that you are trying to decide on what kind of oven to buy: a microwave or a toaster oven. How would you go about comparing/contrasting them?

First, you'd probably decide what features in an oven—toaster or microwave—are important to you. Then perhaps you'd make a list to see how each kind of oven matches up on each feature. Here is one such list:

FEATURES	MICROWAVE	TOASTER OVEN
expense	more expensive	cheaper
cooking time	faster, but doesn't brown	slower, but browns
clean up	cleans easily since no burning	harder to clean

Now you have your three points.

It is only fair and logical to compare and contrast items on the same points. To mention the cooking time of the microwave but not the toaster oven would be both illogical and incomplete. In short, if you are comparing a giraffe and an elephant, you should not compare the height of the giraffe with the bellowing of an elephant. Comparison/contrasts must always be made on the same points.

Once you have the points of your comparison/contrast, you must choose which pattern you will use. The two possible patterns are diagrammed as follows:

PATTERN A

Point 1: Expense

        microwave

        toaster oven

Point 2: Cooking time

        microwave   **SINGLE PARAGRAPH**

        toaster oven

Point 3: Clean up

        microwave

        toaster oven

PATTERN B

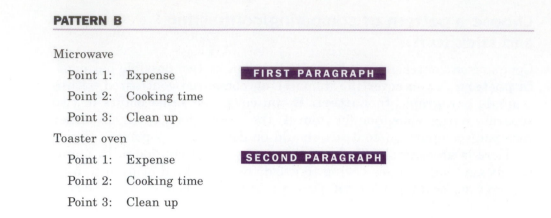

Microwave
    Point 1:   Expense
    Point 2:   Cooking time
    Point 3:   Clean up
Toaster oven
    Point 1:   Expense
    Point 2:   Cooking time
    Point 3:   Clean up

In pattern A, within a single paragraph, you cover both the microwave and the toaster oven on all three points: expense, cooking time, and clean up. In pattern B, on the other hand, using the same three points, you cover the microwave oven in one paragraph and the toaster oven in a separate paragraph. Here is pattern A written out:

> <u>Microwave and toaster ovens are both useful to anyone trying to cook, but they differ in expense, cooking time, and clean up.</u> A microwave oven is more expensive than a toaster oven. Sometimes it is as much as $50 to $100 more, although it is cheaper to operate. Unlike the toaster oven, the microwave saves huge amounts of time because of the speed at which it cooks. For instance, a serving of frozen vegetables can be cooked to perfection in five minutes. A frozen dinner can be ready to eat in ten minutes, and a cup of coffee can be reheated in 30 seconds. A toaster oven takes longer on these jobs. Finally, the microwave is easier to clean up. Because a microwave oven does not brown, it is impossible to burn food, which would then have to be scraped off the rack. The toaster oven, on the other hand, browns food and can sometimes burn it, leaving a sticky mess that's hard to clean. Since speed and ease are most important to me, I think I'll buy the microwave.

Here is pattern B:

> <u>Microwave and toaster ovens are both useful to anyone trying to cook, but they differ in expense, cooking time, and clean up.</u> The microwave oven is more expensive than a toaster oven. Sometimes it is as much as $50 to $100 more, although it is cheaper to operate and saves money on electricity. The microwave is also faster than a toaster oven. For instance, a serving of frozen vegetables can be cooked to perfection in five minutes. A cup of coffee can be reheated in 30 seconds. Finally, the microwave is easy to clean up. Because it doesn't brown, a microwave never burns food, and doesn't make a mess that's hard to clean.
>
> The toaster oven, on the other hand, is a great deal cheaper than the microwave, but it uses more electricity because it cooks more slowly than the microwave. In fact, it can cost almost 50 percent more per month to run. Also, unlike the microwave, the toaster oven browns certain food, such as chicken or fish, which makes

the food look more appetizing. But sometimes the food burns, leaving a sticky mess that's hard to clean. Since speed and ease are most important to me, I think I'll buy the microwave.

Which pattern to use is up to you, the writer. For a long intricate comparison, you might wish to use pattern B, separate paragraphs. In either case you must be sure to match up your compared/contrasted items on the same set of points.

PRACTICING 5

For each of the topics that follow, create two patterns of comparing/contrasting: pattern A, within a single paragraph, and pattern B, between two paragraphs.

1. Two restaurants

PATTERN A	**PATTERN B**
	First paragraph
Point 1: _____	Point 1: _____
Point 2: _____	Point 2: _____
Point 3: _____	Point 3: _____

PATTERN B

Second paragraph

Point 1: _____
Point 2: _____
Point 3: _____

2. Two places you have lived

PATTERN A	**PATTERN B**
	First paragraph
Point 1: _____	Point 1: _____
Point 2: _____	Point 2: _____
Point 3: _____	Point 3: _____

Second paragraph

Point 1: _____
Point 2: _____
Point 3: _____

3. Two loves you have had

PATTERN A	PATTERN B
	First paragraph
Point 1: _____	Point 1: _____
Point 2: _____	Point 2: _____
Point 3: _____	Point 3: _____
	Second paragraph
	Point 1: _____
	Point 2: _____
	Point 3: _____

4. Two pets

PATTERN A	PATTERN B
	First paragraph
Point 1: _____	Point 1: _____
Point 2: _____	Point 2: _____
Point 3: _____	Point 3: _____
	Second paragraph
	Point 1: _____
	Point 2: _____
	Point 3: _____

5. Two candidates in an election

PATTERN A	PATTERN B
	First paragraph
Point 1: _____	Point 1: _____
Point 2: _____	Point 2: _____
Point 3: _____	Point 3: _____
	Second paragraph
	Point 1: _____
	Point 2: _____
	Point 3: _____

PRACTICING 6

Choose one of the topics from Practicing 5 and write a comparison/contrast following Pattern A in a single paragraph.

PRACTICING 7

Choose another topic from Practicing 5 and write a comparison/contrast following Pattern B, using two paragraphs.

Use comparing or contrasting transitions.

Transitions help your reader follow the point-by-point comparison/contrast you are drawing. Without transitions, the points you're comparing and contrasting may blur into one another. Here is an example:

> Reggae and soca are musical forms that differ in rhythm, beat, and message. Reggae originated in Jamaica. Its best-known singer is still Bob Marley. Soca originated in Trinidad with its annual carnivals. The rhythm of reggae is steady, pulsating, and not particularly fast. Soca rhythms can be hypnotically fast, allowing for wild dancing in the streets at carnival time. Reggae has a regular, predictable beat that is best described as a background washboard scraping. Soca's beat can be fairly modulated as in the soca song "Dollar Wine," or erratic, as in that soca favorite "Hot, Hot, Hot." Reggae preaches a message of social justice and Rastafarianism. Soca has no message beyond its flirtatious calls to dance. Reggae is beloved by the ghetto youth and soca by the fun-loving middle class.

Notice how much easier the paragraph is to read with the transitions (underlined) added.

> Reggae and soca, <u>both of which come from the same part of the world</u>, are musical forms that differ in rhythm, beat, and message. Reggae originated in Jamaica. Its best-known singer is still Bob Marley. Soca, <u>on the other hand</u>, originated in Trinidad with its annual carnivals. The rhythm of reggae is steady, pulsating, and not particularly fast. <u>In contrast</u>, soca rhythms can be hypnotically fast, allowing for wild dancing in the streets at carnival time. Reggae has a regular, predictable beat that is best described as a background washboard scraping. This is <u>not so with soca</u>. The beat can be fairly modulated, as in the soca song "Dollar Wine," or crazily erratic, as in that soca favorite "Hot, Hot, Hot." <u>But where the two musical forms differ most is in their message</u>. Reggae preaches a message of social justice and Rastafarianism. Soca, <u>on the other hand</u>, has no message beyond its flirtatious calls to dance. <u>Partly because of these differences</u>, reggae is beloved by the ghetto youth and soca by the fun-loving middle class.

The transitions used in comparison/contrasts are common ones. Of course, some transitions can be used in both comparisons and contrasts. Here is a list of transitions that are most frequently used:

COMPARISON TRANSITIONS	CONTRAST TRANSITIONS
and	although
also	conversely
additionally	however
as well as	in contrast (to)
both	on the other hand
in the same way	whereas
just as . . . so	while
like	the opposite is true
similarly	unlike
too	yet
in addition	
furthermore	

Use these words generously in your own comparison/contrasts and you'll make your writing easier for a reader to follow.

IN A NUTSHELL

To write good comparisons, be sure to do the following:

- Compare things that can be compared.
- State your purpose in the topic sentence.
- Choose a pattern of comparison and stick to it.
- Use transitions.

PRACTICING 8

Underline the transitional words that show contrast or comparison in the following paragraph.

American men are different from Italian men. For one, Italian men often cry to express their sadness. Their culture encourages this outlet in them. On the other hand, American men don't cry because they think crying is unmanly and for sissies. However, American men, for the most part, respect women's rights. Most American men wouldn't consider whistling at a woman passing in the street. Italian men don't hesitate to whistle at a passing woman, to show their appreciation for her good looks. Finally, American men tend to share more in household chores, even though many wives think they could do more. Italian men, on the other hand, are notoriously unwilling to share household chores, which they consider "women's work." Italian men probably suit Italian women best, who know what to expect from them. But some American women would find the Italian man too difficult to live with.

What Do I Need to Look Out For?

Incompleteness in a comparison or contrast is the most common error by far in paragraphs and essays. **Incompleteness** is covering one side of the comparison/contrast but failing to cover the other. Here is an example:

> My neighbors Ida and Ralph are alike in looks but vastly different in personalities. Ida is tall and slender. She wears a size 6 dress and weighs no more than 100 pounds. But her personality is very fiery. She is never afraid to take on new adventures and is always experimenting in the kitchen. Ida took sailplane flying lessons in her sixties. She soloed on her sixty-seventh birthday and got her license a week later. She said she learned to fly because she used to be afraid of heights and wanted to conquer her fear. She's very brave, and I admire her a lot. Ralph is just as tall and thin but doesn't have her spunk.

The student who wrote this paragraph obviously spent too much time on *Ida* and too little on *Ralph.* We get a clear picture of what Ida is like, but no picture at all of Ralph. The comparison/contrast, in short, is incomplete, filling in one side but ignoring the other.

Here is how the student corrected this oversight:

> My neighbors Ida and Ralph are alike in looks but vastly different in personalities. Ida is tall and slender. She wears a size 6 dress and weighs no more than 100 pounds. Ralph is also tall and thin. He's very wiry and weighs only slightly more than Ida. Their personalities, however, are quite different. Ida is very fiery. She is never afraid to take on new adventures. She is always experimenting in the kitchen, and when she was in her sixties, she took sailplane flying lessons. She soloed on her sixty-seventh birthday and got her license a week later. Ralph, on the other hand, is far from fiery. He is as calm as a slow-moving river. Nothing ever gets him upset. He's happy eating the same things for breakfast, lunch, and dinner, day after day. He thought Ida was foolish to start flying in her sixties, but he never said anything because he respects her wishes. The two of them, although very different, have been happily married now for 30 years.

IN A NUTSHELL

Cover both items of a comparison/contrast more or less equally.

PRACTICING 9

Write a paragraph in which you compare and contrast two members of your family. One of the people can be yourself. Be sure to give equal emphasis to both sides.

Unit Test

In the blank provided, write T if the statement is true, F if it is false.

1. _____ To compare means showing similarities; to contrast means showing differences.

2. _____ In real life we rarely use comparison or contrast.

3. _____ The statement "Boston is an older city than San Francisco" shows comparison.

4. _____ "Roller blading and ice skating have much in common" shows comparison.

5. _____ To compare an ice cube with a race car would make an appropriate comparison.

6. _____ If you want to write a comparison or contrast, you should plainly say so in your topic sentence.

7. _____ A good comparison/contrast paragraph sticks to several clear patterns.

8. _____ Your teacher must tell you which pattern to choose.

9. _____ "And," "furthermore," "in addition" are typical contrast transitions.

10. _____ Try to cover both sides of a comparison/contrast equally.

Unit Talk-Write Assignment

Listen to Eddie explaining the difference between a sports nut and a sports fan. Then, in the space provided, turn his spoken words into a well-developed contrast paragraph. Use what you have learned in this unit. Begin with a topic sentence in which you announce what you intend to contrast. Make your points of contrast clear and use standard English.

Spoken Paragraph

I'm not a sports fan, I'm a sports nut. You guys don't know the difference, do you? Well, let me clue you in. A sports fan is someone who every now and again goes to football games, to baseball games, and maybe to check out one or two other sports. A sports nut—almost always a guy—goes to all of them and then watches the video afterwards. You get what I'm saying? A sports fan will support a team when it's in town and when it's away or maybe read in a newspaper the next day how it did. Pretty wishy-washy and wimpy if you ask me. A sports nut will use the Internet to follow the play-by-play if the away game isn't broadcast on radio, and if it is, will naturally listen to it. A sports nut like me lives for sports, eats sports, dream sports, talk sports, and sleep sports. A sports fan can take sports or leave it depending on his mood. A sports nut will kick butt if anyone criticizes his team, regardless of who it is—wife, uncle, nephew, niece, brother, brother-in-law, neighbor, best friend, bookie—it doesn't matter, diss his team, and the sports nut will let you have it. When his team is winning, the sports nut is in 7th Heaven. When his team is losing, the sports nut is in hell. I know what paradise is and when it happened. It was 1995 when the Atlanta Braves beat the Cleveland Indians 1–0 to clinch the World Series. The sports fan will only have a fuzzy memory of what happened. But the sports nut has a scoop on everything and will be able to tell you who scored the only run of the game—David Justice—who was pitching for the Braves—Tom Glavine—and even who caught the final fly ball—outfielder Marcus Grissom. Don't tell me that a sports fan is the same as a sports nut. They ain't. They're as different as night and day.

Written Paragraph

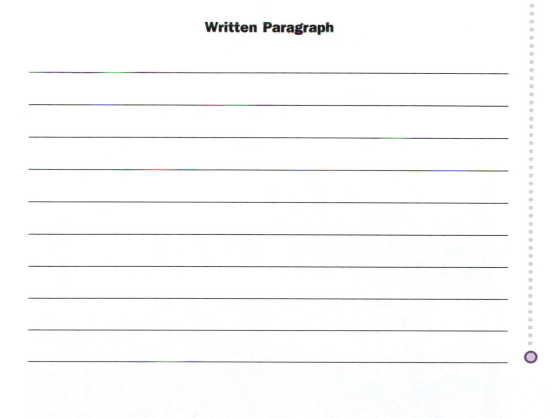

Unit Collaborative Assignment

Get together with a classmate and discuss your opinions on one of the following subjects. List the points on which you agree and disagree.

1. Your attitude toward money

2. The importance of regular exercise

3. Football versus soccer as spectator sports

4. When to go casual and when to dress up

5. Being strict or lenient with children

Unit Writing Assignment

Using the lists you created for the Unit Collaborative Assignment, write a comparison/contrast of your views with those of your classmate. Be sure to treat both sides fairly and to use transitions that stress the comparisons and contrasts.

Photo Writing Assignment

Note the sharp contrast shown in the following photo. Find appropriate points of contrast and develop a comparison/contrast paragraph.

Arguing

"*People should make an attempt to get involved in local politics.*"

You're in college and doing fine. But you wish you had your own computer so you didn't have to go to the computer lab every time you had to write a paper. It's a great lab and the student tutors are really helpful, but sometimes the lab is completely booked when you're free, and you have to go really early in the morning or late at night if you want to meet your deadlines. You must get a computer. But how? You're broke. Even though you work every weekend delivering pizza, you simply can't afford one. You write your parents and ask for a loan, and your mom, ever the practical one, asks you to put your request in writing. She says she'll work on your dad if you make a strong case for needing a computer. You sit down and begin to write:

A computer is the most useful, practical purchase I could make because it would help me become a better student in several ways. First, instead of having to share a crowded computer lab with hundreds of other students, I could write in the quiet of my own room where I can really concentrate. I'd write better papers and do it faster. Second, during peak hours at the lab, students can schedule only a maximum of two hours. There have been times when I'd have revised a paper further, but couldn't get the computer time. If I had my own computer, I would always have the time to write the best possible paper and therefore get a better grade. In fact, having my own computer would probably raise my overall gradepoint average. Not having to get to the lab early in the morning or late at night would leave me with more time to read and study. Finally, doing well in school, I'd probably be motivated to take extra classes and I'd graduate ahead of time. Then I'd be able to pay off the loan earlier. Truly, a computer is just the tool I need to become a better, more efficient student.

What you did was write an argument, trying to persuade your parents to lend you money to buy a computer.

What Am I Trying to Do?

An **argument** is an attempt to persuade someone—a listener or reader—to accept your opinion on a certain subject. Also referred to as *persuasion,* argumentation is part of daily life. We use it to press home our opinions on trivial as well as important topics.

In a way, all writing is argumentation, an attempt to get someone else to see things your way. If you are describing an onion, you are trying to get the reader to see the onion as you do. If you are narrating a horrifying event, you are trying to get your reader to feel your horror.

Argument or persuasion is all around you—from the friend who tries to talk you into letting him use your car, to the teacher who urges you to do better work. Indeed, hardly a day passes when we don't use argumentation. It may be a sports argument, say, that Rod Carew in his prime was a better hitter than any of today's players, or that Nolan Ryan was a better pitcher than Tom Seaver, or that Barry Bonds is a better all-around player than Mark McGuire. It may be about funding a community arts program or about whether you or your sister does more daily chores. Arguments, serious or lighthearted, are part of everyday life.

IN A NUTSHELL

Argumentation is an attempt to persuade someone to your point of view.

PRACTICING 1

Put an *A* before each of the following statements that should be developed as an argument.

1. _____ Student parking should be free; we shouldn't have to buy parking stickers.

2. _____ There's a right and a wrong way to do strength training.

3. _____ "Love" means different things to different people.

4. _____ We should cut back on military spending and put the money into education.

5. ____ There are advantages to living in the country, but I'll take the city any day.

6. ____ I can always count on my sister to cheer me up.

7. ____ Changing a tire is not as hard as it looks.

8. ____ Free medical care is a right, not a privilege.

9. ____ Television does more good than harm.

10. ____ My boss is demanding but fair.

How Can I Do It?

To write a good argument, you must do the following:

- Evaluate your position.
- Give your reasons.
- Cite evidence.
- Refute the opposition.

Evaluate your position.

Writing an argument means taking a position on some issue. Before you try arguing, make sure that you have a sound position and know the facts.

For example, consider this situation: Your student council is thinking of closing the only sandwich shop on campus and installing in its place sandwich-dispensing machines. The council's argument is that the shop is little-used and that the machines will save money. Your view is that the shop serves the evening students well, especially those on tight schedules who can't get to the main cafeteria, some distance away on the north campus. Before dashing off a letter to the student government opposing the machines, you should ask yourself these four questions:

1. *Have I defined the problem clearly?* In other words, what exactly is the student government proposing—to close the shop for good or just temporarily, as an experiment to see how well the machines are received? What kind of vending machines will be installed in place of the shop? What kind of food will they offer? How much will the machine food cost? What savings will the student body realize from closing the shop? In other words, you need to know what you're up against before you can begin to argue.

2. *Have I gathered enough information to form an opinion?* You oppose the closing of the shop because you and other evening students like eating there and hate vending-machine food. In this particular case, beyond learning the details of the proposed closing, you don't need a lot of additional information. Say, however, that someone asks your opinion on increased

security aboard airlines. To have an intelligent opinion on this subject, you would need to have read about it or heard it discussed by experts. In short, before you offer an opinion on any complex matter, you need to be informed.

3. *Does my opinion reflect an honest search for truth, or is it simply self-interest?* The argument that is based entirely on self-interest is generally a weak one. Indeed, looking out only for yourself can hurt someone else. Better by far is an argument based on the public good. So you need to show that many students will also be inconvenienced by closing the sandwich shop, not just you.

4. *Have I tested my position in discussions with others who disagree with it, or do I have a closed mind?* Bouncing your ideas off someone who disagrees with you is a good test of the strength of your argument. Ideally, if you see that the other side has a stronger and more logical case than you do, you should be willing to change your opinion.

Here is a paragraph that reflects a position not carefully evaluated:

> I am against closing the sandwich shop on the south side of campus and replacing it with vending machines. I leave work at 5:30, and it takes me almost an hour to get to campus. Having a sandwich at the shop with other students gives me a half-hour to unwind before my evening class. It would be a great personal inconvenience to me if the shop were closed because I don't have time to get to the main cafeteria, which is on the north side of the campus. Moreover, I don't like machine-vended food. I think it tastes stale. I think the shop should not be closed. If it is, I will have to go without dinner.

Notice that the argument is completely self-centered. Here is a better argument, based on an evaluated position:

> Closing the sandwich shop and replacing it with vending machines, as the student government proposes, will inconvenience many evening students. The projected savings assumes that students will patronize the new machines. Many, however, will not. I have spoken with at least 30 students who say they'd rather skip a meal than eat machine-vended food. Machine-vended food, no matter how quickly it is restocked, does not taste as good as freshly prepared food. Going to the cafeteria is not an option. It is on the north campus and too far away for students rushing to get to evening classes after work. If the shop is losing money, as the student government says, perhaps a slight increase in price could be considered as an alternative to closing the shop altogether. Most evening students on the south campus are prepared to pay a little more to keep the sandwich shop open.

This is a better argument because it is based on a well-defined problem and enough information. Moreover, it reflects a concern for the public good rather than only one person's narrow interests.

PRACTICING 2

Choose one of the topics that follow and take a pro or con position on the statement. Do some research in the library or on the Internet to help you form or confirm your opinion. In the space that follows, apply the four evaluation questions to your opinion.

1. Colleges should require a physical education course for graduation.

2. Everyone should be forced to retire at age 67.

3. Liquor advertisements on billboards should be illegal.

4. All adopted children should be told who their natural parents are.

5. College athletes should be paid to play.

1. Have I defined the problem clearly?

_____

_____

_____

2. Have I gathered enough information to form an opinion?

_____

_____

_____

3. Does my opinion reflect an honest search for truth, or is it simply a personal interest?

_____

_____

_____

4. Have I tested my position in discussions with others who disagree with it, or do I have a closed mind?

_____

_____

_____

Give your reasons.

All arguments turn on a *should*. You think something *should* be this way or that way for certain reasons. Then you support your arguments with those reasons. To be convincing, your reasons must be logical and reasonable. A *logical* reason is one that makes sense. A *reasonable* reason is one that is fair.

Here are some examples of illogical arguments—that is, arguments that make no sense—along with their corrections:

Illogical: We should pass laws to limit the budgets of political campaigns because campaign ads on television are on almost more than the regular programs during an election.

Logical: We should pass laws to limit campaign budgets so that every candidate will have an equal chance—rich or poor.

Illogical: Pooper-scooper laws should be revoked because concrete walkways need fertilizing.

Logical: Pooper-scooper laws should be revoked because they make it difficult for the elderly to walk their pets.

It is illogical to argue that political campaign budgets must be limited because of the frequency of televised campaign ads. The logical argument is that budgets must be limited to put everyone on equal footing. It is illogical to do away with pooper-scooper laws because concrete walkways need fertilizing (they don't, and neither does shoe leather). It is logical to argue that these laws might make it difficult for the elderly to walk their pets.

Here are some examples of unreasonable arguments—that is, arguments that are unfair—along with their corrections:

Unreasonable: Libraries should stay open all night because sometimes I can't sleep and would like to borrow a book.

Reasonable: Libraries should offer more flexible opening hours to accommodate busy working people.

Unreasonable: Weed killers should not be sold because weeds need to live, too.

Reasonable: Weed killers should not be sold because they seep into the soil and poison the groundwater.

It is unreasonable to expect libraries to stay open all night because one patron cannot sleep. It is entirely reasonable to expect libraries to have hours that are convenient to working people. It is unreasonable to argue that weed killers should not be sold because they deprive weeds of life (that's the point). It is reasonable to make this same argument if the weed killers are contaminating the groundwater.

Similarly, a reason may be logical but unreasonable. It is logical for you to argue that you won't do household chores because you're not your parents' slave (you're right, you aren't), but it is unreasonable (everyone in a household should share the chores; neither are your parents your slaves).

To back up an argument with reasons, you first state your position and then your reasons for supporting it. This is what you basically do:

Topic sentence
   Reason 1
   Reason 2
   Reason 3—if there is one

Here is this pattern in practice:

> Our college library is good but its collection of books is small, so students find it hard to get the books they need for their classwork. Therefore, students should be allowed to check out books for only one week instead of the present two. This restriction would allow more students access to the small supply of books. It would also be fairer than the present system, which allows some students to monopolize the books while others can do nothing but wait. When the library has built up its collection, the two-week loan period could be reinstated.

The reasons given are both logical and reasonable. It is logical—that is to say, it makes sense—to shorten the checkout time until more books become available. The argument is also reasonable because it proposes sharing the books among all students rather than permitting a lucky few to monopolize the collection. Your own reasons, when you give them in your arguments, must also be logical and reasonable.

IN A NUTSHELL

The reasons behind your arguments must be both logical and reasonable.

PRACTICING 3

Read the two arguments that follow. Which one gives more logical and reasonable reasons? Explain your choice.

A.

> Dieting is utterly stupid. People spend hundreds of dollars a month on the latest diet fad. They do that because when it comes to dieting, people are copycats. So, there goes another sucker who will lose 20 pounds in one month and gain it all back within six months. I have several friends who have spent hundreds of dollars to go on fad diets, only to admit in the end that the diet did not work. My grandmother, who is from Austria, tells me that in her day nobody dieted; yet, people were not nearly as fat as we are in this country. She says that Americans should walk more; then they wouldn't be so neurotic about dieting. She may be right. Every newspaper advertises some weight clinic, some exercise gym, or some appetite-suppressant pill. I say, eat reasonably, exercise some, and leave the rest to nature.

B.

Following a fad diet plan does not lead to long-term weight loss. I recently read an article in *Reader's Digest* indicating that 85 percent of people who go on diets regain their weight within three to five years. That is why my doctor takes a reasonable approach to dieting. She says that if you need to lose weight, just give up 100 calories a day permanently, and within a year you will have lost 20 pounds. Or, if you want to lose a little faster, just eat an apple at noon instead of lunch. The point is to lose weight slowly and without dramatically altering your eating habits. Also, my doctor believes you must exercise to lose weight. But exercising does not have to involve jogging or working out at an expensive gym. Just park a distance away from where you are driving, walk up stairs whenever possible, and take short breaks to walk down the hall or across the building at work. In other words, my doctor believes that making small but important lifestyle changes leads to long-term weight loss, not going on some extreme diet. I think she's right.

PRACTICING 4

Give at least two logical and reasonable reasons in support of the following topics.

1. Playing a boom box should be banned on public transportation.

Reason 1: _____

_____

Reason 2: _____

_____

Reason 3: _____

_____

2. Smokers should be allowed to smoke in restaurants.

Reason 1: _____

_____

Reason 2: _____

_____

Reason 3: _____

_____

3. Uniforms should be worn in all public high schools.

Reason 1: _____

_____

Reason 2: _____

_____

Reason 3: _____

_____

4. General introductory courses should be optional, not mandatory.

Reason 1: _____

_____

Reason 2: _____

_____

Reason 3: _____

_____

5. Students should take a year off between high school and college to do community service work.

Reason 1: _____

_____

Reason 2: _____

_____

Reason 3: _____

_____

Cite evidence.

Aside from reasons, the next important support of your argument is evidence. Evidence consists of the following:

- Examples
- Facts
- Testimony
- Personal observation

Examples

An **example** is a part used to represent the whole. You say that Larry has a bad temper. Someone asks, "What do you mean?" You say, "Larry became completely irrational, yelling and cursing, when he learned the movie was sold out." This scene gives one example that supports your point about Larry's temper.

The following paragraph likewise uses an example in support of its topic sentence.

<u>Students should be careful about blind dating because it can be risky</u>. For example, my best friend, Marla, went out on a blind date. Her date got drunk, even though he was under the drinking age. On the way home, he nearly wrecked the car. Fortunately, he was pulled over and taken into custody, and she was driven home in a police cruiser.

To use examples, all you have to do is introduce them with a suitable phrase such as *for example, for instance,* or *take the case of,* and then you spell out the example you have in mind. Naturally, any example you use should support your point.

Facts

A **fact** is a statement that is true or can be verified. For instance, the fact that George Washington was born on February 22, 1732, can be confirmed by checking the encyclopedia or any biography of the first president. Some facts are simply accepted by everyone because they have never been proven untrue. That sooner or later all humans die is one such fact.

Here is an example of an argument supported by facts:

> Students who want to save money and live well should sell their cars and ride public transportation. Gasoline in my city is now $1.50 per gallon. My insurance was $890 per half-year, and it cost another $800 per year to license my car. Just selling the car saved me over $2,500 per year in fixed costs. Meanwhile, it costs $1.50 to ride the train to school, with no charge for parking, either.

Facts add believability to a paragraph. Of course, you must always be sure that your facts are indeed facts and not opinions. Ask yourself, can a reader look up this statement and confirm its truth? If not, the statement is an opinion, not a fact.

Testimony

Testimony is expert opinion that backs up your topic sentence. The expert may be someone who is recognized in the field or who has had personal experience with your topic. Here is a paragraph that uses both types of testimony—personal experience and expert opinion:

> Wearing a helmet while riding bicycles on campus should be mandatory. Campus Police Officer Jane Johnson reports that she has investigated at least five serious accidents just this semester in which the rider suffered a severe head injury. In one case, Officer Johnson says, the rider was so seriously injured that he had to leave school. Last week I witnessed a bicycle accident on the road that runs before Old Main. The rider skidded on a slick patch of pavement and hit her head against a tree. I found out later she suffered a concussion that would have been prevented if she'd been wearing a helmet.

Personal observation

Personal observation usually consists of descriptive details and examples based on your experience. Some topics are strictly personal and must be supported mainly by your own observation. Here is such a paragraph that uses both:

> My parents are so unhappy in each other's company that they should get a divorce. My father and mother never talk. When he comes home from work, he heads straight for his room (they have

separate bedrooms). When she comes home, she heads for the television set. They do almost nothing together. For example, they bowl on separate teams on different nights; she eats alone in the kitchen; he eats in his room. They do not even spend holidays together. At Christmas he goes to his brother's house, and she to her sister's. For years they used us children as an excuse for staying married, but we're all grown up now with our own families. There's no reason for them to prolong their misery.

The details this writer uses are not available in any library, but come solely from observation and memory.

IN A NUTSHELL

- Cite evidence to support your arguments.
- Evidence includes examples, facts, testimony, and personal observations.

PRACTICING 5

Decide where you stand on each of the arguments stated that follow. Then present what you consider one good piece of evidence—an example, fact, testimony, or personal observation—to use in support of the argument. Identify the type of evidence in the space provided.

Example:

Argument: We should have stricter laws against trapping wild animals such as bears, foxes, wolves, and mountain lions.

Evidence: Trapping is an exceedingly cruel way to kill animals. Death is not instantaneous. The animal often starves to death.

Type of evidence: Fact

1. **Argument:** Many professional sports have become too expensive for the average fan.

Evidence: _____

_____

_____

Type of evidence: _____

2. Argument: Television programs used to be better than they are today.

Evidence: _____

_____

_____

Type of evidence: _____

3. Argument: Teachers should state their attendance and grade policies in their class syllabus at the beginning of each term.

Evidence: _____

_____

_____

Type of evidence: _____

4. Argument: The mass transit system in my city is efficient (or inadequate).

Evidence: _____

_____

_____

Type of evidence: _____

5. Argument: Teachers should take student evaluations seriously.

Evidence: _____

_____

_____

Type of evidence: _____

PRACTICING 6

Choose one of the topics from Practicing 5 and, after adding more evidence, write a well-supported argument on it.

PRACTICING 7

Choose one of the arguments that follow and write an argument in support of it, using reasons and evidence as your backing.

1. Parents should find alternative ways of punishing children rather than spanking them.

2. Doctors need to find other ways to treat attention deficit or hyperactivity in little kids besides giving them stimulants, antidepressants, or blood-pressure drugs.

3. Despite criticism by many grown-ups, Halloween must be preserved as a part of childhood.

4. Whenever possible, disabled children should be placed in regular classrooms.

5. High school proms have become a shameful waste of money for the students and their parents.

Refute the opposition.

A good argument does not ignore its opposition. Instead, it tries to refute it—to show that the opposition's case is weak. The best way to do this is simply to state the opposing side and then immediately respond. For example, in an argument for gun control, you might acknowledge that some people think gun ownership is a constitutional right. Then you would immediately go on to point out that gun control only *regulates* gun ownership, but does not *abolish* it.

Or, if you are arguing that watching violent movies leads to violent behavior, you might mention the contrary view, namely, that watching violent movies may actually get rid of violence by harmlessly venting it. Then you would refute this view.

It is a good idea to refute the opposition because it shows that you are aware of opposing viewpoints and have thought through both sides. Your reader, who may be thinking, "Yes, but what about this or that?" finds, with a jolt, that not only have you thought about this and that, but that you've answered them.

Here is an example of how to refute the opposition to an argument in favor of coed dorms:

> Now there are those who say that coed dorms will promote sexual activity between students. But the women's and men's dorms are presently located right next to each other and have no restrictions on visiting. Students already have ample opportunity to have sexual relations, and many do. What they do not presently have is the opportunity to just live with each other in the same building (not the same room) and interact like dormmates and friends, rather than like lovers. There are also those who object to unmarried men and women sharing a building on religious grounds. So don't live in the coed dorms if you feel that way. Live in one of the unisex buildings. But don't stop those who don't share your particular morals from living as they please.

This student raises the question of sex in coed dorms as well as religious opposition, and answers both objections.

IN A NUTSHELL

Always mention the opposing view and refute it.

PRACTICING 8

For each argument listed below, state what you think would be one opposing point of view.

1. Obscene literature should be banished from public libraries.

Opposing point of view: _____

_____

2. U.S. residents should simply pay a flat 10 percent federal income tax.

Opposing point of view: _____

_____

3. AIDS tests should be mandated by law for everyone.

Opposing point of view: _____

_____

4. Employers should pay for day care for employees' children.

Opposing point of view: _____

_____

5. Our government should stockpile a variety of antibiotics, to be used in the event of biological warfare.

Opposing point of view: _____

_____

_____

What Do I Need to Look Out For?

Arguments are based on logic and reasonableness. When an argument fails, it is usually because the writer has stated the case illogically. Other pitfalls that you should look out for in writing an argument follow.

- State your position clearly.
- Don't argue the unarguable.
- Watch out for some common fallacies.

State your position clearly.

Don't be timid in expressing your point of view. We're not suggesting that you be obnoxious in making your arguments, only that you be committed. Consider the following examples:

Committed topic sentence:	Coed dorms should be established oncampus for those students who wish to live in them.
Uncommitted topic sentence:	Coed dorms are being tried on many campuses.
Uncommitted topic sentence:	Coed dorms seem okay.
Uncommitted topic sentence:	Coed dorms might or might not work depending on your point of view.

These uncommitted topic sentences do not take a stand. The first mainly gives information, the second waffles, the third is wishy-washy. Oddly enough, an uncommitted topic sentence makes your job as a writer horribly difficult. It is easier to write about anything when you take a definite stand than when you try to tiptoe around the subject, just as it is easier to take a trip when you know where you want to go.

PRACTICING 9

Mark *C* if the sentence is committed and *U* if it is uncommitted. Then, in the spaces that follow, rewrite the uncommitted topic sentences.

1. _____ Political candidates should be limited in the amount of money they can spend on a campaign.

2. _____ It's probably not a good idea to drive without insurance.

3. _____ Playing a team sport teaches valuable lifelong lessons.

4. _____ Giving a tax break for day care seems like a good idea.

5. _____ Maybe something should be done about the potholes on State Street.

6. _____ If you want to succeed, you must do two things: Get a good education and work hard.

7. _____ We need garbage pickup twice a week, not just once.

8. _____ Assisted suicide may or may not be a good idea, depending on your beliefs.

9. _____ It should be just as hard to get married as to get a divorce.

10. _____ Statistics show that cars with airbags are safer.

Rewritten topic sentences:

_____

_____

_____

_____

_____

_____

_____

_____

_____

_____

Don't argue the unarguable.

An issue is arguable if it is expressed in such a way that it can be settled by reasons and evidence. You should always word an issue in a way that makes it arguable. Here are some examples:

Unarguable: Bungee jumping is a truly loathsome sport.
Arguable: Bungee jumping is a dangerous sport.

Unarguable: Tattooing is ugly.
Arguable: Tattooing may be "cool" when you're young, but it has a social cost later.

Unarguable: Smoking should be banned because it is a sin.
Arguable: Smoking should be banned because it is unhealthy.

You cannot prove that a sport is *loathsome,* but you can use statistics to prove that it is *dangerous. Ugly* is a personal opinion that cannot be documented by evidence, but evidence can be cited to show the social consequences of a tattoo. No one can prove with evidence or reasons that an act is a *sin,* but the health hazards of smoking have been amply proven.

To sum up, be sure the point you want to argue is arguable, that is, provable by evidence and reasons.

PRACTICING 10

Check the topic sentence in each pair that is arguable, and state why the other is unarguable.

Example:

_____ **(a).** The Volvo sedan is the best car on the market.

__✔__ **(b).** The Volvo is the safest car on the market.

"Best" cannot be proved by evidence and reasons, but "safest" can.

1. _____ **(a).** Marriage is a rotten institution.

_____ **(b).** Many marriages end in divorce.

_____

_____

2. _____ **(a).** Since the present movie-rating system has not accomplished what it set out to do, it should be abolished.

_____ **(b).** The present movie-rating system could be vastly improved if the movie industry would listen to the public's concerns about violence, sexual diseases, and family problems.

_____

_____

3. _____ **(a).** Birds make by far the best pets in the world.

_____ **(b).** Birds can be excellent companions for elderly people who are lonely and forced to be indoors.

_____

_____

4. _____ **(a).** Having school year-round would help ease the space crunch so that more classes could be offered.

_____ **(b).** Having school year-round would make our educational system the best in the world.

_____

_____

_____

5. _____ **(a).** Modern art is pure garbage, with its wild colors splattered across canvasses.

_____ **(b).** Before you can criticize modern art, you should learn something about it.

_____

_____

PRACTICING 11

Rewrite the following topic sentences to make them arguable.

1. Baseball is the greatest sport in the world.

_____

2. *Titanic* is the best movie of all time.

_____

3. *Mamma Mia's* is the best restaurant in town.

_____

4. Investing in the stock market is a pastime for idiots.

_____

5. Women are superior to men in every possible way.

_____

Watch out for some common fallacies.

A **fallacy** is a misleading or unsound argument. Here are some common fallacies:

- Climbing on the bandwagon
- Attacking the opponent instead of the issue
- Over generalizing
- Citing nonexperts as experts

Have you ever heard (or perhaps said), "But, Mom, everyone is going to Florida for spring vacation!" or "But, Dad, everyone is getting a motorcycle!" **Climbing on the bandwagon** is arguing that an idea is right just because everyone is doing it. Here is an example of the bandwagon fallacy:

The laws against drinking before the age of 21 should be repealed. The fact is that alcohol is widely available to teenagers. In fact, every 18-year-old I know drinks, and regularly.

Attacking the opponent instead of the issue is a common tactic that many of us occasionally use. It varies in degrees of ugliness and is so common in political campaigns as to be a joke. Here is a sample of it:

> To vote for Smith is to throw away your vote on a draft-dodging, pot-smoking radical-liberal from the 1960s.

No mention is made anywhere of what Smith stands for or what policies Smith would try to enact. Only Smith the person (of 40 years ago, no less) is attacked.

The third fallacy, **overgeneralizing,** draws a hasty conclusion from too few instances. For example, if you conclude from one bad experience with a used-car dealer that all used-car dealers are crooks, you're over generalizing. Here is an over generalization made in a paragraph arguing that students are better off living in dorms than renting a room in the neighborhood:

> Another problem is that the rental rooms available in this neighborhood are all dirty, shabby, and roach-infested. I know because I've lived in one.

To conclude that since one rented room was bad that all are likewise bad is to over generalize.

Finally, there's the fallacy of **citing nonexperts as experts.** Television commercials and other advertisements are guilty of this fallacy when they get an actor who plays a doctor on TV to endorse a particular brand of aspirin. An actor is an actor, not a medical expert. Similarly, consider this sentence below:

> Jimmy is right about our math teacher being no good; Jimmy's the best athlete on campus.

Being a good athlete doesn't make Jimmy an expert on math teachers. Indeed, Jimmy may be the best athlete but the worst judge of math teachers. Skill in one area does not necessarily make anyone an expert in another. Be sure that the experts you quote are really experts in the subject on which you are quoting them.

IN A NUTSHELL

When you write an argument, be sure to do the following:

- State your position clearly.
- Argue only the arguable.
- Avoid common fallacies.

PRACTICING 12

Identify the fallacy in each of the following arguments.

1. Everyone knows that playing football builds character.

Fallacy: _____

_____

_____

2. Switching from gas to electric cars is the only way to save the environment.

Fallacy: _____

_____

_____

3. Because religious cults are always driving their members to suicide, our government should make them illegal.

Fallacy: _____

_____

_____

4. If John Smith, who plays a doctor on "ER," endorses Bayer aspirin, that's good enough for me.

Fallacy: _____

_____

_____

5. Bob Jones would make a bad student body president because he's such a jock that he couldn't possibly have the brains to run the student government.

Fallacy: _____

_____

_____

 **Unit Test**

Check the sentence in each pair that more accurately reflects the teaching in this chapter.

Example: _____ **(a).** In social life, as in writing, you should avoid arguments.

___✔___ **(b).** In a way, all writing is argumentation.

1. _____ **(a).** Argument is also referred to as *persuasion*.

_____ **(b).** Argument is also referred to as *intellectual seduction*.

2. _____ **(a).** Be polite and never refute the opposition when you argue.

_____ **(b).** A good argument tries to anticipate the opposition so as to negate it.

3. _____ **(a).** When writing an argument, you need to know exactly what your stand is.

_____ **(b).** Let your argument develop roots as you write from the heart.

4. _____ **(a).** You need to gather information before you declare your stand on an issue.

_____ **(b).** If you feel passionate about your argument, you can be persuasive without knowing the facts.

5. _____ **(a).** Don't bore your readers with facts in your written argument.

_____ **(b).** Facts add believability to a paragraph.

6. _____ **(a).** When writing an argument, your reasons may be illogical so long as they're well stated.

_____ **(b).** When writing an argument, your reasons should be logical and fair.

7. _____ **(a).** The following is a reasonable argument: "Old people shouldn't get jobs that young people want."

_____ **(b).** The following is a reasonable argument: "Because of years of experience, an older person can some times fill a job that a younger person cannot."

8. _____ **(a).** Climbing on the bandwagon is the fallacy of attacking the opponent instead of the issue.

_____ **(b).** Climbing on the bandwagon is the fallacy of believing something only because it is popular.

9. _____ **(a).** When writing an argument, argue only the arguable.

_____ **(b).** You can win an argument by arguing the unarguable.

10. _____ **(a).** To quote the famous movie actress Madonna's stand in an argument against increasing energy rates would add force to your argument.

_____ **(b).** To quote Hal Harvey, president of the Energy Foundation, in an argument favoring wind power energy would add force to your argument.

Unit Talk-Write Assignment

An argument can take many turns and styles. Some arguments are complex and legalistic, such as the argument against prayer in schools; some arguments are simple and emotional, such as the one below. Students in an English class paired up to talk out their arguments on the subject "Something You'd Like to See Changed." After carefully studying this student's argument, rewrite it into an acceptable standard English paragraph. Pay attention to the tips offered in this unit. Feel free to add information to develop the paragraph. Use the blank space provided.

Spoken Paragraph

Call them "rubbernecks," "gawkers," "looky-loos," or whatever you want, but they drive me crazy because they're a menace on the freeway. They slow you down. So, here I am late to work, and all of a sudden the lanes going south slow down and almost come to a dead halt. The snake of cars is not moving. "What's going on?" I mutter to myself. I settle for this snail's pace. I play some nice rap music on the radio. I discover what the delay is all about. Someone's changing a tire in the emergency lane. I don't understand this gawker's effect. I know that one person slowing down can cause hundreds of drivers to slow down even more. One expert says that in our county alone drivers lose a total 1.6 million hours a year to gawking. That's over 6,000 hours every working day. I wish somehow we could all keep driving when we see accidents that are being tended to. I'm sure psychologists would have something to say about why we gawk at disasters. It's probably because somewhere in our deepest nature we are the most curious animals that have ever lived. But on the freeway, we should not gawk at accidents, strange sights, or any other distractions. It's unsafe and it wastes time. I say, "Stop the gawking!"

Written Paragraph

_____

_____

_____

_____

_____

_____

_____

_____

_____

_____

Unit Collaborative Assignment

Break into groups of six. Then choose one of the topics that follow and decide which two students will be for, which two will be against, and which two will be judges. Take ten minutes for the pro and con teams to discuss their positions and come up with reasons and evidence. Present the arguments to the judges, who will critique them according to what you have learned in this chapter.

1. Should we continue ROTC programs on campus?

2. Should teaching assistants be given so much authority in running classes?

3. Should college classes be graded pass/fail rather than with a letter grade?

4. Should we have a volunteer military?

5. Should the college placement office be responsible for getting graduates jobs?

Unit Writing Assignment

Choose one of the topics from the above Unit Collaborative Assignment and argue your stand on it. Be sure to make your reasons logical and fair, to use strong evidence, to refute the opposition, and to avoid fallacies.

Photo Writing Assignment

The following photo shows a billboard in support of a cause. Write an essay in which you argue for or against this position. Begin by evaluating your position, using the questions on page 237. Be sure your topic sentence is clearly committed. Finally, give logical and fair reasons, cite solid evidence, refute the opposition, and avoid fallacies.

16

What Is an Essay?

"Writing essays is good preparation for the kind of business writing you will have to do later in life."

An essay is a related group of paragraphs written to entertain, inform, or persuade. Recall from Unit 3 that all writing more or less serves one of these broad purposes. So far you have been writing paragraphs. The essay is merely a collection of paragraphs about the same subject, and with a more definite beginning, middle, and end.

Writing essays will teach you some important lessons. You will learn how to organize your thoughts on a subject, put them down clearly on paper, and back them up with facts, examples, testimony, reasons, and personal observations. Writing essays will also give you practice in expressing yourself in standard English—the universal language of business. Mastering standard English will help you do well in college and get a good job.

Finally, the classroom essay is usually between 300 and 500 words long, about the size of a memo—the workhorse of business writing. If you go into virtually any kind of business, sooner or later you will find yourself writing memos. Writing essays, in sum, is good preparation for the kind of business writing you will have to do later in life.

An essay consists of three parts: the introduction, the body, and the conclusion. We will deal with each part separately.

The Introduction

The **introduction** of an essay—the opening paragraph—has two main purposes: to grab the reader's attention and to introduce the thesis statement, or main point, of the essay.

To grab the reader's attention, you need a catchy opening, something that will make a reader perk up and want to read on. Here are some examples of opening sentences. Which ones make you want to read on?

> It's midnight, and you're relaxing on the front porch of your home, when suddenly a thunderous explosion rattles your house.
>
> The automobile, owned by most Americans, is a self-propelled vehicle used for travel on land.
>
> The word <u>cannibal</u> comes from the <u>Carib</u> West Indians, a ferocious and warlike people, who skinned their enemies and ate them.
>
> We should all try to be balanced in our political, religious, and social views.

The first and third sentences grab your attention. They make you want to read on to find out more about the explosion and the Caribs' gruesome diet.

Another function of the introduction is to present the **thesis statement**—a single sentence that sums up what the essay is about. Usually, the thesis statement is the last sentence of the first paragraph. Here are some examples of thesis statements:

> The entertainment industry should start giving an Oscar to the best benefit show.
>
> The qualities I like best in a teacher are fairness, knowledge, wit, and compassion.
>
> Religious symbols, such as crosses and menorahs, should be kept out of our public parks.
>
> People usually go into debt for three reasons: unemployment, lack of budgeting, and running credit cards to the limit.

If the topic sentence is a shrimp (statement of small purpose), the thesis statement is a jumbo shrimp (statement of a bigger purpose). The thesis statement, in fact, is like a big topic sentence. It gives the point of the entire essay, whereas the topic sentence gives the point of a paragraph. Basically, that is the only difference between them.

IN A NUTSHELL

The introduction to an essay serves two main purposes:

- To grab the attention of the reader
- To introduce the thesis statement

The introduction to an essay should grab the attention of the reader and introduce the thesis statement.

PRACTICING 1

Underline the thesis sentence in the following opening paragraphs. Then, in the spaces provided, evaluate how well the opening grabs the reader's attention. If you think the opening is dull, write a more catchy one.

1. Atlanta during the 1996 Olympics was very hot. Several days in a row during the first week of competition the temperature topped 90°F with humidity of over 80%. Fortunately, the first week was taken up with mainly swimming. There's no question, as the games once again proved, that sultry weather affects athletic competitions.

_____

_____

_____

2. There was a sudden lurch, a roar, and then the small Japanese car became airborne. I woke up in the back seat to find myself flying in a Toyota. I glanced at Nicky, who was strapped into the seat beside me, and saw terror in her eyes. Someone screamed just before we hit the bottom of the ravine and began to roll. The most terrifying night of my life was the night I almost died in an accident.

_____

_____

_____

3. Why is one place considered ugly and another pretty? Who decides what is pretty and what is not? Chaney Trail in the Angeles Crest Mountains is an ugly recreation area because it has been torn to pieces by off-road bikers.

_____

_____

_____

4. The water was warm and inviting, and some 20 feet below the float was the faint shadow of a shimmering reef. Overhead, the sky stretched in a clear vault of spotless blue. A seagull circled and glided onto the top of a small wave, without making a ripple. I was at my favorite holiday place, Silver Sands in Jamaica.

_____

_____

_____

5. "Four of the things I'd be better without: Love, curiosity, freckles, and doubt." So wrote Dorothy Parker, the American writer. She was right about three—curiosity, freckles, and doubt—but wrong about love. Love is indispensable in life.

_____

_____

_____

The Body

The **body** of an essay consists of all the sub-ideas that prove your thesis statement. Each sub-idea is expressed in a separate paragraph with its own topic sentence.

Here are some examples of thesis statements and the topic sentences of the three paragraphs that make up the body of the essay. Notice that all the topic sentences that follow are already nested in the thesis statements.

Thesis statement:	Before you leave on vacation, take these easy steps to prevent a home burglary.
First topic sentence:	Ask a neighbor to pick up your morning newspaper from the front of your house.
Second topic sentence:	Leave on some lights in the house.
Third topic sentence:	Let friends and neighbors know that you will be gone.

Thesis statement:	It took a while, but after my father's death, I discovered how to deal with grief: accept it, hold on to hope, and keep busy.
First topic sentence:	I simply accepted what had happened.
Second topic sentence:	I held on to the hope that life still offered some goodness.
Third topic sentence:	I kept busy with schoolwork and some social life.
Thesis statement:	A brisk 30-minute walk every day will increase your cardiovascular fitness, tone up your muscles, and help you to relax.
First topic sentence:	A daily, brisk 30-minute walk will help your cardiovascular fitness.
Second topic sentence:	The second benefit of a daily, brisk 30-minute walk is improved muscle tone.
Third topic sentence:	Finally, a daily, brisk 30-minute walk will help you to relax.

IN A NUTSHELL

The body of the essay consists of paragraphs that prove your thesis.

PRACTICING 2

Write three topic sentences for each of the following thesis statements.

1. Whenever I become discouraged about achieving my goals, I think of three people who have overcome serious physical handicaps.

First topic sentence: _____

_____

_____

_____

Second topic sentence: _____

_____

_____

_____

Third topic sentence: _____

_____

_____

_____

2. Horror movies are gory, nerve-racking, and fun.

First topic sentence: _____

_____

_____

_____

Second topic sentence: _____

_____

_____

_____

Third topic sentence: _____

_____

_____

_____

3. Being very short (or very tall) is a special challenge as you
grow up.

First topic sentence: _____

_____

_____

_____

Second topic sentence: _____

_____

_____

_____

Third topic sentence: _____

_____

_____

_____

4. There are three steps to making up your bed properly.

First topic sentence: _____

_____

_____

_____

Second topic sentence: _____

_____

_____

_____

Third topic sentence: _____

_____

_____

_____

5. People who are fanatic patriots are dangerous.

First topic sentence: _____

_____

_____

_____

Second topic sentence: _____

_____

_____

_____

Third topic sentence: _____

_____

_____

_____

The Conclusion

The **conclusion** of your essay summarizes your opinions and leaves the reader with a final thought. A good conclusion does not leave the reader dangling. Rather, it ends the essay gracefully and with a sense of finality. Below are conclusions for the burglary essay and for the essay on overcoming grief:

> Taking these three steps may not guarantee that your house will not be burglarized, but at least you will know that you've done your best to prevent a burglar from stealing your treasures.

> Of course, I still get sad sometimes when I think of my dad. But I now cherish the memories of him, as he would want me to do. I also know that Dad would want me to live my life to the fullest, just as he did.

These conclusions are good because they do not merely parrot back the thesis sentence. Instead, they sum up what the writer has said in the body of the essay and add, as a finishing touch, a final thought.

PRACTICING 3

Which of the pair of conclusions that follow do you think is better? Say why in the lines provided.

1. From an essay about a crotchety uncle:

   (a). So that is why I say my Uncle Charlie is crotchety.

   (b). From cigar smoking to reciting poetry when he's had too much to drink, Uncle Charlie is my most crotchety and colorful relative. Maybe that's why I love him so much.

   _____

   _____

2. From an essay about maintaining a rose garden:

   (a). Gertrude Stein was obviously not a gardener. Only a nongardener would say that "a rose is a rose is a rose." Those of us who work with roses know better. We know that every rose species is uniquely lovely and special. If you start your own rose garden, you will learn that, too.

(b). In conclusion, that is why I say that a rose is not a rose is not a rose, for the reasons given above. Those reasons also show that Gertrude Stein didn't know anything about roses.

3. From an essay on why Monopoly is such a popular board game:

   (a). Bankruptcy, property repossession, a sudden turnaround because of dumb luck: These are all part of the thrill that explains Monopoly's success. Try it. In no time at all, like me, you'll find yourself hooked.

   (b). Monopoly, in sum, is popular because it is like life. As I said in paragraph one, it is an unpredictable game. As I also pointed out in my second paragraph, it is an old game that many people remember playing as children. And as I said in paragraph three, it is a game where you can become very rich or broke. That is why people like Monopoly.

4. From an essay on the joys and risks of riding a motorcycle:

   (a). So you can see, riding a motorcycle brings a sense of freedom, but it also brings many risks.

   (b). It's all included in motorcycle riding—the delight of feeling your hair blown by a breeze at 60 miles per hour to the sudden possibility of a broken leg because of an uncaring driver. The risks are there, but they add to the joy.

5. From an essay on handgun ownership:

   (a). So these are the reasons I oppose handguns. The chances of shooting someone you love are too high. The chances of being shot by your own gun are also too high. Plus, as I said in paragraph two, handguns are only for shooting people, and that's murder. So why would I want to own a handgun?

   (b). My opposition to handguns is based on very practical reasons. Instead of protecting homeowners, the handgun is more likely to imperil them. Statistics clearly show that handguns in the home are mainly used against other family members in tragic accidents or by homeowners in suicides or suicide attempts. The toll is even higher when there are children in the household. Handguns do not make a home safer. In fact, they have the very opposite effect. Given that grim fact, why would anyone want one in the home?

_____

_____

The Whole Essay

The essay has a predictable form that consists of three principal parts. Here it is in visual form:

Title of Essay

Introduction

Thesis statement

Topic sentence: _____

Body

Topic sentence: _____

Body

Topic sentence: _____

Body

Conclusion

The following essay is by Laura Unterman, a student. It follows the five-paragraph format illustrated previously.

In the Land of the Walls, Deserts, and Shwarma

Thesis statement

It is a land of breathtaking beauty, a three-thousand-year-old history grafted onto a rich and lively culture, and this summer I found myself there, in Israel. By car, boat, and on foot, I crisscrossed this ancient land during the sweltering, Middle Eastern summer. When I left, three memories in particular stayed with me, and probably will forever: the Western Wall, the Negev Desert, and the food.

First topic sentence: the Wall

The Western Wall, the only structure remaining from Jerusalem's great temple, evokes powerful emotions. Jews from all over the world come to it to pray. I couldn't believe the emotional outpourings I witnessed. One woman cried as she gently kissed the Wall. A man was so deep in prayer that he was oblivious to being pushed and jostled by others trying to touch the Wall's rough stone surface. People gathered in groups and prayed out loud. Others were lost in silent meditation. As I observed, I came to realize how important the Western Wall is to not just the Israelis, but to Jews all over the world.

Second topic sentence: the Negev Desert

The Negev Desert of Israel is a place of piercing beauty. I spent two weeks there, hiking, camping, and rock climbing. When I first saw the Negev, I was startled. I had expected an endless expanse of sand. Instead, I saw rock formations in hues of brown, red, yellow, and orange, and mountains so perfectly formed they seemed to be the painstaking product of God's own hand. The sky was a crisp blue, and the air was clean and sharp. The plants had a strange and delicate beauty. Even the animals native to the Negev seemed different—almost otherworldly. I will never forget the beauty of the Negev.

Third topic sentence: the Food

My third memory of Israel is as powerful and exotic as my experience with the land and its monuments: It is of delicious food. My budget was tight, and I had to scrimp on everything, but still I delighted in falafel and shwarma—two of the most popular fast-food dishes in Israel. Falafel is a vegetarian dish served in pita bread. Shwarma is pita bread stuffed with lamb or chicken. Both are freshly prepared, hot and delicious, and add a spicy zest to the day's adventures.

Conclusion   The Western Wall, the Negev Desert, and the Middle Eastern food—these are the memories I still have of my summer in Israel. The Wall moved me; the desert awed me; the food left me licking my chops. My total self—mind, soul, and body—were all separately enriched and nourished by this trip.

Laura's essay shows all the characteristics of a good five-paragraph essay.

1. The **introduction** catches our attention with its crisp summary of the experience. It ends with the **thesis statement** *When I had left, three memories in particular stayed with me, and probably will forever: the Western Wall, the Negev Desert, and the food.* Notice that the sub-ideas that will become the topic sentences of the three paragraphs are nested in this thesis statement.

2. The **body** of the essay consists of three paragraphs that prove the thesis statement:

Topic sentence 1.   The Western Wall, the only structure remaining from Jerusalem's great temple, evokes powerful emotions.

Topic sentence 2.   The Negev Desert of Israel is a place of piercing beauty.

Topic sentence 3.   My third memory of Israel is as powerful and exotic as my experience with the land and its monuments: It is of the delicious food.

3. The **conclusion** of the essay gives a sense of finality by returning to the three memories and summarizing the effect each had on the writer. It concludes that each experience enriched and nourished the writer in a different way.

PRACTICING 4

Read the student essay that follows and answer the questions at the end.

Greatness Misunderstood

"Aww, he's just a nut with a crackpot idea." This is how most people respond to someone who suggests something new. People resist change, even change for the better. But history shows that greatness has often been misunderstood and that breakthrough ideas are seldom welcome when they first appear.

One perfect example of misunderstood greatness is Wilbur Wright. When he tried to sell his flying machine to the U.S. government, the officials in charge were highly skeptical. They didn't know anything about the machine since Wright had developed it almost entirely in secret. The government demanded proof—drawings, formulas, and statistics—showing that flying was possible. It demanded budgets detailing the costs of building a flying machine. These bureaucratic demands almost killed Wright's project, but in the end his diligence prevailed and he proved that people could fly.

Brigadier General William (Billy) Mitchell, an American army officer and pilot during World War I, is another example of misunderstood greatness. It was his persistence that forged the airplane into a weapon. Mitchell argued strongly for an independent air force. When his superiors wouldn't listen, he directed the sensational sinking of several war ships in a prearranged bombing—to prove the power of strategic bombing. This stunt led to his court martial in 1925, his suspension for five years, and his resignation from the army in 1926. As a civilian, he continued to argue for a separate air force. Finally, his superiors realized the wisdom of his ideas and, during World War II, the U.S. Air Force was created. Imagine what the Nazis would have done to the world had Mitchell not won his argument, and you can easily grasp the importance of his persistence.

My last example of misunderstood greatness is Frank Lloyd Wright, the father of modern architecture. His idea of beauty was simple geometric forms and vast openness inside buildings. To escape the deadening influence of European architecture, he broke every conventional rule. He was the first to hang cantilevered houses over cliffs. He used cement, glass, and steel to create buildings of astounding beauty. He designed and built the Mile-High Illinois Building, a tripod one-mile high with 528 stories and a taproot foundation that slopes down into solid bedrock. Today his basic designs are evident in buildings everywhere. Yet his work was initially scorned and laughed at.

The lesson to be learned from Wilbur Wright, General Billy Mitchell, and Frank Lloyd Wright is that greatness does not always win the popularity contest. Yale President Kingman Brewster once said, "There is a correlation between the creative and the screwball. So we must suffer the screwball gladly."

1. How does the writer get our attention in the introduction?

_____

_____

_____

2. What is the thesis statement of the essay?

_____

_____

_____

3. What are the topic sentences in the body paragraphs?

First topic sentence: _____

_____

_____

Second topic sentence: _____

_____

_____

Third topic sentence: _____

_____

_____

4. Is the conclusion abrupt, or does it seem to give a sense of finality to the essay? Explain your answer.

_____

_____

_____

_____

IN A NUTSHELL

An essay consists of three parts:

- An introduction with its thesis statement.

- A body of paragraphs, each with a topic sentence that proves the thesis statement.

- A conclusion that gives the essay a sense of finality.

The Title

Put yourself in your instructor's shoes. You have 25 essays to read and grade by tomorrow. Many of them are written, if not on the same, then on similar topics. You come across two: One is titled, *How I Spent My Vacation Last Summer,* the other, *Cooking Beans and Burritos in the Bronx.* Which do you think you'd rather read?

Chances are you'd go for the beans and burritos because it has a splash of color in the title, especially in contrast to the drab *How I Spent My Vacation Last Summer.* What was the beans and burritos essay all about? How one student spent her summer vacation—working in a Mexican restaurant.

The point is that you should use some imagination and make your title sparkly and bright. A title that's plainly descriptive and drab won't attract a reader. Here are some examples. Which of these titles would make you more inclined to read the essay?

About a tightfisted relative:
Aunt Viola
At Heart, A Squirrel

About the benefits of exercise:
Exercise Is Good
The Real Fountain of Youth

About a bad airplane trip:
A Bad Airplane Trip
Turbulence at 35,000 Feet!

About a rotten date:
A Date I Didn't Like
A Night in Purgatory

Our own votes are for the squirrel, the fountain, the turbulence, and purgatory.

Movie producers, newspaper headline writers, and magazine editors all spend considerable time writing catchy titles and captions. So should you. Of course, your title mustn't mislead the way tabloid titles often do (a tabloid headline, "Bigfoot in Brooklyn," could mean that someone there was spotted wearing a size 19 shoe).

PRACTICING 5

Without knowing anything about the essays, underline the title in each pair that makes you want to read the whole work.

1. Cutting Up at the Box Office / Today's Horror Movies

2. The Convertible / The Breeze and I

3. The Danger in Your Back Pocket / Credit Cards

4. Acne Is Bad / The Teenager's Burden

5. Divorce Hurts / Divorce

Unit Test

From the four answers provided, check the one that most agrees with this chapter.

Example: The classroom essay usually contains

_____ **(a).** 1000 to 1500 words.

_____ **(b).** 200 words.

✔ **(c).** 300 to 500 words.

_____ **(d).** As many words as the writer desires.

1. An essay is

_____ **(a).** A collection of paragraphs about the same subject.

_____ **(b).** A collection of paragraphs on different subjects.

_____ **(c).** Exactly three paragraphs and an introduction.

_____ **(d).** The written version of someone's private thoughts.

2. The introduction to an essay exists in order to

_____ **(a).** Introduce the writer to the reader.

_____ **(b).** Grab the reader's attention and introduce the main point.

_____ **(c).** Let the writer warm up at writing.

_____ **(d).** Take up space

3. The main body of the essay consists of

_____ **(a).** The facts and other details that develop the essay.

_____ **(b).** All the words used by the author.

_____ **(c).** The title and conclusion

_____ **(d).** The sub-ideas that prove the thesis

4. The conclusion of an essay

_____ **(a).** Is unimportant.

_____ **(b).** Summarizes the opinions in the essay and gives a final thought.

_____ **(c).** Leaves the reader expecting more.

_____ **(d).** Must be a surprise and leave the reader dangling.

5. The title of the essay should

_____ **(a).** Be the least important part.

_____ **(b).** Always be humorous.

_____ **(c).** Have some sparkle.

_____ **(d).** Be drab.

6. Which of the following titles is the most intriguing?

    ——— **(a).** The War over Lydia's Heart.

    ——— **(b).** Divorce and Fights over Children.

    ——— **(c).** Custody Battles: Why and When.

    ——— **(d).** Children and Divorce.

7. The thesis statement is there to

    ——— **(a).** Assure that the essay is intellectually serious.

    ——— **(b).** Expose the writer's observations.

    ——— **(c).** Sum up the essay in one sentence.

    ——— **(d).** Be a symbol of the entire essay.

8. The purpose of an essay is always to

    ——— **(a).** Inform, persuade, or entertain.

    ——— **(b).** Argue for or against a proposition.

    ——— **(c).** Allow the writer to unload his or her heart.

    ——— **(d).** Define, compare, or narrate.

9. Writing an essay can teach you

    ——— **(a).** How to organize your thoughts.

    ——— **(b).** How to put your thoughts down clearly on paper.

    ——— **(c).** How to back up your points with appropriate details.

    ——— **(d).** All of the above.

10. Once you have learned to write an essay in college, you will

    ——— **(a).** Never use that skill again.

    ——— **(b).** Be prepared to write in business.

    ——— **(c).** Get along better with people.

    ——— **(d).** Know how to use prepositions.

Unit Talk-Write Assignment

Students were asked to write an essay on something from their youth that had a lasting influence on them. Several paired off to talk out their ideas before beginning to write. The following is what one student said.

Read this student's spoken essay and then use it to write a plan for a complete essay. Begin with an attention-getting introduction and clearly stated thesis statement. Then write three topic sentences. Finally, write a conclusion. You will need to add material to create three topic sentences. Use the essay form provided.

Spoken Paragraph

During one of my high school math classes when we were having a test, I watched a couple of students exchanging answers on pieces of torn paper. At first I thought how helpful it would be to set up that kind of communication with a friend so that I could get a decent grade. After all, math is hard and when you're nervous, you make mistakes that you wouldn't usually make. Having a buddy pass me answers to compare with my own would sure save time, and I wouldn't have to study so hard. But then I remembered a story my mom used to read to me when I was a little boy. It's the story of "The Turtle and the Hare." You know, it's a famous story about a bragging hare—by the way, a hare is just a rabbit—who could run like crazy compared with his turtle friend, who just crawled along at a terribly slow pace. The hare used to tease the turtle mercilessly about being so disgustingly slow. One day the turtle challenged the hare to a race. The hare looked at the turtle with a snobby, sarcastic attitude and accepts the challenge, thinking, "You slow poke; you'll lose big time. I'll beat you all to pieces." Of course, the hare immediately jumps far ahead of the turtle. Part way through the race, he stops to sit down on a tree stump and enjoy the scenery. "What a stupid, slow animal that turtle is! How nervy of him to challenge me to a race!" he says to himself. Then the hare takes a nap. Behold, when he wakes up, the plodding turtle has reached the goal and won the race. This story has been with me all of my life, whenever I've been tempted to take shortcuts or to avoid honest work. I keep hearing my mother's voice telling me, "Slow and steady wins the race."

Written Essay

Introduction: _____

_____

_____

_____

Thesis statement: _____

_____

_____

Topic sentence, first paragraph: _____

_____

Topic sentence, second paragraph: _____

_____

_____

_____

Topic sentence, third paragraph: _____

_____

_____

_____

Conclusion: _____

_____

_____

_____

Unit Collaborative Assignment

Choose a classmate and brainstorm an attention-grabbing introduction to an essay about the importance of legible handwriting. Try out several approaches. When you have settled on the best introduction, write it below. Then write a thesis statement, three topic sentences for the body paragraphs, and at least one ending sentence for the conclusion.

Introduction: _____

_____

_____

_____

Thesis statement: _____

_____

_____

_____

Topic sentence, first paragraph: _____

_____

_____

_____

Topic sentence, second paragraph: _____

_____

_____

_____

Topic sentence, third paragraph: _____

_____

_____

_____

Conclusion: _____

_____

_____

_____

Unit Writing Assignment

Write one of the essays you just partially created—about not taking shortcuts or the importance of legible handwriting. When you finish, write an attention-getting title.

Photo Writing Assignment

Study the following picture, and brainstorm ideas for an essay about it. On a separate sheet of paper, write a thesis statement that will serve as the main idea of the essay. Now write down three topic sentences that will support the thesis statement. Finally, write the essay. Be sure the introduction makes the reader want to read on, and the conclusion gives the whole essay a sense of finality. When you are through, write an attention-getting title.

17

The Thesis Statement

"The thesis statement is where you take a stand on the topic."

The **thesis statement** is a single sentence in the opening paragraph that sums up what the essay is about. Every essay should have a thesis statement that functions like a road sign, telling the reader where the essay intends to go.

A thesis statement has three practical aims:

1. It tells in a single sentence what your essay is about: *Fast driving causes accidents and increases air pollution.* We know that this essay intends to discuss the consequences of fast driving, not an encounter with a bear in a campground.

2. It helps you organize your essay: *To do well on an essay exam, you must know the material, understand the question, and organize your answer.* This thesis statement suggests three subtopics for the essay's paragraphs—how knowing the material, understanding the question, and organizing the answer will help you do well on essay exams.

3. It reflects your understanding of the topic and your feelings about it. For instance, to develop the thesis: *Females are the stable element in baboon society* would require an understanding of baboon rituals and communication. Likewise, the thesis: *Affirmative action gives everyone an equal chance* announces clearly that the writer's feelings are in favor of affirmative action.

The thesis statement is where you take a stand on the topic. If you feel that smoking is your right and you're tired of being nagged about it, say so in your thesis statement. Make your stand strong, definite, and clear.

IN A NUTSHELL

The thesis statement of an essay does the following:

- It tells what your essay is about.
- It helps organize the essay.
- It reflects the writer's understanding and attitude toward the topic.

PRACTICING 1

In the space provided, indicate the topic, organizing features, and feelings or understandings suggested by each of the following thesis statements.

Example: Doing crossword puzzles is addicting and educational.

Topic: Crossword puzzles

Organizing features: Two subtopics: what makes doing crossword puzzles addicting and what makes doing them educational

Feelings or understanding: The writer enjoys doing crossword puzzles.

1. Jumping on a trampoline keeps your body in shape while giving you the fun of acrobatics.

Topic: _____

Organizing features: _____

_____

Feelings or understanding: _____

_____

2. Working part-time while attending school full-time places a burden on most students.

Topic: _____

Organizing features: _____

_____

Feelings or understanding: _____

_____

3. To live peacefully in our diverse population, we need to respect each other's religion, nationality, and economic status.

Topic: _____

Organizing features: _____

_____

Feelings or understanding: _____

_____

4. Trout fishing is a sport with a long and colorful history.

Topic: _____

Organizing features: _____

_____

Feelings or understanding: _____

_____

5. The elderly in my neighborhood suffer from no money, no respect, and no companionship.

Topic: _____

Organizing features: _____

_____

Feelings or understanding: _____

_____

Common Faults of the Thesis Statement

The most common faults of thesis statements are as follows:

- Too narrow
- Too broad
- Uncommitted
- Unclear

We'll discuss each fault separately.

The Too-Narrow Thesis Statement

An essay discusses the idea expressed in the thesis statement. It is, however, possible to box yourself in with a too-narrow thesis statement that leaves you with little or nothing to discuss. Here are some examples, along with their revisions:

Too narrow:	My family eats a lot of hamburger because it is inexpensive.
Discussible:	Hamburger is a highly popular food.
Too narrow:	I had my cat declawed to protect my furniture.
Discussible:	A declawed cat makes a good indoor pet.
Too narrow:	Last summer, my brother flew a kite on one of the L.A. beaches.
Discussible:	Kite flying is a popular sport on Los Angeles beaches.

Your thesis statement should have at least one or two key words in it. If it doesn't, it is probably too narrow. **Key words** are words that add a discussible edge to the thesis statement. For example, in the thesis statement *Hamburger is a highly popular food,* the key words are *highly popular.* That is what you must discuss and prove—the popularity of hamburgers. In the thesis statement *A declawed cat makes a good indoor pet,* the key words are *good indoor pet.* You must discuss and prove that a declawed cat does make a good indoor pet. Finally, in the thesis statement *Kite flying is a popular sport on Los Angeles beaches,* the key words are *popular sport.* That kite flying is a popular sport on Los Angeles beaches is what you must prove. You might discuss county-sponsored kite flying contests. You might describe the flocks of kites swarming the beaches on weekends. These details will go a long way toward proving your thesis statement that kite flying is popular.

The point is, your thesis statement must not be too narrow or it will leave you fumbling for something to say. One way to avoid narrowness is to be sure that your thesis statement contains key words that lend it a discussible edge.

PRACTICING 2

In the space provided, check the thesis statement in each of the following pairs that is more discussible. Underline the key words that add a discussible edge.

1. _____ I get a haircut every week.

_____ My haircut reflects my personality.

2. _____ Flying is the safest way to travel.

_____ I usually travel by plane.

3. _____ Housepainting is my job.

_____ Housepainting is a tedious job.

4. _____ Dancing is good aerobic exercise.

_____ I can dance.

5. _____ I made Chinese food for dinner yesterday.

_____ Chinese food is easy to make and healthful.

PRACTICING 3

Insert key words to make the following thesis statements discussible. Indicate in the spaces provided what the inserted words oblige you to discuss and prove.

Example: Joe is my friend.

Revision: Joe is my trustworthy friend.

What I have to do: Find examples that show Joe's trustworthiness.

1. Volkswagen has introduced a new bug.

Revision: _____

What I have to do: _____

2. I photographed my grandfather.

Revision: _____

What I have to do: _____

3. Our family has a reunion every year.

Revision: _____

What I have to do: _____

4. Yesterday I watched several shows on MTV.

Revision: _____

What I have to do: _____

5. I lift weights.

Revision: _____

What I have to do: _____

The Too-Broad Thesis Statement

A thesis statement is too broad if it commits you to a topic too big to cover in a brief essay. The solution to a too-broad thesis statement is to pare it down to a more manageable size. Here are some broad thesis statements with their more manageable revisions:

Which of the two do you think is a better thesis statement? We cast our vote for the second.

The first thesis statement is not altogether bad, but it would be harder to develop than the second. It hinges on one key word: *disaster*. In writing about how your fishing trip was a disaster, you'd probably eventually come up with the topics of thunderstorms, vicious mosquitoes, and bad food. Therefore, in addition to writing, you'd also have to be looking—for topics.

In the second thesis statement you can concentrate on the writing. Your topics of *thunderstorms, vicious mosquitoes,* and *bad food* are already nested in the thesis statement. You know exactly what to write about and in what order. The second thesis statement is a good thesis statement for these reasons:

It is not too narrow.	It gives three reasons why the fishing trip was a disaster; one reason would *not* have been enough.
It is not too broad.	The three topics—*thunderstorms, vicious mosquitoes,* and *bad food*—can be nicely covered in a short essay. You don't have to write a book.
It is committed.	We know exactly the writer's opinion of the fishing trip—it was a disaster.
It is not unclear.	The language is plain and straightforward with no wordiness or pompousness.
It has key words that suggest a structure for the essay.	The writer knows what support to provide and in what order.

PRACTICING 7

Mark *G* beside the good thesis statement in each pair and then explain why it is good.

1. _____ **(a).** Last Thanksgiving was an awful holiday.

_____ **(b).** Last Thanksgiving was an awful holiday because I quarreled with my sister, burned the turkey, and fell off a ladder.

Reason: _____

_____

2. _____ **(a).** Stephen King writes readable books.

_____ **(b).** Stephen King's books are so good because they are about normal people who get into supernatural situations.

Reason: _____

_____

3. ____ **(a).** Recharging the cartridges of laser printers saves money, recycles a useful part, and helps the environment.

____ **(b).** Recharging the cartridges of laser printers is worthwhile.

Reason: _____

_____

4. ____ **(a).** *Consumer Reports* magazine helps me make buying decisions, brings me up to date, and informs me of product recalls.

____ **(b).** *Consumer Reports* magazine helps me.

Reason: _____

_____

5. ____ **(a).** I enjoyed my vacation in Destin, Florida.

____ **(b).** Destin, Florida, is a great undiscovered vacation spot with something for everyone.

Reason: _____

Unit Test

Circle *T* if the statement is true; circle *F* if it is false.

Example: T ⒡ A thesis statement keeps you from taking a stand on an issue.

1. T F The thesis should be stated in a single sentence.

2. T F The thesis statement can help you organize your essay.

3. T F The four common faults of a thesis statement are (1) showing too much emotion, (2) dealing with only one side of the issue, (3) not using enough examples, (4) being prejudiced.

4. T F Narrow thesis statements are not helpful because they often leave you with nothing to discuss.

5. T F "A stapler is a handy office gadget" is too narrow to be a good thesis statement.

6. **T**   **F**   "The last 75 years have witnessed many superb baseball pitchers" is too broad to be a good thesis statement.

7. **T**   **F**   A tactful writer will always write an uncommitted thesis statement.

8. **T**   **F**   The following is an uncommitted thesis statement: "Stem cell research should probably continue because it may find the cure for cancer."

9. **T**   **F**   An unclear thesis statement is sometimes the result of trying to impress rather than to communicate.

10. **T**   **F**   The following is a good thesis statement: "By using clever marketing strategies, many clothing companies have turned web surfers into buyers."

Unit Talk-Write Assignment

Spoken Opinions

The subject is prayer in public schools. Here are four different opinions, offered informally and in spoken form, by four students. Use these ideas—as well as your own—to write a good thesis statement. It should have a discussible edge and committed opinion. It should also have key words that will suggest the structure for an essay. Use standard English.

1. Why would anyone not want prayer in the schools? Prayer is wonderfully comforting, and it is part of all religions. Prayer is universal. I don't know what I'd do without prayer. When my mother was very sick, I prayed for her, and she recovered.

2. Catholics pray holding beads in their fingers. Buddhists pray surrounded by incense. Shintoists clap their hands to pray. Muslims bow towards Mecca to pray. You could go on and on, describing how people around the world pray. Prayer belongs in schools because it belongs everywhere.

3. Praying in school is wrong because it forces students to pray in a certain way, which not all students may believe in. Why can't we just pray at home or in our house of worship? God will hear us.

4. I'm against prayer in schools. One-minute prayers are allowed, and the next thing you know, they're required. No one says you can't pray now—just do it silently. But don't tell me I have to pray in school using someone else's prayers.

Thesis Statement

_____

_____

_____

_____

Unit Collaborative Assignment

Pair up with a classmate. Each person should choose a topic from the list below and write a thesis statement. Exchange thesis statements with your partner and take turns critiquing them. Be sure the thesis statement is not too narrow, too broad, uncommitted, or unclear, and that it includes key words.

1. What to do about stalkers
2. Spike Lee's (or another director's) movies
3. How to avoid losing your temper
4. Cultural diversity on campus
5. Final examinations should (or should not) be abolished.

Unit Writing Assignment

Write an essay using the thesis statement you wrote for the Unit Collaborative Assignment.

Photo Writing Assignment

Study the following picture. Then write a thesis statement about how you think the person in the foreground of the picture is likely to feel 20 years from now about doing this act. Create a committed thesis statement, and write a five-paragraph essay.

18

Organizing Your Essay, from Beginning to End

"The beginning of your essay is what your reader sees first and where you make an important first impression."

Every essay has three parts: a beginning, middle, and end. The beginning, called the **introduction,** consists of an opening paragraph and includes the thesis statement. The **body,** or middle of the essay, includes paragraphs that support and prove the thesis. The **conclusion,** or end, consists of a final paragraph that brings the essay to a close.

Even in essays that are otherwise not alike, these three parts still play the same role. We will discuss the role of each part and give advice for writing catchy introductions, solid supporting paragraphs, and effective conclusions.

The Introduction

Here is what a typical introduction looks like:

- Opening sentences (grabbers)
- Transition
- Thesis statement

To illustrate how all three parts work in the introduction, we're going to build a typical introductory paragraph from scratch. This is the model we will use as our pattern:

Introduction

Grabber: three to six sentences that pull in the reader.

Transition (if necessary): sets the stage for the thesis.

The thesis: single sentence that sums up the essay.

An example of an opening paragraph that contains all these necessary parts follows.

Grabbers	Bang! The explosion shattered the stillness of the house. An object whizzed through the wall, smashed through a picture hanging on the wall, and flew over the streets of New York. I sat stunned in my chair, unable to move. Then I got up to investigate. In the next room my little brother, six years old, sat sobbing on the
Transition sentence (underlined)	floor. Beside him was my mother's handgun that had just gone off accidentally. <u>This incident taught me a lesson.</u> Handguns are dangerous
Thesis statement	to own because they provide little protection, can be used in the heat of a quarrel, and often cause deadly accidents.

We'll discuss each separate part in some detail.

Opening sentences (grabbers)

The opening sentences, or grabbers, pull the reader in. This is the readers' first bite of your offering, and how it tastes will really make a difference in how they receive your essay. If you begin with the usual humdrum fare, your readers might chew on, but only reluctantly. Here are some techniques to help you write catchy grabbers.

1. Begin with a quotation or catchy saying.
Beginning with a quotation allows you to use someone else's clever words to get your essay started. Standard reference works such as *Bartlett's Familiar Quotations* or *The Oxford Dictionary of Quotations* are good sources of quotations. Other books, magazines, and newspapers are also rich sources. For example, one student opened her essay on books that she loves with this quotation:

> "When I am dead, I hope it may be said, 'His sins were scarlet, but his books were read.' " So wrote the English writer Hilaire Beloc. He didn't need to worry. His books are read. In fact, he happens to be one of the writers whose books I love. . . .

In this example, a student uses a catchy saying to open an essay about being in charge of your life:

> "You get what you tolerate." I heard my father say this a hundred times, but I didn't realize what it meant until one day when I

was complaining about my girlfriend Jenny's lack of consideration. Suddenly I understood. I had a part in how she was treating me. I was letting myself be a doormat. That day I learned a valuable lesson: I never have to be a victim in life.

Here are some tips for opening with quotations or sayings:

- Don't use this opening all the time: Anything in excess soon becomes stale.

- Identify the person you quote unless he or she is so famous as to be immediately recognizable (e.g., Martin Luther King Jr., Abraham Lincoln, William Shakespeare).

- Make sure your quotation is short—a sentence or two at the most.

- Choose a quotation that's spicy and insightful, something with a real zing to it.

ESL Advice!

Don't be embarrassed to use any exotic statement or saying from your own culture as a grabber. What might seem trite to you could well be an eye-opener for American readers. To make sure your grabber works as you intend it to, try it out on a native student.

---

2. Describe a personal experience.

We all like to hear about personal experiences and tend to get pulled into them quickly. The paragraph about the handgun, for example, opens on a personal experience. Here is another such introduction, about the difficulty of parking on campus:

Grabbers

    The rain was pouring down in huge, shimmering sheets. I could barely see where I was driving. When I turned into the campus parking lot, I moved my head as close to the windshield as possible in order to see, but I could barely make out the outlines of parked cars. After I had circled the student parking lot three times, I finally found a spot up in what we call "monkey heaven"—a narrow parking area behind the technical building—blocks away from the science building. <u>I learned that night what every student who drives to school here knows.</u> Because of overcrowding and the scattered layout of the buildings, our campus desperately needs a multilevel parking structure located in a central position and open to all students.

Transition sentence (underlined)

Thesis statement

This opening is sometimes referred to as opening "in the middle of things" because it places the reader right in the middle of a dramatic situation. Then it ties in the experience with the point of the thesis statement.

Here are some tips for opening with a personal experience:

- Make the opening situation dramatic.

- Keep it brief.

- Connect it with a transition sentence to the thesis statement.

3. Ask a question.

Asking a question gets to the point of your thesis statement immediately. Here is an example:

> Do you suddenly change into a monster the moment you get behind a steering wheel? Many people do. They live the calm life of Dr. Jekyll until they slide behind the wheel of a car, and then they turn into an ugly Mr. Hyde. Such, for example, is the case of my Aunt Matilda, who drives a taxi for a living. My Aunt Matilda has two contrasting personalities, the one when she is out of a car and another uglier one when she is behind the wheel of her taxi.

Although the thesis statement itself should never be worded as a question, a question is a zippy opening because it pulls in readers by addressing them directly. Plus, it immediately raises the topic of your thesis statement.

4. Give a startling fact or statistic.

Facts and statistics make punchy grabbers. Here are some examples:

From an essay on how we celebrate Memorial Day:	In 1868, General John A. Logan, Commander in Chief of the Grand Army of the Republic, did a wonderful thing. He created Memorial Day.
From an essay on having a car stolen:	In 1991, over 200,000 people were arrested for car theft, according to the <u>Information Please Almanac</u>. I was one who had a car stolen that year. . . .
From an essay on suffering through the flu:	It killed 20,000,000 people in 1918, 500,000 in the United States. I'm talking about the flu. . . .

Here are some tips for opening with facts:

- Be sure your facts are indeed facts and not opinions.

Fact:	The *Washington Post* is published in Washington, D.C.
Opinion:	I think the *Washington Post* is a great newspaper.

- Use only specific, not general, facts.

General fact:	It is sad to realize that many people die from heart problems caused by smoking.
Specific fact:	Every year in the United States, 170,000 people die from heart problems caused by smoking.

One way to check that your opening sentences create a real grabber is to read them aloud as if you were using them to start a conversation. Or, better yet, read them aloud to a friend. Does your friend want to hear more? If the answer is no, you have a little more work ahead. If you make three or four false starts, that's fine. Keep trying. Eventually, you will write a snappy introduction that will grab your reader.

The introduction, in turn, also consists of three parts:

- Grabber sentences that pull the reader in.

- A transition sentence that ties in the grabbers to the thesis statement.

- The thesis statement.

IN A NUTSHELL

An essay consists of three parts:

- Introduction.

- Body.

- Conclusion.

PRACTICING 1

Write a grabber for each of the following topics.

1. A time you said "yes" when you should have said "no"

_____

2. A memorable Halloween experience

_____

3. Being surprised

_____

4. Earliest childhood memories

_____

5. A very good friend

_____

Transition sentence

After the grabber comes the **transition,** a sentence that ties your introduction to the thesis statement. Sometimes a transition is necessary, but sometimes it is not, depending on the wording of your grabber. In this paragraph, for example, which we quoted earlier, the transition is clearly necessary:

Grabbers

Bang! The explosion shattered the stillness of the house. An object whizzed through the wall, smashed through a picture hanging on the wall, and flew over the streets of New York. I sat stunned in my chair, unable to move. Then I got up to investigate. In the next room my little brother, six years old, sat sobbing on the

Transition sentence (underlined)

floor. Beside him was my mother's handgun that had just gone off accidentally. <u>This incident taught me a lesson.</u> Handguns are dangerous

Thesis statement

to own because they provide little protection, can be used in the heat of a quarrel, and often cause deadly accidents.

In the following paragraph the grabber ties in so naturally with the thesis statement that a transition is unnecessary:

My hands were trembling. A cold sweat washed over my brow. When the teacher told us to begin, I was in such a state I could hardly turn the page. I tried to begin by answering the first question, but before I could write, I had to stop my knees from knocking. I was sure that everyone in the room could hear my quaking. <u>Test taking is always an ordeal for me because of my fear of doing poorly, my nervousness, and my tendency to overprepare.</u>

The grabber leads so naturally to the thesis statement at the end that a transition is unnecessary.

In your own opening paragraphs, your ear and common sense will tell you whether you need a transition. Read the paragraph aloud. If the grabber seems to flow naturally into the thesis statement, you need no transition. However, if the grabber seems to need tying into the thesis statement, use a transition sentence.

Thesis statement

The thesis statement ends the introduction. In Unit 17 we discussed the thesis statement at length. We said it was a single sentence in the opening paragraph that sums up what the essay is about. Every essay must have a thesis statement. It is like a road sign, telling your reader where your essay intends to go. The thesis statement is usually the last sentence of the opening paragraph. If you wish to refresh yourself on the thesis statement, review Unit 17.

In summary, when you write your own opening paragraph, be sure to include a grabber, a transition sentence (if your ear tells you that one is necessary), and a thesis statement.

IN A NUTSHELL

In addition to the grabber, the introduction also contains two other parts:

- A transition sentence (if necessary).
- The thesis statement.

PRACTICING 2

Choose one of the five topics listed below and write an introduction to pull in your audience. Your introduction should include a grabber, transition sentence (if necessary), and thesis statement. Keep your work. You will need it for Practicing 4.

1. The first time you did something.

2. A disappointment with your family.

3. Evaluating a current movie (good or bad).

4. Working in a group.

5. A difficult experience.

The Body

In writing the body of your essay, you will use the strategies learned earlier in this book. Which strategy you will use depends on your thesis statement. Some essays, in fact, may require paragraphs developed by different strategies. For example, if you are writing an essay on anger, you might define anger in one paragraph, give examples of it in another, and explain the process you use to control your own temper in a third. Other essay assignments—for example, to compare two people—may require you to focus on one strategy only—comparing/contrasting.

Indeed, many thesis statements have topics that lead naturally to one particular strategy over another. If you were asked, for example, to tell a love story, you would naturally use narration, not argumentation, to develop an essay on that topic.

Here is a table listing the various strategies you might use in developing an essay. The second column lists the unit that covered the particular strategy. The last column gives an example of a topic that might be developed by that strategy. Use the table to review any strategy you're unsure of as you prepare to write your own essays.

STRATEGY	UNIT	USES	EXAMPLE TOPIC
Narration	8	To tell a story	My appendicitis operation
Description	9	To describe	My beloved cat, Fluffie
Illustration	10	To give examples	The stresses of college life
Process	11	To explain anything step by step	How to make good compost
Definition	12	To pinpoint the meaning of a word	What is romance?
Classification	13	To sort into types	Four types of teachers
Comparing and contrasting	14	To find similarities and differences between two things	Baseball versus football
Argumentation	15	To debate a point	Drinking on campus should be banned

Using the strategies to develop paragraphs that support the thesis statement is just one technique that you would use in writing the body of your essay. Here are other techniques you would also practice:

- Stick to the thesis statement.

- Link your paragraphs.

- Write solid paragraphs.

Stick to the thesis statement.

The best way to stick to the thesis statement is to underline its key words. In Unit 17 we defined *key words* as words that add a discussible edge to the thesis statement. These, in effect, are the ideas that the body of your essay must support and prove. For example, let us say that this is your thesis:

> Driving at night is <u>harder</u> to do than driving at day because of the <u>problems</u> caused by <u>poor visibility</u>, <u>fatigue</u>, and the occasional <u>drunk driver</u>.

By underlining the key words, you know exactly what three ideas you must cover in the body of your essay: (1) problems caused by poor visibility, (2) problems caused by fatigue, and (3) problems caused by drunk drivers.

Stick to the topics you promised to cover in your thesis. Not to do so is like being a server at a restaurant and bringing stew when you promised pancakes. If you need a refresher course on sticking to the topic, review Unit 7.

Link your paragraphs.

In Unit 7 we also discussed how to link sentences *within* a paragraph to help your reader follow your train of thought. Paragraphs, too, must be linked or your reader might get lost. In the following section we will discuss how to link the paragraphs of an essay.

1. Repeat key words from the thesis statement.
Here is an example:

Thesis statement:	Driving at night is <u>harder</u> than driving during the day because of the <u>problems</u> caused by <u>poor visibility</u>, <u>fatigue</u>, and the occasional <u>drunk driver</u>.

Here is how repetition would be used in the topic sentences of the paragraphs:

Topic sentence of first paragraph:	Driving at night is harder because of the problems caused by poor visibility.
Topic sentence of second paragraph:	Driving at night is harder because of the problems caused by fatigue.
Topic sentence of third paragraph:	Driving at night is harder because of the problems caused by the occasional drunk driver.

2. Use transitional words and sentences.
Transitional words like *first, second, third,* and *finally* help the reader to see the relationship between paragraphs. Other expressions are *nevertheless, in contrast, in addition, another point is, an example that comes to mind is,* and *therefore.* These words may be combined with an opening sentence—either the topic sentence or a new one written just for the transition—to link two paragraphs. Here are some examples:

Opening sentence of first paragraph:	<u>First</u>, driving at night is harder because the visibility is poor.
Opening sentence of second paragraph:	<u>In addition</u>, fatigue is a problem for the night driver.
Opening sentence of third paragraph:	<u>Finally</u>, the night driver must cope with the occasional drunk driver.

Here is how a specially written transition sentence could be used to link paragraph three to the previous paragraphs:

The problems faced by night drivers don't end here, however. In fact, the worst problem may be drunk drivers.

3. Repeat words and ideas.

This is the "step back, then step forward" approach. First you step back to the ending of the preceding paragraph, then you step forward to the topic of the new paragraph.

Here is an example. This is the first paragraph from the essay on night driving. Notice how the opening sentence of the next paragraph first steps back and then steps forward into the new topic:

> First, driving at night is harder because the visibility is poor. It is, of course, harder to see at night because of darkness. Added to the darkness is the uneven glare from roadside lighting, which makes visibility even poorer. But the worst problem of all is that many drivers do not dim their lights for an oncoming car. Nothing can blind a driver quicker than the dazzling lights of an inconsiderate oncoming motorist. On two-lane highways, many accidents are caused by this temporary blindness. My uncle, for example, ran his car off the road and into a ditch because a semitruck blinded him with its bright lights. The driver of the truck didn't even stop and may not even have known that he or she had caused an accident.

Step back: But even the blinding lights of oncoming trucks don't cause as many nighttime traffic accidents as an even more common problem—fatigue.

Step forward: Fatigue is . . .

Write solid paragraphs.

If an essay can be said to have a meat-and-potatoes section, it is the body, where you prove your thesis. In the body of the essay your evidence and supporting details must be solid. Use all the techniques about paragraph writing that you've learned in this book. If you need to review a topic, use the following table.

TO REVIEW THIS TOPIC	SEE THIS UNIT
The importance of standard English	2
Questions to ask about your audience	3
The three main purposes for writing	3
Writing clear topic sentences	4
Including sharp details in your paragraphs	5
Strategies for writing paragraphs	8–15
The whole essay	16
The thesis statement	17

IN A NUTSHELL

To write the body of your essay, follow these tips:

- Stick to your thesis statement.
- Link your paragraphs.
- Write solid paragraphs.

Here are some ways to link paragraphs:

- Repeat key words from the thesis statement.
- Use transitional words and sentences.
- Repeat words and ideas.

PRACTICING 3

For each thesis statement below, name the strategy you would use to develop it into an essay. Then, choosing one of the thesis sentences, write three topic sentences that support its main point.

1. Seat belts have repeatedly proven their value in saving lives.

Strategy: _____

2. The meaning of the word *terrorist* is clear.

Strategy: _____

3. Saving money, even a little at a time, can bring surprising benefits.

Strategy: _____

4. My old neighborhood and my new neighborhood are as different as night and day.

Strategy: _____

5. My first day at camp was the most horrible day of my life.

Strategy: _____

6. There are three types of animal lovers.

Strategy: _____

7. Forsythia in bloom is the loveliest of all flowering bushes.

Strategy: _____

8. It's easy to plan a wedding if you begin early.

Strategy: _____

9. The hardest job I ever had was selling brushes door-to-door.

Strategy: _____

10. Bikes should be banned from the pedestrian pathways on campus.

Strategy: _____

Thesis sentence selected: _____

Topic sentence for paragraph 1: _____

Topic sentence for paragraph 2: _____

Topic sentence for paragraph 3: _____

PRACTICING 4

Return to Practicing 2 and the introduction you wrote for an essay. Now write a three-paragraph body that will prove your thesis statement. Be sure that you stick to your thesis statement. Save your work; you will need it for Practicing 5.

The Conclusion

The conclusion to your essay is a final, short paragraph that wraps up the essay. This is your "goodbye" to the reader. Unlike the introduction, which has a three-part form—grabber, transition (if necessary), and thesis statement—the conclusion has no special subsections. In some essays, the conclusion may be nearly as long as the introduction; in others it may be only a sentence or two. Your aim in the conclusion is to tie up all loose ends and leave the reader with a sense of completion.

Even though conclusions vary, there are some well-known ones that are best avoided because they add nothing but filler to an essay. The first is the *so-as-you-can-see* ending. Here is an example:

> So, as you can see from what I've written, the proposal to raise the parking fees on campus is bad for the reasons I've given.

If you've given the reasons, you don't need to say that you've given them. Just giving them is enough.

Another stale ending is the *in-conclusion-my-thesis-statement-proves-that* or *states-that* ending. Your thesis statement by now has already been proved. You don't need to rehash it.

> In conclusion, my thesis statement states that family vacations are seldom fun for teens because they deny teens the company of their friends, force them to do things they're not interested in, and usually stick them with baby-sitting. For these very reasons, I am against family vacations if teens have to go on them.

Here are three good ways to end an essay:

1. Give one final thought.

In this conclusion you add one last insightful comment on the topic. Here is an example:

Thesis statement:	Garage sales have become popular because they allow people to get rid of their clutter, earn a little extra money, and meet their neighbors and other people.
Conclusion:	Over the years the garage sale has grown up. Aside from all their other functions, garage sales have become a huge recycling enterprise that operates on the principle, "One person's junk is another's treasure." Garage sales, in fact, ease the pressure on the landfills. Plus, garage sales are fun!

The final thought is that garage sales, in addition to everything else, are also fun.

2. Suggest an action.

Here is an example from an essay on ways to increase your vocabulary:

Thesis statement:	You can increase your vocabulary in three simple steps: Jot down each word you read or hear whose meaning you don't know and look it up later; write down the definition and memorize it; use the new word as soon as possible.
Conclusion:	It pays to increase your word power. You are judged not only by the clothes you wear, which show the outer person, but by the words you use, which show the inner. Begin today to practice the three-step method of building your vocabulary, and within a few months you will find that the image of your inner person has been greatly improved—almost as much as your outer self would be improved by new clothes.

The suggestion—practicing the three-step method for increasing vocabulary will improve the inner person—is the final shot of this ending paragraph.

3. Ask a thought-provoking question.

A thought-provoking question leaves your reader thinking about a point raised by your essay. It is a natural impulse in most of us to want to answer a question, or at least to think about how we would answer it. We are therefore left thinking. An example follows.

Thesis statement: Test taking is always an ordeal for me because of my fear of doing poorly, my nervousness, and my tendency to overprepare.

Conclusion: At the end of every test, I always feel as if I've tried my hardest but been hampered by my nervousness. I also know that no matter whether I was nervous or not, some tests have an important effect on my life. An SAT result, for example, might determine where I can go to college. Yet, I can't help thinking I would do better on tests if they didn't make me so nervous. And I can't help wondering: Is it fair for society to put so much stock in a single event, especially one where my nervous nature might cause me to do worse than I otherwise would?

We are left to puzzle over this question: Indeed, is it fair?

IN A NUTSHELL

In your conclusions avoid these endings:

■ The *so-as-you-can-see* ending.

■ The *in-conclusion-my-thesis-statement-states* ending.

Among the various ways of ending an essay are these:

■ Give one final thought.

■ Make a suggestion.

■ Ask a final question.

PRACTICING 5

Complete the essay you started in Practicing 2 and continued in Practicing 4. Write a forceful conclusion, using one of the methods suggested above.

The Whole Essay

No matter what kind of essay you write or on what topic, it will consist of the three parts we just discussed—the introduction, body, and conclusion. Keep in mind what the shell of an essay looks like.

Title of Essay

**Introduction
Grabber, followed
by transition
(if necessary)
Thesis statement**

_____
_____
_____
_____
_____

Topic sentence: _____

Body

Topic sentence: _____

Body

Topic sentence: _____

Body

Conclusion

You can use this shell for writing an essay on any topic. Before you begin writing your essay, copy down this shell and use it as your model to be filled in with different words, depending on your topic.

Here is this pattern used in an actual student essay:

Title of essay   Sweating It Out

**Introduction
(Grabber)**   My hands were trembling. A cold sweat washed over my brow. When the teacher told us to begin, I was in such a state I could hardly turn the page. I tried to begin by answering the first question, but before I could write I had to stop my knees from knocking. I was sure that everyone in the room could hear my quaking.

**Thesis
statement**   Test taking is always an ordeal for me because of my fear of doing poorly, my nervousness, and my tendency to overprepare.

**First
paragraph:
developed
by narration**   I have a tremendous fear of doing poorly when I sit down to take a test, and no matter how hard I try, I can't seem to shake the feeling. But I know exactly where I got it from and how it began. I was in first grade and taking a

test that would determine who got into the "Discovery Program," which was for gifted kids only. Our teacher was a substitute, and she cracked a joke about how the test would show who among us were horses and who were donkeys. We all wanted to be horses, not donkeys, but as I took the test, I kept saying to myself, "This is going to make you look like a donkey." And it did. I didn't get into the program, but my best friend did. I was so ashamed that when I was given another chance to take the test in third grade, I begged my mother not to make me.

Second paragraph: developed by definition of *nervousness*

My nervousness is another reason I don't test well. By <u>nervousness</u> I don't mean "fear." I think I have as much courage as anyone my age. I have done the usual stupid things and taken my share of risks. The nervousness I'm talking about is a raw physiological reaction to situations where I feel stress. My palms sweat; my heart races; I become confused and feel as if the ground itself might swallow me up. Yet this feeling comes over me in situations that pose no physical risk, like meeting a new girl, for example. My doctor told me that I'm adrenaline sensitive. When I asked him what that meant, he said it meant that I was a nervous person. And I am. I just can't help the extreme way that my body reacts to stress.

Third paragraph: developed by comparison/ contrast

Finally, I have a tendency to overprepare for a test. When I compare myself and the way I prepare for a test with the way my best friend, Jason, prepares, I see right away that I'm overdoing it. For a psych test we had last week, Jason read the chapter through twice and skimmed it once, the night before the test. In contrast, I read it six times, all the way through. Some sentences and paragraphs I knew by heart. Even the morning of the test I was still hitting the books whereas Jason was talking about baseball. Then the test began, and I broke out in a cold sweat and became confused—from knowing too much, I think. I did all right, but no better than Jason, who didn't work as hard but who managed to stay cool.

Conclusion: ends with a question

At the end of every test, I always feel as if I tried my hardest but was hampered by my nervousness. Yet, I also know that no matter whether I was nervous or not, some tests have an important effect on my life. An SAT result, for example, might determine where I can go to college. Yet I can't help thinking I would do better at tests if they didn't make me so nervous.

And I can't help wondering: Is it fair for society to put so much stock in a single event, especially one where my nervous nature might cause me to do worse than I otherwise would?

Unit Test

Check the response that most accurately answers the question.

Example: What are the three parts of an essay?

     (a). Thesis statement, example, and conclusion.

     (b). First paragraph, second paragraph, and third paragraph.

✔ **(c).** Beginning, middle, and end.

     (d). Supporting evidence, details, and facts.

1. What are the three parts of a typical introduction?

     (a). Title, subject, and anecdote.

     (b). Opening sentences, transition, and thesis statement.

     (c). Appeal to reader, mention of subject, and introduction of author.

     (d). Outline of the essay, major points of the essay, thesis statement.

2. What is the function of a grabber?

     (a). It pulls the reader into the essay.

     (b). It takes the reader's attention away from the thesis.

     (c). It alerts the reader to the fact that the essay is ending.

     (d). It is a one-sentence summary of the essay.

3. Which of the openings that follow is the best for an essay on how education should not smother students' creativity?

     (a). In my opinion, no school should stop students from thinking.

     (b). When a young person is forbidden to express himself/herself, that person tends to follow any loud voice.

     (c). Is conformists all we want our students to be?

     (d). The writer Robert Lindner once wrote, "Our schools have become vast factories for the manufacture of robots."

4. Why do personal experiences make good openers?

_____ **(a).** Everyone likes to hear about a personal experience.

_____ **(b).** They are always sad and make the reader feel lucky.

_____ **(c).** They are usually unimportant, so you don't have to pay attention.

_____ **(d).** They do not make good openers.

5. Which of the following is a good tip for using facts?

_____ **(a).** Always get your facts from a book.

_____ **(b).** Be sure your facts are facts and not opinions.

_____ **(c).** Repeat your facts several times throughout the essay.

_____ **(d).** Make sure your facts are not politically biased.

6. What technique can help you stick to your thesis statement?

_____ **(a).** Copying it on a post-it and pasting it on your refrigerator.

_____ **(b).** Not thinking about anything else as you write.

_____ **(c).** Telling your roommate to remind you of it.

_____ **(d).** Underlining its key words.

7. Why is it necessary to link your paragraphs?

_____ **(a).** Your page will look better.

_____ **(b).** Your reader can take a breath.

_____ **(c).** Your reader can follow your train of thought.

_____ **(d).** Your paper will be shorter.

8. What is a solid paragraph?

_____ **(a).** One that is full of information.

_____ **(b).** One that repeats the key words of the thesis.

_____ **(c).** One that reveals a sense of humor.

_____ **(d).** One that uses all of the techniques of writing good paragraphs.

9. What should your aim be in writing your conclusion?

_____ **(a).** To tie up all lose ends and leave your reader with a sense of completion.

_____ **(b).** To greet your reader one more time.

_____ **(c).** To say goodbye to your reader.

_____ **(d).** To repeat your introduction and title.

10. A good essay will always be

—— **(a).** funny.

—— **(b).** long.

—— **(c).** well-organized.

—— **(d).** full of big words.

Unit Talk-Write Assignment

What follows is a student's rambling talk about an old-fashioned institution—the milkman. Search through this spoken material to extract the following ingredients for an essay: a grabber to introduce the essay, a thesis to control the essay, three topic sentences to form the body of the essay, and a final sentence to conclude the essay. Use the space that follows to write the skeleton of your essay.

Spoken Paragraph

Rats! Out of milk again. Now I've got to stop everything I'm doing and run to the store. What a bummer! How I wish we had Mr. Garrett to deliver milk, cream, cheese, orange juice, and eggs directly to our house. When I visit my grandmother in California, I enjoy the fact that she has a friendly milkman who takes good care of his route customers. Mr. Garrett delivers dairy products every Tuesday and Thursday morning. The guy is on such friendly terms with his customers that he actually steps into their kitchens to check the refrigerator's stock. Then he might say, "Mr. B, you have plenty of fresh milk until Thursday. No need to add any." Then he leaves, but not before telling one of his funny jokes. He's like a member of every family on his route. Even watch dogs don't bite him. They just jump on him with friendly yelps because they're so tickled to see him. He has been known to jump into the middle of a roughhouse fight between neighborhood kids, separating them while he reminds them that their mothers wouldn't like how they're behaving. I heard he even prayed with a couple on his route who planned to get a divorce. With someone like Mr. Garrett watching your fridge and making sure you're stocked, you never have to bother with last-minute runs to the market. By the way, if Grandma wants an extra order, like chocolate milk or ice cream, she just leaves a note on the door, and, like magic, Mr. Garrett fills her order. I sure do wish they'd bring back the old-fashioned personal milkman.

Written Essay

Title of Essay

Introduction: _____
_____
_____

Thesis statement: _____
_____
_____

Body: _____
(First topic sentence)   _____
_____
_____

Body: _____
(Second topic sentence) _____
_____
_____

Body: _____
(Third topic sentence)   _____
_____
_____

Conclusion: _____
_____
_____
_____

Unit Collaborative Assignment

Join with three other classmates and plan an essay on one of the following topics.

1. Are our thoughts as important as our action?
2. Being tolerant of others.
3. Moral responsibility.
4. The pleasures of being alone.
5. An emotional experience.

Use the essay shell given in this unit. Working together, write:

- A thesis statement.
- An attention-grabbing opener.

- Three topic sentences for the body of the essay.
- A suitable conclusion.

Unit Writing Assignment

Write a complete essay on the group topic you chose and developed in the Unit Collaborative Assignment above. Or, if you prefer, choose one of the other topics and develop it into an essay.

Photo Writing Assignment

Study the following picture of a football game. Then write an essay of five paragraphs (introduction, three-paragraph body, and conclusion) in which you argue that playing football (or another team sport) teaches important values. Ask yourself these questions as you develop your essay:

- Do I have an attention-grabbing opener?
- Did I place my thesis statement at the end of the first paragraph?
- Do the three body paragraphs support the thesis statement?
- Does my ending wrap up the essay?

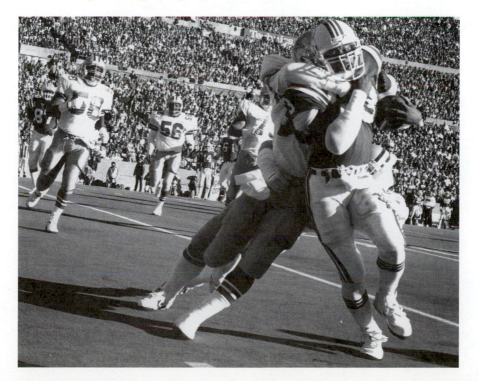

19

Revising, Editing, and Proofreading

"Revising means, literally, seeing again."

Writing a good essay requires us to play two roles. First, we must be writers, putting words down on the page. Then we must become readers, putting ourselves in the reader's shoes to evaluate what we have written.

This is what you did as a writer:

You wrote a thesis statement.

You wrote an attention-getting introduction.

You supported your thesis statement, beginning each paragraph with a topic sentence.

You wrote the first draft.

Now, to improve and correct your work, you must take the role of reader. Here is what you must do:

- Revise what you have written.

- Edit your revised essay.

- Proofread your essay before you hand it in.

So far, we have mainly discussed your role as a writer. In this unit we will focus on your role as a reader. Naturally, there is some carryover from one role to the other. For example, as you pore over your work from the reader's viewpoint, you will occasionally become the writer again to correct or improve it.

Revising

Revising means, literally, "seeing again." It is during this stage that you have the chance to make your writing better. Indeed, most writers do their best work during revision. Here is where you shift paragraphs, add details, scrap sentences, cut deadwood, substitute words—in short, do anything necessary to improve the writing.

However, don't revise immediately. Instead, after you have completed your first draft, put it aside for a while—if you can—to let it "settle." Then pick it up a few days later and give it a fresh look. Don't worry if you're not satisfied with it. Most writers feel exactly the same way about their first drafts—dissatisfied. In any case, no matter how rough your draft seems, at least you now have something to work with.

One good way to start the revision process is to read your paper aloud—to someone else or to yourself. Reading your paper aloud gives you a sense of how it sounds. A checklist you can use appears on the inside cover of this book.

Notice that the Revising Checklist tells you the units that you need to review if you're unsure how to answer a particular question. Don't be reluctant to go back and review an earlier unit. Indeed, the advice in these units is more likely to sink in only after you actually try to apply it to your own writing. You learn to ride a bicycle in much the same way: not by reading, but by doing.

Revising, like writing, is a uniquely personal process. It can be done in many different ways. Some students like to scribble on their papers, circling words that need deleting or improving, rewriting passages that are muddled, using arrows to add or move sections. A few students hate messiness and revise by writing a second draft on a clean sheet of paper. Still other students go immediately to their computers to work on screen, moving sentences and paragraphs around and adding inserted material. No matter what your style, it is a good idea to double-space your first draft. The added space on the page makes rewriting *much* easier.

Using talk skills to revise your work

Talking can help with revision. Start by reading your work aloud to a partner or friend. Reading aloud forces you to pay attention to every word and not skip any words or sentences. It also helps you to tell how your writing sounds to someone else. Does it sound choppy? Or, do you have a sentence that goes on and on—and on?

To use talk skills to revise, do the following:

- Read your essay aloud to a friend.

- Ask your friend what you can do to improve it.

- Apply every question on the Revising Checklist to your first draft.

- Make changes as you or your friend think of them.

- If you don't understand a question on the Revising Checklist, review the unit where it is discussed.

ESL Advice!

If you're having trouble with idiomatic English, try reading your essay aloud to a native student and ask for suggestions.

If you are working with someone in your class, you will have to take turns going over each other's material. Be patient with each other. The mutual give-and-take will help you both learn how to revise.

If you must work alone, follow the same steps given above. If you feel funny about reading your work aloud, do it in private. Reading your work aloud lets you use your speaker's ear to help judge the writing. Finally, don't be afraid to scribble mercilessly over your first draft. Scratch out and rewrite sentences to your heart's content. First drafts are supposed to look beaten up. If yours is clean and nice, ask yourself honestly: Am I being too easy on myself?

PRACTICING 1

Here is the first draft of an essay that needs to be improved. Read it carefully and then complete the Revising Checklist.

My girlfriend Tiara doesn't get along with my friends. After puzzling over the possible reason, I have decided that Tiara is so needy for attention that her stunning looks can't save her from the annoyance people feel in her presence.

Now, Tiara makes heads turn because she looks exotic. She is from the Middle East and has huge black eyes, creamy skin framed by silky black hair, with a figure to die for. But here is a typical example of what she does. We're in the same geology class, and last Saturday, the teacher organized a field trip to Red Rock Canyon, a desert area filled with unusual geological formations. Who knows how long these rocks have been there and how many winds and rain storms washed over them? Time has ravished many spots of nature. We were to meet at 9:00 A.M. in front of the library to board a college bus that would take us to our destination. At 9:10 Tiara was nowhere in sight, so the driver waited another fifteen minutes. As the bus was ready to pull out, there she came running, with a mane of newly dyed bright purple hair flying in the wind and wearing short shorts, an orange tube top, and flimsy little sandals. "Wait for me!" She shouted happily, and, of course, we did. People who make other people wait are rarely popular. Resentment was written all over the faces of those she had inconvenienced. Worse yet, on the trip she couldn't walk with those flimsy sandals and she kept skinning her legs and knees. Needless to say, she also spent a lot of time pulling up her tube top. By the end of the day, everyone was so disgusted with her.

REVISING CHECKLIST	RESPONSES
1. Do I have a clear thesis statement that controls m̲y̲ essay? (Unit 17)	1. _____
2. Do I get my reader's atten-tion in the introduction? (Unit 18)	
3. Do my body paragraphs have clear topic sentences? (Units 5 and 18)	3. _____
4. Do I support my thesis statement by using the strategies effectively? (Units 8–15)	4. _____
5. Do I stick to the point I make in the thesis state-ment? (Unit 7)	5. _____
6. Do I link the paragraphs of my essay? (Units 7 and 18)	6. _____
7. Is my purpose clear (to entertain, inform, or per-suade)? (Unit 3)	7. _____
8. Have I taken my audience into account? (Unit 3)	8. _____

REVISING CHECKLIST	RESPONSES

9. Have I used standard English throughout? (Unit 2)

9. _____

_____

_____

_____

10. Do I close my essay with a sense of finality? (Unit 18)

10. _____

_____

_____

Now apply the Revising Checklist inside the front cover. Go over the essay point by point. Note problems.

PRACTICING 2

Using your marked Revising Checklist, revise the essay about Tiara. Add new material if necessary.

_____

_____

_____

_____

_____

_____

_____

_____

_____

_____

_____

PRACTICING 3

Now work with a partner to critique each other's revised essays. Begin by comparing your marked Revising Checklists. Did you identify the same major problems?

Then both partners should read their revised essays. Since there is always more than one way to write or say anything, your revisions won't match. But the same revising principles apply. Apply the Revising Checklist to each other's work.

IN A NUTSHELL

Revising means making big changes in your writing. To revise, you should:

- Use the Revising Checklist in this unit.
- Read your essay aloud to a partner.

PRACTICING 4

Choose one of the broad topics listed below to generate a thesis statement for a short essay. Use brainstorming, clustering, or any other method you find helpful to gather ideas. Then write a first draft and revise it using the Revising Checklist. Keep your revised paper because in the next section you will learn how to edit it.

1. Television
2. College
3. Family
4. Music
5. Sports

Editing

When you **revise,** you make big changes. You sharpen your thesis statement or decide to use another strategy to support your point. You might drop one example and choose another that fits better, or you might add a definition. You might rewrite your conclusion to give the essay a better ending.

When you **edit,** you make smaller—but no less important—changes. You look at every sentence to catch errors in grammar, spelling, punctuation, and capitalization. You also check for whether you have used standard English throughout. Editing is an important stage of writing and can make a significant difference in how your final copy looks.

Naturally, revising and editing can overlap. You can catch a big mistake during the editing process, just as you might find a little one as you revise. The trick is to be flexible and open-minded, remembering that your overall aim is to make your essay better.

Editing requires a keen eye. Read your writing slowly and carefully. Concentrate hard on the page as you look for errors that need correction.

Using talk skills to edit

You can use talk skills to edit with a partner, just as you did for revising, or you can edit in a group. To edit in a group requires a little planning ahead, but it is well worth the effort. Form a group of five or six students and agree on a time you will meet to edit. Each student should bring to the edit meeting copies of his or her essay—one for each member of the group.

At the meeting, sit in a circle. One student reads aloud to the group, pausing after each sentence so the group can make editing suggestions. For example, someone might spot a misspelled word. Someone else might ask if a comma is needed before the *and.* You yourself might see a word that is unnecessarily capitalized. After you have read, paused, and discussed each sentence of the first student's essay, the next student reads, and so on, until everyone's essay has been group edited.

The advantages of group editing are obvious. First, several pairs of eyes are better than one. Your friends can point out errors that you didn't even know you made. Second, you can correct these errors and submit a better essay. Finally—and most importantly—you will learn from your mistakes so you won't make them next time. You will learn the rules of grammar, punctuation, capitalization, and spelling and become a better writer.

An Editing Checklist appears inside the front cover of this book. It includes questions about the 20 most frequent writing errors that students make. Part VI discusses each of these errors and gives practice exercises for you to check your understanding. Notice that each question in the Editing Checklist tells you which error in Part VI to check if you are having a particular problem. For example, are you writing a lot of fragments? Check Error 1. Are you having trouble using commas correctly? See Errors 13 and 14.

As with the Revising Checklist, the information in parentheses tells you where to get help with each problem.

IN A NUTSHELL

Editing means going over your material to catch errors of grammar, punctuation, capitalization, and spelling.

To edit your work, you should:

- Use the Editing Checklist.
- Read your essay aloud to a partner or form an editing group.

PRACTICING 5

Edit the two paragraphs that follow. Use the Editing Checklist.

Computers and fax machines are making it possible for people to start businesses in there homes. An example of this new trend is my neighbor mrs. lilly Hammond who graduated from kent law school several years ago and past her bar exams, but could not afford to rent an office for her legal practice. Turning her back bedroom into an office and dealing with her clients at home. She likes the arrangement, both financially and personally because she saves money. And can be home for her children.

My retired computer science teacher, who runs a business from his house. Advising people who need help with their computers. He just left some flyers around the Neighborhood, letting people know that can help them set up their computers show them how to use a new computer program and get glitches out of older programs. I am told that this man is making good money through his home-based business.

PRACTICING 6

Here are two more paragraphs for you to edit, using the Editing Checklist as a guide.

The T-shirt is one of the best fashion inventions of all time, it allows the wearer, whether male of female, to be comfortable. I happen to be male and love to dress informal but yet attractive. It use to be that I felt dressed up only when I wore a white shirt with a tie. Now, I just wear a black cotton T-shirt under a sport coat of any color except Navy. Its' such a relief to sit at a movie or in a restaurant without feeling that your neck is getting a rash from the stiff shirt or that your being strangled by a tie noose.

I've seen women devoted to T-shirts as well. In fact, this summer I spied several girls wearing long T-shirts as dresses that walked along the shopping mall of our city. Looking relaxed yet attractive. Some of these T-shirts were striped to give a naval look others had gold letters stitched on them, such as "DKNY," which apparently stands for "Dona Karen of New York," a well-known designer. Quite a few revealed colored patches of cats, birds, dogs, or flags. But what they all had in common was a sense of comfort. I think T-shirts as a proper fashion statement should be promoted and I'll risk a fashion arest to say so.

PRACTICING 7

Edit the essay that you wrote and revised for Practicing 4. Use the Editing Checklist on the inside cover.

Proofreading

Proofreading means giving your paper one final check for errors you might have missed. Don't rush. Proofreading is crucial to catch any errors that escaped your eye during both revising and editing—

accidentally omitted words, misspellings, and punctuation slipups. In fact, you might ask a classmate to exchange papers for proofreading. At this stage, a writer is often too close to the paper to spot errors easily seen by a stranger's eyes. Indeed, writers often see what they *intended* to write rather than what they actually wrote. If you can't find someone to proofread your work and have only yourself to rely on, we advise you to read slowly, one word at a time.

If you are writing on a computer, be sure to use a spell-check program on your essay. Bear in mind, however, that the spell-check process is not foolproof. A word may be spelled correctly but still misused. For instance, a spell check will not catch the error in the sentence *We baked to dozen cookies.* No spell-check program knows the difference between *to, too,* and *two.*

IN A NUTSHELL

After you've produced a first draft, you should put your paper through the following steps:

- Revising
- Editing
- Proofreading

Student Essay in Progress

In this section we present a student essay in progress. We include:

- The first draft with its revisions
- The second draft with its editing
- The final draft, all proofread

First draft with notes for revising

Having Good Manners   *needs attention-getting opening*

unclear

(When they are young parents teach their kids about   *Explain what manners are*

manners.)Parents always want their kids to have good

manners. When people have good manners there polite

and aren't rude. People use thier manners all of the time

need clear plan of development –   everyday.(Having good manners is important to make   *make thesis clear*

use consistent point of view

1. business friends and to get a job.)If (you) don't have good manners
2. friends
3. family   then no one will like you. Having good manners can be as

simple as saying thank you and please. When you are at

work, you must be polite to your boss and the other
organize ideas more clearly

people around you. If somebody is trying to get a job then

they need to dress nicely and act polite. Nobody will hire a

guy whose slopy and rude. *explain why - give examples*

If you want to have any friends then you need good

manners. If your friends throwing a party, you should tell

give more examples them if you are coming or not. Throwing a party is fun, but
off topic of manners

it is also takes lots of planning. You had to figure out who

to invite and what kind of food to have. (Then knowing how

Fragment

much stuff to buy.) When people dont say if they are

coming then you don't know how much to buy.

unclear People with bad manners are (geeks.) They dont have
Slang

any friends and no one likes them. You should have good

Be more specific manners all of the time. (Even at home.) When someone
Fragment

calls at home, you should take a message and not forget.

give examples

That is rude. It is a bummer to live with rude people even

if their your family. That is why we need manners. *re-write conclusion Focus on why manners are important.*

Edited first draft

The Importance of Good Manners

Keep your elbows off of the table. Don't slurp your soup. Say

"please." Most of us have heard our parents say these phrases

many times before. Did our parents simply enjoy enforcing these

rules, or do good manners actually have a purpose in life? As we

grow, manners, or the socially correct way of acting, become more

and more important. Good manners are necessary to succeed in

business, social, and family situations.

In the work place, good manners can make the difference

and staying unemployed. *to set up an* *one*
between getting a job or not. When calling up for an interview, you

should be polite and professional to the person answering the

phone. ~~Another example of good manners is to~~ arrive^ing at the
 is another way to impress the boss.
interview on time and well dressed ^Wearing jeans or shorts is
 not appropriate   *it is polite to*
~~sloppy~~. Several days after the interview ~~you can~~ send a letter
                                 his or her   *Having good manners like these will*
thanking the interviewer for ~~their~~ time.
impress people in business situations, and can increase one's success in the work place.
        Manners are ^also important in social situations such as parties. ~~If~~
 When a friend   *also* *with a party invitation, one*
~~someone~~ calls ~~to invite you to a party,~~ ~~you~~ should check the date
        accept or decline   *Responding promptly to an*
and ~~respond quickly~~. ~~Calling back about the~~ invitation is an
                                                                    one
example of good social manners. When attending the party, ~~you~~

                                                        A
should not bring people along who weren't invited. ~~G~~uest who
        five or six other   *be*
shows up with ~~a whole bunch of~~ people will probably not ~~get~~
 again   *ing*
~~anymore~~. When ~~you~~ leaves the party it is polite to thank the host
        he or she   *s*   *Friends will feel appreciated when they are*
and ask if ~~they~~ needed any help cleaning up. *treated this way.*
It is easy to forget about using   with family members but manners become very important
        ~~G~~ood manners ~~are vital for a happy home life when dealing with~~   *when*
people live together   We can be considerate to relatives by   ing
~~your family members~~. ~~One example is to~~ remember^ to relay phone
                It can be upsetting
messages. ~~I get really mad~~ when messages are forgotten or

written down wrong. Another problem can result from borrowing
                                                     One
items without asking or returning them. ~~You~~ should always ask

permission to borrow something, like clothes or even toothpaste.

Being polite and returning borrowed items quickly will keep family

members happy. Another way to ~~to~~ respect family members with
                                             entering
good manners is to knock on doors before ~~barging in~~ a room
                                                        This type of
because everyone appreciates having some privacy. ~~B~~ehavio^r ~~like~~

~~this~~ will improve relationships and keep the house peaceful.
                        using
        Many people believe that ~~to use~~ good manners is not
                        is
important, or ^an old fashioned way of behaving. However, parents

realize that manners are important and they teach their children
                                                        Although
how be polite so ~~that~~ they can achieve many things. ~~S~~itting up
        remembering to   *seem like*   *using*
straight and ^saying "thank you" may ~~be~~ a lot of trouble, ~~but~~ good
        keep employers, friends, and family happy.
manners will ~~lead to success~~.

Final draft

The Importance of Good Manners

"Keep your elbows off of the table." "Don't slurp your soup." "Say 'please.'" Most of us have heard our parents say these phrases many times. Did our parents simply enjoy enforcing these rules, or do good manners actually have a purpose in life? As we mature, manners, or the socially correct way of acting, become more and more important. Good manners are necessary to succeed in business, social, and family situations.

In the work place, good manners can make the difference between getting a job and staying unemployed. When calling to set up an interview, one should be polite and professional to the person answering the phone. Arriving at the interview on time and well dressed is another way to impress the boss. Wearing jeans or shorts is not appropriate. Several days after the interview it is polite to send a letter thanking the interviewer for his or her time. Having good manners will impress people in business situations, and can increase one's success in the work place.

Manners are also important in social situations such as parties. When a friend calls with a party invitation, one should check the date and either accept or decline. Responding promptly to an invitation is an example of good social manners. When attending the party, one should not bring people along who weren't invited. A guest who shows up with five or six other people will probably not be invited again. When leaving the party it is polite to thank the host and ask if he or she needs any help cleaning up. Friends feel appreciated when they are treated this way.

It is easy to forget about using good manners with family members, but manners become very important when people live together. We can be considerate to relatives by remembering to relay phone messages. It can be upsetting when messages are forgotten or written down wrong. Another problem can result from borrowing items without asking or not returning them. One should always ask permission to borrow something, like clothes or even toothpaste. Being polite and returning borrowed items quickly will keep family members happy. Another way to respect family members with good manners is to knock on doors before entering a room because everyone appreciates having some privacy. This type of behavior will improve relationships and keep the house peaceful.

Many people believe that using good manners is not important, or is an old-fashioned way of behaving. However, parents realize that manners are important and they teach their children how to be polite so they can achieve high goals. Although sitting up straight and remembering to say "thank you" may seem like a lot of trouble, using good manners will keep employers, friends, and family members happy.

Unit Test

Fill in the blank with the word or words that most accurately complete the sentence.

Example: To improve and correct your writing requires you to be a <u>reader</u>.

1. Writing an essay requires you to play two ___roles___.

2. The literal meaning of *revising* is ___seeing again___.

3. One good way to start revising is to ___read___ your essay aloud to a friend.

4. If you don't understand something on the Revising Checklist, refer to the appropriate ___unit___ where it is discussed.

5. The changes you make when editing are usually ___smaller___ than those made when revising.

6. Group editing is good because several ___eyes___ are better than one.

7. Giving your paper one final check for errors is called ___proofreading___.

8. The student paper in this chapter was written in ___three___ (give number) full drafts.

9. It is best to always ___wait___ a few days before revising an essay.

10. It is a good idea to ___double space___ your first draft to allow space for rewriting.

Unit Talk-Write Assignment

What follows is a *spoken* paragraph expressing one participant's views from a panel discussion on the topic of fathers (or in some cases mothers) who don't make child support payments. It is your job to rewrite these spontaneously expressed ideas into a brief essay on the same subject. Your essay should include an introduction, body, and conclusion. Use the material plus what you know and have read about the topic to write three solid paragraphs. Write in the space provided and use any additional paper you need to do at least three drafts.

Spoken Paragraph

I'm embarrassed to admit this, but my own dad hasn't give my mom a penny toward our support for the last two years. He lives in Montana, and my mom got tired of dinging him all the time. Sure, she could get a lawyer on him, but she doesn't have that kinda money. In fact, she has to work extra hours in order to pay our bills. It's hard on her as a single parent and it leaves us kids home alone a lot more. Even Saturdays and Sundays when she waitresses. Parents who neglect to support their children don't have any idea how furious and bitter children get about this. They see the parent as a loser or a real jerk. Of course, some times I suppose the parent could be out of a job or in some kind of financial mess. But still, if you had the kids, you have to support the kids. You don't just walk away. You ought to have to make up any back payments. I heard where one father moved to a different state so it would be easier for him to hide from making child support payments. How can any parent be so stone hearted that he doesn't give a rip about his own flesh and blood. No wonder some kids don't talk to their fathers for the rest of their lives. I guess the only way to make sure that parents fulfill their obligations to their children is to send them to jail when they don't. Did you hear about the bill that's before Congress now? About making it a felony for parents to cross state lines in order to not pay child support? Some states already have laws to imprison delinquent parents, but they aren't always enforced. We should start enforcing these laws, too. I happen to know several cases where the kids are getting no support—zero, zilch. I say, if you're old enough to have kids, you're old enough to be responsible and pay for them. Period.

Written Essay

_____

_____

_____

_____

_____

_____

_____

_____

_____

_____

_____

_____

_____

_____

_____

_____

_____

_____

Unit Collaborative Assignment

Of all the revising task writers have to do, perhaps the most difficult and time consuming is proofreading. By the time the writer gets around to doing it, the material is so familiar that it seems stale and mistakes are hard to see.

Get together with a classmate and try your hand at proofreading the paragraph that follows. Altogether, you should find 10 errors.

Some inventions have one inventor, but more typically, an invention will have several inventors each contributing a little part to the final product. For example take the case of the bicycle. Most historians concedes that the first bicycle—even though it wasn't a bicycle as we think of the world nowadays—came from the invention of an two-wheeled wooden hobbyhorse in 1791. No one knew who invents it, but a local aristocrat in Paris was seen riding it around Parisian parks. You rode it by stradling a padded saddle and propell it with your feet on the ground like a scooter. This contraption eventually become known as a *velocifere.* Later, in 1817, a German noble man hadded a front wheel that could be steered. Finally, a Scotish blacksmith contributed a forked frame and added treadles that, when pressed by the feet, send power to the rear wheel. That device is considered by many to be the first true bicycle.

Unit Writing Assignment

Use brainstorming or any other technique to gather ideas for an essay on one of the following topics. Be sure that you have a clear thesis statement, topic sentences opening every body paragraph, paragraphs developed with strong evidence, and a strong conclusion. Then revise and edit your essay. Use the Revising and Editing Checklists. Carefully proofread before you submit the final draft to your instructor.

1. How a modern invention changed our lives.

2. The importance of preserving our national parks.

3. A recent fad that you consider good or bad.

4. A controversial issue that's been in the news.

5. How terrorists and their threats have changed your life.

Photo Writing Assignment

The following photo shows a Boy Scout troop. Write an essay about any youth program, such as scouting, 4-H, summer sport camp, or a religious youth organization in which you were involved, saying how it affected you for good or ill. Use the Revising and Editing Checklists to revise and edit. Your teacher may ask you to hand in all three drafts—the first draft, the revised draft, and the edited and proofread final draft.

20

The Sentence

"When we read a sentence, we know who did what or what happened and to whom."

A sentence is a group of words that expresses a complete thought. This completeness is what your speaker's ear uses to recognize a sentence. If someone said to you, "match," you'd probably reply, "What?" meaning, "What do you mean?" If, however, someone said, "If I had a match, I would light the fire." You might reply, "Oh, let me find one." You respond differently because the second statement is complete enough for you to understand it.

Subject and Verb

To be complete, every sentence must have a subject and a verb. In its simplest form, the **subject** is someone who does something:

> The <u>bird</u> sang.
> <u>Dick</u> shouted.
> <u>Mary</u> fell.

Naturally, the subject of a sentence can also be *something* rather than *someone*:

> The <u>car</u> stopped.
> The <u>bell</u> rang.
> <u>Jealousy</u> destroys.

The word that tells what the subject does or did is called the **verb.** From these examples, we know that the bird *sang,* Dick *shouted,* and Mary *fell.* We also know that the car *stopped,* the bell *rang,* and jealousy *destroys.*

Each of these examples is called a **kernel sentence.** A kernel sentence is the smallest sentence possible. Here are some other kernel sentences:

Jump!

Hurry!

Watch out!

These kernel sentences are commands. The subject (you) is implied:

(You) jump!

(You) hurry!

(You) watch out!

Every sentence—no matter how long and complex—contains a kernel sentence. For example:

The bird sang.

Although we can add words to it, making it longer and more detailed, its kernel will still be *the bird sang.* Here are some examples with added words:

Early in the morning, <u>the bird sang</u>.

<u>The bird,</u> spreading its yellow wings, <u>sang</u>.

Despite black clouds and thunder rolls, <u>the bird sang</u>.

<u>The bird sang</u> as if his heart were broken.

Perched on a tree limb, <u>the bird sang</u> until noon.

When we read a sentence, we know who did what or what happened and to whom. Therefore, to find the subject of a sentence, simply do this: First identify the verb. Then ask "Who?" or "What?" in front of it. The answer will be the subject. So, for example, in the sentence *The bird sang* we know that the verb is *sang.* If we ask "Who sang?" the answer is the subject, *the bird.*

PRACTICING 1

Underline the subject once and the verb twice in each of these sentences.

1. The man ate.

2. The clouds drifted.

3. The baby giggles.

4. The bomb exploded.

5. Knives cut.

PRACTICING 2

Underline the kernel sentence in each of these sentences.

1. Greg leaped into the air.
2. Gathering yellow pansies, Marcia lifted the basket.
3. The townspeople voted for the incumbent mayor.
4. The soccer players, victorious grins on their faces, left the field.
5. As the whole family sat down to dinner, she announced her divorce.
6. My hometown named our largest park after Ben Jones, who won a medal in the 1972 Olympics.
7. Jimmy cornered me in the drugstore.
8. Some hideous person stole three of our bikes.
9. Mr. Hightower ran down the road in his underwear.
10. Rain or smog, we walk at 6:00 every morning.

IN A NUTSHELL

Every sentence contains a kernel sentence consisting of a subject and verb.

Prepositional Phrases

Sometimes it's easy to spot the subject of a sentence, but sometimes it isn't. For example, what is the subject of this sentence?

One of Mary's friends gave her a surprise party.

If we apply the test of asking "Who?" before *gave*, we find that *one* is the subject. Because the prepositional phrase *of Mary's friends* comes before the verb *gave*, you might mistake *Mary's friends* for the subject.

A **preposition** is a word that shows the relationship between two things; a prepositional phrase is a group of words beginning with a preposition. A preposition always has an **object**—usually a noun or pronoun that follows it. The preposition and its object make up the prepositional phrase. Here is an example:

Ginger placed the napkin in the napkin ring.

Here the preposition is *in,* and the object is *napkin ring*. Remember this formula:

PREPOSITION	+	OBJECT	=	PREPOSITIONAL PHRASE
on		the table		on the table
to		the sea		to the sea
of		the college		of the college
from		the store		from the store

Below is a list of the most common prepositions:

about	beside	inside	to
above	besides	into	toward
across	between	like	through
after	beyond	near	throughout
against	by	of	under
along	despite	off	underneath
among	down	on	until
around	during	out	up
at	except	outside	upon
before	for	over	with
behind	from	past	within
below	in	since	without
beneath			

One way to avoid mistaking a preposition for the subject of a sentence is to cross out all the prepositional phrases in any sentence whose subject you're trying to find. Here are some examples:

The captain ~~of the baseball team~~ encouraged the players.
The top ~~of the mountain~~ could not be seen.

IN A NUTSHELL

One way to avoid mistaking a preposition for the subject of a sentence is to cross out all the prepositional phrases in any sentence whose subject you're trying to find.

PRACTICING 3

Cross out the prepositional phrase(s) in each of the sentences below. Then identify the subject by circling it.

1. Tom went up the block and down the street.

2. After the lecture, we went into the Orange Room for coffee.

3. She ran out the door without her keys.

4. I'll have a chocolate sundae with fudge sauce and nuts on top.

5. She backed into the driveway without her glasses.

6. We turned into the left lane and stopped at the next light.

7. From the other side we watched.

8. Fred walked around the tent and into the woods.

9. We waited in the lobby for Nick and Steffie, but they were already in their seats.

10. During the night, snow drifted against the door.

PRACTICING 4

Create a prepositional phrase for each of the following prepositions. Then use it in a complete written sentence.

1. on

_____

_____

2. under

_____

_____

3. without

_____

_____

4. from

_____

_____

5. near

_____

_____

6. between

_____

_____

7. behind

_____

_____

8. off

_____

_____

9. like

_____

_____

10. throughout

_____

Action Verbs and Linking Verbs

Verbs tell us who did what action in a sentence. However, what about a verb like _is?_ What action does _is_ describe? In fact it describes no action because _is_ is a linking verb.

There are two main kinds of verbs: action verbs and linking verbs. **Action verbs** describe an action. They tell us that the subject did a particular something. Here are examples:

Jack **answered** the question.

The dog **chewed** the bone.

Jerry **served** the drinks.

A **linking verb** connects the subject to other words that say something about it. Here are some examples:

My family **is** poor.

Grandpa **looks** happy.

The cheese **smells** bad.

That music **sounds** odd.

The linking verb _is_ connects the subject _family_ to the word _poor,_ which is the family's condition. Likewise, _Grandpa_ is linked to _happy_ by the linking verb _looks, cheese_ to the word _bad_ by the linking verb _smells,_ and _music_ to the word _odd_ by the linking verb _sounds._ Linking verbs are said to be _linking_ because they _link_ the subject to other words that tell us something about the subject.

SOME COMMON LINKING VERBS

am	sound
are	look
has been	appear
is	seem
was	taste
were	smell
feel	

Note: Some linking verbs can also act as action verbs, depending on their role in the sentence. Here are some examples:

To smell

Linking: That cheese *smelled* rotten.
Action: The rat *smelled* the cheese.

To taste

Linking: The strawberries *taste* sweet.
Action: The soldiers *taste* the water.

PRACTICING 5

Circle the linking verb(s) in each of the following sentences.

1. Addictions are dangerous.
2. Missy is a tiny parakeet.
3. Harry Pendergast was my dad's banker.
4. Her car looked old and battered.
5. Most people appear honest.
6. Does the apple pie taste as good as it looks?
7. College freshmen often feel insecure.
8. The sky looks overcast.
9. Cheeseburgers are popular everywhere.
10. My cousin has been my best friend.

Be careful not to confuse an infinitive with the preposition *to* followed by a noun or a pronoun.

Infinitive: Jennifer decided to skip the party.

Preposition: Jennifer went to the party.

IN A NUTSHELL

Verbals—words that look like verbs but do not act like verbs—come in three kinds: gerunds, participles, and infinitives.

- Gerunds act as nouns.
- Participles act as adjectives.
- Infinitives consist of *to* plus a verb.

PRACTICING 10

Underline only the infinitives in the following sentences. Do not underline if *to* is a preposition.

1. How do you plan to win?
2. I plan to offer the job to Jim.
3. Don't forget to visit your elderly aunt.
4. We prefer to walk to the library.
5. Many students try to cram for tests.
6. He hesitates to drive at night.
7. I ran to see what had happened to her.
8. They did not want to risk their reputations for him.
9. Just cut some string and bring it to me.
10. Peter's pulse began to quicken.

PRACTICING 11

Underline the verb and circle the infinitive in the following sentences.

Example: The wind <u>began</u> (to blow).

1. We are expecting to settle in Kentucky.
2. All the mothers preferred to stay with their children.
3. Her brother likes to tease her.
4. All of us would like to speak fluent English.

5. Try to keep all the tickets in one envelope.

6. He will certainly have to apologize.

7. To be happy is not my main goal in life.

8. He insisted on his right to leave the country.

9. I plan to cook dinner on Monday.

10. Bullets, real and psychological, aim to kill.

Compound Subjects and Verbs

A sentence with more than one subject is said to have a **compound subject.** Here are some examples:

Mary and Madeline shopped.
The woman and her dog ran.
My roommate and I argued.

A sentence may also have more than one verb—called a **compound verb.** Here are some examples:

Mary walked and shopped.
The woman waved and yelled.
My roommate huffed and puffed.

Compound subjects and verbs may occur in the same sentence:

Mary, Helen, and Isa walked and shopped.
The woman and her friend waved and yelled.
My roommate and I argued, made up, and laughed.

PRACTICING 12

Underline the compound subjects in the following sentences.

1. My boss and his daughter came to my birthday party.

2. Politeness and civility seem to be characteristics of the past.

3. Spaghetti, a green salad, and fresh bread are my favorite meal.

4. A fool and his money are soon parted.

5. Museums, monuments, and castles invite tourists to visit them.

6. Bears, wolves, foxes, and other wild animals should be protected.

7. Newspapers and magazines are great to read on the airplane.

8. Looks plus talent are a good combination.

9. Love and marriage go together like a horse and carriage.

10. Action and freedom are an important part of U.S. history.

PRACTICING 13

Underline the compound verbs in the following sentences.

1. The crook staggered and disappeared.

2. Expensive gifts often displease and embarrass.

3. The French king captured the throne and governed the people.

4. She arched her brows and smiled.

5. We stood in line and talked.

6. Shawna made breakfast and walked the dog.

7. Michael jumped from the car and ran into the house.

8. The vine climbed and curled along the fence.

9. She delicately peeled and ate the orange.

10. Ronnie slept and snored all night.

 **Unit Test**

In the following paragraph, underline all subjects once and verbs (including helping verbs) twice. Circle the verbals (gerunds, participles, and infinitives).

I love to visit Lucinda's Bonjour Café. Everyone should have a private oasis of that kind—a warm, comforting place. Bonjour Café is not an elegant restaurant like restaurants uptown with thick carpets, damask drapes, and someone to check your overcoat. It is just a cozy, clean little shop with a display cabinet full of fresh pastries and a coffee machine for making great capuccino. The motley clientele includes all kinds of old people from the retirement home across the street, small business owners renting in the neighboring mall, and people simply wanting to interrupt their day with a fresh, homemade lunch. Lucinda owns and operates the shop. She is the reason it attracts such a faithful clientele. Lucinda's warm hospitality and her French effervescence are a strong magnet. She goes out of her way to be kind to those frail oldsters limping in on walkers, and she never forgets to ask people about the good or bad events in their lives. My closest friends and I love to meet at Bonjour for lunch or for an afternoon snack. Lucinda will be there to welcome us like long lost members of her family.

Unit Talk-Write Assignment

Listen to this informal conversation between two friends who confide their fears in one another. From this dialogue, develop an essay of at least three body paragraphs defining courage. You may use examples from your own life and memory or from the dialogue between Ted and Bob. After you have completed and edited your essay, underline several examples of verbal forms that you have used (gerunds, participles, and infinitives).

Spoken Dialogue

Ted: Yesterday I had a real scary experience.

Bob: Oh, yeah? What happened?

Ted: I was flying home from San Francisco, and the plane got into some heavy turbulence. It scared the daylights out of me.

Bob: Yeah, I know what you mean. I don't like to fly, either.

Ted: You ever notice how some things scare some people and other things don't? The woman in the seat beside me, for instance, slept through the whole thing. She was even snoring. I couldn't believe it.

Bob: Yeah, like my dentist was telling me the other day, he's got a patient who falls asleep in the chair every time. Can you believe that? Sleeping in a dentist's chair? I could never do that.

Ted: Me, neither. Dentists scare the heck out of me.

Bob: Me? I can't stand tight places. When I broke my wrist last year, I had to have an MRI. I panicked in the tube. I thought I would pass out. It felt like I was in a coffin. Yet the technician was telling me that some people find the experience quite relaxing.

Ted: I'm afraid of running water. I can dive and swim in a lake or in the ocean without any problems. But put me in a river, and I freak.

Bob: Yeah? I'm okay in a river or in the ocean or in a lake. Just don't take me into the deep woods. I'm likely to go bananas.

Ted: I wonder why? I'm not afraid of woods. Just of running water.

Bob:　Not me. I think I could go over Niagara Falls if I had to.

Ted:　Must be something to do with our early childhood experiences.

Bob:　I guess.

Ted:　Kinda makes you wonder, doesn't it? Like, I mean, what's courage anyway?

Bob:　Yeah? Like, for instance, me getting into a river, which is a thing I'm not afraid of, doesn't take any courage. But climbing into an MRI tube, now that's a whole different story.

Ted:　That would be a piece of cake for me. I'd probably fall asleep in there. But put me on a riverbank, and I begin to shake like a leaf.

Bob:　Shoot! That's not scary. That doesn't take any courage.

Ted:　It does, for me. Like, going into the deep woods, for me anyway, doesn't take any courage. I've never had an MRI, but I'm not afraid of tight places, and I'm sure one wouldn't bother me in the least. None of that takes courage for me. But if you ever see me standing in a river, when I get out give me a medal, cause that took guts.

Bob:　So maybe courage is, like, not rescuing someone from a burning building but, like, I mean, doing what you're afraid of—facing up to your fears.

Ted:　That's deep, man. So maybe the soldier who charges a machine gun nest and blows away the enemy, is only doing it because he's not afraid of it. Him doing that is like you going over Niagara Falls.

Bob:　Yeah. Or like you getting an MRI.

Ted:　Who knows. This is too deep, and I gotta get to class. See you later, Buddy.

Bob:　Hang in there.

Written Paragraph

_____

_____

_____

_____

_____

_____

_____

_____

_____

_____

_____

_____

_____

_____

_____

_____

_____

_____

_____

_____

_____

Unit Collaborative Assignment

Choose a partner to whom you ask the questions below and who must write down an answer in a complete sentence. Exchange roles and have your partner ask you the same questions to which you write your answers in complete sentences. Exchange papers. Circle the subject and underline the verb in your partner's paper, while your partner does the same to yours. Do you agree on all the subjects and verbs? In case of disagreement, ask your instructor.

1. Where would you like to spend your next vacation?

2. Why have you chosen this destination?

3. Whom would you choose as a traveling companion?

4. What characteristics make him or her a good companion?

5. How would you describe the place?

6. How expensive or inexpensive is it?

7. What activities would you pursue?

8. How long would you stay?

9. How would this place enrich you?

10. How would you sum up your attitude toward this place?

Unit Writing Assignment

Use the sentences you wrote in the Unit Collaborative Assignment to write about your ideal vacation spot. You may wish to add some additional sentences.

Photo Writing Assignment

Write an essay imagining what you would do if your neighborhood were being evacuated because of a hurricane or tornado. What thoughts would be uppermost in your mind? What possessions would you take with you? Who might be with you? Where would you seek shelter? After you have completed the assignment, including revising and editing, go back over the essay and underline the kernel sentence in each sentence, all participles once, gerunds twice, and infinitives three times.

21

Building Sentences

Every sentence must have a subject and a verb: To this rule, there is no exception. Not every construction with a subject and verb, however, is a sentence. It could be a **dependent clause.**

Dependent and Independent Clauses

A **clause** is a group of words with both a subject and a verb. If a clause makes sense on its own and is a complete sentence, it is called an **independent clause.** The following are independent clauses and, therefore, complete sentences:

> He cleaned his glasses.
> They took the bus home.
> We are saving money for a vacation.

What about the following passages?

> When he cleaned his glasses
> If you take the bus
> While we saved money for a vacation

Each of the above clauses has a subject (*he, you, we*) and a verb (*cleaned, take, saved*), but none makes complete sense. These are **dependent**

clauses—a group of words with a subject and verb that must be connected to an independent clause to make sense.

> John could see the crack—when he cleaned his glasses.
>
> If you take the bus, get off at Maple Street.
>
> While we saved money for a vacation, we didn't feel deprived.

Your ear for language is the best judge of whether a clause makes sense or not and is therefore independent or dependent. Many dependent clauses begin with a telltale sign—one of these words:

who	which
whom	that
whose	

These words are called **relative pronouns.** They get that name because they show how a dependent clause is *related* to a main clause.

A dependent clause may also begin with one of these words, called **subordinating conjunctions:**

after	if	so that	whenever
although	in order that	than	where
as if	now that	that	wherever
because	once	though	whether
before	provided that	unless	while
even if	rather than	until	why
even though	since	when	

Typically, it is these linking words that make a clause dependent. In fact removing the subordinate conjunction changes a dependent clause into an independent one. Here are some examples:

Dependent: Until you forgave him.
Independent: You forgave him.

Dependent: Because you served on the jury.
Independent: You served on the jury.

ESL Advice!

If you don't trust your ear to tell a dependent from an independent clause, look for the presence of a relative pronoun or subordinate conjunction. Either one will help you identify the construction as a dependent clause.

IN A NUTSHELL

- Clauses are either dependent or independent.

- One telltale sign of a dependent clause is the use of a relative pronoun or subordinating conjunction in its beginning.

PRACTICING 1

In the blanks provided, write *D* if the clause is dependent and *I* if the clause is independent. For each clause you label *D,* underline the word that makes the clause dependent.

1. _____ Who spoke with a high, nasal voice.

2. _____ He imagined himself walking down the street.

3. _____ The cover was torn and dirty.

4. _____ Although no one spoke.

5. _____ Rather than covering up the mistake.

6. _____ They stood there with their hats on.

7. _____ Since it is such a beautiful day.

8. _____ That she decided to become a nun.

9. _____ If war could have solved the problem.

10. _____ The temptation is to rush.

PRACTICING 2

In each blank, write an independent clause to complete the sentence.

1. _____ , who won first prize.

2. If you agree, _____ .

3. _____ , where I collapsed from fatigue.

4. Now that he has graduated, _____ .

5. _____ while watering the lawn.

6. Before you give him the gift, _____ .

7. While I'm trying to finish the story _____ .

8. _____ whenever he opens his mouth.

9. If we ask him to join us for lunch, _____ .

10. _____ where we finally found a piece of land for sale.

Three Basic Sentence Types

There are three basic sentence types: simple, compound, and complex. All three sentence types are commonly used in writing and talking. We will discuss each separately.

The simple sentence

A **simple sentence** consists of a single independent clause. First graders routinely write simple sentences such as these:

> I like Billy.
>
> Peggy is mean.
>
> I like green beans.

But the simple sentence, in spite of its name, is not always short, crisp, and childlike. It can be expanded if given more than one subject or verb. Here are some examples:

Simple sentence with plural subject:	The hens and chicks scratched for bugs.
Simple sentence with one subject and three verbs:	Too many people speak without thinking, read without understanding, and work without goals.

Another way to expand the simple sentence is to add **modifiers,** words that describe and explain the subject or verb. Here are some examples:

Simple sentence:	The chicken scratched for bugs.
First expansion:	The chicken, a big, beautiful Rhode Island Red, scratched for bugs.
Second expansion:	The chicken, a big, beautiful Rhode Island Red, scratched for bugs in the dusty barn-yard.

PRACTICING 3

Expand the simple sentences below by adding subjects, verbs, or modifiers.

1. The bed is old.

_____

2. The wife took the stand.

_____

3. The old man sat on the bench.

_____

4. A book can be a good friend.

_____

5. My cousin throws money away.

_____

6. Foolish friends are a burden.

_____

7. To face reality is sometimes difficult.

_____

8. The two cars crashed.

_____

9. My aunt tells wonderful stories.

_____

10. All the foods I like are fattening.

_____

The compound sentence

A **compound sentence** consists of two or more simple sentences joined by a coordinating conjunction. There are seven **coordinating conjunctions:** *and, but, for, or, nor, so,* and *yet.* The simple sentences in a compound sentence should express ideas of equal importance. Here are some examples

Simple: Comic strips entertain. Sermons inspire.
Compound: Comic strips entertain, and sermons inspire.

Simple: Jason must get some sleep. He will get sick.
Compound: Jason must get some sleep, or he will get sick.

Simple: He was athletic. He didn't practice. He lost the match.
Compound: He was athletic, but he didn't practice, so he lost the match.

Simple: She had never ridden a bicycle.
Compound: She had never ridden a bicycle, nor had I. (Notice the change in subject and verb order in a *nor* clause.)

Notice that a comma comes immediately before the coordinating conjunction that joins the sentences.

PRACTICING 4

Use a coordinating conjunction to join each pair of simple sentences into a compound sentence. Write your answers below the sentences.

Example: Money is important. Money can create greed.

1. The dog fetched the bone. Those watching enjoyed the sight.

   _____

   _____

2. I telephoned my grandmother. I congratulated her on her 75th birthday.

   _____

   _____

3. I have dieted for one month. I have not lost any weight.

   _____

   _____

4. The doctor made a house call. He had forgotten his medical bag.

   _____

   _____

5. John will straighten out the living room. It will look good for company.

   _____

   _____

6. Give me a big hug. I need to feel loved.

   _____

   _____

7. The moon is bright and golden. We should go for a walk.

_____

_____

8. I have studied all day. I still don't feel ready for the test.

_____

_____

9. Everyone has left. The room is empty.

_____

_____

10. I drank some strong coffee. Now I can't sleep.

_____

_____

The complex sentence

The **complex sentence** consists of one **or more** independent clauses joined to one or more dependent clauses. Unlike the compound sentence, which connects two equal ideas, the complex sentence emphasizes one idea over the other. The less important idea is said to be *subordinate*. Naturally, the more important idea is expressed in the independent clause:

> Alicia's heart is broken because her sweetheart left.

Alicia's broken heart is the main idea; the less important idea is why it is broken—because her sweetheart left.

Common sense and your ear for language will help you decide which of two ideas is more important and therefore belongs in the independent clause. Here are, for example, two sentences:

> I hung out the American flag. I went to the post office.

If you want to emphasize *going to the post office,* you will put it in the independent clause:

> After I hung out the American flag, I went to the post office.

If you want to emphasize *hanging the American flag,* you will put it in the independent clause:

> Before I went to the post office, I hung out the American flag.

Bear in mind the words that signal a dependent cause. You may wish to review the relative pronouns and subordinating conjunctions on page 356 before you do the exercises.

PRACTICING 5

Join the following sentences into complex sentences using a relative pronoun or subordinating conjunction. Be sure to express the most important idea in the independent clause.

Example: *(Although anger)* Anger causes suffering.*(, indifference)* Indifference is even worse.

1. I congratulated Henry. He was pleased.

   _____

2. We are at a crossroads. We shall succeed or fail.

   _____

3. I bought a Chevrolet. It has more room than a Honda.

   _____

4. We need a curfew on our street. The noise pollution is terrible.

   _____

5. She acts very mature. She is the youngest.

   _____

6. He put down the heavy box. He rang the doorbell.

   _____

7. Skydiving is exciting. It is extremely dangerous.

   _____

8. Children often feel responsible for their parents' divorce. They suffer guilt.

   _____

9. Moving away can be difficult. It often means losing old friends.

   _____

10. I love suspense movies. They keep me awake at night.

    _____

PRACTICING 6

Write a series of sentences on one of your favorite activities—something you really enjoy. Each sentence should be of the specific type listed below.

1. Simple sentence with more than one subject:

_____

2. Simple sentence with more than one verb:

_____

3. Simple sentence with modifiers:

_____

4. Two compound sentences:

   (a). _____

   (b.) _____

5. Three complex sentences:

   (a). _____

   (b.) _____

   (c). _____

PRACTICING 7

Exchange papers with a classmate and discuss the sentences you wrote in Practicing 6. Help each other make any necessary corrections.

The Statement, the Question, the Command, the Exclamation

So far, we've been discussing sentences as grammatical units and classifying them according to their structure. But sentences can also be classified by purpose. Sentences, whether simple, compound, or complex do not always make straightforward statements. Some times they ask questions, give commands, or offer exclamations. Here are some examples:

Simple statement:	The table has not been set.
Simple question:	Has the table been set?
Simple command:	Set the table immediately!
Simple exclamation:	How nicely the table is set!

Compound statement:	Charities receive a lot of money, and they have an obligation to use it wisely.
Compound question:	Do charities receive a lot of money, and do they use it wisely?
Compound command:	Sir, your charity has received a lot of money, but stop wasting it!
Compound exclamation:	How amazing to realize the huge amount of money charities receive and how often they waste it!
Complex statement:	Because diabetes causes heart disease, it is life threatening.
Complex question:	Since diabetes causes heart disease, is it life threatening?
Complex command:	Let's cure diabetes since it is a life-threatening disease!
Complex exclamation:	How sad it is to realize that 20 million people are at risk of becoming seriously ill each year because diabetes is a life-threatening disease!

PRACTICING 8

In the space provided, label the sentences that follow as *S* for simple, *CO* for compound, and *CX* for complex.

Example: _CX_ Was she crying because he left?

_____ **1.** Get out and never come back!

_____ **2.** If the dog bites you, will you sue the owner?

_____ **3.** Why is Ariana so determined?

_____ **4.** How beautifully the lake shimmers and how mysteriously it laps the shore!

_____ **5.** Although you are tired, will you help me?

Sentence Variety

Writers seldom write in only one sentence type for the same reason that good cooks season their food with more than just salt. Any sentence pattern that is overused will quickly seem boring. Variety is the key to a good writing style and can be achieved easily if you use a mix of simple, compound, and complex sentences. The following is a ho-hum passage:

Rap music started during the 1970s. It comes from African chanting. It also comes from chatting. Rap music means "chat music." It contains. . . .

This passage consists of a string of simple sentences. Notice how it is immediately improved when the sentences are varied:

Rap music, which started during the 1970s, comes from African chanting. It also comes from chatting. Rap music means "chat music," and it contains. . . .

This sort of sentence variation is exactly what you instinctively do in your everyday talking. It is what you must also try to do in your writing.

PRACTICING 9

Rewrite the following paragraph to eliminate the choppy effect of too many simple sentences. Read the sentences aloud to determine the relationship between them. Then reduce the number of simple sentences by combining some into compound and complex sentences.

Hairdressers often function as therapists for their clients. They listen to all kinds of personal confessions. I have my hair cut once a month. I am always surprised by what I overhear. Once I heard a women literally broadcast her husband's affair. She told the entire salon. She was speaking above the noise of the blow drier. She was not aware of how loud she was. I have pondered why such intimacy exists between hairdressers and clients. For one thing, hair dressers are service oriented. They are kind to their clients. Also, hairdressers do not belong to most clients' normal social groups. Hairdressers can be objective. They can be uninvolved listeners. Many hairdressers understand human nature. They offer good advice. They offer practical advice. They can help with personal problems.

Unit Test

1. Write a simple sentence with modifiers about the clothing you are wearing today.

2. Write a complex sentence beginning with *Although*. Be sure to place a comma following the dependent clause.

3. In the spaces provided tell whether the sentence is simple *(S)*, compound *(C)*, or complex *(X)*.

   (a). _____ Before we arrive home, let's count the money.

   (b). _____ Think hard, and you will find the answer.

   (c). _____ This pottery, which is made by Hopi Indians, is expensive.

   (d). _____ When I receive your letter, I'll answer it.

   (e). _____ This is a dull, gray morning, but the sun is peaking through the clouds.

4. In the paragraph that follows, underline all independent clauses.

   Parents must preach what they practice. They must not preach morality that they themselves ignore. For instance, Peggy's parents constantly tell her to be more frugal and to quit buying clothes that sit unused in her closet. I find that rather ironic since Peggy's mother wears a different outfit every day and buys only from Neiman Marcus, Saks Fifth Avenue, or some other expensive store. How can Peggy absorb the message of frugality from a spendthrift mother? Then there are my friend Ray's parents. Because they want him to become a lawyer, they criticize him if he ever gets a C. They don't let him go out more than once on a weekend. "You won't get into law school," they say. But I never see Ray's parents without a glass of beer or Scotch in their hands. They drink all the time. Now what kind of hypocrisy have we here? We have parents who preach a gospel of hard work and deprivation while they party. One basic principle of child rearing is this: Parents must preach only those moral principles that they themselves observe.

5. Rewrite the following paragraph to eliminate the choppy effect of too many simple sentences.

   Train watching is an old tradition. It is an American tradition. We do not use trains the way people do in Europe. In Europe people regularly use trains for transportation. They travel from city to city by hopping on a train. But here in the United States, trains are relatively rare. Perhaps that is why people love to watch trains. Retired men especially love to watch trains. They love to watch trains arrive. They love to watch trains depart. My home town is Glendale, California. My home town has a strong tradition of train watching. Every morning a group of men gathers at the Metrolink Station. They gather soon after dawn. These men have little in common. What they do have in common is their love for trains. To them watching trains is wonderful entertainment. Watching trains is cheap, too. They watch freight trains. They watch passenger trains. Every train has its special attraction. When it rains, these men sit in their cars. They watch from the driver's seat. That isn't as much fun. They would rather stand at the rail. They would rather talk about the trains. They would rather talk about the train's exotic destinations. The men have a nice camaraderie. There is another perk to being a train watcher. The train engineer gives an extra toot on the whistle as a train passes. He acknowledges this special band of spectators.

Unit Talk-Write Assignment

When we talk, most of us pay little conscious attention to sentence variety. But the more sophisticated we become in language, the more we are likely to naturally vary our sentences. The following spoken comments—about keeping a neighborhood looking attractive—lack sentence variety. On a separate sheet of paper, rewrite the passage to add sentence variety by using coordinating or subordinating clauses. Be sure to use standard English.

Spoken Paragraph

I don't believe in neighborhood yard police. Every hedge doesn't have to be clipped like every other hedge on the street. Home owners create a home that reflects their taste. But, gee whiz, some yards look trashy. Some yards look like second-hand car lots. One guy up the street keeps a truck on his front lawn. He keeps two motorcycles. He keeps all kinds of weird looking motors. He lets his grass grow tall. He lets his grass get dry. He lets it get brown. I believe in individual freedom. His yard goes too far. Here are some rules I would suggest. They are general. They are easy. Keep all vehicles inside the garage. Keep the garage door down. Trim hedges weekly. Mow the lawn weekly. Water the lawn when the weather is hot. Get rid of all weeds. Get rid of dry tree limbs. If you have children, keep their toys inside when they aren't using them. Keep their bicycles inside when they aren't using them. Mend broken fences. Paint fences when necessary. A peeling fence is super ugly. A fence with broken slats is super ugly. Follow these simple rules. They will make a big difference. People should keep up their own property. Then the combined properties will make a pretty neighborhood. The neighborhood won't look like a shanty town.

Written Paragraph

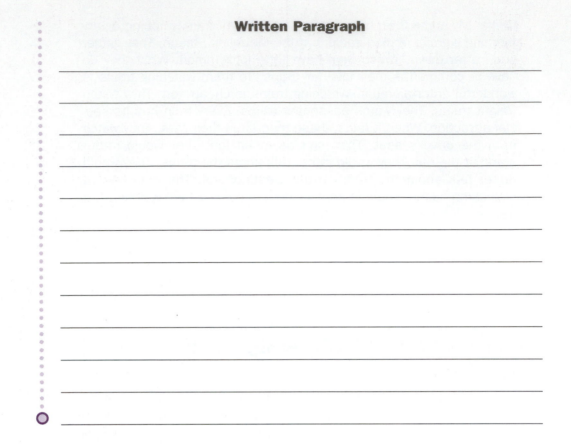

Unit Collaborative Assignment

Get together with two or three classmates to talk about what really bugs you (for example, your boss at work, drivers who don't signal a turn, a roommate who is sloppy, textbooks that are boring). When one student is speaking, the others should write down some of the sentences. When everyone has discussed his or her "bug," take turns presenting and classifying the written sentences as simple, compound, or complex.

Unit Writing Assignment

Using the ideas you accumulated during the Unit Collaborative Assignment, write about some specific aspect of your life or society that annoys you. Make a special effort to use sentence variety.

Photo Writing Assignment

Write an essay discussing the advantages or disadvantages of being an identical twin. To support your view, use your observations or imagination to describe situations in which twins might be involved. You may want to add some humor to your essay. After you have completed the assignment, including revising and editing with a view toward sentence variety, find one example of each type of sentence—simple, compound, and complex. At the bottom of your paper, write and label each sentence.

The 20 Most Common Sentence Errors

This part of *Writing Talk* deals with sentence errors that we all make occasionally. The errors are not arranged in any particular order, and run the range from fragments to misspellings. If you find yourself routinely making any of these errors, review the appropriate material and work the exercises.

Error 1

Sentence Fragments

A **sentence fragment** is only part of a sentence. It is a "wannabe" sentence that lacks either subject, verb, or sense. Sometimes the omission occurs because the writer is "on a roll" and flying across the page. It's fine to write fast and get all your thoughts down in a hurry, but then you must always proofread for errors.

Here are some examples of fragments:

Lost his wallet.	**(Missing subject)**
Mary's job.	**(Missing verb)**
Despite his charm.	**(Missing sense)**

A fragment can spring from one of several causes. If you learn to recognize these, you will be able to avoid fragments in your own writing.

Fragments Caused by a Missing Subject

When you include the verb but forget to write the subject, the result will be a fragment. Here are some examples:

Lenny made a date with Fern. Then never showed up.
After the party they had double milk shakes. Also apple pie.

In these examples the writer mistakenly thought that the subject of the first sentence also applied to the second group of words. It does—but the second thought must be formally joined to the first by a conjunction such as *and* or *but*. If you forget the conjunction, you must write the two thoughts as separate, complete sentences.

Lenny made a date with Fern, but he never showed up.

or

Lenny made a date with Fern. Then he never showed up.
After the party they had double milk shakes and apple pie.

or

After the party they had double milk shakes. They also had apple pie.

PRACTICING 1

Correct the following fragments caused by a missing subject. You can either join the fragment to the sentence before or rewrite it as a separate sentence.

1. The children were excited. And ran into the gym.

_____

_____

2. Murphy found out that he was adopted. Then searched for his biological mother.

_____

_____

3. Grandma put on the rented ice skates. Stood up and let go of the railing. And started to skate as if she were still a teenager.

_____

_____

4. He locked the door. Or at least thought he did.

_____

_____

5. The courtship was passionate. But burned out in two months.

_____

_____

Fragments Due to -ing Words

Some fragments are triggered by an *-ing* word such as, say, *puffing*. Here are some examples:

He sat there with contentment. Puffing on his cigar.
I remained at my desk. Playing with some yellow silly putty.

Why beginning with an *-ing* word often leads to a fragment is something of a puzzle. Possibly, the writer mistakes the *-ing* word for a full verb, but it isn't.

To correct a fragment due to an *-ing* word, either join it to the sentence that went before (use a comma to set off the first part of the sentence), or rewrite it as a separate sentence:

He sat there with contentment, puffing on his cigar.
I remained at my desk, playing with some yellow silly putty.

or

He sat there with contentment. He puffed on a cigar.
I remained at my desk. I played with some yellow silly putty.

PRACTICING 2

Correct the *-ing* fragments by rewriting the sentences below.

1. The lions slept in the sun. Snoring contentedly.

_____

_____

2. Max and I stood at the bus stop. Waiting for Joe.

_____

_____

3. Dad loves soy sauce. Pouring it on everything.

_____

_____

4. Judy loves to create romance. Using candlelight for every dinner she cooks.

_____

_____

5. I am a registered Democrat. Voting often, however, for Republican legislation.

_____

_____

Fragments Due to "To" Constructions

A third common type of fragment is triggered by *to* constructions. Two examples follow:

> We are trying to save money. To pay our bills.
>
> Melany read the newspaper. To see if the Trojans had won the game.

As before, you can correct this type of fragment by either joining it to the sentence before or rewriting it as a separate and complete sentence:

> We are trying to save money to pay off our bills.

> or

> We are trying to save money. We want to pay off our bills.
>
> Melany read the newspaper to see if the Trojans had won the game.

> or

> Melany read the newspaper. She wanted to see if the Trojans had won the game.

Note that you could also move the *to* construction to the beginning of the combined sentence. If you do this, put a comma after the *to* construction.

> To pay off our bills, we are trying to save money.
>
> To see if the Trojans had won the game, Melany read the newspaper.

PRACTICING 3

Correct the following *to* fragments by either joining them to the sentences before or rewriting them as separate sentences.

1. The students went on a trail hike. To clean up the environment.

_____

_____

2. The hog was created as a scavenger. To clean the earth.

_____

_____

3. He wanted desperately to persuade her. To quit calling him "Snooky."

_____

_____

4. She stood outside the office waiting for enough nerve. To speak to her professor.

_____

_____

5. Try to get some spirit and loyalty. To cheer the team on.

_____

_____

Fragments Due to Dependent Words

You have learned about fragments caused by omitted subjects, *-ing* words, and *to* clauses. You have also learned two main ways of correcting fragments—by joining the fragment to the sentence before or by rewriting the fragment as a separate sentence.

We come now to a fourth kind of fragment. This one is triggered by misused relative pronouns and subordinate conjunctions. *This fourth type of fragment is corrected in only one way: by joining it to the sentence before.* Here is a list of relative pronouns that can cause fragments:

who

whom

whose

which

that

Here are examples of fragments caused by unconnected relative pronouns:

We looked at the flat tire. <u>Which</u> was beyond repair.

We have a week to pay our landlord, Mrs. Smith. <u>Who</u> has been most patient.

Here are the corrections:

We looked at the flat tire, which was beyond repair

We have a week to pay our landlord, Mrs. Smith, who has been most patient.

As you can see, both fragments were corrected by joining them to the sentence before. Indeed, both were caused by the writer's use of a period instead of a comma.

Similarly, a fragment can be caused by the misuse of a subordinate conjunction. As with relative pronouns, this type of fragment can only be corrected in one way—by joining it to the sentence before. Here is a list of subordinate conjunctions:

after	although	as if
because	before	even if
even though	if	in order that
now that	once	provided that
rather than	since	so that
than	that	though
unless	until	when
whenever	where	wherever
whether	while	why

Here are some examples of fragments caused by unconnected subordinate conjunctions:

<u>Although</u> his desk is messy. He runs a well-organized program.
<u>Wherever</u> he lives and works. Discord breaks out.

To correct such fragments, simply join them to the neighboring sentence:

Although his desk is messy, he runs a well-organized program.
Wherever he lives and works, discord breaks out.

Note that if the dependent clause comes first, it is separated from the independent clause by a comma:

Incorrect: Since it was raining. We brought along our umbrellas.
Correct: Since it was raining, we brought along our umbrellas.
Or: We brought along our umbrellas since it was raining.

PRACTICING 4

Rewrite the following fragments by joining them to a neighboring sentence.

1. Even though the old roof is leaking. We are not getting a new one.

_____

_____

2. She bought a new watchband. Which looks very expensive.

_____

_____

3. Ask him about his family. If you see pictures of children on his desk.

_____

_____

4. Find out more about his background. Before you hire him.

_____

_____

5. Purchase one good outfit each season. Rather than a dozen cheap ones.

_____

_____

Fragments Due to Added Details

Details added to a sentence can also cause a fragment. Beware of the words listed below. They often lead to added-detail fragments.

especially	including
except	not even
particularly	such as
in addition	for example

Here are three examples of fragments caused by added details:

No one knew exactly what they were feeling. Not even the boss.

They won several prizes. Including a trip to Hawaii, a new car, and a refrigerator.

Abraham Lincoln saw violence as the supreme threat to America. Particularly war.

To correct a fragment caused by added details, simply attach the details to the previous sentence, adding any words necessary. Use a comma to set off the added details.

No one knew exactly what they were feeling, not even the boss.

They won several prizes, including a trip to Hawaii, a new car, and a refrigerator.

Abraham Lincoln saw violence as the supreme threat to America, particularly war.

If the additional detail fragment is long, you can make it into a separate sentence:

Fragment: Fred tends to antagonize people because he acts like a real jerk. For example, never being on time, talking only about himself, interrupting others, and talking with his mouth full.

Corrected: Fred tends to antagonize people because he acts like a real jerk. For example, he's never on time, talks only about himself, interrupts others, and talks with his mouth full.

PRACTICING 5

Correct the following fragments caused by added details by joining them to the sentence before.

1. Rick is so paranoid he's put three locks on his door. In addition to installing a security system.

   _____

   _____

2. She can't stand to be touched. Except by her own sister.

   _____

   _____

3. I suffer from allergies all year round. Ragweed, treemold, and dust.

   _____

   _____

4. We gave her some excellent suggestions for staying out of debt. Including creating a budget.

   _____

   _____

5. A major problem of our industrialized world is job boredom. Such as the boredom of factory assembly jobs.

   _____

   _____

Error No. 1 Review

The following paragraph contains fragments. Correct each error by one of the methods you have learned.

I often wonder how old people manage to stay happy. Especially when their health fails. One afternoon I expressed this wonderment to my 85-year-old grandmother. Because I felt it important to find an answer. She was in her wheel chair. Having suffered a broken hip last year. I sat in a chair next to her. Thinking about how frail she had gotten. Though I didn't really know exactly what words to use. I finally took courage and asked, "Grandma, how do you handle being confined to a wheel chair? When you were always so active?" She thought for an instant. Then she said, "Getting old is not for sissies. Not even for people who are not sissies. Especially if you have lost your health and mobility. But, as long as I have my mind, I can enjoy something every day. For instance, your visit right now. It's such fun to hear about your college life. Particularly the classes you are taking and the friends you are making." What she was really telling me was that people have to make the best of their situation. Which is true at any age. Not just when you're old. I felt inspired by her attitude.

Error 2

Run-On Sentences

A **run-on sentence** is actually two sentences written as one. There are two main types of run-on sentences: the fused sentence and the comma splice.

The **fused sentence** consists of two sentences joined—or fused—without any punctuation between them:

We drove to Las Vegas it is an exciting city

Here is how the sentence should be written:

We drove to Las Vegas. It is an exciting city.

The second type of run-on sentence is the **comma splice**—two full sentences separated by a comma instead of a period:

We took a day trip to Hoover Dam, it's so impressive.

Here is the sentence, corrected:

We took a day trip to Hoover Dam. It's so impressive.

PRACTICING 1

In the blanks provided write *FS* if the run-on sentence is fused and *CS* if it is spliced. Then correct the error.

1. _____ Stop talking to me I have no time for this.

2. _____ You must be on time, he will be angry if you aren't.

3. _____ Golf is a very hard game it is probably the hardest game of all.

4. _____ It was a lovely evening, there wasn't a cloud in the sky.

5. _____ Take the bus save gas money.

Correcting Run-On Sentences

There are four ways to correct run-on sentences. Take, for example, this one:

> I'm in a good mood you are in a better mood.

To correct it, you can do one of the following:

■ Put a period at the end of the first sentence:

> I'm in a good mood. You are in a better mood.

■ Put a semicolon at the end of the first sentence:

> I'm in a good mood; you are in a better mood.

■ Put a coordinating conjunction at the end of the first sentence (note that a comma goes before the conjunction):

> I'm in a good mood, but you are in a better mood.

■ Use a subordinating conjunction (note that a comma is placed between the two clauses):

> Though I'm in a good mood, you are in a better mood.

Note that no comma is needed if the independent clause comes first as in the example that follows:

> I'm in a good mood, though you are in a better mood.

PRACTICING 2

Correct the following run-ons in all four possible ways.

1. He missed his plane he had to take a later flight.

Insert a period: _____

Insert a semicolon: _____

Insert a coordinating conjunction and comma: _____

_____

_____

Insert a subordinating conjunction and comma: _____

_____

_____

2. I like to play chess I'm no good at the game.

Insert a period: _____

Insert a semicolon: _____

Insert a coordinating conjunction and comma: _____

_____

_____

Insert a subordinating conjunction and comma: _____

_____

3. I'll go to the bookstore we can drive your car.

Insert a period: _____

Insert a semicolon: _____

Insert a coordinating conjunction and comma: _____

_____

_____

Insert a subordinating conjunction and comma: _____

_____

_____

4. She lived for a while in Mexico she was not happy there.

Insert a period: _____

Insert a semicolon: _____

Insert a coordinating conjunction and comma: _____

_____

_____

Insert a subordinating conjunction and comma: _____

_____

_____

5. Many men have courted Cathy none has been successful.

Insert a period: _____

Insert a semicolon: _____

Insert a coordinating conjunction and comma: _____

_____

Insert a subordinating conjunction and comma: _____

_____

_____

PRACTICING 3

Correct the following run-on sentences using one of the four possible ways.

1. Jennifer is a lucky person she should play the lottery.

_____

_____

2. The political season is upon us, there are daily ads on the television for the candidates.

_____

_____

3. Worms are beneficial to the soil they are everywhere.

_____

_____

4. Shop lifting is not just a nuisance crime it is paid for by honest shoppers.

_____

_____

5. Speeding is a common traffic offense it is not as bad as reckless driving, though.

_____

_____

6. My landlord is very punctual he's always on-time to collect the rent.

_____

_____

7. Don't sneeze on me, I don't want your cold.

_____

_____

8. I'm madly in love with my neighbor she doesn't even know I exist.

_____

_____

9. Men are vainer than women they just hide it better.

_____

_____

10. Many people read for pleasure, on the other hand, more people read for business.

_____

_____

Error No. 2 Review

The following long paragraph contains fused sentences and comma splices. Correct each error in any way you choose.

One summer I worked as a lifeguard at the local pool, I found the job surprisingly difficult. Chief among my difficulties was keeping the rough housing kids in line, especially the teenagers, I found that frequently they would defy my authority. Since I was a teenager myself, it was a constant struggle to control them, I had to really put my foot down. One day an incident occurred that taught all of us a lesson. Some boys were horsing around in the deep end, dunking each other and splashing I told them to stop but they wouldn't listen they kept right on, churning up the water and disturbing other swimmers I yelled at them repeatedly. Finally, I said to myself, that's it, this has to stop and it has to stop right now. I got off my lifeguard stand and went down to the pool deck to really let them have it when I thought I saw the vague outline of a submerged swimmer. I screamed at the boys to stop their splashing they screamed right back at me. I dove in they started to splash me, too, but in spite of all the foam I swam to the bottom, found an unconscious swimmer, and brought him to the surface. While someone called the paramedics, I worked on the boy the other teenagers suddenly become very serious they stopped all the horsing around. By the time the paramedics arrived, I had pumped most of the water out of the victim's lungs he was conscious and talking. He said he had had a seizure because of all the splashing he had been unable to attract attention and get help. For the rest of the summer, those boys never gave me any more trouble I think they realized that they had almost caused someone to drown.

Error 3

Lack of Subject-Verb Agreement

Subjects and verbs must agree in number: that is the one rule of subject-verb agreement. A singular subject always takes a singular verb; a plural subject always takes a plural verb. Most of the time, this rule is plain and easy to follow, as in the following sentences:

Peggy admires Fred.

The workers admire Fred.

Peggy, a singular subject, takes the singular verb *admires. Workers,* a plural subject, takes the plural verb *admire.*

We are also likely to come across sentences like these:

Jack don't want company.

There is pickles in the refrigerator.

He, a singular subject, is incorrectly paired with the plural verb *don't. Pickles,* a plural subject, is incorrectly paired with the singular verb *is.*

Subject-verb agreement errors are typically caused by some common words and grammatical situations. Here they are, in no particular order:

■ *Don't, was,* and *wasn't:*

Incorrect: He don't remember his promise.
Correct: He doesn't remember his promise.

Incorrect: You was right again.
Correct: You were right again.

■ *Each, every, either/or,* and *neither/nor:*

Incorrect: Each of us are to blame for the mistake.
Correct: Each of us is to blame for the mistake.

Incorrect: Either of the shirts are the right size.
Correct: Either of the shirts is the right size.

■ Prepositional phrase between a subject and verb:

Incorrect: One of the three television sets are broken.
Correct: One of the three television sets is broken.

■ Sentences beginning with *there/here:*

Incorrect: There is too many potatoes to peel.
Correct: There are too many potatoes to peel.

Incorrect: Here is the best solutions to the problem.
Correct: Here are the best solutions to the problem.

■ Questions:

Incorrect: Where is the warm blankets?
Correct: Where are the warm blankets?

■ Compound subjects joined by *and, or, either/or,* or *neither/nor:*

Incorrect: The doctor and nurse was talking.
Correct: The doctor and nurse were talking.

Incorrect: The doctor or the nurse were upset.
Correct: The doctor or the nurse was upset.

■ The indefinite pronouns *each, everyone, anybody, somebody,* and *nobody:*

Incorrect: Each of the passengers wish to get off here.
Correct: Each of the passengers wishes to get off here.

■ *Who, which,* and *that:*

Incorrect: Larry is one of those people who gives cheap gifts.
Correct: Larry is one of those people who give cheap gifts.

We'll take up these situations one by one.

Do, Don't, Was, and Wasn't

Subject-verb disagreements are often caused by the words *do* and *don't,* *was* and *wasn't.* Here are the correct forms of *to do:*

SINGULAR	PLURAL
I do	We do
You do	You do
He, she, it does	They do

Here are examples of agreement errors made with *do* and *don't*:

Incorrect: She do her assignments on time.
Correct: She does her assignments on time.

Incorrect: He don't realize what time it is.
Correct: He doesn't realize what time it is.

Was and *wasn't* are also often involved in many subject-verb agreement errors. Here are the correct forms:

SINGULAR	PLURAL
I was	We were
You were	You were
He, she, it was	They were

Here are some examples of errors commonly made with this verb:

Incorrect: You was in the kitchen.
Correct: You were in the kitchen.

Incorrect: They was eating taffy apples.
Correct: They were eating taffy apples.

PRACTICING 1

Underline the correct verb in parentheses.

1. They (was, were) sitting in the bleachers.
2. That answer (doesn't, don't) make sense.
3. (Wasn't, Weren't) you already up by 6:30 this morning?
4. Donna, you (was, were) supposed to get dessert.
5. Matthew (doesn't, don't) always act on principle.

Each, Every, Either/Or, and Neither/Nor

The words *each, every, either,* and *neither* all take a singular verb. Here are some examples:

Each dog, cat, and owner was (not were) listed by name.
Every skirt and blouse is (not are) being ironed and folded.
Neither of the senators votes (not vote) for more college funds.
Either of the photos is (not are) flattering to her.

Don't be confused by the prepositional phrase—for example, *of the photos*—that usually follows *each, every, either,* or *neither.* Cross it out and the verb choice will be clear.

Either/or and *neither/nor* are also trouble-spots. Here are some examples:

Incorrect: Neither the pitcher nor the catcher were any good this season.

Correct: Neither the pitcher nor the catcher was any good this season.

Incorrect: Neither the teacher nor the student were in the wrong.
Correct: Neither the teacher nor the student was in the wrong.

If one subject joined by *either/or* or *neither/nor* is singular and one is plural, the verb should agree with the nearer subject.

Incorrect: Either the coyotes or our dog bark all night.
Correct: Either the coyotes or our dog barks all night.

Incorrect: Either our dog or the coyotes barks all night.
Correct: Either our dog or the coyotes bark all night.

PRACTICING 2

Underline the correct verb in parentheses in the following sentences.

1. Neither of the sandwiches (has, have) mayonnaise.

2. Each of the contestants (hold, holds) a little flag.

3. Every house on the block (is, are) blue.

4. Either the criminal or the victims (is, are) being interviewed now.

5. Neither the cherries nor the apricots (has been, have been) picked.

Phrases Between a Subject and Its Verb

A prepositional phrase that comes between a subject and verb can cause an agreement error. Here is a list of common prepositions:

about	along	behind	between
above	among	below	beyond
across	around	beneath	by
after	at	beside	despite
against	before	besides	down

during	near	past	underneath
except	of	since	until
for	off	throughout	up
from	on	through	upon
in	out	to	with
into	outside	toward	within
inside	over	under	without
like			

Here is a typical agreement error caused by a prepositional phrase coming between a subject and verb:

Only one of his many movies have won an Oscar.

The prepositional phrase *of his many movies* comes between the subject *one* and the verb *have*. However, the subject is still *one*, and *one* is always singular. Cross out the prepositional phrase and the subject is immediately clear:

Only one ~~of his many movies~~ has won an Oscar.

PRACTICING 3

Cross out all prepositional phrases in the sentences that follow. Circle the subject and underline the correct verb.

1. The bicycles leaning against the ladder (is, are) for sale.

2. The sheets on the bed (look, looks) like silk.

3. That box of cans and bottles (go, goes) to the recycling center.

4. Out of season, a pound of cherries (costs, cost) more than $5.00.

5. The vase on the piano (is, are) filled with pink silk flowers.

Sentences Beginning with There/Here

Subject-verb agreement errors can easily occur in sentences that begin with *there is, there are, here is,* and *here are.* Here are some examples:

Incorrect: There <u>was</u> three women sitting in the back row.
Correct: There <u>were</u> three women sitting in the back row.

Incorrect: Here <u>is</u> the black buttons to sew on my coat.
Correct: Here <u>are</u> the black buttons to sew on my coat.

In all these examples the writer is confused by *there* or *here,* which strike the ear as singular. Neither *here* nor *there,* however, is the subject of the sentence. If you're confused by such sentences, reword them to make the subject come before the verb, and the mistake will quickly become visible.

> Two women were sitting in the back row.
> The black buttons to sew on my coat are here.

PRACTICING 4

Underline the correct verb in parentheses. Circle the subject.

1. Here (is, are) Linda Palmer's application.

2. There (is, are) the Colorado Rockies.

3. There (is, are) times in life that try my soul.

4. Here (is, are) the books you requested.

5. There (was, were) two clouds on either side of the rainbow.

Questions

Most sentences that we write or speak are statements, such as these:

> The stars are out.
> The apple is green.

In these, and in most statements, because the subject comes before the verb, it is easy to spot an agreement error.

On the other hand, when we ask a question, the verb typically comes before the subject:

> Where are the stars?
> What color is the apple?

With the subject following the verb in a question, it is easy to make an agreement error, such as this one:

> When is Keith and Samantha leaving?

To use the correct plural verb *are* requires a speaker or writer to guess that a plural subject—*Keith and Samantha*—lies ahead. Sometimes we guess wrong.

If you're in doubt about the subject-verb agreement in a question, simply reword it as a statement. So, for example, we have:

> Keith and Samantha (is/are) leaving soon.

It is now evident that the plural are is the correct verb since *Keith and Samantha* refer to two people.

PRACTICING 5

Underline the correct verb form in the following questions.

1. Who (is, are) those men standing on the corner?
2. When (do, does) Simone and Mary arrive?
3. Where (is, are) the knives and forks?
4. How many raffle tickets (has, have) Marvin sold?
5. Why (was, were) the fans cheering?

Compound Subjects Joined by And, Or, Either/Or, or Neither/Nor

Sentences that look like this can give writers trouble:

singular noun + and + singular noun

Here are some examples:

The bride and groom looks happy.
Luck and hard work is a winning combination.
Cobwebs and dirt covers the window.

In all these sentences the writer was fooled by what seemed to be a singular subject. However, just as one plus one make two, one singular subject plus another singular subject joined by *and* always make a subject plural. The sentences should therefore read:

The bride and groom <u>look</u> happy.
Luck and hard work <u>are</u> a winning combination.
Cobwebs and dirt <u>cover</u> the window.

Although two singular subjects joined by *and* always take a plural verb, two singular subjects joined by *or* require a singular verb:

Steak and chicken <u>are</u> on the menu.

but

Steak or chicken <u>is</u> on the menu.
Burt and Gus <u>are</u> driving to Florida.

but

Burt or Gus <u>is</u> driving to Florida.

Two plural nouns joined by or take a plural verb:

Usually the class presidents or vice-presidents sit on stage.

What happens when a sentence has two subjects, one singular and one plural, joined by *or*? In that case the verb agrees with the *nearer* subject:

The vice-presidents or <u>the president sits</u> next to the guest speakers.

but

The president or the <u>vice-presidents sit</u> next to the guest speakers. The same rule applies with two subjects joined by *either/or* and *neither/nor:* The verb agrees with the nearer subject:

Either the coach or the <u>co-captains unfurl</u> the flag.

but

Either the co-captains or <u>the coach unfurls</u> the flag.

PRACTICING 6

Complete the following sentences using a correct singular or plural verb form.

1. Neither Heidi nor her pals _____ .

2. Cash or credit cards _____ .

3. Either the drummer or the guitarists _____ .

4. Two sweaters or one coat _____ .

5. Either chocolate or butterscotch _____ .

PRACTICING 7

Underline the correct verb in parentheses in the following sentences.

1. Her limpid blue eyes and golden hair (have, has) enormous appeal.

2. Wages and salaries (are, is) the same thing.

3. Chocolate chip cookies and ice cream (is, are) a favorite food of Flora's.

4. A solid education and a strong character (was, were) required of all applicants.

5. My parents and my boyfriend (urges, urge) me to finish college.

The Indefinite Pronouns Each, Everyone, Anybody, Somebody, and Nobody

Indefinite pronouns are so called because they refer to no specific—or definite—person. The following indefinite pronouns always take a singular verb:

another	everyone	nothing
anybody	everything	one
anything	nobody	somebody
anyone	none	
everybody	no one	

Here are some examples:

Everybody <u>has</u> (not have) the duty to protect our freedoms.

Everyone <u>opposes</u> (not oppose) the new mall.

Nobody <u>wishes</u> (not wish) him more luck and happiness than we do.

Another <u>makes</u> (not make) a different point entirely.

PRACTICING 8

Underline the correct verb in parentheses.

1. None of the sardines (has, have) been eaten.

2. Everyone (has, have) a mind with which to decide.

3. One of the paramedics (comes, come) from Guadalajara.

4. Somebody (is, are) hiding behind that bush.

5. None of the restaurants (is, are) open.

Who, Which, and That

Who, which, and *that* are often used to replace nouns in dependent clauses. When they are so used, they should agree with the *closest* preceding noun. An example follows.

Incorrect: My mother is one of the reporters who covers City Hall.

Correct: My mother is one of the reporters who cover City Hall.

The closest noun that went before *who* is not *mother* but *reporters*. It is *reporters* that therefore determines the case of the verb.

In fact the sentence is a blend of two smaller sentences:

My mother is one of the reporters. The reporters cover City Hall.

The *who* stands for *reporters,* not for *mother.*
Here are other examples:

Leon or Ray is one of the climbers who <u>are</u> going to attempt the the pinnacle.	(**climbers,** not Leon or Ray, is the closest noun before **who**)
Among my greatest fears and worries is encountering a snake that spits poison.	(**snake,** not **fears** or **worries,** is the closest noun before **that**)

PRACTICING 9

Circle the closest noun preceding *who, which,* or *that* in the following sentences. Then underline the correct verb.

1. She is among those scientists who (believe, believes) in Martians.

2. Fabio is one of several students who (merit, merits) an award.

3. The barn is one of the buildings that (need, needs) painting.

4. Patsy is among the seniors who (is, are) dissatisfied.

5. The trunk and suit cases, which (look, looks) sturdy, fall apart easily.

Error No. 3 Review

The following paragraph contains subject-verb agreement errors. Rewrite the paragraph, making all required corrections.

One of my strongest wishes are to have a flower garden filled with roses, pansies, sweet peas, and other colorful blossoms. But no one realize more than I do that tending a flower garden is constant work. Once you decides to plant a flower garden, you have to take care of it regularly. You has to pull out the weeds that quickly grows, and you has to water regularly. It don't matter if you are tired and prefer watching T.V.; the garden call you when it need tending. There's the various weather problems to consider as well. For instance, a hot sun or strong winds ruins flowers. A heavy, pelting rain destroys blooms, too. Children and animals is another problem. They has little awareness of flowers and will trample them as they runs or plays.

Aunt Bee is among my relatives who has a spectacular flower garden. Either she or her two sons works in it every single day to keep it beautiful. Nobody know better than they how much work a garden takes. Until I am sure that I have plenty of time to devote to a flower garden, I guess I'll just enjoy gardens that has been grown by my friends and relatives.

Error 4

Incorrect Verb Forms

Verbs are either regular or irregular. Regular verbs form the past tense by adding -d or -ed. They also form the past participle by adding *-d* or *-ed*. The past participle generally refers to actions in the distant, rather than the immediate, past. It requires a helping verb, either *have, has,* or *had.* Here are some examples of common regular verbs:

PRESENT TENSE	PAST TENSE	PAST PARTICIPLE
charge	charged	have, has, or had charged
live	lived	have, has, or had lived
bake	baked	have, has, or had baked
hike	hiked	have, has, or had hiked
heave	heaved	have, has, or had heaved

Here are some examples of these words in sentences:

Past:	He lived in California for a year.
Past participle:	He has lived in some exotic places.
	He had lived in New York many years ago.

Past:	They baked the cake yesterday.
Past participle:	They have baked many cakes.
	They had already baked the birthday cake.

Don't let your ear fool you into dropping the *-d* or *-ed* endings of past tense verbs. Although this is a common mistake we all occasionally make in everyday speech, you must not make it in your writing.

EAR ALERT

Dropped ending:	They were suppose to do better.
	They were not use to the heat.
Correct:	They were supposed to do better.
	They were not used to the heat.

PRACTICING 1

Change the underlined regular verb in each sentence to the past participle. Remember to use *has, have,* or *had.* Write out the entire sentence.

1. They <u>decide</u> not to go.

_____

2. Maxine <u>bought</u> a new computer.

_____

3. Her mother <u>worked</u> as my father's accountant.

_____

4. The dog <u>sniffs</u> at the fire hydrant.

_____

5. We <u>row</u> every day on the lake.

_____

Omitting the Helping Verb in a Past Participle

EAR ALERT

In some slangy talk it is common to drop the helping verb in a past participle—an act your ear might even excuse. However, dropping the helping verb, whether your ear approves or not, is always wrong in writing. Here are some examples:

Dropped verb:	I seen that movie.
Written form:	I <u>have</u> seen that movie.

Dropped verb:	We been around the block twice.
Written form:	We <u>have</u> been around the block twice.

Dropped verb:	Why Harry brought flowers?
Written form:	Why <u>has</u> Harry brought flowers?

PRACTICING 2

Rewrite each sentence below in the lines provided, inserting the helping verb where it belongs.

1. He been a cocky kid since he was young.

_____

2. She said she given enough for one day.

_____

3. The refrigerator frozen the food.

_____

4. You eaten yet?

_____

5. They fallen from a high place.

_____

PRACTICING 3

The paragraph that follows contains errors in the use of past participles. First underline each error; second, rewrite the paragraph with the correct past participles.

My budget fallen on hard times lately. No matter how hard I try, it been real hard to make ends meet. If I work a full shift, I clear $120 per week. Last year this use to be enough to pay my bills, but this year it isn't. It costs me about $60 per week for rent. That leaves me with about half of what I take home. For food, I use to budget $20 per week, but this year for some reason, that simply isn't enough. I'm more likely to spend at least $30 for food, and that means eating a lot of junk. Last year I could occasionally go out for a hamburger, but not this year. So after rent and food, I have about $30 left for everything else. I'm suppose to pay car insurance and tuition and everything on that. That means, if I want to go to movie, which costs about $7, or nearly a third of my weekly pay that's left, I really have to think hard. I ask myself, what could happened that I'm so broke this year? I think it's because everything gone up. What used to cost $5 last year, now costs about $7. Gaso line gone up, too, and it seems I'm buying more gas. Maybe my car become a gas guzzler. I don't know. All I know is that I can barely make ends meet.

_____

_____

_____

_____

_____

_____

_____

_____

_____

Irregular Verbs

Verbs are **irregular** if their past tense is not formed by adding *-d* or *-ed*. For example, if the rule for changing tenses were applied to *bring*, its past tense should be *bringed*. It isn't—it's *brought*. *Bring* is therefore an irregular verb.

Below is a list of irregular verbs that many of us use every day. Remember, the past participle always requires the use of the helping verbs *have, has* or *had*.

SOME COMMON IRREGULAR VERBS

PRESENT	PAST	PAST PARTICIPLE
arise	arose	arisen
be	was	been
bear	bore	borne
become	became	become
begin	began	begun
break	broke	broken
bring	brought (not *brung*)	brought
build	built	built
burst	burst (not *busted*)	burst
catch	caught	caught
buy	bought	bought
choose	chose	chosen
cling	clung	clung
come	came	come
dive	dove	dived
do	did (not *done*)	done
draw	drew	drawn
drink	drank	drunk
drive	drove	driven
eat	ate	eaten
fall	fell	fallen
feed	fed	fed

PRESENT	PAST	PAST PARTICIPLE
feel	felt	felt
fight	fought	fought
fly	flew	flown
forgive	forgave	forgiven
freeze	froze	frozen
get	got	gotten
go	went	gone
grow	grew	grown
hang (clothes)	hung	hung
hang (execute)	hanged	hanged
have	had	had
hold	held	held
hurt	hurt (not *hurted*)	hurt
know	knew	known
lead	led	led
lay	laid	laid
lie	lay	lain
lose	lost	lost
make	made	made
mean	meant	meant
meet	met	met
pay	paid	paid
put	put	put
read	read	read
ride	rode	ridden
ring	rang	rung
rise	rose	risen
run	ran	run
say	said	said
see	saw (not *seen*)	seen
seek	sought (not *seeked*)	sought
sell	sold	sold
set	set	set
shake	shook	shaken
shine	shone	shone
shrink	shrank	shrunk
sing	sang	sung
sink	sank	sunk
sleep	slept	slept
speak	spoke	spoken
spend	spent	spent

PRESENT	PAST	PAST PARTICIPLE
spin	spun	spun
spit	spat	spat
spring	sprang (not *sprung*)	sprung
stand	stood	stood
steal	stole	stolen
sting	stung	stung
stink	stank (not *stunk*)	stunk
strike	struck	struck
strive	strove	strove
swear	swore	sworn
swim	swam (not *swum*)	swum
swing	swung	swung
take	took	taken
teach	taught	taught
tear	tore	torn
tell	told	told
think	thought	thought
throw	threw	thrown
understand	understood	understood
wake	woke	woken
weave	wove	woven
wear	wore	worn
win	won	won
wring	wrung	wrung
write	wrote	written

PRACTICING 4

Complete the following chart. Refer to the list of irregular verbs beginning on page 404, if in doubt.

PRESENT	PAST	PAST PARTICIPLE
1. seek	_____	_____
2. sell	_____	_____
3. steal	_____	_____
4. ring	_____	_____
5. fly	_____	_____
6. teach	_____	_____
7. hurt	_____	_____

PRESENT	PAST	PAST PARTICIPLE
8. strive	_____	_____
9. hang (execute)	_____	_____
10. spit	_____	_____

PRACTICING 5

In the following sentences, the past tense is used incorrectly. Write the correct form in the spaces provided.

1. His mother <u>waked</u> him up to go to work. _____

2. She <u>weared</u> that blouse yesterday. _____

3. I <u>throwed</u> the ball to the pitcher. _____

4. They <u>selled</u> themselves short. _____

5. I could have <u>ate</u> the whole cake. _____

6. The worker <u>striked</u> for better pay. _____

7. I've <u>fighted</u> that battle before. _____

8. Because of the yeast, the bread had <u>raised</u>. _____

9. I found out I <u>payed</u> too much for the battery. _____

10. She <u>swinged</u> in the park all morning. _____

Problems with irregular verbs

Two problems are common with the everyday use of irregular verbs:

- Using the simple past instead of the past participle.

Incorrect: She has wove two rugs.
Correct: She has woven two rugs.

Incorrect: They have tore the book.
Correct: They have torn the book.

- Using an incorrect form of the past participle.

Incorrect: He had brung his rollerblades to school before.
Correct: He has brought his rollerblades to school before.

Incorrect: She has broke the remote control.
Correct: She has broken the remote control.

Beware of these two common errors.

PRACTICING 6

Some of the underlined past participles that follow are correct, some are incorrect. If the participle is correct, write C in the blank; if it is incorrect, write the corrected participle in the blank.

1. I have <u>wore</u> that many times. _____

2. They couldn't have <u>sang</u> any worse. _____

3. The president has <u>saw</u> to the problem. _____

4. They have <u>drug</u> the boat through the mud flat. _____

5. Because of the freezing weather, the pipes have <u>busted</u>. _____

6. In another move or two, he will have <u>sprang</u> the trap. _____

7. Because she washed my jeans in too hot water, they have <u>shrunk</u>. _____

8. She has <u>wrote</u> him three times. _____

9. I have <u>drew</u> my own conclusions. _____

10. You have <u>ran</u> away from home for the last time. _____

Problem Verbs

A few verbs seem to give the entire English-speaking world trouble. They are *lie/lay, sit/set,* and *rise/raise.*

Lie/lay

Here are the principal parts of these two verbs:

PRESENT	PAST	PAST PARTICIPLE
lie	lay	lain = to rest in a horizontal position like a sleeper
lay	laid	laid = to set down something, as you might do a book

TO LIE	TO LAY
I like to lie on the grass.	She lays (what?) the tile in the bathroom.
The dog is lying on the grass.	She is laying (what?) the tile in the bathroom.
Yesterday I lay on the grass.	Yesterday she laid (what?) the tile in the bathroom.
I have lain on the grass too long.	She must have laid (what?) the tile in the bathroom.

PRACTICING 7

Underline the correct verb in parentheses.

1. (Lie, Lay) the portable phone on the desk.

2. I have been (lying, laying) plans in my dreams.

3. He was (lain, laid) to rest with all military honors.

4. She was tired and went to (lie, lay) down.

5. She complains that all he does is (lie, lay) around watching television.

Sit/set

Here are the principal parts of *sit* and *set:*

PRESENT	PAST	PAST PARTICIPLE
sit	sat	sat = to rest on one's bottom
set	set	set = to place something somewhere

TO SIT	TO SET
He sits at the head of the table.	The child sets (what?) his toys by his bed.
She is sitting by the window.	He is setting (what?) the toys in a row.
The crew sat in the cockpit.	Last night he set (what?) the bear next to the giraffe.
They have always sat in the front row.	Did he set (what?) the toys on the table?

PRACTICING 8

Underline the correct verb in parentheses.

1. They (sat, set) in the bleachers, hoping to catch a fly ball.

2. I'm (sitting, setting) the groceries on the counter.

3. (Sit, Set) yourself down on the sofa and listen to me play the piano.

4. She (sat, set) the socket wrench set on the bench.

5. (Sit, Set) with me under a tree and listen to the bird sing.

Rise/raise

Here are the principal parts of *rise* and *raise:*

PRESENT	PAST	PAST PARTICIPLE
rise	rose	risen = to get up or move up on your own
raise	raised	raised = to lift up someone or something

TO RISE	TO RAISE
Let us rise and be counted.	You should not raise (what?) your hopes too much.
I am rising early to greet the dawn.	She is raising (what?) the hem two inches.
Everyone rose when the anthem was played.	They raised (what?) the flag.
The audience has risen.	She has raised (what?) an objection.

PRACTICING 9

Change the underlined word(s) by substituting *rise* or *raise*. Do not change the tense of the original.

1. <u>Lift</u> the banner above your head. _____

2. The moon <u>came up</u> over the ocean. _____

3. The entire team had <u>stood up</u> to watch the home run. _____

4. Victory <u>pulled up</u> their spirits. _____

5. He <u>got up</u> late today. _____

Lie/Lay, Sit/Set, Rise/Raise: Does It Really Matter?

Even if students don't ask the question, "Does it really matter if I say *lie* or *lay?*" they often think it. The answer is, yes, it does matter.

True, if you commanded *Lay down!* instead of *Lie down!* your dog would probably obey just as quickly. "If I'm understood when I incorrectly say *lay* instead of *lie,* or *lie* instead of *lay,* what does using the correct form matter?"—that is what many students wonder. Being understood, however, is no substitute for being correct. Furthermore, being correct is what makes you understandable.

Language does change, and as the years roll by, we predict that one day *lie* and *lay* will have the same meaning in grammar books. Until that day comes, these differences do matter. For example, you might scribble this memo to your boss: "Dear Boss, I lay the contract on your desk before I left." Upon reading it your boss might mutter, "No, you didn't. You laid it there. If you can't get that right, how can I trust you with this important contract? I'm giving the account to Nancy." In other words, these little differences are important because they matter to people.

Of course, they don't matter if you work for a dog.

Error No. 4 Review

The paragraph below contains errors in the past tense and past participles of irregular verbs. Find and correct all the errors.

When I began working at Gary's Restaurant, I was lead to believe that I would soon be given a rise in pay. Mrs. Smith, my supervisor, even complimented me when I was hired, telling me that I brung a lot of experience to the company. Now as I set here writing this letter, I cannot help but feel that I was misleaded. I don't want to rise this point and belabor it, but when the pipes in the kitchen busted, I was the one who saved the food in the walk-in. Furthermore, in my six months of employment here, I have never shrinked from doing my duty. Whatever my supervisor told me to do, I always did it as well as I understanded the request. Nobody has ever wringed work out of me. I'm always the first to volunteer. I have wrote this letter because I feel not only mistreated, but also misleaded. As I drived to work today, I thinked to myself that Gary's is a good place to work. But now my confidence has been shook. Now that I have spoke my honest opinion, I hope that I will get the pay increase I deserve. I hope by this letter I have not fell out of favor. But as I have always been brung up to believe, honesty is the best policy.

Error 5

Incorrect Forms of <u>Do,</u> <u>Be,</u> and <u>Have</u>

Even if you've spoken English all your life, verbs can still be troublesome. Part of the problem is that we don't speak and write verbs the same way. In speech we sometimes drop the tense endings of verbs when we shouldn't, as in this sentence:

She laugh all the time.

Or, we add an ending when we shouldn't:

They laughs all the time.

In the first sentence, since *she* is singular, the verb must also be singular—*laughs*. In the second sentence, since *they* is plural, the verb must also be plural—*laugh*.

You can make these mistakes in everyday speech—we all occasionally do—and be forgiven. You should not, however, make them in writing. The standards for grammar are stricter in writing than in speech, meaning that you must always write verb tenses correctly.

Present Tense Endings

In standard English you must use the correct endings with verbs. You cannot use a plural ending with a singular subject, or a singular ending with a plural subject. Here are the correct endings for regular verbs in the present tense:

PRESENT TENSE—SINGULAR

INCORRECT	CORRECT
I walks	I walk
you walks	you walk
he, she, it walk	he, she, it walks

PRESENT TENSE—PLURAL

INCORRECT	CORRECT
we walks	we walk
you walks	you walk
they walks	they walk

Present tense problems

There are two kinds of problems that commonly occur with verbs in the present tense:

- Dropped *-s/-es* endings for *he, she,* and *it.*

Incorrect: He take the train to work.
Correct: He takes the train to work.

Incorrect: She make pancakes for breakfast.
Correct: She makes pancakes for breakfast.

Incorrect: It hurt my feelings.
Correct: It hurts my feelings.

- Unnecessary *-s/-es* for *we, you,* and *they.*

Incorrect: We visits Gram every weekend.
Correct: We visit Gram every weekend.

Incorrect: You always smiles, even in sad times.
Correct: You always smile, even in sad times.

Incorrect: They both plays the accordion.
Correct: They both play the accordion.

Problems with dropped and added endings occur, as we said, because we are less precise in our speech than we must be in our writing. If you make such errors regularly in your speech, your ear may not be particularly helpful in catching them. In that case you should simply memorize the correct endings.

PRACTICING 1

In the blanks provided write *C* if the verb is correct and *NC* if it is not.

1. _____ Bernice and I drives in the same car pool.

2. _____ We try to pay our electricity bill.

3. _____ Our neighbor keep trying to win the lottery.

4. _____ Jeremy buy Melinda's affection.

5. _____ She repeat herself constantly.

PRACTICING 2

In the passage that follows, strike out any incorrect verb and write the correct form above it.

Most of my friends likes to watch soccer. During the World Cup season, we sits in front of my TV all day long to watch the competition. My friend Danny always support the team from Brazil, but I cheer for the Italian team with Baggio, who wear a braid down his back. That seem cool to me. The penalty kicks excites everyone the most. Then we screams and yells at the top of our voices. If the kicker make a goal, we goes crazy. If the goalie intercept the ball, we explodes. Soccer get you involved, no matter what side win.

Past Tense Endings

Here are the correct endings for regular singular verbs in the past tense:

PAST TENSE——SINGULAR

INCORRECT	CORRECT
I walk	I walked
you walk	you walked
he, she, it walk	he, she, it walked

Here are the correct endings for regular plural verbs in the past tense:

PAST TENSE——PLURAL

INCORRECT	CORRECT
we walk	we walked
you walk	you walked
they walk	they walked

With both singular and plural verbs, we can be careless in our speech and drop the *-ed* ending. In writing, however, you must *always* use the *-ed* ending with regular verbs in the past tense.

Incorrect: I pick up the mail yesterday.
Correct: I picked up the mail yesterday.

Incorrect: He drop several hints.
Correct: He dropped several hints.

PRACTICING 3

In the blank at the end of each sentence, write the past tense of the underlined verb.

1. The mechanical teddy bear <u>dance</u> a jig. _____

2. Studies <u>suggest</u> that TV violence is bad. _____

3. Despite my pleadings, Betty <u>continue</u> to smoke. _____

4. Some countries <u>remain</u> neutral during the war. _____

5. He <u>manage</u> to turn the tiny argument into a major problem. _____

6. Beverly <u>challenge</u> her opponent. _____

7. Jack and Jill <u>decide</u> to go up the hill. _____

8. I secretly <u>open</u> the door to the safe. _____

9. The strange voice on the telephone <u>ask</u> my name. _____

10. They <u>litter</u> the grass with cans and wrappers. _____

Problems with -ing Verbs

Verbs ending in -*ing* describe an action that is either happening now or is ongoing. All -*ing* verbs need a helping verb.

He is eating in the kitchen.

He was eating in the kitchen.

He has been eating in the kitchen.

He had been eating in the kitchen, but now he eats in the dining room.

Two kinds of problems can occur with -*ing* verbs:

- *Be* or *been* is used instead of the correct helping verb.

Incorrect: She be eating in the kitchen.

Correct: She is eating in the kitchen.

or

She has been eating in the kitchen.

Incorrect She been studying in the library.

Correct: She was studying in the library.

or

She has been studying in the library.

■ The helping verb is completely omitted.

Incorrect: They bragging too much.
Correct: They are bragging too much.
                They were bragging too much.
                They have been bragging too much.
                They had been bragging too much.

PRACTICING 4

Rewrite the following sentences to correct the misuse of *be* or *been,* or to insert the missing helping verb.

Example: The birds be chirping outside my window.

             The birds are chirping outside my window.

1. My car be needing a lube job.

_____

2. She forcing her son to give up college.

_____

3. My father buying a house near the train station.

_____

4. How your mother be coming along with her knitting?

_____

5. Marcy hoping that she can marry next year.

_____

6. They be ignoring all of his advice.

_____

7. Margaret sitting under an elm tree when the lightning struck.

_____

8. Every young person be searching for a way to feel important.

_____

9. Dylan expecting to inherit some money from an uncle.

_____

10. Schwarz be waiting for him in the adjoining room.

_____

Difficult Verbs

Verbs can be hard to master. Few are harder than the three verbs we probably use more than any others in the language: *be, have,* and *do.*

To be

To be is commonly used both as a verb on its own and as a helping verb. Here is a listing of the forms of the verb *to be:*

PRESENT TENSE—SINGULAR TO BE

INCORRECT	CORRECT
I be, I ain't	I am, I am not
you be, you ain't	you are, you are not
he/she/it be, he/she/it ain't	he/she/it is, he/she/it is not

PRESENT TENSE—PLURAL TO BE

INCORRECT	CORRECT
we be, we ain't	we are, we are not
you be, you ain't	you are, you are not
they be, they ain't	they are, they are not

PAST TENSE—SINGULAR TO BE

INCORRECT	CORRECT
I were	I was
you was	you were
he, she, it were	he, she, it was

PAST TENSE—PLURAL TO BE

INCORRECT	CORRECT
we was	we were
you was	you were
they was	they were

As you can see—indeed as you already know from repeated use— *to be* is an irregular verb. As both a verb and a helping verb, it is often incorrectly spoken. All of these sentences below, for example, are wrong, even if your ear tells you otherwise.

I ain't staying in New York.

The lake be dangerous because the wind be blowing hard.

You was rude to step in front of her.

If these are forms that you commonly use in your daily speech, be especially careful not to trust your ear with *to be*. Instead, you should memorize its correct forms.

Here is how these sentences should be written:

I am not staying in New York.

The lake is dangerous because the wind is blowing hard.

You were rude to step in front of her.

PRACTICING 5

The following passage contains several errors in the use of the verb *to be*. In the space provided, rewrite the passage, correcting all errors. (Hint: you should find eight errors.)

Today I be sad. It be the third anniversary of my dad's death. Believe me, even after three years, it ain't easy to lose your dad. He been my best friend. We went fishing and camping together every year. We was simply best buddies. Last summer I hiked where my dad and I had hiked along a lake high up in the Sierras. I be feeling sick with my heavy heart. My mom tried to comfort me by reminding me that I have some great memories. But that can't make up for the present loss. Right now, I wish he and I was sitting down to plan one of our famous outings. But it can't happen. He be gone forever.

_____

_____

_____

_____

_____

_____

_____

_____

_____

_____

_____

To have

To have, like *to be,* is commonly used both as a verb and a helping verb. Also like *to be,* it is an irregular verb. Here are its main forms:

PRESENT TENSE—SINGULAR TO HAVE

INCORRECT	CORRECT
I has	I have
you has	you have
he/she/it have	he/she/it has

PRESENT TENSE—PLURAL TO HAVE

INCORRECT	CORRECT
we has	we have
you has	you have
they has	they have

PAST TENSE—SINGULAR TO HAVE

INCORRECT	CORRECT
I has	I had
you has	you had
he/she/I have	he/she/it had

PAST TENSE—PLURAL TO HAVE

INCORRECT	CORRECT
we has	we had
you has	you had
they has	they had

To have is so often misused in daily speech that you should be cautious about trusting your ear to judge its correctness. These sentences below, for example, are all incorrect:

She have two nieces and two nephews.
Benny have a nifty new Honda convertible.
They has a party yesterday.

Here are the correct forms:

She has two nieces and two nephews.
Benny has a new Honda convertible.
They had a party yesterday.

Error No. 5 Review

Fill in the blanks with the correct form

1. Yesterday Julie (insist) _____

2. Melvin (be) _____ the g

3. They both (be) _____ go

4. Last May, Elvira (decide) _____

5. Miranda (do) _____ follo

6. David still (eat) _____ t

7. She (hide) _____ her sp

8. If you (be) _____ satisfi

9. The roof (have) _____ a

10. (Do) _____ she always

11. Jessie (have) _____ told

12. City Hall (have) _____ t

13. If she (swim) _____ to
    _____ strong.

14. You have (do) _____ the

15. The door (have) _____

The paragraph that follows cont *be,* and *have* verbs. Rewrite the paragra should be able to find 22 errors.)

If I be a waitress, I would try to be
many waitresses nowadays doesn't offer
would approach the customer with a smile
just grab my notebook and ask, "What wo
day at Benny's coffee shop, where my bes
fast, the waitress at our table ask us abo
surprised at such a cold attitude, and my
order for pancakes. After she be taking
to another customer and talk, talk, talk w
the kitchen. I be real offended. We was i
erately ignore our needs. Well, finally she
place it on the table, she spill some cof
dishes because she be so rough. Most p
ant meal or enjoy, but not this one. She ju
to get our check. I have no idea why she
ress, I be trying hard to please my custo

Fill in the correct form of the verb *to have* in the following sentences.

Example: She <u>has</u> to be on time.

1. Judith _____ a free ticket to the game.

2. You _____ to take him to the bus.

3. The Baxters _____ two beautiful daughters.

4. He _____ my raincoat, and I must _____ it tomorrow.

5. I _____ got to live alone, and Mother _____ to understand why.

6. _____ they mentioned the problem?

7. Where _____ Pete been?

8. She _____ embarrassed me too often.

9. Everyone _____ to follow the regulations.

10. We _____ two computers, but our neighbors _____ only one.

To do

The verb *to do,* like *to be* and *to have,* is used both as a verb and a helping verb. Here are its correct forms:

PRESENT TENSE—SINGULAR TO DO

INCORRECT	CORRECT
I does	I do
you does	you do
he/she/it do	he/she/it does

PRESENT TENSE—PLURAL TO DO

INCORRECT	CORRECT
we does	we do
you does	you do
they does	they do

PAST TENSE—SINGULAR TO DO

INCORRECT	CORRECT
I done	I did
you done	you did
he/she/it done	he/she/it did

INCORRECT

we done

you done

they done

EAR ALERT

The main probl
differently than it
these sentences bel

He don't have th

I does whatever

She done her h

Here are the corre

He doesn't have

I do whatever I'

She did her hom

or

She has done h

PRACTIC

Use the correct

1. He _____

2. She _____

3. _____

4. How _____

5. Melissa ra

6. I _____

7. _____
due today?

8. Where _____

9. _____

10. _____

Error 6

Passive Voice

English has two voices; the active and the passive voice. The **active voice** stresses *who* did an act. The **passive voice** stresses *to whom* or *to what* an act was done. Most of us usually speak in the active voice because it is simpler and more direct.

Active voice: The cashier gave us our change.

Passive voice: Our change was given to us by the cashier.

Because it hides the doer, the passive voice is often preferred by writers who wish to avoid naming names. Here is a case in point.

The tax return was lost.

Who lost the tax return? The active voice would have told us:

Bill lost the tax return.

In writing you should mainly use the active voice. It is livelier and stronger than the passive voice and more like everyday talk. The passive voice is occasionally used in scientific reporting, where what was done is more important than which researcher did it:

The chemical mixture was heated.

It is also occasionally used in instances where an act is more important than its cause:

The fishing village was destroyed by a tidal wave.

Here the important fact is the destruction of the village. That it was destroyed by a tidal wave is secondary.

PRACTICING 1

Read the paired sentences aloud and write *A* in the blank beside the sentence in the active voice.

Example: __A__ **(a).** Louise made the coffee.

_____ **(b).** The coffee was made by Louise.

1. _____ **(a).** The package was advertised by the travel agent.

   _____ **(b).** The travel agent advertised the package.

2. _____ **(a).** Initiative is crushed by bureaucracy.

   _____ **(b).** Bureaucracy crushes initiative.

3. _____ **(a).** Mrs. Stanhope spoke to the letter carrier.

   _____ **(b).** The letter carrier was spoken to by Mrs. Stanhope.

4. _____ **(a).** The people were misled by the cult.

   _____ **(b).** The cult misled the people.

5. _____ **(a).** The boat was stopped by the Coast Guard.

   _____ **(b).** The Coast Guard stopped the boat.

6. _____ **(a).** I enjoyed the lecture.

   _____ **(b).** The lecture was enjoyed by me.

7. _____ **(a).** The play was staged by the Drama Club.

   _____ **(b).** The Drama Club staged the play.

8. _____ **(a).** An invasion of ants interrupted the picnic.

   _____ **(b).** The picnic was interrupted by an invasion of ants.

9. _____ **(a).** The developer obtained the building permit.

   _____ **(b).** The building permit was obtained by the developer.

10. _____ **(a).** A strong case was made by the prosecuting attorney.

    _____ **(b).** The prosecuting attorney made a strong case.

PRACTICING 2

Rewrite the sentences below to change verbs to the active voice from the passive voice.

Example: The marshmallows were enjoyed by the Boy Scouts.

Answer: <u>The Boy Scouts enjoyed the marshmallows.</u>

1. An ace was served by the tennis champion.

_____

2. The home was inspected by the building inspector.

_____

3. The movie was enjoyed by everyone.

_____

4. The sugar water was relished by the humming birds.

_____

5. A screenplay was written by my neighbor.

_____

6. The candidate was backed by women's groups.

_____

7. Jogging is done by many people for exercise.

_____

8. The statue was removed by the protestors.

_____

9. The law was passed by the Senate.

_____

10. The taxi cab was summoned by the doorman.

_____

PRACTICING 3

Rewrite these sentences to put them in the active voice.

1. A bad fall was suffered by the polevaulter.

_____

2. The car was fixed by the mechanic.

_____

3. Encouragement was given to the class by the dean.

_____

4. New soles were put on the shoes by the shoemaker.

_____

5. The order was placed by Jim.

_____

6. A standing ovation was given to the player.

_____

7. The plane was guided in by the air controller.

_____

8. The poor homeowners were robbed by the slick-talking con man.

_____

9. The wonderful tarts were made by him.

_____

10. An incentive was offered by the sales manager.

_____

11. A lively tune was played by the band.

_____

12. Our snow was shoveled by our neighbor's son.

_____

13. The oven was cleaned by me.

_____

14. The syllabus was handed out by the professor.

_____

15. A safety flare was shot off by the lifeguard.

_____

Error No. 6 Review

Rewrite the following paragraph in the active voice.

Last summer our house was painted by me. The job took about two weeks. First, the exterior was washed using warm water and a mild detergent. Then all the chinks and pores in the walls were sealed with putty. It was not an easy job. After the putty had had a chance to dry, the exterior could be painted. A latex paint was used because it is easy to apply and cleans up with water. A whole week was needed to finish this part of the job. I was very careful to apply the paint evenly because I did not want to have to apply two coats. A color was used that was very close to the original color. Our house is a two-story house, which meant that a ladder was needed to do the second story. This was the hardest part of the job. It meant working 35 or 40 feet high, which was not easy. The paint can had to be balanced on the top rung of the ladder while I worked. Plus it was very hot, and I had to keep coming down to drink water. But when the job was finished, a great deal of satisfaction was felt by me. I had to pat myself on the back. Even my dad said that a good job was done.

_____

_____

_____

_____

_____

_____

_____

_____

_____

_____

Error 7

Shift in Tense

I f you begin a sentence in the present tense, you must end it in the present tense. If you begin in the past tense, you must end in the past tense. For example, look at this sentence:

Larry blew a tire, and then just keeps on driving.

The problem with the sentence is that it begins with a verb in the past tense and ends with a verb in the present tense. Larry is made into a time-traveler—hopping from the past to the present in one breath. To be correct, the sentence must read:

Larry blew a tire, and then just kept on driving.   **(All past tense)**

or

Larry blows a tire, and then just keeps on driving.   **(All present tense)**

Your tense use must be consistent. You must not shift tenses unless there is a logical reason. Yet because we mix up our verb tenses all the time in everyday speech, your ear might mislead you into making the same mistake in writing. Be alert to this possible error. Make sure your verbs in a written sentence all use the same tense.

PRACTICING 1

Correct the shifts in verb tense in these sentences.

1. The teacher writes the assignment on the board, and then left the room with no comment.

_____

_____

2. When I warned her that the road was slippery, she simply pays no attention.

_____

_____

3. He memorizes the entire Bill of Rights, but failed the test anyway.

_____

_____

4. When clouds covered the moon, the lovers leave the park.

_____

_____

5. I had barely started my laundry when the washing machine floods all over the floor.

_____

_____

6. She grabbed the pen on the desk and hurriedly signs the contract.

_____

_____

7. The night before her wedding, Annie had dinner with her best friends and weeps for two hours.

_____

_____

8. When the first snow falls, the men in the neighborhood got out their shovels to clear the walk ways.

_____

_____

9. All of us lustily sang "I've Been Workin' on the Railroad," and then we eat three huge pizzas.

_____

_____

10. He climbed to the top of the hill and builds a fire.

_____

_____

PRACTICING 2

Correct the shifts in verb tense in these sentences.

1. Mary recognized the car and is yelling, "There goes the thief!"

_____

_____

2. For twenty years he has kept the secret and never tells a soul.

_____

_____

3. We stop recruiting volunteers and had started to work.

_____

_____

4. Tom envied Lud and wants to take over his job.

_____

_____

5. The clouds looked menacing, so we pull up our stakes and leave the camp.

_____

_____

6. I look out the window and saw three fire engines.

_____

_____

7. They paid for her tuition and gave her spending money, but she never shows an ounce of gratitude.

_____

_____

8. He is a carpenter and has received good benefits.

_____

_____

9. Although I felt dizzy, I manage to cross the stream on the rope bridge.

_____

_____

10. Most of the stories are old, but we listened with fascination.

_____

_____

PRACTICING 3

Complete the sentences below, using the correct verb tense.

1. She set the table, while he _____.

2. People gathered around the accident and then the fire truck _____.

3. Before the curtain rose, the actor _____.

4. When the wind howls outside our windows, _____.

5. We made reservations for 7:00, which _____.

6. They did apologize, so _____.

7. Francis walks two miles every day, but _____.

8. They applauded the mayor and then _____.

9. December was mild, but January _____.

10. He leaves the cap off the toothpaste, and _____.

Error No. 7 Review

Rewrite the following paragraph to correct all shifts in tense.

My mother is so funny. Once she watched a TV program about regular car maintenance. Then, for weeks afterward, she gives our family long harangues about getting the oil changed regularly and replacing a weak battery. "Won't you feel silly if you were in a busy intersection and your car stalled," she must have asks me every night. And practically all day Saturday, there she is in the garage, checking some hose or gasket or belt. She visited every neighbor and points out the dangers of ignoring an oil leak or bad brakes. "Watch out for uneven tire wear," she preaches to everyone. My father was embarrassed that Mom is so forward about telling our neighbors how to run their lives. He tells her that if she wanted to take good care of her car, fine, but that she should allow the neighbors to make their own decision about their own cars.

_____

_____

_____

_____

_____

_____

_____

_____

_____

Error 8

Shift in Point of View

Writing is easier to read if it uses the same point of view throughout. You may choose a first person, second person, or third person point of view:

FIRST PERSON	SECOND PERSON	THIRD PERSON	
I	you	he, she, it, one	SINGULAR
we	you	they	PLURAL

Here are some examples:

Incorrect: When a <u>person</u> sees an accident, <u>you</u> should immediately offer assistance.

Correct: When <u>you</u> see an accident, <u>you</u> should immediately offer assistance.

or

When <u>one</u> sees an accident, <u>one</u> should immediately offer assistance.

Here is a paragraph containing many shifts:

How <u>we</u> wake up in the morning affects how <u>you</u> view the rest of the day. If <u>you</u> start the day off badly, <u>we'll</u> be in a bad mood for the rest of the day. Start off strong and cheerful, and <u>one</u> will be facing the day with a positive outlook. On the other hand, if <u>we</u> wake up in a so-so mood, chances are good that <u>your</u> so-so mood will carry over through the rest of the day and make it so-so. There's no mystery in this: It's simply a matter of common sense. The mood <u>you</u> wake up in sets the tone for the rest of <u>one's</u> day.

Here is the correction using *you*. *You, we,* or *one* would all be correct as long as you don't shift from one pronoun to another.

How <u>you</u> wake up in the morning affects how <u>you</u> view the rest of the day. If <u>you</u> start the day off badly, <u>you'll</u> be in a bad mood for the rest of the day. Start off strong and cheerful, and <u>you</u> will be facing the day with a positive outlook. On the other hand, if <u>you</u> wake up in a so-so mood, chances are good that <u>your</u> so-so mood will carry over through the rest of the day and make it so-so. There's no mystery in this: It's simply a matter of common sense. The mood <u>you</u> wake up in sets the tone for the rest of <u>your</u> day.

PRACTICING 1

Correct the shifts in point of view in the following sentences by crossing out and rewriting words when necessary.

1. When I went to San Francisco, we had a wonderful time.

2. They stood in line all day, which is what you have to do if you want to get tickets.

3. In spite of my attempt to do the right thing, you could see there was no way to win.

4. A person should study hard if you want to be a success in college.

5. The counselor at the school is a sympathetic person that one can share your troubles with.

6. If one intends to drive for a long time, you should try to get enough sleep the day before.

7. To overcome your bad habits, we should all practice will power.

8. For someone to succeed in a new job, we must be willing to watch and learn.

9. One's love of ice cream can easily overcome your desire to stay on a diet.

10. I don't play the lottery because you know you can't win.

PRACTICING 2

Complete each of these sentences using a pronoun. Do not shift point of view.

1. When you go out on a blind date, _____.

2. If a person exercises, _____.

3. Even though I'm a big baseball fan, _____.

4. If you pay attention to the big things _____.

5. I made several phone calls, but _____.

6. You should floss twice a day if _____.

7. A person who likes poetry _____.

8. If someone wants to save money grocery shopping, _____.

9. A person who likes Chinese food should _____.

10. Should you feel restless, _____.

PRACTICING 3

Rewrite the following sentences to correct the shifts in point of view.

1. If you like to read, one should try the local library.

_____

_____

2. One should not talk too much if you don't know the subject well.

_____

_____

3. When you go on a trip, one should always have your insurance paid up.

_____

_____

4. A person can get good bargains if you shop at outlet stores.

_____

_____

5. Someone can make new friends in a city if you join a health club.

_____

_____

6. One only has to listen to know that you can't take anything they say at face value.

_____

_____

7. Broccoli will help one's digestion, but carrots will help your night vision.

_____

_____

8. As you walk into the room, one can hear the people babbling away.

_____

_____

9. When I bought my blender, you could never tell that it would come in so handy.

_____

_____

10. One must try hard at everything one does, or you'll never know if you could succeed.

_____

_____

Error No. 8 Review

Rewrite the following paragraph to correct the shifts in point of view.

As part of freshmen orientation week, some colleges organize a hike in the mountains or even an overnight camping trip. Now, to me that sounds like a good idea. Imagine how we could bond while you're fighting off mosquitoes, building a fire, or sharing our dried food inside your tents. Starting one's freshmen week with a lecture, an English placement test, and an explanation of the campus rules we're supposed to follow is dull by comparison. But a one or two-day hike by a lake or in the Sierras encourages students to make new friends quickly while you enjoy a few hours of hiking, cycling, trail exploring, or even canoeing. Then you could gather around a campfire at night while the freshmen ask questions of the older students, who can reassure us that college is fun as well as hard work. I think such an orientation would give me confidence as we face college life.

_____

_____

_____

_____

_____

_____

_____

_____

_____

_____

Error 9

Unclear or Missing Referent

If writing were baseball, the pronoun would be a relief pitcher whose job is temporarily to relieve nouns, who are the starters. In both speech and writing the **pronoun** is a word used in place of a noun.

The **referent** of a pronoun is the noun it replaces. Consider this sentence:

Elaine works, but she is getting her degree at night.

The pronoun is *she*; its referent—the word it refers to—is *Elaine*.

Most of the time, the referent of a pronoun is perfectly clear from the context of a sentence. However, sometimes it isn't. Sometimes a referent is either unclear or altogether missing.

Unclear Referents

Here is an example of an unclear referent:

Peggy told Denise that she had made a grave error.

In the above sentence the referent of the pronoun is unclear. We do not know whether Peggy or Denise made the grave error. Here is the same sentence rewritten to avoid the unclear referent:

Peggy told Denise, "You have made a grave error."

or

Peggy told Denise that Denise had made a grave error.

Sometimes the unclear referent is not a person, but an action, feeling, or episode.

Unclear: The service was slow, and the food was cold when it arrived, which really upset Herbert.

Was Herbert upset because the service was slow, because the food was cold, or both?

Clear: Not only was the service slow, but the food was cold, both of which upset Herbert.

Another example follows:

Unclear: The population of the United States is aging, which means that in the future young people will have much more contact with older people. Many people think this is a good thing.

What does *this* refer to? We do not know. It could refer to the fact that more of the U.S. population is older rather than younger, that young and old will interact more in the future, or both.

Clear: The population of the United States is aging, which means that in the future, young people will have much more contact with older people. Many people think such increased contact will benefit both young and old.

Note that sometimes to get around an unclear referent, you may need to rewrite one sentence into two.

PRACTICING 1

Rewrite the following sentences so that the pronouns refer clearly to only one referent.

1. Marty decided to move to Costa Rica and study medicine, which his parents couldn't understand.

_____

_____

2. She scraped the hand rails and the stairs and painted them.

_____

_____

3. It was hot, the line was long, and the clerk was slow, which really tried Jack's patience.

_____

_____

4. My father told my brother that he was a good father but a bad husband.

_____

_____

5. Betty was a good friend of Mary's until she moved to New York.

_____

_____

6. Alexa held a lipstick in one hand and blush powder in the other, putting it on as we laughed about the new styles.

_____

_____

7. Ben told Richard he had been a loyal friend.

_____

_____

8. Stanley and Merle's room was a chaotic mess because he left everything on the floor or on the bed.

_____

_____

9. We have made great progress in cleaning up our environment, but we still have a long way to go. This surprises many people.

_____

_____

10. Mom and Aunt Lottie went shopping even though she had a bad cold.

_____

_____

Missing Referents

In both speech and writing we often use pronouns with missing referents. This is especially true of the pronouns *they* and *it*. Here is an example:

> Although my grandfather and father were farmers, I have no interest in it.

What is it? We have a fuzzy idea that by it the writer means *farming,* but the word *farming* does not appear in the sentence.

Usually the best way to rewrite such a sentence is to omit the pronoun and provide the missing noun.

Although my grandfather and father were farmers, I have no interest in farming.

Here are some more examples:

Missing: Between games, they announced the score.

Who is this mysterious *they* in the sentence?

Clear: Between games, the announcer called out the score.

Incorrect: It says to yield to the driver approaching from your right.

Correct: The sign says to yield to the driver approaching from your right.

Now we know the identity of the unnamed *it*.

The requirement that every pronoun have a specific and clear referent is not picky. In everyday talk we do not observe such exactness in pronoun use because we can always ask "What?" and get an answer. In writing, however, there's no second chance. Every pronoun must therefore have a specific referent.

PRACTICING 2

Rewrite the following sentences to clarify the pronoun reference.

1. It says the shirt comes in plum, mango, and lime green.

_____

_____

2. My boyfriend is a great cook, but I have no interest in it.

_____

_____

3. They did not allow us to touch the Indian weavings.

_____

_____

4. I deposited the money in my bank, but they haven't posted the correct balance.

_____

_____

5. We were in the middle of registering when they informed us that the class was closed.

_____

_____

6. They refused to give me a refund even after I wrote a strong letter.

_____

_____

7. If you don't have a ticket, they won't let you in.

_____

_____

8. See; it says this is a dead-end street.

_____

_____

9. They say one should not beg a lover to stay faithful.

_____

_____

10. It has an alarm that goes off when you open the door from the outside.

_____

_____

PRACTICING 3

Rewrite the following sentences to correct the pronoun errors.

1. Maggie treated Jeanne and her mother to dinner.

_____

_____

2. When Vladimir lent money to Gorsky, he did not know he would go bankrupt.

_____

_____

3. It says the police caught the burglar.

_____

_____

4. Fred insisted to Woody that his wife was not to blame.

_____

_____

5. There is a big difference between the politicians of the past and those of today. They lack nobility.

_____

_____

6. We found a pressed rose in the book that my grandmother gave my grandfather.

_____

_____

7. They allow you to make three separate payments.

_____

_____

8. The nurse told Emma that her name was unusual.

_____

_____

9. They say that gelatin is good for your nails.

_____

_____

10. If your Persian cat will not eat raw fish, boil it.

_____

_____

Error No. 9 Review

Rewrite the following paragraph to eliminate all the pronoun reference problems.

My friend, Lucy, loves her cat, Fluffy, so much that she purrs constantly. When she takes her to the veterinarian, she orders a limousine so she can hold her and pet her, and so she can feed her little pieces of shrimp, which I think is a bit extreme. Once Lucy told a neighboring woman that she was noble because she loved cats. They say that women who love cats make good mothers. It wouldn't surprise me. Now, I admire cats because they have such independent spirits, but I do not intend to get one. The other day Lucy's cat held a real mouse in one paw and a toy mouse in the other, eating it as she frisked and pranced. As long as cat owners outnumber cats, they will not be a problem.

_____

_____

_____

_____

_____

_____

_____

_____

_____

Error 10

Lack of Pronoun Agreement and Sexism

A pronoun and its referent (the noun it replaces) must agree in number. Singular nouns require singular pronouns. Plural nouns require plural pronouns. Here are some examples:

The bride put on *her* veil.

The attendants picked up *their* flowers.

In the first sentence the singular noun *bride* requires the singular pronoun *her*. In the second sentence the plural noun *attendants* requires the plural pronoun *their*.

Although pronoun agreement is often not a problem, it can be when we try to find a pronoun to replace an indefinite pronoun.

An **indefinite pronoun** is a pronoun that refers to no one in particular. Here is a list of common indefinite pronouns (they are always singular):

INDEFINITE PRONOUNS

one	nobody	each
anyone	anybody	either
everyone	everybody	neither
someone	somebody	

Study these sentences:

Incorrect: Each of the men carry a bottle of water.

Correct: Each ~~of the men~~ carries a bottle of water.

(**Each** requires a singular verb. Remember, cross out the prepositional phrase if you are confused about the subject.)

Incorrect: Either Harriet or Nancy will give me their paycheck.

Correct: Either Harriet or Nancy will give me her paycheck.

(***Either*** **is singular.**)

In both speech and writing, to avoid being sexist, we often use the plural *their* to refer to many indefinite pronouns that are singular. We say, for example, and it sounds perfectly right to our ear:

Someone put their keys on the table.

Technically speaking, this use is wrong. *Their* is plural; *someone* is singular. On the other hand, the singular pronoun *his* is sexist:

Someone put his keys on the table.

It is sexist because *someone* could be a female, a possibility the pronoun ignores.

The best way to correct an agreement problem is by rewriting the sentence. You can change the wrong pronoun either to singular or plural. Here is an example:

Incorrect:	Everyone who donates $50 will get their name on a plaque.
Correct:	If you donate $50, you will get you name on a plaque.
Correct:	People who donate $50 will get their names on a plaque.

Here is another example:

Incorrect:	Did everyone have their coffee?
Correct:	Did you have your coffee?
Correct:	Did every diner have coffee?

PRACTICING 1

Correct the agreement errors in the following sentences both ways that you've learned—by changing to the singular and to the plural.

1. Is everybody bringing their date to the party?

Singular: _____

Plural: _____

2. Everyone should help themselves to dessert.

Singular: _____

Plural: _____

3. Nobody knows for certain what their future holds.

Singular: _____

Plural: _____

4. If anyone needs help, they should ask me.

Singular: _____

Plural: _____

5. Would everyone who saw the accident give me their names?

Singular: _____

Plural: _____

6. If everyone did what they were told, the world would be a better place.

Singular: _____

Plural: _____

7. If someone tries hard, they will be sure to succeed.

Singular: _____

Plural: _____

8. If someone has a problem with a coworker, they should try to work it out privately.

Singular: _____

Plural: _____

9. Will everyone please tell us their names?

Singular: _____

Plural: _____

10. Neither Dennis nor Derrick sent in their money.

Singular: _____

Plural: _____

Sexism in Writing

You have just learned how to avoid the sexist use of indefinite pronouns. Sexism in writing is even worse when a singular pronoun automatically assigns the male sex to professionals:

> Every police officer should wear his badge at all times.

The use of *his* in the above sentence suggests that every police officer is a man, which is both sexist and untrue. On the other hand, using *his* or *her* is correct but clumsy. Another solution is to make the whole sentence plural, using the neutral pronoun *their*. The possible nonsexist choices follow.

Incorrect: Every police officer should wear his badge at all times.

Correct: Every police officer should wear his or her badge at all times.

Correct: Police officers should wear their badges at all times.

Their includes both men and women, and it is not as clumsy as *his* or *her*.

On the other hand, sometimes we are quick to assume that some professions are dominated by women. For example, we may refer to nurses, secretaries, and grade school teachers as *she*. This is also sexist because both men and women can be nurses, secretaries, and grade school teachers. Here is an example of this type of sexism in writing:

Incorrect: A teacher should be a good role model for her students.

Correct: A teacher should be a good role model for his or her students.

Correct: Teachers should be good role models for their students.

If you are facing a pronoun agreement problem that you simply cannot rewrite in the plural, then use *his* or *her*. If the choice is between being sexist or being clumsy, we think it is better to be clumsy.

PRACTICING 2

Rewrite the following sentences to correct the sexist bias.

1. When a plumber is finished working, he shouldn't leave a mess for the customer.

_____

_____

2. A hair stylist should always keep her station clean.

_____

_____

3. A good secretary keeps her boss organized.

_____

_____

4. A flight attendant should be sure her uniform is clean and pressed.

_____

_____

5. You could call a lawyer and find out what he thinks.

_____

_____

6. A social worker visits her clients regularly to check their progress.

_____

_____

7. A criminal who breaks the law repeatedly should serve his full jail term.

_____

_____

8. A reporter must check his facts carefully.

_____

_____

9. An anthropologist in the field should take care of his digging tools.

_____

_____

10. If your doctor doesn't give you an itemized bill, ask him for one.

_____

_____

PRACTICING 3

Rewrite the following sentences to correct the agreement errors and sexism.

1. Everyone should call their mother at least once a month.

_____

_____

2. Neither Nicole nor Sally turned in their homework.

_____

_____

3. A professor should be available to help her students.

_____

_____

4. Either my dog or my cat will get their shots today.

_____

_____

5. Everyone knows that they should not walk on the grass when it is wet.

_____

_____

6. A good boss plans her day efficiently.

_____

_____

7. Nobody in their right mind would do such a thing.

_____

_____

8. An architect needs his blueprints to present his ideas.

_____

_____

9. Everybody wanted their refund by mail.

_____

_____

10. An obstetrician should be considerate of his pregnant patients.

_____

_____

Error No. 10 Review

Rewrite the following paragraph to correct all pronoun agreement and sexism errors.

One problem I have with our neighborhood grocery store is that they hide flawed fruits and vegetables behind fruits and vegetables that are perfect. For instance, the other day, I was in the mood for a juicy nectarine. So, I drove to Tim's Market. In the back of the store, I spied a bin heaped with gorgeous yellowish red nectarines. With glad anticipation I gently palpated the top row of the heap to confirm that each of the globes were perfectly ripe—just ready to be eaten in heavenly juicy bites. Everyone around me were also admiring the fabulous display. No one indicated that they suspected anything wrong with the fruit. But when I started lifting off the top nectarines, I found that the nectarines in the layers underneath were bruised, small, or hard. Each of these nectarines were of inferior quality. None were like the large, attractive, ripe fruit adorning the top layer. It seems to me that when someone owns a grocery store, they should not pretend that all the fruit they sell is top quality. Damaged fruit and vegetables should be placed in a special bin to be sold at a lower price. Every grocery owner should respect his clients enough to be truly honest in his marketing strategies.

_____

_____

_____

_____

_____

_____

_____

_____

_____

_____

_____

_____

Error 11

Trouble with Comparisons and Superlatives

···

Adjectives and adverbs are **modifiers,** words that describe and explain. **Adjectives** describe a noun or a pronoun by narrowing it down to a specific type, such as in the following cases:

I envy that thin girl. **(Which girl? The *thin* one.)**

She feels lonely. **(How does she feel? She feels *lonely*.)**

The apples look ripe. **(How do the apples look? They look *ripe*.)**

Adverbs describe verbs, adjectives, and other adverbs in the following ways:

- They tell *how.*
- They tell *when.*
- They tell *where.*
- They tell *to what extent.*

Many adverbs end in *-ly*, but not all. These are all adverbs: *neatly, roughly, slowly, totally, considerably, really, yesterday, nearby*. Here are some more examples:

She ran very quickly. **(*Very* tells how she ran—describes the adverb *quickly*.)**

We're leaving soon. **(*Soon* tells when we're leaving—describes the verb *leaving*.)**

He stood here. **(*Here* tells where he stood—describes the verb *stood*.)**

They are terribly late. **(*Terribly* tells to what extent they are late—describes the adverb *late*.)**

Comparisons

Adjectives and adverbs are often used to make comparisons between two things. The rules for making comparisons are straightforward:

- For an adjective or adverb of one syllable, add *-er*.

The bread is warm.	**(One-syllable adjective)**
The rolls are warmer.	

He swallowed hard.	**(One-syllable adverb)**
She swallowed harder.	

- For an adjective or adverb of more than one syllable, add *more*.

The book was shocking.	**(Adjective of more than**
The movie was more shocking.	**one syllable)**

Our camp rebelled openly.	**(Adverb of more than**
Their camp rebelled even	**one syllable)**
more openly.	

- For an adjective or adverb that ends in *y*, drop the *y* and add *-ier* in the comparative.

She's lucky at love.
She's luckier at cars.

Jerry is funny.
Mary is funnier.

PRACTICING 1

Write the comparative form of each word listed below.

Example: long   <u>longer</u>

beautiful   <u>more beautiful</u>

1. messy _____

2. blunt _____

3. furious _____

4. desirable _____

5. cold _____

6. goofy _____

7. mean _____

8. clumsy _____

9. intelligent _____

10. happy _____

Double comparisons

A common mistake often heard in everyday speech is the **double comparison,** using both *-er* and *more.*

Incorrect: Phoenix is more hotter than San Francisco.
Correct: Phoenix is hotter than San Francisco.

Incorrect: Bunny is more quieter than Lisa.
Correct: Bunny is quieter than Lisa.

PRACTICING 2

Rewrite the following sentences to correct the comparisons.

1. Wayne has the more relaxeder attitude.

_____

_____

2. The sooner you leave, the more faster you will get there.

_____

_____

3. Her hairdo is attractiver than Joyce's.

_____

_____

4. This story is more sadder than I expected.

_____

_____

5. She was at peace and more serener than before.

_____

_____

6. Squirrels are much more quicker than rabbits.

_____

_____

7. Where freedom is concerned, Americans are more luckier than most other citizens.

_____

_____

8. When can we afford a more better car?

_____

_____

9. He traveled frequentlier than he had told me.

_____

_____

10. The ocean was dangerouser than it looked.

_____

_____

Superlatives

The comparative form of adjectives and adverbs is used to express a difference between two things.

> The first bell is loud.
> The second bell is louder.   **(Comparative)**

To express differences among three or more things, you must use the superlative form of an adjective or adverb.

> The first bell is loud.
> The second bell is louder.   **(Comparative)**
> The third bell is loudest.   **(Superlative)**

> The salmon is fresh.
> The swordfish is fresher.   **(Comparative)**
> The trout is freshest of all.   **(Superlative)**

The rules for changing adjectives and adverbs into the superlative form are simple:

- For an adverb or adjective of one syllable, add *-est*.

dark	darker	darkest
light	lighter	lightest
short	shorter	shortest

He was the shortest of all the basketball players.

Notice that some adjectives or adverbs double the final consonant: glad-der/gladdest, sadder/saddest, dimmer/dimmest, bigger/biggest.

■ For an adjective that ends in *y,* drop the *y* and add *-iest.*

funny	funnier	funniest
fancy	fancier	fanciest
petty	pettier	pettiest

Marty was the craziest of them all.

■ For an adjective or adverb of two or more syllables, add the word *most.*

wonderful	more wonderful	most wonderful
fortunate	more fortunate	most fortunate
interesting	more interesting	most interesting

Loons make the most dreadful sound at night.

PRACTICING 3

In the blanks provided, write the correct superlative forms of the words below.

1. merciful _____

2. skinny _____

3. sweet _____

4. carefully _____

5. pushy _____

6. smoothly _____

7. thoughtful _____

8. hideous _____

9. unusual _____

10. thick _____

Problems with superlatives

When you use superlatives, watch out for these common errors of every-day speech:

■ Use the superlative only when you are speaking of *more than two things.*

Incorrect: She is the most qualified of the two applicants.

Correct: She is the more qualified of the two applicants.

Incorrect: This is the funniest of the two scenes.

Correct: This is the funnier of the two scenes.

■ Do not use both an *-est* or an *-iest* ending and *most*.

Incorrect: That is the most kindest gesture imaginable.

Correct: That is the kindest gesture imaginable.

Incorrect: She has the most sunniest disposition.

Correct: She has the sunniest disposition.

PRACTICING 4

Rewrite the following sentences to correct the errors in forming the superlative.

1. Isn't this place the most wonderfulest you could ever imagine?

_____

_____

2. Both models on the cover are the beautifulest.

_____

_____

3. This is the most hardest math assignment I have ever been given.

_____

_____

4. Older people can give you the most wisest counsel of all.

_____

_____

5. Of the three, she is the most youngest.

_____

_____

6. Have the judges given out the gold medal to the most worthiest of the three athletes?

_____

_____

7. Many people find Irish storytellers the interestingest of all English language writers.

_____

_____

8. Miami's the most hottest city imaginable in the summer.

_____

_____

9. Our choir has the most talentedest singers.

_____

_____

10. The biggest cities are bound to harbor the corruptest criminals.

_____

_____

PRACTICING 5

For the following sentences, first decide if a comparative or superlative form is needed. Then write the correct form.

Example: It was the (beautiful) <u>most beautiful</u> rainbow I'd ever seen.

1. She was the (fanatic) _____ person I have ever met.

2. Of the two dogs, the boxer was the (friendly) _____ .

3. The Arco Building seemed the (high) _____ building I had ever seen.

4. Of all the office managers, she was the (efficient) _____ .

5. A ripe peach is (sweet) _____ than a ripe plum.

6. Of the two candles, the red one was the (pretty) _____ .

7. Uncle George was the (ambitious) _____ member of my dad's family.

8. Consider the three routes, then take the (fast) _____ .

9. We were asked to relate the (embarrassing) _____ moment of our childhood.

10. The bridge is (slippery) _____ than the road when it rains.

Error No. 11 Review

Rewrite the passage that follows to correct all incorrect comparatives or superlatives.

When there is a choice at the grocery store, I always ask for a plastic bag rather than a paper one. First of all, plastic bags are usefuller than paper ones because you can use them as small garbage can liners or as handy travel bags. Second of all, plastic bags are more stronger than paper ones. If a paper bag gets the least bit damp, it tears, and all of its contents spill out—sometimes causing the embarrassingest situation imaginable. People rush to your aid thinking, "This shopper is more clumsy than a clown." Besides, plastic bags preserve trees because to make paper bags you have to cut down trees. I show off that I am more ecologicaler than shoppers with paper bags when I exit from the grocery store. Using plastic instead of paper grocery bags is one of the most easiest ways to be environmentally conscious.

_____

_____

_____

_____

_____

_____

_____

_____

_____

Error 12

Dangling or Misplaced Modifiers

A **modifier** is a word or phrase that describes. Modifiers are adjectives, adverbs, or words or phrases that function as adjectives or adverbs. What a modifier describes in a sentence depends not only on what it says, but also where it is put.

Snapping violently, the tourists ran from the alligator.

Here *snapping violently* is a modifier. Because of its place in the sentence, however, it modifies *tourists* rather than *alligator*. Such a modifier is said to dangle.

Dangling Modifiers

A **dangling modifier** is a word or phrase at the beginning of a sentence that mistakenly modifies the word immediately following. When a modifier begins a sentence, *the word it modifies must come immediately after*. Otherwise, the modifier will be unconnected to the word the writer meant it to modify. In short, it will dangle. Here are some examples:

Dangling: Dipping below the horizon, I watched as the sun set.

Dangling: Confused and upset, the crowded store caused the little girl to lose her mother.

Dangling: Screeching, we looked for our binoculars as the owl flew by.

To correct these sentences, place the word being modified immediately after the modifier and rewrite as necessary.

Correct: Dipping below the horizon, the sun set as I watched.

Correct: Confused and upset, the little girl lost her mother in the crowded store.

Correct: Screeching, the owl flew away as we looked for our binoculars.

Sometimes correcting a dangling modifier results in the passive voice. In this case, restructure the sentence completely. Here is an example:

Dangling:	Hiding under a rock, I found a little lizard.
Correct but passive voice:	Hiding under a rock, a little lizard was found by me.
Correct and active voice:	I found a little lizard hiding under a rock.

PRACTICING 1

Rewrite these sentences to correct the dangling modifiers.

1. Fluttering wildly, I caught the butterfly in my net.

_____

_____

2. Newly polished, the guests marveled at the gleaming silverware.

_____

_____

3. Hurrying through the grocery store, my shopping bag seemed especially heavy.

_____

_____

4. Old and broken, she left the couch behind when she moved.

_____

_____

5. Drooping pitifully, I watered the plant.

_____

_____

6. Drenched from the recent rain, he still watered the lawn.

_____

_____

7. Weeping on stage, the audience was enthralled by the actor.

_____

_____

8. Pounded by waves and sinking at the stern, I watched the ship go down.

_____

_____

9. As an athlete, weight training is very important.

_____

_____

10. Wearing my new glasses, the stars in the sky looked beautiful.

_____

_____

Misplaced Modifiers

A modifier tends to modify the nearest noun. For example, notice how the meaning of the following sentence changes as we move the modifier **only:**

She went into the pool wearing her only bikini.	**(She owned only one bikini. *Only* is modifying *bikini*.)**
She went into the pool wearing only her bikini.	**(She wore nothing but a bikini. *Only* is modifying *wearing*.)**

A **misplaced modifier** is too far from the word it is meant to modify and, as a result, it doesn't convey the correct meaning or it gives the sentence an unintended, funny meaning. Here are some examples of misplaced modifiers with unintentional meanings:

Misplaced: The fisherman caught a bass with a chuckle.
Misplaced: I climbed a tree with new shoes on.
Misplaced: She bicycled to Burlington to visit her grandmother wearing a bike helmet.

Because of a misplaced modifier, we have *a bass with a chuckle, a tree with new shoes,* and *grandmother wearing a bike helmet.* A misplaced modifier is corrected by rewriting the sentence. You must reword the modifier or move it closer to the word it modifies. Here are possible corrections:

> With a chuckle, the fisherman caught a bass.
> With new shoes on, I climbed the tree.
> Wearing a bike helmet, she bicycled to Burlington to visit her grandmother.

To avoid the confusion of misplaced modifiers, always place a modifier immediately in front of the word it is meant to modify. This is especially true of one-word modifiers such as *almost, even, hardly, nearly, only,* and *often.* Because these words limit what follows, it is important where they occur in a sentence. Remember the bikini example at the beginning of this section. Another example follows.

> He just baked a cake.   **(He did it a moment ago.)**
> He baked just a cake.   **(He didn't bake bread.)**

PRACTICING 2

First underline the misplaced modifier in each sentence below. Then rewrite the sentence so that the modifier is correctly placed.

Example: I put money in the bank <u>with a smile</u>.

<u>With a smile, I put money in the bank.</u>

1. Jonathan gave his dog a bone with a pat on the head.

_____

_____

2. At the ceremony, he retired with honors in his uniform.

_____

_____

3. The pool table seemed tilted to the customers.

_____

_____

4. We saw huge fir trees skiing down the slope on both sides.

_____

_____

5. Josephine barbecued ribs for 20 people on the grill.

_____

_____

6. The jogger ran past the dog wearing a funny hat.

_____

_____

7. Spaghetti is most delicious when it is eaten on a patio with meat balls.

_____

_____

8. She almost handed out candy to the trick-or-treaters for two hours.

_____

_____

9. We saw the ocean waves sitting on a deck.

_____

_____

10. The young lovers admired the moon going on a stroll.

_____

_____

Error No. 12 Review

Underline the dangling and misplaced modifiers in the following paragraph. Then rewrite the sentences correctly in the spaces below. You should find six errors.

My favorite place during the summer is the beach. Relaxing on the sand, the waves roll in peacefully. Seagulls look for crabs overhead. When I'm on the beach, my mind is full of nothing but relaxation and pleasant dreams playing in the sand. Buzzing noisily, I ignore the hordes of flies. Occasionally, I wade into the surf and enjoy watching the waves up close with my shoes on. Thinking neither of work nor school, the beach is pure pleasure. In fact, when I'm on the beach, I think of nothing at all, except how lovely it is to be there.

_____

_____

_____

_____

_____

_____

Error 13

Omitted Commas
Part I

Punctuation marks are the traffic signs of writing. They are the visible marks that tell the reader when to slow down, when to speed up, and when to stop. In spoken sentences punctuation is heard as pauses, upbeats, and downbeats.

The Comma (,)

You hear the comma as a half-pause. Sometimes the comma just makes listening or reading easier, but sometimes it is crucial to meaning. Here is an example:

> Still, water was important to many primitive tribes.
> Still water was important to many primitive tribes.

The difference in the meanings of these two sentences depends on where the comma is placed. In the first sentence, *still* means "nonetheless" or "nevertheless." In the second sentence, *still* serves as an adjective describing *water*.

In this section we will cover two hard-and-fast rules of comma usage.

Commas with coordinating conjunctions

Place a comma in front of coordinating conjunctions (*and, but, or, for, nor, so, yet*) that link independent clauses (see Unit 21).

> He dated Mabel, but he did not fall in love with her.
> I am obsessed with neatness, and my girl friend is, too.
> He wrote me three letters, so I finally answered him.

Do not use a comma before *and* if it is not followed by an independent clause.

> **Incorrect:** He read a magazine, and watched TV.
> **Correct:** He read a magazine and watched TV.

PRACTICING 1

Finish the following sentences by adding another independent clause and a coordinating conjunction. Remember to use a comma.

Example: The clouds were beautiful.

<u>The clouds were beautiful, but they brought heavy rain.</u>

1. The earth is mother to us all _____
2. I love movies _____
3. On July 4 we always have a picnic _____
4. Make a fresh pot of coffee _____
5. Love is what makes the world happy _____
6. Fred plays the violin in private _____
7. We're good friends _____
8. Many people are utterly sincere _____
9. The dew was on the rose _____
10. Jane should stop feeling sorry for herself _____

Commas with introductory words, phrases, and clauses

Use a comma after introductory words, phrases, and clauses.

Words: Therefore, we beg you to be patient.
Well, I am not the least bit surprised.
Derrick, I'll take full responsibility.

Phrases: Seen from the top of the hill, the church was small.
Having expressed my view, I withdrew from the argument.
By the way, you owe me $10.00.

Use a comma after a dependent clause only if it comes at the beginning, but not at the end, of a sentence:

If at first you don't succeed, try again.

but

Try again if at first you don't succeed.
When I get a raise, I'm getting a new suit.

but

I'm getting a new suit when I get a raise.

PRACTICING 2

Insert commas where needed. Mark *C* for correct if no comma is needed.

1. _____ No they cannot enter without paying a fee.

2. _____ If he is a great man then many men are great.

3. _____ Although he had a headache Clarence continued to run.

4. _____ Take a left on Elm Street and then a right at the first light.

5. _____ She made a budget but she is not sticking to it.

6. _____ Nevertheless high heels are bad for your posture.

7. _____ I have two job interviews tomorrow and one on Monday.

8. _____ When we live by the sword we perish by the sword.

9. _____ First of all finding happiness should not be your primary goal.

10. _____ He hates to give speeches but he always accepts when it's for a good cause.

PRACTICING 3

Insert commas where needed. In the spaces provided, state the rule that makes the comma necessary.

Example: Ted, your dad is looking for you.

Rule: A comma follows an introductory word. _____

1. Because I am a woman I believe that mothers influence sons.

Rule: _____

2. Serena please pass the salt and pepper.

Rule: _____

3. She accepted the gold trophy and he accepted the blue ribbon.

Rule: _____

4. If we had known the consequences we would have stayed at home.

Rule: _____

5. Additionally he stole her wallet.

Rule: _____

6. The lightening bolt flashed across the sky and rain poured from the heavens.

Rule: _____

7. From where I sit I have observed some fascinating people.

Rule: _____

8. Although he hates routine he orders his coffee at 7:00 A.M. every morning.

Rule: _____

9. Are they planning to pick you up or are you driving alone?

Rule: _____

10. If you hate your job your health is bound to be affected.

Rule: _____

Error No. 13 Review

Correct the passage that follows by placing commas where they belong.

Parents and grandparents who don't learn to use the Internet are behind the time and their situation will only get worse. From a common sense point of view computer literacy is a modern requirement. If you think about it learning to use computers today is equivalent to learning to drive a car fifty years ago. The school in my home town sponsors several media literacy classes and our local community college offers special workshops in using the Internet. These classes teach older adults basic skills and how to connect with the World Wide Web. They even receive tips on how to supervise their children's use of the Internet. My mother has not yet taken advantage of these classes. Therefore she knows nothing about the technology her children use every day. However our neighbor took a computer course and enjoyed it very much. If this neighbor's enthusiasm influences my mother to sign up for the class I'll be thrilled. She might then become technologically literate and part of the twenty-first century.

Omitted Commas
Part II

In Error 13 you learned two rules for using commas:

1. Place a comma in front of coordinating conjunctions (*and, but, or, for, nor, so, yet*) that link independent clauses.

2. Use a comma after introductory words, phrases, and clauses.

In this section you will learn two more hard-and-fast rules for using commas: (1) Use commas to separate items in a series, and (2) place commas around words that interrupt the flow of a sentence.

Use commas to separate items in a series.

We can talk, daydream, play cards, or read.
They swam, played football, and threw the Frisbee.
The soft, furry leaves feel like velvet.
We will research the facts, gather support, and publicize our cause.

Do not, however, use commas unnecessarily with words in a series.

Do not use a comma before "and" if only two items are mentioned.

Incorrect: He reads novels, and poetry.
Correct: He reads novels and poetry.

Do not use a comma between modifiers unless you can insert the word "and" between them.

Incorrect: She carried beautiful, red roses.
Correct: She carried beautiful red roses.

You wouldn't say *She carried the beautiful and red roses,* so you shouldn't use a comma. You would, however, use a comma between the modifiers of this sentence:

A fresh, brisk breeze blew off the ocean.

You could insert an *and* between the modifiers, and the sentence would still sound right:

ESL Advice!

If you can't hear the incorrectness of the sentence, memorize the rule.

A fresh and brisk breeze blew off the ocean.

Do not use a comma before the first item in a series or after the last.

Incorrect:	We went, to sightsee, to shop, to dine out, and to enjoy, ourselves.
Correct:	We went to sightsee, to shop, to dine out, and to enjoy ourselves.
Incorrect:	She put, her shoes, her handbag, and her suitcase, in the trunk of the car.
Correct:	She put her shoes, her handbag, and her suitcase in the trunk of the car.

PRACTICING 1

Insert commas as necessary to separate items in a series.

1. They jumped over rocks trees and bushes.

2. We can do the job with a little luck a little effort and a little perseverance.

3. I love you more than chocolate marshmallows apple pie and fudge brownies.

4. You need paper pencil and your textbook.

5. Bright sparkling water gushed from the beautiful old fountain.

6. They ate pasta bread and peanuts to get ready for the race.

7. I have a dog a cat a bird and a snake.

8. Do you prefer yams bananas or plantains?

9. My mother my father my sister and my brother live with me.

10. I like to watch baseball football tennis and soccer on television.

PRACTICING 2

Strike through the unnecessary commas in the following sentences.

Example: The old lady put down her coat, and hat.

1. She runs, lifts weights, and eats plenty of fresh vegetables, to keep fit.

2. I love my house, and my garden.

3. My neighbors include, a Jamaican, an American, and an Armenian.

4. My ugly, blue car is in the garage.

5. Pack sandwiches, fruit, drinks, and cookies, for the picnic.

6. I love Beethoven, and Chopin.

7. Among my uncle's favorite foods, are ice cream, apples, peaches, and apricots.

8. The brand, new Jeep belongs to my roommate.

9. The card games we like include, canasta, gin, poker, and hearts.

10. The band played blues, and rock and roll.

Place commas around words that interrupt the flow of a sentence.

In talking it is natural to pause before and after words that interrupt the flow of thought. In writing, this pause is signaled by a comma. Interruptions include the following:

1. Expression.

You understand, of course, that the position is temporary.

2. Descriptive phrase.

The lighthouse, tall and majestic, stood among the rocks.
Mr. Golub, our mail carrier, is always very pleasant.

3. Prepositional phrase.

The ice, on which the skaters glided, shone in the moonlight.

4. Unessential clauses that begin with *who, whose, which, when, where,* or *that.*

Elaine, who went to Oakland Community College, now lives in Detroit.

A clause containing information that is *not* essential to understanding a sentence is enclosed by commas.

Ms. Jones, who works at Benson's, witnessed the accident.

(Because Ms. Jones is named, the information in the clause is not essential to identify her as the woman who witnesses the accident.)

On the other hand, the clause containing information essential to understanding the sentence is not set off by commas.

The woman who works at Benson's witnessed the accident.

Now the information in the clause is essential to identify who witnessed the accident—*the woman who works at Benson's,* since we don't know her name.

Commas needed:	The poet read "Daddy," which I'd never heard.
Commas not needed:	The poet read a poem that I'd never heard before.

Most of the time, relative clauses with *which* need commas while relative clauses with *that* do not.

Commas needed:	The horse Anchovy, which I often ride, is in the stable.
Commas not needed:	The horse that I often ride is in the stable.

PRACTICING 3

Underline the words that interrupt the flow of the sentence, then place commas around them.

Example: My uncle who now has gray hair is also my best friend.

My uncle, who now has gray hair, is also my best friend.

1. The beloved teacher who had taught for 50 years finally retired.

2. The divorce which no one expected was final last week.

3. He realized of course that he would never make his plane.

4. My mother a champion rug hooker never took lessons in her art.

5. The old cat purring furiously rubbed up against my leg.

6. The police officer who is also our crossing guard always looks out for the small children.

7. Mr. Smith by the way is a champion chess player.

8. Self-confidence a key ingredient in success can be developed.

9. The garden around which we strolled is very well cared-for.

10. You are nevertheless mistaken on that point.

PRACTICING 4

Insert the omitted commas in the following sentences. Use all four rules that you have learned in Errors 13 and 14. Then, in the spaces provided, state the rule. If no comma is needed, state the rule that makes it unnecessary.

1. I spoke to him repeatedly but he wouldn't listen.

Rule: _____

2. You need a walking stick a backpack and a compass for the hike.

Rule: _____

3. Of course it is your right to decline.

Rule: _____

4. My uncle Harry who wears a hearing aid was at my graduation.

Rule: _____

5. Peter will you answer the bell?

Rule: _____

6. I wore my new blue blazer.

Rule: _____

7. They had however other plans.

Rule: _____

8. She heard my voice and came into the room.

Rule: _____

9. My best friend who is also my accountant went with me.

Rule: _____

10. Because you're so nice I wanted to give you a gift.

Rule: _____

Error No. 14 Review

Rewrite the following paragraph to add commas where needed.

Even with a plan it's easy to get derailed. For example when I started college my goal was to become a pediatric nurse. I concentrated on getting good grades so I studied hard working long hours into the night. My science classes required a tremendous amount of reading memorizing and hours of lab work. But in the spring of 1998 I enrolled in a drama class as an elective. I was chosen to be in the school musical and I started to hang out with other drama students. They were all one big bad influence. They spent their days and evenings in the auditorium instead of the classroom. Being young and naïve I took to these devil-may-care people faster than you can say "ambisol." As a result my career goals crashed burned and went up in smoke. I neglected reading assignments cut class and skipped labs. All I did was hang around with my new theater friends pretending we were headed for Broadway and fame. When my mother noticed my grades slipping she warned me that my new friends were bad for me but of course I didn't listen. Fortunately the school newspaper panned my performance and I came to my senses. I also realized that I was hurting my mother the person I loved most. So I quit drama and started studying. I am now back to my original hopes and dreams bolstered by diligence and determination.

Error 15

Apostrophe Problems

T he apostrophe (') has two uses, to show possession and to indicate a contraction.

Use the apostrophe to show possession.

The chart below shows how apostrophes are used to show possession or ownership. For a singular noun, always add *'s*. However, to form the possessive of a plural noun ending in *s*, add only the apostrophe. If the plural does not end in *s*, add *'s*.

SINGULAR (ALWAYS ADD 'S)	PLURAL
dog's tail	dogs' tails
boss's desk	bosses' desks
woman's hat	women's hats
Genevieve Smith's home	the Smiths' home

PRACTICING 1

Make the following nouns possessive. First decide if the noun is singular or plural. Then decide if you need only an apostrophe or *'s*.

1. The Browns barbecue
2. The cat dish
3. The doctors offices
4. The person mood
5. The children games
6. The car windshield
7. The Moses Ten Commandments
8. The politicians photograph
9. The churches towers
10. The barnyard smell

Use the apostrophe to show an omission in a contraction.

Apostrophes are used to show omitted letters in contractions, such as *don't (do not)* or *isn't (is not)*. Contractions are commonly used in informal writing. Here are some common contractions:

cannot	can't
could have	could've
could not	couldn't
did not	didn't
do not	don't
has not	hasn't
have not	haven't
he is	he's
I am	I'm
I would	I'd
it is	it's
let us	let's
she is	she's
should have	should've
should not	shouldn't
they are	they're
they are not	they aren't
was not	wasn't
who is	who's
will not	won't
would have	would've
would not	wouldn't

EAR ALERT

In speech we can hear these contractions. What we cannot hear is exactly where the apostrophe goes—where the letter was actually omitted.

wouldn't, not would'nt   **(The apostrophe marks the omission of the *o*.)**

they're, not theyr'e   **(The apostrophe marks the omission of the *a*.)**

Remember to put the apostrophe exactly where the letter is missing.

Do not use apostrophes unnecessarily.
Only use an apostrophe with a possessive.

Incorrect: The mother's are having a bakesale for Oakton School.
Correct: The mothers are having a bakesale for Oakton School.

To test whether a noun is possessive or not, turn it into an *of* phrase.

The baby's blanket is wet.   **(baby's blanket =**
                                    blanket of baby =
                                    possessive)

The quiz answers' are on the sheet.   **(answers' are =**
                                        the are of the answers =
                                        not possessive)

Do not use apostrophes with the pronouns his, hers, its, ours, yours, or theirs.

Incorrect: The scarf is hers'.
Correct: The scarf is hers.

Incorrect: Put the CD back in it's case.
Correct: Put the CD back in its case.

It's is a contraction—short for *it is*. If you unravel the contraction, you get:

Put the CD back in it is case.

which makes no sense.

PRACTICING 2

Rewrite the following sentences to use contractions whenever possible.

Example: They did not obey the rules.

   They didn't obey the rules. _____

   1. You should not rollerblade without knee pads.

   _____

   _____

   2. I could not have cared less.

   _____

   _____

   3. Lou will not take out the garbage.

   _____

   _____

4. He was not at all impressed with their answer.

_____

_____

5. They said they had not seen him.

_____

_____

6. If he could have attended the meeting, he would have.

_____

_____

7. Why have you not finished your homework?

_____

_____

8. If you did not owe me $10 dollars I would not be so skeptical.

_____

_____

9. I am afraid it is too late for apologies.

_____

_____

10. Who is going to carry in the cake?

_____

_____

PRACTICING 3

Insert apostrophes where needed.

1. Despite health warnings, peoples desire for junk food continues.

2. Were wondering how long hes going to defy the law.

3. According to him, its someone elses fault.

4. Ten artists are displaying their paintings at John Kellers new gallery.

5. Shes afraid of lightning, but he isnt.

6. Africas wild life attracts many photographers.

7. The storys ending puzzled many readers.

8. My cousin inherited Aunt Idas old piano.

9. The governments leaders would only meet in neutral territory.

10. Marvs tattoos have become infected.

PRACTICING 4

Every sentence below has one apostrophe error. It may be missing an apostrophe (or *'s*) in a possessive or in a contraction. Sometimes the error is an unnecessary apostrophe. Add apostrophes (or *'s*) where they are needed. Strike out all unnecessary apostrophes.

1. Lets fetch Grandpa's coat so he won't be cold.

2. Wasn't he the biggest coward youve ever seen?

3. Put the trophy in it's place on the mantle.

4. Don't be so sure that the bracelet is her's.

5. The contract is asking for two weeks vacation per year.

6. Put an apple and two cookies's in his lunch box.

7. Its my opinion that students shouldn't get an A on a late paper.

8. The Rodmans' and the Joneses attended the game.

9. Its not up to me to give you a pass.

10. Most of the actors faces had been made up to look old

Error No. 15 Review

The passage that follows contains ten misplaced or missing apostrophes. Rewrite the passage to correct these errors.

The best taste in the world belongs to chocolate. Whether dark cocoa or light milk chocolate, it's creamy texture delights my pallet. But chocolate is addicting, and once I start eating it, I ca'nt stop. Lately Ive read that doctors attitudes have changed toward chocolate. Doctors used to warn that chocolate caused tooth decay, headache's, and all manner of other illnesses. But now some medical researchers have found that chocolate is a mood elevator and even an aphrodisiac. I think it was my mothers fudge that started me on the road to being a chocolaholic. No one elses fudge could compare with her's. I used to sit in my room with a large square of

Mom's fudge on a porcelain saucer, and I felt so comforted and queenly as I bit into one nutty piece after another. You woul'dve thought I was in heaven. Other desserts are lovely, but they just dont compare with good chocolate.

_____

_____

_____

_____

_____

_____

_____

_____

_____

Error 16

Trouble with Quotation Marks

Your ear may tell you when a pause means a comma, but sometimes your ear is of little use in identifying the correct punctuation. For certain punctuation marks, you must simply learn the rules. In this unit you will learn how to use quotation marks correctly.

Use quotation marks to indicate a person's exact words.

One of the two main written uses for quotations marks ("") is to indicate a person's exact words—called a direct quotation. Direct quotations can be reported in a number of different ways, all requiring quotation marks.

> He remarked, "This is rather difficult."
> "This is rather difficult," he remarked.
> "This," he said, "is rather difficult."
> "This is difficult," he remarked. "And it doesn't get any easier."

Begin every quotation with a capital letter.

Do not, however, use a capital letter for the second part of a divided quotation that is *not* a full sentence.

> "I work at the zoo," she said, "because I love animals."

Here the second part of the divided quotation is not a full sentence, so a comma is used after *said,* but no capital letter.

> "Give me the money," his father said. "I'll put it in the bank for you."

Here the second part of the divided quotation is a full sentence. A period follows *said* and the second part of the quotation begins with a capital letter.

Do not use quotation marks in indirect quotations.

An indirect quotation—rewording what someone has said—does not require quotation marks. Often an indirect quotation is announced by the words *that, what,* or *if.* Some examples follow.

Direct quotation:	Peter said, "Go ahead and start without me."
Indirect quotation:	Peter said that we should go ahead and start without him.
Direct quotation:	The butler asked, "Shall I serve tea, Madam?"
Indirect quotation:	The butler asked if he should serve tea.

PRACTICING 1

Add the required quotation marks.

Example: I'm betting on your horse, said the gambler, because he's the fastest.

"I'm betting on your horse," said the gambler, "because he's the fastest."

1. Whatever you do, don't look back, said the guide.

2. I'm a man of the ocean, said the sailor. That's why I hate land.

3. Why was I ever born? the teenager asked.

4. To do the dishes, his mother replied. That's why you were born.

5. Alexander wondered, Where have all the flowers gone?

6. I do not, she said, always fall asleep during the sermon.

7. I don't eat anything with eyes, explained the vegetarian.

8. Jumping through the hoop, the tiger seemed to be saying, I'm tired of this.

9. I shower only on Sunday, the old gentleman remarked. I never shower on Monday.

10. The auctioneer cried, Going, going, gone!

PRACTICING 2

Place quotation marks only around the exact words of the speaker; leave the sentence unchanged if the quotation is indirect.

1. John wondered what had happened at the party.

2. Let me guess, Josephine said. You must be the new mail carrier.

3. Tony asked his editor if she had gone crazy.

4. As a matter of fact, the editor replied, I have—from deadlines.

5. The police recommended that we file a report.

6. Happy birthday, we all shouted, and many happy returns.

7. She suggested that we stay for cake and coffee.

8. Walter explained that only one replacement would be hired.

9. Are you here to apply for the job? he asked. Please fill out this application.

10. It's getting late, she said. Are you nearly finished?

Using other punctuation with quotation marks

Commas and periods always go inside the quotation marks.

> "The food is very spicy," said Hal.
> "Eat slowly," she suggested, "and drink plenty of water."

Question marks and exclamation points go either inside or outside, depending on the sentence.

> **Inside:** "Why are you asking?" the lawyer wondered.
> **Outside:** Who just asked, "Why are you asking"?

In the first example the spoken words make up a separate question; in the second example the spoken words are part of the question.

> "Duck!" Paul screamed.
> Paul keeps screaming, "Duck"!

In the first example the spoken words make up a separate command; in the second the spoken words are part of the command.

PRACTICING 3

The sentences that follow use other punctuation marks in connection with quotation marks. In the spaces provided, write *C* if the sentence is correctly punctuated and *NC* if it is not. Correct the sentence if it is incorrectly punctuated.

Example: __C__ "What are you doing?" he asked.

1. _____ The acrobat cried, "I missed you"!

2. _____ "How much is your rent?" he asked.

3. _____ The gentleman grumped, "So you say", adding, "but I know better."

4. _____ Who said, "Give me liberty, or give me death"?

5. _____ "Find yourself a job"! she bawled.

6. _____ "Give me a break!" he cried.

7. _____ Who just said, "I'm tired of this movie?"

8. _____ "Sir," she remarked bitterly, "you are no gentleman".

9. _____ "I will not"! she snapped.

10. _____ They asked, "Now, what's the matter"?

Use quotation marks to indicate titles of short works

Use quotation marks to indicate the titles of short works, such as magazine articles and short stories. Underline or italicize the titles of long works.

SHORTER WORKS	LONGER WORKS
magazine article—"Outlet Shopping"	magazine—*Consumer Reports*
newspaper article—"City Council Approves New Train Station"	newspaper—*The Cleveland Press*
book chapter—"The Child from Ages 2 to 6"	book—*Child Development*
poem—"America"	poetry collection—*The Collected Poems of Allen Ginsberg*
song—"Buffalo Soldier"	movie—*Shane*
editorial—"Stand Up for Your Rights"	television series—*Frasier*

PRACTICING 4

Use quotation marks or underlining as required.

Example: Stay Young is an essay that appears in an anthology titled Readings for Writers.

"Stay Young" is an essay that appears in an anthology titled <u>Readings for Writers</u>.

1. Chapter 3 is entitled Purpose and Thesis.

2. My favorite Bob Marley song is No Woman No Cry.

3. Running in the Family is an amusing book.

4. My uncle's favorite book is A Passage to India.

5. Did you see the movie Titanic?

6. I read an interesting editorial in the Atlanta Constitution; it was called "Enough Already."

7. The Jamaica Journal is an informative magazine about Jamaica.

8. I love the television series The Nanny.

9. Saving Private Ryan is a realistic but gory movie.

10. His favorite play is Death of a Salesman.

Error No. 16 Review

Add the missing quotation marks where needed. Some sentences are correct.

My aunt and I have a private book club between us. Every week, we try to read a book together and then discuss it afterwards. Sometimes we choose a book that's too big to be read in a week, and it takes us longer. The last book we read together was The Nightmare Years by William L. Shirer. My aunt's favorite chapter in that book is chapter 4, which is entitled The Year Off in Spain, 1933. I like the way he writes, said my aunt. I especially like his plain style. I agree, I replied, because he gets right into his subject quickly and without any fussiness. What do you mean by fussiness? my aunt wondered. I explained that I meant Shirer is not a pretentious writer. He's always down-to-earth and to the point, I added. My aunt agreed with me. She said she found that trait also in his most famous book, The Rise and Fall of the Third Reich, which we had read last year. He writes that way, said my aunt, because he used to be a newspaper reporter for the Chicago Tribune. He learned his writing trade in the newsroom. When we're finished reading this book, we intend to read Berlin Diary, Stranger Come Home, and The Rise and Fall of Adolf Hitler, which are other books by Mr. Shirer.

Error 17

Incorrect Capitalization Part I

Because capital (uppercase) and lowercase letters sound the same, your ear cannot help you with capitalization: *Penny,* the name, sounds the same as *penny,* the noun, meaning "a one-cent coin." To learn capitalization, you must know the rules. Here are the first set of rules (you will learn additional rules in the next section, Error 18):

- Capitalize the first word in a sentence or direct quotation.
- Capitalize names of individual persons and the word I.
- Capitalize family relationships used as names.
- Capitalize the names of nationalities, religions, races, tribes, and languages.
- Capitalize after a colon if what follows is a full sentence.
- Capitalize the names of the days of the week, months of the year, holidays, and religious occasions.
- Capitalize the names of specific places, including monuments.
- Capitalize the names of companies, clubs, political groups, and other official organizations.

Here are these rules of capitalization, one by one.

Capitalize the first word in a sentence or direct quotation.

Children often feel insecure.

Ralph Sockman said, "The test of courage comes when we are in the minority; the test of tolerance comes when we are in the majority."

"The fault," she insisted, "is in us."

Notice that in the third example, *the* is capitalized because it begins a new sentence; however, *is* remains lowercase because it is part of the first sentence.

PRACTICING 1

Correctly capitalize the following sentences.

1. Jessica complained vigorously. she said she felt deprived.

2. "can you give me a map?" she asked. "my sense of direction is terrible."

3. Carmen laughed, "he'll be fine if you just leave him alone."

4. I want to be remembered as a helpful person. helpful people are saints.

5. Run for your life! don't stay under the tree.

Capitalize names of individuals and the word I.

Give the note to Miss Ehrlich, not to Captain Douglas.
Our family doctor is Ruth Kazan.

Notice that nicknames are also capitalized.

He was known by his buddies as Big Shoulder Beans.

PRACTICING 2

Capitalize the names of individuals in the following sentences.

1. All Americans revere abraham lincoln.

2. I hate it when my dad's college pals call him shorty.

3. Laurence bradley, carolyn costaldo, and jose guiterrez are scheduled to talk at Career Day.

4. The greatest Sioux leader was sitting bull.

5. Many cities have named streets after the great civil rights leader, martin luther king.

Capitalize family relationships used as names.

Here comes Uncle Joe, drunk as a lord.
After Grandpa Justin had lunch, we went to the park.
Please don't give Mom so much trouble.

Notice that you do not capitalize *mother, father, grandmother, grandfather, uncle, aunt, cousin,* and so forth when these terms are preceded by *my, your, our,* or any other possessive word.

Ask Grandma if she'd like more tea.

but

Ask your grandma if she'd like more tea.

His aunt raises golden retrievers.

> but

Auntie Meg raises golden retrievers.

PRACTICING 3

Capitalize wherever necessary. Write *C* In the blank if the sentence is correct.

1. _____ My mother grew up on a farm in West Texas.

2. _____ I was so mortified that I never wanted to see aunt Ruby again.

3. _____ Her grandmother could ride a horse like a cowboy in a rodeo.

4. _____ My uncle Frank never mentions his brother, Norm.

5. _____ If you take dad to the airport, remind him to call mom.

Capitalize the names of nationalities, religions, races, tribes, and languages.

I love Chinese, Vietnamese, and Italian food.

The Baptist, Methodist, and Catholic churches are sponsoring a community picnic on Sunday.

Denise Chavez writes about the Mexican-American community in New Mexico.

Native Americans of the Southwest include the Zunis, Navajos, Apaches, and Utes.

Most people in Montreal speak both French and English.

PRACTICING 4

Fill in the blanks as indicated.

Example: In high school, I took (language) <u>Spanish</u>.

1. My best friend is (nationality) _____ .

2. Someone who is bilingual speaks two languages fluently, such as _____ and _____ .

3. People who live in Canada are _____ , and people who live in Mexico are _____ .

4. There are many Protestant denominations, including _____ , _____ , and _____ .

5. The (races) _____ , _____ , and _____ must learn to appreciate each other's cultures.

Capitalize after a colon if what follows is a full sentence.

Here is a command I can respect: "Love your neighbor as yourself."

but

The following ingredients are needed: eggs, flour, sugar, and milk.

PRACTICING 5

If the sentence is capitalized correctly, leave it alone. Write over any lowercase letters that should be capitalized.

Example: Dear Sir: ~~we~~ W regret that the table you ordered is still not in stock.

1. Please enclose the following papers: the bank statement, the tax return, and the application.

2. The poem begins as follows: "despair is a green snake with black wings."

3. Follow these directions: Dig a trench, hammer some stakes into the ground, and set up the tent.

4. Here are the virtues I am anticipating: loyalty, courage, and faith.

5. This is what I advised him: continue to take your medicine and see what happens.

Capitalize the days of the week, months of the year, holidays, and religious occasions.

Labor Day always falls on Monday.
My favorite time to snow ski is in January or February.
Halloween is becoming a very popular holiday.
Every Easter, I attend church services at sunrise.

Note that the seasons of the year are not capitalized.

I love the fall when all the leaves take on brilliant hues.
In the spring, people's thoughts turn to love.

PRACTICING 6

In the spaces provided, mark *C* if the sentence is properly capitalized and *NC* if it is not. Then correct the errors.

1. _____ Many Americans celebrate palm sunday as well as passover.

2. _____ Next Summer I plan to visit Guadalajara.

3. _____ I attend night school on tuesdays and wednesdays.

4. _____ Does school close on Martin Luther King Day?

5. _____ Every Christmas I eat candy until I'm sick.

Capitalize the names of specific places, including monuments.

Last summer we visited Mount Rushmore.
Some day I want to visit the Leaning Tower of Pisa in Italy.
Who engineered the Golden Gate Bridge?
I attend New York University and hope to graduate this year.
Follow Anderson Blvd. all the way to Stocker Road.
Park right in front of Brown's Bakery Shop.

Do not capitalize the names of places that are not specific:

He walked down the street toward the bakery shop.

but

He bicycled down Maple Street to Brown's Bakery Shop.

PRACTICING 7

Correct the capitalization errors in these sentences.

1. The hurricane hit miami and tampa before heading up the coast to south carolina.

2. Thousands of people visit yellowstone national park and mount rushmore each year.

3. My mother was born in the small town of haskell, texas; my father came from limerick, ireland.

4. First I have to stop at wagner's drug store and then at five star cleaners, which is right next door.

5. New orleans is on lake pontchartrain, which empties into the gulf of mexico.

Capitalize the names of companies, clubs, political groups, and other official organizations.

You can still get "full serve" at some Standard Oil stations.

"Bonjour" is the name of our French Club.

My brother switched from the Republican Party to the Democratic Party.

I belong to the National Organization for Women.

The Federal Bureau of Investigation (FBI) is headquartered in Washington.

PRACTICING 8

Underline the words that should be capitalized in the following sentences.

1. Our college uses national-international student programs (NISP) for its international study programs.
2. Belonging to the sorority alpha sigma alpha has helped me make friends on campus.
3. Several of my friends work at pacific bell telephone company.
4. Our next-door neighbor has been elected to the house of representatives.
5. She works at flossmore general hospital.

Error No. 17 Review

Correct all the capitalization errors in the following essay.

I love santa fe, new mexico. When you drive through the center of town, you would never guess that this is a state capital. The small town square is bordered on all sides by fabulous shops displaying authentic indian jewelry, rugs, and pottery. At the center of the square is a pretty little park where you can watch tribal dances and listen to hispanic music. One side of the square is called "governor's mansion." Along its front is a portal, where craftspeople from the various pueblos of the area display their wares. They sell hopi kachina dolls, zuni fetishes, navajo silver jewelry, and acoma pots. When I visit santa fe, I always stop by the wheelwright museum because it has a wonderful gift shop, where I can buy antique hopi kachinas. I also love to drive out to the little town of susuque for some delicious mexican tamales, smothered in red salsa and accompanied by freshly mashed guacamole. There's a picturesque little catholic church with a classic black steeple standing at the side of the road. If I have the time, I like to hike in bandalero state park or take a drive to some of the famous rock formations, like ship's rock or camel rock. All houses in santa fe are made of adobe so that when you drive up hyde park road toward the ski lift, you might actually think you're in a foreign country like iraq or in some mexican village. The new mexico sky in santa fe is gorgeous—filled with giant white puffy clouds that are a magical backdrop for lightning storms at night. Santa fe may not be as wild and exciting as chicago or new york city, but it is stunning in its rustic and artistic charms.

Incorrect Capitalization
Part II

I n the last section, Error 17, you learned these rules for capitalizing correctly:

- Capitalize the first word in a sentence or direct quotation.

- Capitalize names of individual persons and the word *I*.

- Capitalize family relationships used as names.

- Capitalize the names of nationalities, religions, races, tribes, and languages.

- Capitalize after a colon if what follows is a full sentence.

- Capitalize the names of the days of the week, months, holidays, and religious occasions.

- Capitalize the names of specific places, including monuments.

- Capitalize the names of companies, clubs, political groups, and other official organizations.

Now you will learn these other capitalization rules:

- Capitalize names of commercial products.

- Capitalize titles of books, magazines, essays, poems, stories, plays, articles, films, television shows, songs, and cartoons.

- Capitalize titles used in front of a person's name.

- Capitalize specific college courses.

- Capitalize areas of the country.

- Capitalize historical eras and events.

- Capitalize abbreviations of familiar organizations, corporations, people, countries, time, and titles.

- Capitalize the opening and the first word of the closing of a letter.

Capitalize the names of commercial products.

I use Tide because it works as well as any other laundry detergent.

Do not capitalize types of products.

We need paper towels, spaghetti sauce, and peanut butter.	**(These are merely types of products, not brand names.)**

but

Post oatmeal is good for you.	**("Post" is a brand name, but "oatmeal" is a type of food.)**

PRACTICING 1

Capitalize the names of commercial products in the following sentences.

1. I love hershey's chocolate.

2. My favorite milk additive is carnation.

3. I always use gillette shaving cream.

4. The most popular car of the 1960s was the volkswagen.

5. To repel mosquitoes, off works really well.

Capitalize titles of books, magazines, newspapers, essays, poems, stories, plays, articles, films, television shows, songs, and cartoons.

Book:	Have you read *Hearts* by Hilma Wolitzer?
Magazine:	I subscribe to *Discover* magazine.
Newspaper:	*The Washington Post* is a respected newspaper.
Essay:	Her essay is entitled "Affirmative Action and Women: Off the Cuff Comments."
Poems:	I love Lorena Bruff's poem, "The Cello."
Story:	"A Worn Path" is a moving short story.
Play:	She was wonderful in *King Lear*.
Article:	Read the article called "Shakespeare in the Bush."
Film:	*Civil Action* is a powerful movie.

Television Show:	I always watch "60 Minutes" on Sunday night.
Song:	Bob Marley's "War" uses the words of a speech as its lyrics.
Cartoon:	I miss "The Far Side" cartoons.

Notice how words are capitalized in titles. The beginning word is always capitalized. The first word after a colon is also always capitalized. Certain words are not capitalized, however, unless they come at the beginning.

Do not capitalize:

- The article *a, an,* or *the* unless it is the first word

- The coordinating conjunctions *and, but, yet, or, nor, so,* and *for*

- Short prepositions such as *of, from, by, in, up,* and *out* (capitalize prepositions of five or more letters, such as *about, among, between, behind, through, though,* and *without*)

PRACTICING 2

Correctly capitalize the titles in the following sentences.

1. I read an article in science fiction digest entitled "UFO's appear in farmer's field."

2. Paul Laurence Dunbar wrote a poem called "we wear the mask."

3. Two of my favorite television shows are "wheel of fortune" and "mad about you."

4. *A farewell to arms* can be found in the book, *collected short stories of ernest hemingway.*

5. First she sang "fly me to the moon" and then "moon over miami."

Capitalize titles used in front of a person's name.

President George W. Bush, Governor Zell Miller, Secretary of State Madeline Albright, General H. Norman Schwarzkopf, Jr., Attorney General Janet Reno, Mrs. Miller, Mr. Planter, Ms. Lowery

but

George W. Bush, the president of the United States; Zell Miller, governor of Georgia; Madeline Albright, secretary of state; H. Norman Schwarzkopf, Jr., retired general; and Janet Reno, attorney general of the United States

PRACTICING 3

In the blank in front of each sentence, write *C* if the sentence is correct and *NC* if it is incorrect. Correct by writing above the word.

1. _____ Warren Christopher was once the Secretary of State.
2. _____ My congratulations to Mr. Smith and miss james.
3. _____ One day a woman will be President of the United States.
4. _____ Richard Nixon was once vice president.
5. _____ They said that Congresswoman McKinney would speak.

Capitalize specific college courses.

I aced the exam in Algebra 100.

> but

All my life I've hated algebra.
I am taking Introduction to Psychology.

> but

Classes in psychology are very popular.
Language courses are always capitalized.
I'm taking French 100.
I'm planning on studying Chinese.

PRACTICING 4

Capitalize the names of specific college courses.

1. The hardest class I ever took was introduction to speech.
2. Last semester I got an A in anthropology and a B in spanish.
3. He says he is taking religion 101.
4. I made a fool of myself in introduction to acting.
5. My favorite class is introduction to prison literature.

Capitalize areas of the country.

People in the Midwest sometimes talk like Canadians.
We decided to move to the South.
I'll never live on the West Coast.

Do not capitalize compass directions or areas of the country used as adjectives.

Go south for two blocks, then turn north.
My mother speaks with a western clip.

PRACTICING 5

Fill in the blanks with an area of the country or a compass direction. Capitalize correctly.

Example: Her favorite aunt lives on the <u>East Coast</u>.

1. On the _____ side of the mountains, was a valley.

2. We drove all night, always heading _____ .

3. Thirteen years ago I moved from the _____ Coast to the _____ Coast.

4. If I could choose, I'd live in the _____ .

5. Go _____ on Berkford, and then turn _____ on Nancy Creek.

Capitalize historical eras and events.

In the Age of Reason humans tried to make sense of their world.
I wish I had lived during the Medieval Period.
Poetry from the Romantic Age was largely about nature.
Many Americans were hurt during the Depression.
The Battle of the Bulge was the last great battle of World War II.

PRACTICING 6

Mark *C* beside the sentence in each pair that is correctly capitalized.

1. _____ **(a).** Custer was killed in the battle of little big horn.

_____ **(b).** Custer was killed in the Battle of Little Big Horn.

2. _____ **(a).** The Civil War pitted American against American.

_____ **(b).** The civil war pitted American against American.

3. _____ **(a).** In the Victorian age people were very prudish.

_____ **(b).** In the Victorian Age people were very prudish.

4. _____ (a). The modern age is characterized by many good novels.

   _____ (b). The Modern Age is characterized by many good novels.

5. _____ (a). World War I was settled by the Treaty of Versailles.

   _____ (b). World war I was settled by the treaty of versailles.

Capitalize abbreviations of familiar organizations, corporations, people, countries, time, and titles.

Organization:	FAA, NCAA, MADD
Corporation:	GE, AT&T, MCI
People:	JFK, FDR, LBJ
Countries:	U.S.A. or USA, U.K, or UK
Time:	12:00 A.M., 2:30 P.M.
Titles:	Benjamine Stein, Sr.; Felicia Baquero, M.D.; Theodore Munch, Ph.D.; Carolyn Wu, D.D.S.

PRACTICING 7

Complete the following sentences with an appropriate abbreviation.

1. The abbreviation for the Soviet Union was _____ .

2. The Boy Scouts of America is sometimes abbreviated _____ .

3. The Food and Drug Administration, or _____ , is an important government agency.

4. Alcoholics Anonymous is known as _____ , and the Automobile Association of American is known as _____ .

5. John Chavez is both a medical doctor, or _____ and a doctor of philosophy, or _____ .

Capitalize the opening and the first word of the closing of a letter.

Dear Madame,

My dear Joseph,

Dear Dr. Pevitts,

Sincerely,

Sincerely yours,

Best regards,

Love and kisses,

PRACTICING 8

Write a letter about yourself as part of your application to be admitted to college. Capitalize correctly.

Error No. 18 Review

Correct all the capitalization errors in the following letter.

april 1st, 1999

Dear Peter,

this is a hard letter to write since I do not convey bad news well. I have signed up for three classes, all of which I like. I'm enrolled in introduction to freshman composition, economics 101, and us history from the revolutionary war to the civil war. I expect to do well in all of them because I am determined to study hard and get good grades. What's the bad news? Well, it is this: the girl you like so much—the one from the south who speaks in such a charming way—is in all my classes. What's more, on her own and without any prompting whatsoever from me, she has decided to sit right next to me in every class. I told her that you would not like that, especially since you come from the northeast and have a very jealous nature. You know what she said? She said she didn't care if you were secretly a cia agent from Washington, d.c., she intended to sit where she pleased. What can I do? I'm just a kid from the west coast who is used to free spirited california girls. I told you you should've stayed at citrus college rather than transferring to riverside university, but you wouldn't listen. Now, because of your thoughtlessness, I'm stuck with the prettiest girl in town.

yours sincerely,

John

P.S. I don't work for the fbi, but this is a fib. Happy april fools' day!

Misspelled Words
Part I

Before the existence of dictionaries, words were spelled entirely by ear or by whim. *Slow* might be spelled *sloe, slo,* or *slough.* With the appearance in the eighteenth century of the first English dictionary, however, spelling gradually became standardized to the point that children today compete in spelling bees.

Even if we never get skilled enough at spelling to enter a spelling bee, we can all become better spellers by observing some simple rules.

Tips for Improving Your Spelling

1. Sound out words. For instance, the word *government* contains an "n" if you say it aloud slowly. The word *find* has a final "d" sound and should not be spelled *fine.* Saying a word aloud can definitely help you to spell it correctly.

2. Make up your own memory tricks for remembering the spelling of problem words. For example, *cemetery* is spelled with all *e's* because it is so eerie; the *principal* is your pal; dessert has two *s's* because it is doubly good.

3. Use a dictionary. Looking up words regularly will help make you familiar with any quirks in their spellings. Ask your teacher to recommend a good dictionary.

4. Keep a list of words you often misspell and refer to it when you proofread your writing.

5. If you write with a computer, the first rule of spelling is simply this: Use the spell checker that comes with your writing program. Most programs have spell checkers built into them. However, even sophisticated spelling checkers go only so far. Although they catch such misspellings as *heighth* for *height* and *occassion* for *occasion,* they don't tell you if you've incorrectly used *its* for *it's* or *their* for *there* or *they're.*

Rules for Spelling

Spelling in English is not always as clear-cut as we would like. Nearly every rule has an exception. Nevertheless, learning the rules and the exceptions will make you a better speller.

As you go over the rules, bear in mind the difference between vowels and consonants.

Vowels:	*a, e, i, o, u,* and sometimes *y*
Consonants:	all other letters of the alphabet

Using ie and ei

Remember the age-old rule: "*i* before *e* except after *c* or when sounded as *ay* as in *neighbor* or *weigh.*"

niece

relieve

believe

but

ceiling

receive

deceive

EXCEPTIONS

either	leisure	species
caffeine	neither	their
financier	seize	weird
foreigner	science	
height	society	

PRACTICING 1

Underline the correct spelling of each word-pair in parentheses.

1. (Neither, Niether) Fred nor Mark is going to the club brunch.

2. They bought (their, thier) tickets in advance.

3. What is that (wierd, weird) sound?

4. A good (neighbor, nieghbor) is as valuable as silver or gold.

5. What do you like to do in your (leisure, liesure) time?

6. Drinks that contain salt are just as bad as those that contain (caffeine, caffiene).

7. You cannot live a serene life if you flout the rules of (soceity, society).

8. She has always done well in (sceince, science) courses.

9. If you (believe, beleive) that, I have a bridge to sell you.

10. She left a (breif, brief) e-mail message for me.

Changing y to i

When you add an ending to a word that ends in a consonant plus *y,* change *y* to *i*. Keep the final *y* when it is preceded by a vowel.

try + ed = tried

worry + er = worrier

silly + ness = silliness

buy + er = buyer

sway + ing = swaying

EXCEPTIONS

horrify	horrifyingly
lady	ladylike
carry	carrying
cry	crying (but crier)
worry	worrying
study	studying

PRACTICING 2

Combine the following words with the ending shown to the right and place the correct word in the blank provided.

Example: study   +   es   =   studies

1. testify   +   es   =   _____

2. merry   +   ily   =   _____

3. muddy   +   ed   =   _____

4. mortify   +   es   =   _____

5. lazy   +   ily   =   _____

6. bury   +   ing   =   _____

7. obey   +   ing   =   _____

8. fry   +   ed   =   _____

9. lonely   +   ness   =   _____

10. beauty   +   ful   =   _____

The final silent *e*

When you add endings that start with a vowel, such as *-al, -able, -ence,* or *-ing,* drop the final *e*. When you add an ending that starts with a consonant, such as *-ment, -less,* or *-ly,* keep the final *e*.

Here are some examples for you to study:

bride	+	al	=	bridal
like	+	able	=	likable
emerge	+	ence	=	emergence
take	+	ing	=	taking
manage	+	ment	=	management
love	+	less	=	loveless
polite	+	ly	=	politely

EXCEPTIONS

argue	+	ment	=	argument
courage	+	ous	=	courageous
judge	+	ment	=	judgment
manage	+	able	=	manageable
nine	+	th	=	ninth
notice	+	able	=	noticeable
true	+	ly	=	truly

PRACTICING 3

Place a *C* to the left of the word that is spelled correctly.

Example: _____ pleasureable

    _C_ pleasurable

1. _____ likeable   _____ likable
2. _____ management   _____ managment
3. _____ desperately   _____ desperatly
4. _____ arguement   _____ argument
5. _____ dosage   _____ doseage
6. _____ movable   _____ moveable
7. _____ managing   _____ manageing
8. _____ useable   _____ usable
9. _____ judgement   _____ judgment
10. _____ supposing   _____ supposeing

Doubling the final consonant

In one-syllable words
To add *ed, ing, er,* or *est* to a one-syllable word, double the consonant if it is preceded by a single vowel.

pin	+	ed	=	pinned
trim	+	ing	=	trimming
thin	+	er	=	thinner
sad	+	est	=	saddest

PRACTICING 4

Add the indicated endings to the words listed below and spell them correctly in the blanks provided.

Example: set (ing)   setting

1. dip (ed) _____
2. stop (ing) _____
3. dig (ing) _____
4. flop (ed) _____
5. knit (ed) _____
6. run (er) _____
7. slam (ed) _____
8. drop (ing) _____
9. blab (ed) _____
10. big (est) _____

In multi-syllable words
To add *ing* or *ed* to words of more than one syllable, double the final consonant if the following is true:

- The stress is on the final syllable:

com-mit′
be-gin′
oc-cur′

- The last three letters consist of a consonant/vowel/consonant:

commit
begin
occur

Therefore:

commit	+	ed	=	committed
begin	+	ing	=	beginning
occur	+	ed	=	occurred

Now, consider these words:

travel = traveling   **(Do not double because the accent is on the first syllable: *tra'-vel*.)**

benefit = benefited   **(Do not double because the accent is on the first syllable: *be'-ne-fit*.)**

repeat = repeating   **(Do not double because the last three letters do not fit the consonant/vowel/consonant pattern.)**

PRACTICING 5

In the blanks on the right, add *ed* and *ing* to the following words.

	ED	**ING**
Example: admit	admitted	admitting
1. prefer	_____	_____
2. unwrap	_____	_____
3. expel	_____	_____
4. remit	_____	_____
5. defer	_____	_____

PRACTICING 6

Add *ed* and *ing* to the following words.

1. travel	+	ed _____	+	ing _____
2. suspect	+	ed _____	+	ing _____
3. profit	+	ed _____	+	ing _____
4. label	+	ed _____	+	ing _____
5. defect	+	ed _____	+	ing _____

Forming plurals

Most words form their plurals by simply adding s.

SINGULAR	PLURAL
sled	sleds
egg	eggs
sister	sisters
rag	rags

However, there are a few exceptions that you should master.

Words ending in -s, -ss, -z, -x, -sh, or -ch

Words ending in *-s, -ss, -z, -x, -sh,* or *-ch* form their plurals by adding *-es,* an extra syllable for easier pronunciation.

SINGULAR	PLURAL
lens	lenses
kiss	kisses
buzz	buzzes
box	boxes
wash	washes
church	churches

PRACTICING 7

Form the plurals of the following words.

1. fox _____
2. crash _____
3. beach _____
4. buzz _____
5. dash _____
6. mix _____
7. bush _____
8. quiz _____
9. kiss _____
10. bus _____

Words ending in -o
If a word ends in an *-o* preceded by a vowel, add *-s.*

rodeo	rodeos
patio	patios
zoo	zoos
radio	radios
video	videos

If a word ends in an *-o* preceded by a consonant, add *-es:*

hero	heroes
potato	potatoes
echo	echoes
buffalo	buffaloes

EXCEPTIONS

alto	altos
grotto	grottos
memo	memos
motto	mottos
photo	photos
piano	pianos
solo	solos

PRACTICING 8

Write a sentence for each of the following words using the **plural** form.

1. potato

_____

2. video

_____

3. motto

_____

4. echo

_____

5. radio

_____

6. tomato

_____

7. zoo

_____

8. hero

_____

9. piano

_____

10. solo

_____

Words ending in -f
Most words ending in *-f* (or *-fe*) change the *f* to a *v* and add *-es*

SINGULAR	PLURAL
half	halves
calf	calves
leaf	leaves
wife	wives

EXCEPTIONS	
roof	roofs
safe	safes
chief	chiefs
proof	proofs

PRACTICING 9

Form the plurals of the following words.

1. leaf _____

2. roof _____

3. half _____

4. safe _____

5. wharf _____

6. chief _____

7. thief _____

8. knife _____

9. calf _____

10. hoof _____

Irregular plurals

Some words form irregular plurals.

SINGULAR	PLURAL
woman	women
foot	feet
ox	oxen
mouse	mice

PRACTICING 10

Form the plural of the following words.

1. goose _____

2. man _____

3. mouse _____

4. louse _____

5. woman _____

Words that do not change

Some words have the same spelling for singular and plural.

SINGULAR	PLURAL
deer	deer
fish	fish (or fishes)
sheep	sheep
species	species
series	series
moose	moose

PRACTICING 11

Turn the following words into plurals and then write a sentence using the plural.

Example: deer <u>deer</u>

<u>We saw a herd of deer at the saltlick.</u>

1. fish _____

_____

2. mouse _____

_____

3. moose _____

_____

4. series _____

_____

5. sheep _____

_____

PRACTICING 12

Circle the word in each pair that is correctly spelled.

1. halfs, halves

2. measurless, measureless

3. admited, admitted

4. expeled, expelled

5. pianos, pianoes

6. benefitted, benefited

7. mouses, mice

8. biggest, bigest

9. tomatoes, tomatos

10. slopy, sloppy

11. heros, heroes

12. writing, writting

13. likable, likeable

14. permited, permitted

15. occurring, occuring

16. peceive, receive

17. argument, arguement

18. hieght, height

19. coppying, copying

20. wives, wifes

Error No. 19 Review

Rewrite the following passage to correct all misspelled words (there are 15).

Scuba diving terrifys me. Although I have recieved a diploma admiting me to the elite group of certified scuba divers, I have never conquered my fear when under water. Niether my fearless brother nor my athletic sister hasever been able to releive my nervousness. Once I put on my scuba diving suit and grab my gear in readyness for a diving expedition, all I can think about is getting back home. I don't mind the cold water; I don't mind the tight divving suit. My bigest problem is the foriegn world that greets me under water. For instance, there are the slimmy sea weeds brushing against my face and making me afraid that they will start wraping around my neck or around the valves of my oxygen tank. I don't even enjoy seeing the multi-hued fishes swiming because I'm so scarred that among them might be a hidden shark. As for the darkness at depths of more than thirty feet, I just want to get back up to the world above the sea waves. Beleive me, I'm always utterly grateful to climb back on board the boat and head back to shore.

_____

_____

_____

_____

_____

_____

_____

_____

_____

_____

_____

_____

Error 20

Misspelled Words
Part II

English spelling is difficult. Words are often not spelled the way they sound. *Raccoon* sounds like it should have a "k" but doesn't. *Threw* sounds like *through* but is spelled differently. *Though, cough,* and *through* look like rhyming words but actually are not pronounced at all alike. Given that English has a vocabulary of over 400,000 words, it's a wonder that we spell as well as we do.

Some words—called **homophones**—sound exactly alike but have different spellings and meanings. Other words are not exactly homophones but are similar enough to be confused often. Study the following examples:

altar (a raised platform in church)	alter (to change)
it's (it is)	its (pronoun: *Its engine was throbbing.*)
accept (to receive with consent: *They accept our offer.*)	except (excluded: *Every one cried except Peter.*)
advice (noun: *I gave my advice.*)	advise (verb: *I advise you to leave.*)

Homophones and Frequently Confused Words

Learn the meaning and spelling of these homophones and frequently confused words. Errors in spelling can change the meaning of writing. *Angel* spelled correctly will still confuse your reader if you really meant *angle.*

accept—to take or receive/**except**—excluding, other than, but for

> They accept our thanks.
> I work every day except Sunday.

access—a means of approach/**excess**—more than the usual

> She had access to my room.
>
> Drinking to excess is not good.

advice—recommendation (noun)/**advise**—to caution, to warn (verb)

> The lawyer's advice is to do nothing.
>
> I advise you not to move.

affect—to influence, to change/**effect**—to bring about (verb); consequence, result (noun)

> Watching too much television affected my sanity.
>
> The new supervisor effected some good changes.
>
> It will have an effect on my pocket book.

altar—a raised platform in a church/**alter**—to change

> They exchanged wedding vows at the altar.
>
> The coach should alter the pitcher's motion.

bare—without covering or clothing/**bear**—to bring forth, to endure (verb); an animal (noun)

> The playing field was bare of any grass.
>
> Every year the mares bear foals.
>
> I can't bear going to the dentist.
>
> As I hiked past the river, I spotted a bear.

capital—value of goods, money; a principal city/**capitol**—a building in which legislators meet

> Investors should not squander their capital.
>
> Nashville is the capital of Tennessee.
>
> The capitol was a scene of heated debate.

cite—to quote/**site**—place or scene/**sight**—ability to see

> He loves to cite Shakespeare's words.
>
> The site for the monument was chosen by a committee.
>
> He claims to have the gift of second sight.

course—a path; subjects taken in school/**coarse**—rough in texture

> The obstacle course took us over mountains.
>
> I'm taking a course in literature.
>
> The sheets felt coarse.

desert—a dry land (noun); to abandon (verb)/**dessert**—something sweet served at the end of a meal

> We're going to the desert for the weekend.
>
> Don't desert me at the altar.
>
> My favorite dessert is strawberry shortcake.

forth—forward/**fourth**—next after third

> The settlers went forth into the wilderness.
>
> The fourth rule is this: Always study hard.

its—possessive form of it/**it's**—contraction of it is

> The cat licked its fur.
>
> It's too bad you have to go.

lose—to misplace or come to be without/**loose**—to be free from restraint

> Don't lose your keys.
>
> He tripped over his loose shoelace.

passed—went by/**past**—an earlier time; beyond

> We passed like ships in the night.
>
> That's all in the past.
>
> She walked past without saying a word.

piece—part of a whole/**peace**—opposite of war

> Give me a piece of that pie, please.
>
> We all want peace.

personal—private, intimate/**personnel**—employees

> That happens to be my personal business.
>
> He was hired by the personnel office.

principal—first in rank; the chief or head/**principle**—an accepted rule or belief

> Elmwood School has a new principal.
>
> Many arguments have been started over a principle.

quiet—making no noise; peaceable/**quite**—completely or entirely

> All's quiet on the street.
>
> Now I'm quite lost.

sole—only; the bottom of the foot/**soul**—the spirit

> She was the sole survivor.
>
> The shoemaker mended the sole of my shoe.
>
> She had a beautiful soul.

their—ownership/**there**—in that place/**they're**—contraction of they are

> Their coats are hanging in the closet.
>
> Put it over there.
>
> They're always very friendly.

to—a preposition; part of any infinitive/**too**—also, excessively/
two—second

> I'm going to the mountains.
>
> I'm too tired to talk.
>
> You should go, too.
>
> That's too much whipped cream.
>
> She ate two hot dogs.

who's—contraction of who is/**whose**—the possessive case of who
> Who's driving with me?
>
> Whose scarf is this?

your—the possessive case of you/**you're**—contraction of you are
> I found your notebook.
>
> You're the boss.

Although these are, of course, not the only homophones—English is riddled with many others—these are some you are most likely to encounter.

PRACTICING 1

Underline the correct word choice for each sentence below.

1. You have (access/excess) to many computers.

2. It will have a severe (affect/effect) on my budget.

3. (Its/It's) too late to (altar/alter) my plans.

4. This is my (forth/fourth) trip to New York.

5. I drove (past/passed) her house with my heart pounding.

6. (There/Their/They're) lies the problem.

7. She said that (its/it's) a matter of (principal/principle).

8. Are you (quite/quiet) finished?

9. He gave me a (piece/peace) of his mind.

10. (Whose/Who's) bringing the salad?

PRACTICING 2

Write a sentence for each of these pairs of homophones.

1. principal _____

   principle _____

2. capital _____

   capitol _____

3. personal_____

personnel_____

4. course _____

coarse _____

5. sole _____

soul _____

Commonly Misspelled Words

Below is a list of words that are commonly misspelled. If you regularly have trouble with any words on this list, memorize the correct spelling.

LIST OF COMMONLY MISSPELLED WORDS

accidentally	daily
acquaintance	definite
acquire	dependent
address	design
already (not to be confused with *all ready*)	device (not to be confused with *devise*)
all right (always two words, just like *all wrong*)	disappearance
answer	embarrass
anxious	environment
arithmetic	especially
athletics	exaggerate
attendance	exercise
awful	existence
awkward	familiar
believe (not to be confused with *belief*)	fascinate
breathe (not to be confused with *breath*)	foreign
business	forty
calendar	fragrant
cemetery	friend
changeable	fulfill
chief	government
choose (not to be confused with *chose*)	grammar
conscience (not to be confused with *conscious*)	harass
	height
	hindrance
	incredible
	independent

interesting	proceed
irresistible	receive
judgment	recognize
library	referred/referring
literature	relieve/relief
maintenance	resemblance
mathematics	restaurant
medicine	reverence
million	ridiculous
miracle	sandwich
miscellaneous	seize (not to be confused with *size*)
mischief	separate
necessary	several
neighbor	similar
noticeable	sincerely
nuisance	succeed
occasion	surprise
occur/occurrence/occurred	temperature
offered	than (not to be confused with *then*)
parallel	thorough
peculiar	tragedy
politics	truly
possess	unnecessary
practically	until
precede	usually
preferred	vegetable
prejudice	visitor
preparation	weird
privilege	writing

PRACTICING 3

Each of the following sentences contains a misspelled word from the list above. Write the corrected version in the blank provided.

Example: Their *existance* was in doubt. <u>existence</u>

1. They met each other accidentaly. _____

2. My strong point is athaletics. _____

3. It was not easy to chose between them. _____

4. She can be very changable. _____

5. On this particular point, his judgement was flawed.
   _____

6. He has his own upholstery bisness. _____

7. I'm so dependant on her. _____

8. Maintenence said the problem was with the water heater. _____

9. Mathamatics has always been my worse subject. _____

10. It was not necessery to do more. _____

PRACTICING 4

Circle the *correctly* spelled word in each of the following word-pairs.

1. miscellanous/miscellaneous

2. neighbor/naighbor

3. embarrass/embarress

4. conscience/conscence

5. ocasion/occasion

6. occurence/occurrence

7. poletics/politics

8. vegatable/vegetable

9. preparation/preperation

10. tragidy/tragedy

Error No. 20 Review

The paragraph that follows contains 20 of the spelling errors mentioned in this section. Correct each error.

When I was in grammer school, I made freinds with a foriegn exchange student. His name was Adam, and he was an intaresting kid. He came from England, and was very independant even though he was only eight years old. Early in our acquaintence, we decided to swap accents. So on a dayly basis, we would sit on the playground and try to talk like each other. I was from the South and had a southern accent, while he spoke like a Londoner, which I found irresestible. But much to our suprise, we found that we couldn't do it. Its very hard to capture another person's accent. Trying to do it makes you sound rediculus, or piculiar, to say the least. The other kids used to tease us, which embarassed us. It was hard enough allready for Adam to get adjusted without the nuisence of being teased for the way he sounded. We decided to stop the silly buseness of switching accents and just be ourselves. Many years later, on a social ocasion, I met Adam again. By then he was in his mid 20s and had remained in Atlanta. We talked about how the other kids used to harrass us and laughed about it. Not until later did I recanize a funny fact: Adam had ackwired a southern accent and now spoke exactly as I did!

READINGS

The readings in this part are organized according to the writing strategies that you learned earlier. They show how professional writers use the same techniques. The introduction, "Help for Your Reading," and the headnotes preceding each selection will help you get the most out of the readings. Use the questions that follow the readings to test your understanding of the material you've read.

Help for Your Reading

You can improve your reading with a few commonsense techniques. Here are some suggestions to help you read the selections in this book.

1. Scan the whole piece before you read.

Before you begin to actually read an essay, short story, or poem, casually look it over. Pay attention to the title—especially in the case of poems and short stories. The title is often a clue to the meaning of the piece. Turn the pages of an essay to see its major divisions, if any. Some essays are subdivided by heads; others appear as solid blocks of print. Scanning the heads as you turn the pages will tell you what an essay is about and what points it covers. Note the number of pages. What you are doing is looking over the essay as if it were a map for an upcoming trip. You are finding out how far you have to go and what kind of ground you have to cover.

2. Read the headnote first.

The **headnote** is the paragraph that precedes each writing selection. It gives you a general idea of what the reading is about and any surprises or twists you should look for. The headnote may also alert you to the work's main points. Through the headnote, the editors can whisper advice in your ear as you get ready to tackle the selection.

3. Write your reactions in the margins of the pages.

Get rid of the old-fashioned idea that writing in a book is a sin. If the book belongs to someone else or to the library, writing in it is definitely a sin. Otherwise, writing in a book is not sinful, but useful. Feel free to underline words or ideas. Scribble your reactions in the margin as you read. Writing down your reactions helps you become an active, rather than a passive, reader. When you react to a piece of writing, you involve yourself in it and are likely to get its point better than if you simply sit and read between snores. If a description is particularly sad, you might note: "This passage is gloomy." If the author's opinion annoys you, show your irritation by jotting down your reaction, whether it be, "That's a typical closed-minded opinion," or simply, "Rubbish." Another good use of marginal writing is to summarize in a phrase what the whole paragraph is about, so that when you reread, you can go straight to your summaries.

4. Underline key ideas.

All writing consists of two parts—a point and its proof. As shown in this text, most nonfiction paragraphs make a point and then try to prove it, using facts, examples, or reasons. To understand a paragraph, you must know its main point, usually found in the topic sentence. The topic sentence can be the opening sentence of a paragraph, or, less commonly, the closing sentence. An alert reader learns, therefore, to pay special attention to opening and closing sentences. Underlining the topic sentence is an excellent way to help you keep the main idea in mind as you read the rest of the paragraph. Consider this passage:

> I have found over the years that the most effective way for me to write an essay is simply to begin writing. Some friends of mine begin by doing research or by making an outline, but neither way works for me. What I do is sit down with a pen and pad and begin scribbling. At this point, I'm too shaky about what I want to say to use a computer. In fact, when I first start, I haven't the faintest idea what I'm going to say. My goal is simply to get something down on paper, anything. But once I have my first sentence, I'm ready to begin. It's a little bit like a diner sitting down to eat a meal, which does not really begin until the first bite. I may change that first sentence; I might not even use it in the final paper. But I have to have it to begin the writing. From there I might limp to a second sentence or even to a third. Or I might have a real outburst of creativity and draft an opening paragraph. Then I might go to the library or log on the Internet for information about my topic that I might use in the paper. But none of this can I do until I have that one sentence. I know this is a peculiar way of doing things, but that's how I write an essay, and I say "do what works for you."

The topic sentence is the key to the meaning of the paragraph. The rest of the paragraph supports and explains the topic sentence.

Also pay close attention to signal words, words that announce some important idea. Here are some examples, with the signal words underlined:

The most significant reaction of all, however, came from the eyewitnesses.

One often overlooked fact is that interest rates on personal loans are not tax deductible.

Of particular significance is the way the women themselves feel.

Perhaps most important, you must exercise to lose weight.

These signal words are clues to ideas the author considers particularly important.

5. Think about what you have read.

Every paragraph or so, stop and think about what you have just read. Make a mental summary—preferably aloud—to be sure you fully understand what you are reading. If you have trouble doing this, read the passage again, and perhaps even a third time, until you understand it.

6. Look up unfamiliar words in the dictionary.

Often **context**—surrounding words or sentences—will suggest a word's meaning. In the paragraph below, notice how context tells what the word *cacique* means:

> When Columbus first discovered the West Indies, he was greeted by a naked, peaceful people. His journals show that while he was slightly surprised at the lack of metal tools and weapons, he marveled that everyone—men and women, as well as children—went around totally naked. Even the *caciques,* who were shown great respect by their people, were surrounded by advisers, and occasionally sported ornamental gold bracelets

and necklaces that signified their high rank, were also stark naked, a fact Columbus found remarkable.

What is a *cacique?* Obviously, from the context of the paragraph, a cacique was a leader of these peaceful people.

Sometimes context tells us all we need to know about the meaning of a word. Consider this sentence: "The cows had to be herded back to their *byre* for milking." Although you may have no idea what the word byre means if you see it standing alone, in the context of this sentence, you are sure it must mean something like "barn," "stable," or "cowshed."

7. Reread.

Your first reading of an essay, short story, or poem will provide a general picture of the work. You will understand its broad outline, get its main idea, and absorb its general point of view. But in order to become a better writer, you must read, and reread, line by line and even word by word. Poems, especially, need rereading because so much meaning is contained in relatively few words. So rid yourself of the idea that five minutes before class starts you can skim the reading assignment and know it. Good writing requires careful rereading.

Narrating

Daddy Tucked the Blanket

Randall Williams

Looking back, most adults can remember being embarrassed about something in their backgrounds. The story that follows highlights the shame that comes from being poor. As you read, try to place yourself in the narrator's shoes; how would you have reacted under the same circumstances? Which details contribute most vividly to the portrait of a ramshackle house? What really matters in a home—a luxurious environment or a loving one?

1 About the time I turned 16, my folks began to wonder why I didn't stay home any more. I always had an excuse for them, but what I didn't say was that I had found my freedom and I was getting out.

2 I went through four years of high school in semirural Alabama and became active in clubs and sports; I made a lot of friends and became a regular guy, if you know what I mean. But one thing was irregular about me: I managed those four years without ever having a friend visit at my house.

3 I was ashamed of where I lived. I had been ashamed for as long as I had been conscious of class.

4 We had a big family. There were several of us sleeping in one room, but that's not so bad if you get along, and we always did. As you get older, though, it gets worse.

5 Being poor is a humiliating experience for a young person trying hard to be accepted. Even now—several years removed—it is hard to talk about. And I resent the weakness of these words to make you feel what it was really like.

6 We lived in a lot of old houses. We moved a lot because we were always looking for something just a little better than what we had. You have to understand that my folks worked harder than most people. My mother was always at home, but for her that was a full-time job—and no fun, either. But my father worked his head off from the time I can remember in construction and shops. It was hard, physical work.

7 I tell you this to show that we weren't shiftless. No matter how much money Daddy made, we never made much progress up the social ladder. I got out thanks to a college scholarship and because I was a little more articulate than the average.

8 I have seen my Daddy wrap copper wire through the soles of his boots to keep them together in the wintertime. He couldn't buy new boots because he had used the money for food and shoes for us. We lived like hell, but we went to school well-clothed and with a full stomach.

9 It really is hell to live in a house that was in bad shape 10 years before you moved in. And a big family puts a lot of wear and tear on a new house, too, so you can imagine how one goes downhill if it is teetering when you move in. But we lived in houses that were sweltering in summer and freezing in winter. I woke up every morning for a year and a half with plaster on my face where it had fallen out of the ceiling during the night.

10 This wasn't during the Depression; this was in the late 60's and early 70's.

11 When we boys got old enough to learn trades in school, we would try to fix up the old houses we lived in. But have you ever tried to paint a wall

that crumbled when the roller went across it? And bright paint emphasized the holes in the wall. You end up more frustrated than when you began, especially when you know that at best you might come up with only enough money to improve one of the six rooms in the house. And we might move out soon after, anyway.

The same goes for keeping a house like that clean. If you have a house **12** full of kids and the house is deteriorating, you'll never keep it clean. Daddy used to yell at Mama about that, but she couldn't do anything. I think Daddy knew it inside, but he had to have an outlet for his rage somewhere, and at least yelling isn't as bad as hitting, which they never did to each other.

But you have a kitchen which has no counter space and no hot water, **13** and you will have dirty dishes stacked up. That sounds like an excuse, but try it. You'll go mad from the sheer sense of futility. It's the same thing in a house with no closets. You can't keep clothes clean and rooms in order if they have to be stacked up with things.

Living in a bad house is generally worse on girls. For one thing, they **14** traditionally help their mother with the housework. We boys could get outside and work in the field or cut wood or even play ball and forget about living conditions. The sky was still pretty.

But the girls got the pressure, and as they got older it became worse. **15** Would they accept dates knowing they had to "receive" the young man in a dirty hallway with broken windows, peeling wallpaper and a cracked ceiling? You have to live it to understand it, but it creates a shame which drives the soul of a young person inward.

I'm thankful none of us ever blamed our parents for this, because it **16** would have crippled our relationships. As it worked out, only the relationship between our parents was damaged. And I think the harshness which they expressed to each other was just an outlet to get rid of their anger at the trap their lives were in. It ruined their marriage because they had no one to yell at but each other. I knew other families where the kids got the abuse, but we were too much loved for that.

Once I was about 16 and Mama and Daddy had had a particularly vio- **17** lent argument about the washing machine, which had broken down. Daddy was on the back porch—that's where the only water faucet was—trying to fix it and Mama had a washtub out there washing school clothes for the next day and they were screaming at each other.

Later that night everyone was in bed and I heard Daddy get up from **18** the couch where he was reading. I looked out from my bed across the hall into their room. He was standing right over Mama and she was already asleep. He pulled the blanket up and tucked it around her shoulders and just stood there and tears were dropping off his cheeks and I thought I could faintly hear them splashing against the linoleum rug.

Now they're divorced. **19**

I had courses in college where housing was discussed, but the soci- **20** ologists never put enough emphasis on the impact living in substandard housing has on a person's psyche. Especially children's.

Small children have a hard time understanding poverty. They want the **21** same things children from more affluent families have. They want the same things they see advertised on television, and they don't understand why they can't have them.

Other children can be incredibly cruel. I was in elementary school in **22** Georgia—and this is interesting because it is the only thing I remember about that particular school—when I was about eight or nine.

After Christmas vacation had ended, my teacher made each student **23** describe all his or her Christmas presents. I became more and more uncomfortable as the privilege passed around the room toward me. Other children were reciting the names of the dolls they had been given, the kinds of bicycles and the grandeur of their games and toys. Some had lists which seemed to go on and on for hours.

It took me only a few seconds to tell the class that I had gotten for **24** Christmas a belt and a pair of gloves. And then I was laughed at—because I cried—by a roomful of children and a teacher. I never forgave them, and that night I made my mother cry when I told her about it.

In retrospect, I am grateful for that moment, but I remember wanting **25** to die at the time.

Vocabulary

semirural (2)	deteriorating (12)
class (3)	impact (20)
shiftless (7)	substandard (20)
articulate (7)	psyche (20)
teetering (9)	affluent (21)
trades (11)	

Understanding What You Have Read

Check the correct answer in the blank provided.

1. According to the narrator, it is difficult to keep an old house clean because

   _____ (a). everything in it is deteriorating.

   _____ (b). you have no sense of pride in it.

   _____ (c). you don't have enough money to buy cleaning products.

   _____ (d). the windows keep letting in dirt.

2. Having a shabby house because of being poor is more difficult on girls than on boys because

   _____ (a). girls are more sensitive.

   _____ (b). boys don't care about luxurious surroundings.

   _____ (c). boys know they can make money once they finish school and start working.

   _____ (d). girls spend more time doing house chores and they receive dates at home.

3. The parents in this story fought with each other but did not abuse their children because

   _____ (a). the children would have ganged up on them.

   _____ (b). the parents loved the children too much.

   _____ (c). the uncles and aunts always protected the children.

   _____ (d). the local social workers watched out for child abusers.

4. After the violent quarrel about the washing machine, what did the father do to the mother?

   _____ (a). He bought her a new washing machine.

   _____ (b). He apologized and promised to quit blaming her.

_____ **(c).** He wept with shame.

_____ **(d).** He went to her room and pulled the blanket over her shoulders.

5. What happened after Christmas to humiliate the narrator?

_____ **(a).** He was told that his parents could not pay his tuition.

_____ **(b).** A student accused him of living in a dirty shack.

_____ **(c).** He had to tell the class that he received only a belt and a pair of gloves for Christmas.

_____ **(d).** The church gave him some ugly, secondhand clothes.

Thinking About What You Have Read

1. In paragraph 5, the narrator says that words are too weak to tell us what it was like to be poor. Do you think the narrator succeeded in conveying what it is like to be poor? Give reasons for your answer.

2. We are never told exactly why the parents got a divorce. What is your guess? Imagine the circumstances that led to the divorce.

3. In his final paragraph, the narrator writes, "I am grateful for that moment. . . ." What could have caused his gratitude for having felt so deeply embarrassed? Can you think of a painful moment in your own life for which you now feel grateful? Explain how the gratitude evolved.

4. What are some of the psychological effects of being poor, especially on children? How can some of these effects be avoided or lessened?

5. Despite the poverty described, how do you feel about the narrator's father? What kind of man is he? Does he possess characteristics that make him a good father? If so, what are they?

Writing Assignments

1. Write a short narrative essay about something that happened to you in the past that embarrassed you. How would you react to that same incident today?

2. Support the following main idea, taken from paragraph 20 of the story: Substandard housing has an impact on a person's psyche, especially that of a child. If possible, narrate a personal experience to prove your point.

The Circuit

Francisco Jiminez

Most students consider school and learning a nuisance to endure between weekends and holidays. But here is an entirely different take on going to school that you might not have thought of—by a migrant worker child who actually hungered for learning and felt deprived when his family's nomadic lifestyle kept him out of school. The narrator acquaints us with the harsh labor in the fields and the poverty and drudgery that is the farm laborers' lot. As you read the story, look for the techniques of a good narrative that you learned in Unit 8. Analyze the pacing of the story by focusing on which events are recreated in detail and which are glossed over to move the story along.

1   It was that time of year again. Ito, the strawberry sharecropper, did not smile. It was natural. The peak of the strawberry season was over and the last few days the workers, most of them braceros, were not picking as many boxes as they had during the months of June and July.

2   As the last days of August disappeared, so did the number of braceros. Sunday, only one—the best picker—came to work. I liked him. Sometimes we talked during our half-hour lunch break. That is how I found out he was from Jalisco, the same state in Mexico my family was from. That Sunday was the last time I saw him.

3   When the sun had tired and sunk behind the mountains, Ito signaled us that it was time to go home. "Ya esora," he yelled in his broken Spanish. Those were the words I waited for twelve hours a day, every day, seven days a week, week after week. And the thought of not hearing them again saddened me.

4   As we drove home Papá did not say a word. With both hands on the wheel, he stared at the dirt road. My older brother, Roberto, was also silent. He leaned his head back and closed his eyes. Once in a while he cleared from his throat the dust that blew in from outside.

5   Yes, it was that time of year. When I opened the front door to the shack, I stopped. Everything we owned was neatly packed in cardboard boxes. Suddenly I felt even more the weight of hours, days, weeks, and months of work. I sat down on a box. The thought of having to move to Fresno and knowing what was in store for me there brought tears to my eyes.

6   That night I could not sleep. I lay in bed thinking about how much I hated this move.

7   A little before five o'clock in the morning, Papá woke everyone up. A few minutes later, the yelling and screaming of my little brothers and sisters, for whom the move was a great adventure, broke the silence of dawn. Shortly, the barking of the dogs accompanied them.

8   While we packed the breakfast dishes, Papá went outside to start the "Carcanchita." That was the name Papá gave his old '38 black Plymouth. He bought it in a used-car lot in Santa Rosa in the winter of 1949. Papá was very proud of his little jalopy. He had a right to be proud of it. He spent a lot of time looking at other cars before buying this one. When he finally chose the "Carcanchita," he checked it thoroughly before driving it out of the car lot. He examined every inch of the car. He listened to the motor, tilting his head from side to side like a parrot, trying to detect any noises that spelled car trouble. After being satisfied with the looks and sounds of the car, Papá then insisted on knowing who the original owner was. He never did find out from the car salesman, but he bought the car anyway. Papá figured the original owner must have been an important man because behind the rear seat of the car he found a blue necktie.

Papá parked the car out in front and left the motor running. "Listo," he **9**
yelled. Without saying a word, Roberto and I began to carry the boxes out
to the car. Roberto carried the two big boxes and I carried the two smaller
ones. Papá then threw the mattress on top of the car roof and tied it with
ropes to the front and rear bumpers.

Everything was packed except Mamá's pot. It was an old large galva- **10**
nized pot she had picked up at an army surplus store in Santa María the
year I was born. The pot had many dents and nicks, and the more dents
and nicks it acquired the more Mamá liked it. "Mi olla," she used to say
proudly.

I held the front door open as Mamá carefully carried out her pot by both **11**
handles, making sure not to spill the cooked beans. When she got to the
car, Papá reached out to help her with it. Roberto opened the rear car door
and Papá gently placed it on the floor behind the front seat. All of us then
climbed in. Papá sighed, wiped the sweat off his forehead with his sleeve,
and said wearily: "Es todo."

As we drove away, I felt a lump in my throat. I turned around and looked **12**
at our little shack for the last time.

At sunset we drove into a labor camp near Fresno. Since Papá did not **13**
speak English, Mamá asked the camp foreman if he needed any more
workers. "We don't need no more," said the foreman, scratching his head.
"Check with Sullivan down the road. Can't miss him. He lives in a big white
house with a fence around it."

When we got there, Mamá walked up to the house. She went through **14**
a white gate, past a row of rose bushes, up the stairs to the front door.
She rang the doorbell. The porch light went on and a tall husky man came
out. They exchanged a few words. After the man went in, Mamá clasped
her hands and hurried back to the car. "We have work! Mr. Sullivan said
we can stay there the whole season," she said, gasping and pointing to an
old garage near the stables.

The garage was worn out by the years. It had no windows. The walls, **15**
eaten by termites, strained to support the roof full of holes. The dirt floor,
populated by earth worms, looked like a gray road map.

That night, by the light of a kerosene lamp, we unpacked and cleaned **16**
our new home. Roberto swept away the loose dirt, leaving the hard ground.
Papá plugged the holes in the walls with old newspapers and tin can tops.
Mamá fed my little brothers and sisters. Papá and Roberto then brought
in the mattress and placed it on the far corner of the garage. "Mamá, you
and the little ones sleep on the mattress. Roberto, Panchito, and I will
sleep outside under the trees," Papá said.

Early next morning Mr. Sullivan showed us where his crop was, and after **17**
breakfast, Papá, Roberto, and I headed for the vineyard to pick.

Around nine o'clock the temperature had risen to almost one hundred **18**
degrees. I was completely soaked in sweat and my mouth felt as if I had
been chewing on a handkerchief. I walked over to the end of the row, picked
up the jug of water we had brought, and began drinking. "Don't drink too
much; you'll get sick," Roberto shouted. No sooner had he said that then
I felt sick to my stomach. I dropped to my knees and let the jug roll off my
hands. I remained motionless with my eyes glued on the hot sandy ground.
All I could hear was the drone of insects. Slowly I began to recover. I poured
water over my face and neck and watched the dirty water run down my
arms to the ground.

I still felt a little dizzy when we took a break to eat lunch. It was past **19**
two o'clock and we sat underneath a large walnut tree that was on the side
of the road. While we ate, Papá jotted down the number of boxes we had
picked. Roberto drew designs on the ground with a stick. Suddenly I noticed

Papá's face turn pale as he looked down the road. "Here comes the school bus," he whispered loudly in alarm. Instinctively, Roberto and I ran and hid in the vineyards. We did not want to get in trouble for not going to school. The neatly dressed boys about my age got off. They carried books under their arms. After they crossed the street, the bus drove away. Roberto and I came out from hiding and joined Papá. "Tienen que tener cuidado," he warned us.

20   After lunch we went back to work. The sun kept beating down. The buzzing insects, the wet sweat, and the hot dry dust made the afternoon seem to last forever. Finally the mountains around the valley reached out and swallowed the sun. Within an hour it was too dark to continue picking. The vines blanketed the grapes, making it difficult to see the bunches. "Vámonos," said Papá, signaling to us that it was time to quit work. Papá then took out a pencil and began to figure out how much we had earned our first day. He wrote down numbers, crossed some out, wrote down some more. "Quince," he murmured.

21   When we arrived home, we took a cold shower underneath a water-hose. We then sat down to eat dinner around some wooden crates that served as a table. Mamá had cooked a special meal for us. We had rice and tortillas with "carne con chile," my favorite dish.

22   The next morning I could hardly move. My body ached all over. I felt little control over my arms and legs.

23   This feeling went on every morning for days until my muscles finally got used to the work.

24   It was Monday, the first week of November. The grape season was over and I could now go to school. I woke up early that morning and lay in bed, looking at the stars and savoring the thought of not going to work and of starting sixth grade for the first time that year. Since I could not sleep, I decided to get up and join Papá and Roberto at breakfast. I sat at the table across from Roberto, but I kept my head down. I did not want to look up and face him. I knew he was sad. He was not going to school today. He was not going tomorrow, or next week, or next month. He would not go until the cotton season was over, and that was sometime in February. I rubbed my hands together and watched the dry, acid-stained skin fall to the floor in little rolls.

25   When Papá and Roberto left for work, I felt relief. I walked to the top of a small grade next to the shack and watched the "Carcanchita" disappear in the distance in a cloud of dust.

26   Two hours later, around eight o'clock, I stood by the side of the road waiting for school bus number twenty. When it arrived I climbed in. Everyone was busy either talking or yelling. I sat in an empty seat in the back.

27   When the bus stopped in front of the school, I felt very nervous. I looked out the bus window and saw boys and girls carrying books under their arms. I put my hands in my pant pockets and walked to the principal's office. When I entered I heard a woman's voice say: "May I help you?" I was startled. I had not heard English for months. For a few seconds I remained speechless. I looked at the lady who waited for an answer. My first instinct was to answer her in Spanish, but I held back. Finally, after struggling for English words, I managed to tell her that I wanted to enroll in the sixth grade. After answering many questions, I was led to the classroom.

28   Mr. Lema, the sixth grade teacher, greeted me and assigned me a desk. He then introduced me to the class. I was so nervous and scared at that moment when everyone's eyes were on me that I wished I were with Papá and Roberto picking cotton. After taking roll, Mr. Lema gave the class the assignment for the first hour. "The first thing we have to do this morning is finish reading the story we began yesterday," he said enthusiastically. He

walked up to me, handed me an English book, and asked me to read. "We are on page 125," he said politely. When I heard this, I felt my blood rush to my head; I felt dizzy. "Would you like to read?" he asked hesitantly. I opened the book to page 125. My mouth was dry. My eyes began to water. I could not begin. "You can read later," Mr. Lema said understandingly.

For the rest of the reading period I kept getting angrier and angrier with myself. I should have read, I thought to myself. **29**

During recess I went into the restroom and opened my English book to page 125. I began to read in a low voice, pretending I was in class. There were many words I did not know. I closed the book and headed back to the classroom. **30**

Mr. Lema was sitting at his desk correcting papers. When I entered he looked up at me and smiled. I felt better. I walked up to him and asked if he could help me with the new words. "Gladly," he said. **31**

The rest of the month I spent my lunch hours working on English with Mr. Lema, my best friend at school. **32**

One Friday during lunch hour Mr. Lema asked me to take a walk with him to the music room. "Do you like music?" he asked me as we entered the building. **33**

"Yes, I like corridos," I answered. He then picked up a trumpet, blew on it, and handed it to me. The sound gave me goose bumps. I knew that sound. I had heard it in many corridos. "How would you like to learn how to play it?" he asked. He must have read my face because before I could answer, he added, "I'll teach you how to play it during our lunch hours." **34**

That day I could hardly wait to get home to tell Papá and Mamá the great news. As I got off the bus, my little brothers and sisters ran up to meet me. They were yelling and screaming. I thought they were happy to see me, but when I opened the door to our shack, I saw that everything we owned was neatly packed in cardboard boxes. **35**

Vocabulary

sharecropper (1)	clasped (14)
signaled (3)	blanketed (20)
original (8)	hesitantly (27)
galvanized (10)	

Understanding What You Have Read

Check the correct answer in the blank provided.

1. What is the meaning of the opening sentence of the story—"It was that time of year again?"

    _____ **(a).** It was time to move to the next farm.

    _____ **(b).** It was time for the flu season to begin.

    _____ **(c).** It was time to enjoy a summer vacation.

    _____ **(d).** It was time to buy new clothes for work.

2. The father is very proud of

    _____ **(a).** his children.

    _____ **(b).** the living quarters in which the family lived.

    _____ **(c).** the family dog.

    _____ **(d).** his black '38 Plymouth.

3. Where had the mother found the pot she liked so much?

_____ **(a).** At her grandmother's home in Mexico.

_____ **(b).** At a Macy's sale.

_____ **(c).** At an army surplus store.

_____ **(d).** At a church rummage sale.

4. When the family worked for Mr. Sullivan, they stayed in

_____ **(a).** a garage.

_____ **(b).** the local Y.M.C.A.

_____ **(c).** tents.

_____ **(d).** barracks built for the help.

5. Who was Mr. Lema?

_____ **(a).** The local sheriff.

_____ **(b).** The owner of the vineyard.

_____ **(c).** The narrator's teacher.

_____ **(d).** The narrator's father.

Thinking About What You Have Read

1. What were some of the conditions that made the work in the fields extremely difficult? List them.

2. Were there any causes for joy in the life described? If so, what were they?

3. Why did the boys run and hide when the school bus came down the road? What does this indicate about the lives of these migrant laborers?

4. Why does the narrator rejoice when the grape season is over? Why is he ashamed of facing his brother at the breakfast table (paragraph 24)?

5. What is the meaning of the sentence "I saw that everything we owned was neatly packed in cardboard boxes"?

Writing Assignments

1. Narrate an incident in which you experienced a great disappointment.

2. Tell a story about a funny, sad, or nostalgic family dinner.

Describing

My Grandmother, the Bag Lady

Patsy Neal

The description that follows is heartrending in the honesty of its descriptive details. We cannot help but be moved by the author's view of her grandmother, whose world has shrunken to the dimensions of a bag, containing all of her possessions, attached to her walker. Those of us who have watched parents or grandparents deteriorate, as this grandmother has, recognize the symptoms and weep for the fate of anyone that lonely and that frightened. As you read, underline sensory details that you consider particularly vivid. Does the writer use any metaphors or similies?

1   Almost all of us have seen pictures of old, homeless ladies, moving about the streets of big cities with everything they own stuffed into a bag or a paper sack.

2   My grandmother is 89 years old, and a few weeks ago I realized with a jolt that she, too, had become one of them. Before I go any further, I had best explain that I did not see my grandmother's picture on TV. I discovered her plight during a face-to-face visit at my mother's house—in a beautiful, comfortable, safe, middle-class environment with good china on the table and turkey and chicken on the stove.

3   My grandmother's condition saddened me beyond words, for an 89-year-old should not have to carry around everything she owns in a bag. It's enough to be 89, without the added burden of packing the last fragments of your existence into a space big enough to accommodate only the minutest of treasures.

4   Becoming a bag lady was not something that happened to her overnight. My grandmother has been in a nursing home these last several years; at first going back to her own home for short visits, then less frequently as she became older and less mobile.

5   No matter how short these visits were, her greatest pleasure came from walking slowly around her home, touching every item lovingly and spending hours browsing through drawers and closets. Then, I did not understand her need to search out all her belongings.

6   As she spent longer days and months at the nursing home, I could not help noticing other things. She began to hide her possessions under the mattress, in her closet, under the cushion of her chair, in every conceivable, reachable space. And she began to think that people were "stealing" from her.

7   When a walker became necessary, my mother took time to make a bag that could be attached to it, so that my grandmother could carry things around while keeping her hands on the walker. I had not paid much attention to this bag until we went to the nursing home to take her home with us for our traditional Christmas Eve sharing of gifts.

8   As we left, my grandmother took her long, unsteady walk down the hallway, balancing herself with her walker, laboriously moving it ahead, one step at a time, until finally we were at the car outside. Once she was safely seated, I picked up her walker to put it in the back. I could barely lift it. Then I noticed that the bag attached to it was bulging. Something clicked, but it still wasn't complete enough to grasp.

At home in my mother's house, I was asked to get some photographs **9** from my grandmother's purse. Lifting her pocketbook, I was surprised again at the weight and bulk. I watched as my mother pulled out an alarm clock, a flashlight, a small radio, thread, needles, pieces of sewing, a book and other items that seemed to have no reason for being in a pocketbook.

I looked at my grandmother, sitting bent over in her chair, rummaging **10** through the bag on the walker, slowly pulling out one item and then another, and lovingly putting it back. I looked down at her purse with all its disconnected contents and remembered her visits to her home, rummaging through drawers and through closets.

"Oh, Lord," I thought with sudden insight. "That walker and that purse **11** are her home now."

I began to understand that over the years my grandmother's space of **12** living had diminished like melting butter—from endless fields and miles of freedom as a child and young mother to, with age, the constrictions of a house, then a small room in a nursing home and finally to the tightly clutched handbag and the bag on her walker.

When the family sent her to a nursing home, it was the toughest deci- **13** sion it had ever had to make. We all thought she would be secure there; we would no longer have to worry about whether she had taken her medicine, or left her stove on, or was alone at night.

But we hadn't fully understood her needs. Security for my grandmother **14** was not in the warm room at the nursing home, with 24-hour attendants to keep her safe and well fed, nor in the family who visited and took her to visit in their homes. In her mind her security was tied to those things she could call her own—and over the years those possessions had dwindled away like sand dropping through an hourglass: first her car, sold when her eyes became bad and she couldn't drive; then some furnishings she didn't really need. Later it was the dogs she had trouble taking care of. And finally it would be her home when it became evident that she could never leave the nursing home again. But as her space and mobility dwindled, so did her control over her life.

I looked at my grandmother again, sitting so alone before me, hair **15** totally gray, limbs and joints swollen by arthritis, at the hearing aid that could no longer help her hear, and the glasses too thick but so inadequate in helping her to see . . . and yet there was such dignity about her. A dignity I could not understand.

The next day, after my grandmother had been taken back to the nurs- **16** ing home and my mother was picking up in her room, she found a small scrap of paper my grandmother had scribbled these words on:

"It is 1:30 tonight and I had to get up and go to the bathroom. I cannot **17** go back to sleep. But I looked in on Margaret and she is sleeping *so* good, and Patsy is sleeping too."

With that note, I finally understood, and my 89-year-old bag-lady grand- **18** mother changed from an almost helpless invalid to a courageous, caring individual still very much in control of her environment.

What intense loneliness she must have felt as she scribbled that small **19** note on that small piece of paper with the small bag on her walker and her small purse next to her. Yet she chose to experience it alone rather than wake either of us from much-needed sleep. Out of her own great need, she chose to meet our needs.

As I held that tiny note, and cried inside, I wondered if she dreamed **20** of younger years and more treasured possessions and a bigger world when she went back to sleep that night. I certainly hoped so.

Vocabulary

plight (2)	rummaging (10)
minutest (3)	diminished (12)
mobile (4)	constrictions (12)
conceivable (6)	inadequate (15)
laboriously (8)	invalid (18)

Understanding What You Have Read

Check the correct answer in the blank provided.

1. Was the grandmother the kind of bag lady we expect to encounter on a city street?

   _____ **(a).** Yes, except she had money.

   _____ **(b).** No, because she was only 55 years old.

   _____ **(c).** No, because she had a room in a good nursing home.

   _____ **(d).** Yes—she wanted to live in the streets with other home-less women.

2. According to the author, becoming a bag lady was something that happened

   _____ **(a).** after the grandmother had a stroke.

   _____ **(b).** gradually over time.

   _____ **(c).** overnight.

   _____ **(d).** because no one loved her.

3. Who made the bag the grandmother could use to hang on her walker?

   _____ **(a).** The author.

   _____ **(b).** The grandmother's nursing home attendant.

   _____ **(c).** Some women who belonged to a church organization.

   _____ **(d).** The author's mother.

4. How did the family feel when they sent the grandmother to a nursing home?

   _____ **(a).** They were happy they were no longer responsible for her.

   _____ **(b).** It was the toughest decision they ever had to make.

   _____ **(c).** They were unhappy because the nursing home was expensive.

   _____ **(d).** They were too busy with other matters to care deeply.

5. At the end of the essay, the author describes her grandmother as a

   _____ **(a).** courageous, caring individual.

   _____ **(b).** childish, whimpering creature.

   _____ **(c).** domineering, demanding patient.

   _____ **(d).** senile woman who had lost all her faculties.

Thinking About What You Have Read

1. Why do you think the bag and its contents became so precious to the grandmother?

2. The portrait of this grandmother is mostly sad, but the author does offer some beauty in her portrayal. Point to the paragraph in which this occurs.

3. How does the author feel about her grandmother's plight? How do the other members of the family feel?

4. In paragraph 11, the author has a sudden insight. What does she realize? Do you agree with her conclusion? Why or why not?

5. How does the author define security in her grandmother's life? Be specific in your answer.

Writing Assignments

1. Describe the mental and physical state of an older person whom you know well. Try to be as understanding as possible of the person's attitudes and ways.

2. What will you like to be when you are 89? Describe the person you imagine yourself to be. Use specific details.

Black Cadillac

Bart Edelman

Except for the fact that this piece is written in stanzas with short lines, it is really more like an essay than a poem. If you read thoughtfully, you will get a clear image of what a Cadillac looked like in the fifties. Black was the color preferred by owners who wanted to drive a sleek, impressive car. As you read, also try to figure out the little drama that is developing. What is the conflict? How is it resolved? How do you feel about the ending?

The elongated fins,   1
A flying fish on wheels—
Grandpa's shiny new Cadillac
Floated down the block at twilight
And beached itself on the concrete sand.
Three toots of the horn
Brought us screaming from the house;
We swept around the immaculate sedan
And gazed in astonishment . . .
He'd really done it this time.   10

Grandpa stood in his pinstriped suit
With his back to us,
Whistling "Take Me Out To The Ballgame"
And smoking a Tareyton;
He jingled a pocketful of change,
Stroked a long string of keys
And turned towards us, grinning.
"So what do you think?
Anyone up for a ride?
It's only the shank of the evening.   20
I think we need to go nightlifin'.
Get inside and put your pajamas on.
We'll be out 'til the wee hours."

Past the frown on Mother's face we dashed,
Ready for adventure.
From our bedroom we heard
The exchange of raised voices,
Cross words,
A painful drawn out sigh,
Then nothing but silence   30
And an engine ignited.

By the time we reached the street,

He was gone;

We could barely make out

The slippery tail

Flipping in the wind,

Swimming far out to sea

As if it had never been there.

Mother told us calmly

That he had other stops to make,   40

But we knew the reason he didn't stay—

Why she always chased him away.

Months later,

When Grandpa came calling for us,

Willing to explain,

He was driving an old brown Chevrolet.

Vocabulary

elongated (1)   shank (20)
immaculate (8)   ignited (31)

Understanding What You Have Read

Check the correct answer in the blank provided.

1. To what does the poet compare Grandpa's Cadillac?

_____ **(a).** A leopard.

_____ **(b).** A fish.

_____ **(c).** A black velvet blanket.

_____ **(d).** A pinstriped suit.

2. Grandpa wants to take his grandchildren

_____ **(a).** to the nearest coffee shop for ice cream.

_____ **(b).** to prayer meeting at church.

_____ **(c).** for a ride and some night life.

_____ **(d).** to hunt for night frogs at the pond.

3. Cross words are exchanged between

_____ **(a).** the grandfather and the mother.

_____ **(b).** the children and the mother.

_____ **(c).** the children and the grandfather.

_____ **(d).** the neighbor and the grandfather.

4. After the cross words, what happens?

_____ **(a).** The children get into the car.

_____ **(b).** The mother leaves in the car with the grandfather.

_____ **(c).** The car can't start due to a dead battery.

_____ **(d).** The grandfather drives off alone.

5. The next time the children see the grandfather, he is driving

_____ **(a).** a Mercedes Benz.

_____ **(b).** a Honda.

_____ **(c).** a Chevrolet.

_____ **(d).** a BMW.

Thinking About What You Have Read

1. What is the conflict in this poem? Between which characters does it take place?

2. Why do you think the grandfather bought the black Cadillac?

3. Do you consider the grandfather lovable or not? How would you feel if he were your grandfather?

4. What kind of person is the mother? Why does she behave the way she does?

5. What do you think happened between the time of the incident narrated and the next time the grandfather came to visit?

Writing Assignments

1. Describe your grandfather. What did he look like? What kind of personality did he have? How did you feel about him? If you do not remember your own grandfather, describe someone else's.

2. Describe the car of your dreams. Include the make, the style, the color—anything that will make this car seem real to your reader.

A View from Mount Ritter

Joseph T. O'Connor

Sometimes a harrowing experience can enhance your character, nudging you toward maturity and self-esteem. This is exactly what happened to the narrator of this essay who, as a high school student, joined an expedition to the top of Mount Ritter in northeast California. In recounting his frightening adventure, he focuses on the fury of a mountain storm to create a dominant impression. As you read, notice how his choice of words throughout provides concrete, vivid description that is rich in sensory detail.

"I hate this," I thought. We were on our way to the top of Mount Ritter in northeastern California. You would think everyone, near one of the tallest ridges in the Sierra Nevadas, would be in high spirits. But on this particular day the rain fell in torrents. Quarter-size hailstones pelted our protective helmets as thunder echoed through the canyons. **1**

It was the second week of my mountain expedition in California. The first week there had not been a cloud in the sky, but on Tuesday of week two, a dark cover crept in from the west, painting the sunlit, blue sky black. The storm came in so fast we didn't even notice it until our shadows suddenly disappeared. **2**

"Here it comes," our guide warned. As if God himself had given the order, the heavens opened, just a crack. Huge drops began falling but abruptly stopped, as if to say, "You know what's coming; here's a taste." As we began searching for shelter, a bolt of lightning ripped open the blackish clouds overhead and in unison thunder cracked, leaving everyone's ears ringing. We were in the midst of a huge July thunderstorm. Ethan, our guide, had said that during the summer in the high Sierras it might rain twice, but when it does, it's best not to be there. Suddenly lightning struck a tree not 20 feet from where I was standing. **3**

"Lightning positions!" Ethan yelled frantically. A little too frantically for my taste. I thought he was used to this kind of thing. As scared as I was, squatting in a giant puddle of water and hailstones, with forks of lightning bouncing off the canyon walls around me, I couldn't help chuckling to myself at the sight of Ethan's dinner-plate-size eyeballs as he panicked like an amateur. Soon after the lightning died down some, we hiked to the shelter of nearby redwoods to put on rain gear. While we prayed for the rain to subside, I watched the stream we stood beside grow into a raging, white-water river. Another expeditioner, Mike, and I were under a full redwood donning our not-so-waterproof equipment when I realized we were standing on a small island. **4**

"Mike! Let's go!" I yelled, my exclamation nearly drowned out by the roar of water surrounding us and another roll of thunder. **5**

"I'm way ahead o' ya!" he screamed in his thick New York accent, and his goofy smile broke through the torrents. "Ya ready?" **6**

"Yeah!" I yelled back, and jumped from our island into the knee-deep water. He followed as we slopped through the storm, losing our footing every few feet. **7**

The unforgiving downpour lasted all day and into the night as we stumbled down the rocky cliffs seeking the driest place to set up camp. It was dusk before we found a small clearing in a pine forest, and began what was to be the worst night of my life. We constructed our tents in the dark, fumbling with the ropes with our frozen hands and finishing just as a stiffness like rigor mortis set in. We lay awake all night, shivering in our wet **8** sleeping bags while rain poured down and a small stream made its way through our tent.

It's funny how these memories keep coming back to me as if it was **9** just yesterday. All this happened last summer, after my junior year in high school. I had decided to attend a mountaineering program in the Sierras. Two weeks in the back country with no sign of civilization. It sounded exciting and slightly dangerous, and I've always been up for a good adventure. I found out on that trip that nature is underestimated. The experience was the most invigorating, fulfilling, stimulating two weeks of my life. For the first time since I could remember, my head was crystal clear. I felt born again, only 2 weeks old. On top of Mount Ritter, 13,000 feet above sea level, I was entranced at the sight of the orange-red sun as it peeked over the glistening peaks far off in the east. Cumulous clouds appeared transparent as they glowed bright red in the morning glory.

The wonder of all I'd experienced made me think seriously about what **10** comes next. "Life after high school," I said to myself. "Uh-oh." What had I been doing for the last three years? I was so caught up in defying the advice of my parents and teachers to study and play by the rules that I hadn't considered the effects my actions would have on me.

"Youth is wholly experimental," Robert Louis Stevenson wrote. Sure, **11** there will be mistakes, but there will also be successes. I was a confused kid. Everyone—my parents, teachers and coaches—offered suggestions, but I chose to ignore them. I had "potential," they told me. As a typical teen, I thought I could make it on my own. I didn't want any help, and the more people tried to give it the more distant I grew. I was the kid who thought he could be perfect at anything without any preparation. I was lost in the daydream that I didn't need to study; I was going to play professional soccer. My game was good and I thought that practice, or getting good grades, for that matter, was unnecessary. Stubbornness and rebellion can be terrible things if they get out of control.

"To get back one's youth one has merely to repeat one's follies." A day **12** before my awakening on that fateful July sunrise, I would have disagreed with this quotation from Oscar Wilde. But after recognizing the results of my own follies for the first time, I thoroughly agree.

This year, my final year in high school, I've at last cleared my head and **13** buckled down. Judging by the past semester, I'm on the right track. My D average has U-turned into this report card's three B's and one A, landing me on my first Honor Roll. I intend to be on the Principal's List after this semester; then I hope to graduate and attend a community college in northern California, near the mountains, before transferring to a four-year school.

Thanks to that morning's conversion, I am a new person. Now, I know **14** I'll have to work hard. The sun streaming over the eastern Sierras wiped out the dark clouds that blurred my vision. Jonathan Harker in Bram Stoker's "Dracula" must have felt exactly the same way when he wrote in his journal: "No man knows 'till he has suffered from the night how sweet and how dear to his heart and eye the morning can be."

Vocabulary

torrents (1)	stimulating (9)
pelted (1)	entranced (9)
abruptly (3)	defying (10)
subside (4)	potential (11)
donning (4)	conversion (14)
rigor mortis (8)	

Understanding What You Have Read

Check the correct answer in the blank provided.

1. The trip described took place

   _____ (a). in a dream after having gone river rafting.

   _____ (b). one summer after the narrator's junior year in high school.

   _____ (c). when the narrator was 5 years old.

   _____ (d). shortly before the narrator was married.

2. The expeditioners did not notice the storm coming until

   _____ (a). their shadows suddenly disappeared.

   _____ (b). the birds starting chirping frantically.

   _____ (c). the leader yelled, "Put up the tents!"

   _____ (d). lightening suddenly struck a camper.

3. While donning rain gear, the narrator suddenly noticed that

   _____ (a). a deer was seeking shelter under the same tree.

   _____ (b). a forest ranger appeared out of nowhere.

   _____ (c). he was standing on a small island.

   _____ (d). all the other campers were sleeping soundly.

4. The heavy rain

   _____ (a). washed away the tents.

   _____ (b). gradually turned into a warm summer drizzle.

   _____ (c). caused a beautiful rainbow to appear.

   _____ (d). lasted all day and into the night.

5. As a typical teen, the narrator

   _____ (a). thought he could make it on his own.

   _____ (b). grew more and more distant as people tried to help him.

   _____ (c). believed he could be perfect without preparation.

   _____ (d). all of the above.

Thinking About What You Have Read

1. Why was this experience important in changing the narrator's outlook on life and his plans for the future?

2. How does the narrator make the storm seem real to the reader? Give specific examples of vivid language used.

3. The narrator also uses comparisons—similes and metaphors—to make his description vivid. Find examples and tell why each is effective.

4. Which paragraph, in your opinion, describes the most difficult part of the experience? Give reasons for your answer.

5. Would you have enjoyed the experience described in this essay? Why or why not?

Writing Assignments

1. Using O'Connor's essay as a model, write an essay describing a striking aspect of nature you once experienced. Try to make the scene come to life for your reader.

2. Write an essay in which you narrate an incident in your past that contributed dramatically to your growth toward maturity.

Illustrating

So Who Makes Up All Those Signs that Tell Us What We Mustn't Do?

Bailey White

Perhaps, like the author, you have wondered who in the world thinks up all of the signs posted in public places to make people behave. If you have, then the essay that follows will speak familiarly to you. If you have not, then maybe the next time you encounter a sign that forbids you to do something, you will remember this essay. Notice how the author uses numerous examples—real and imaginary—to illustrate his point.

I was leaning over the little railing, looking down into the Devil's Millhopper, an interesting geological formation and the focal point of a Florida state park. Waterfalls plunge 120 feet into a bowl-shaped sinkhole, maidenhair ferns and moss grow in little crevices along the steep, sloping sides of the gorge, and a beautiful mist rises. I stood there feeling a reverence for those spectacles of the natural world. I felt the slow sweep of geologic time, I felt the remnants of the spiritual significance that place had had for the Indians who lived there for thousands of years; I felt the wonder and awe the European explorers experienced when they peered into that chasm for the first time. **1**

Then another feeling crept over me, a deep, almost atavistic,* longing. It was the urge to throw something into the Devil's Millhopper. I looked around. A stone or a stick would do, but what I really wanted was a piece of food, the nibbled end of a hot-dog bun or a wedge of chocolate cake without icing. Then I noticed the sign, one of those tastefully unobtrusive state park signs: "Do Not Throw Food Or Trash In Gorge." **2**

It was 4 A.M. and I was at the Los Angeles bus station, my next-to-last stop on a dreary transcontinental trip—three days and three nights on a Greyhound. My back ached, my knees ached, my head ached. Ever since El Paso, Texas, my seatmate had been an old man who chain-smoked Marlboro cigarettes and sucked and slobbered over a perpetual ham sandwich that kept oozing out of a greasy crumple of wax paper. I longed for a bath in my own bathtub at home, and then a deep sleep in my own bed, stretched out full length between clean sheets. But, I thought, pushing open the door of the bus station restroom, if I can just wash my feet and my hair I will be all right. I lined up my soap, my washrag and my little bottle of shampoo on the back of the sink and took off my shoes and socks. Aah, I thought. Then I saw the sign on the mirror: "Do Not Wash Hair Or Feet In the Sink." **3**

A few weeks ago I went into our little downtown restaurant and saw that it had replaced its tired old salad bar with a gorgeous saltwater aquarium with sea anemones, chunks of living coral and big, slow-moving, colorful fish with faces I could almost recognize. I spent my whole lunchtime staring into **4**

*Throwback.

that tank, mesmerized by the fish as they gracefully looped and glided, sending the tentacles of the sea anemones into slow swirls and fanning out the tall grasses. When I finished my sandwich I noticed that there were a couple of crumbs left on my plate, just the size to pinch between thumb and finger.

Oh, I thought, to pinch up those crumbs and dip my fingers down into the water, breaking through the smooth surface into the coolness and silence of that peaceful world. A fish would make a looping turn, his odd exophthalmic eyes would rotate slowly in their sockets and fix upon the crumbs. Then he would angle up, and I would feel for just one exquisite instant those raspy fish lips grating across my fingertips. With rising delight and anticipation, I pinched up a crumb, two crumbs. I scrabbled across to the plastic top of the tank, found the little door, lifted it open—and then I saw the sign: "Do Not Feed The Fish." **5**

"We Prohibit Climbing In Any Manner From Or Along the Canyon Rim." **6**

"Do Not Pick Flowers." **7**

"No Smoking, Eating Or Drinking." **8**

"No Swinging From Vines In Trees." **9**

"No Pedestrian Traffic In Woods." **10**

"No Fishing." **11**

"No Swimming." **12**

"No Trespassing." **13**

Don't get me wrong. I approve of these necessary and useful prohibitions. But sometimes I wonder: Who makes them up and how does he know so well the deep and touching urges of human beings to pick flowers, picnic in unusual spots, walk in the woods, climb canyon walls, swing from vines and feed already well-nourished animals? I imagine a sour, silent little man skulking around in public places, watching us furtively with squinty eyes and scribbling notes on his bulging pad with a gnawed pencil. In national parks he disguises himself as a tourist in reflective sunglasses and plaid Bermuda shorts. "Bryce Canyon," he notes with a smirk. "Urinating on hoodoos and off cliffs." In zoos he wears khaki and lurks in the shadows, hiding behind a bag of peanuts. "Touching the giraffe's tongue through fence wire . . . feeling the camel's hump," he scribbles. **14**

At night he goes home and, in his stark-white workshop illuminated with fluorescent lights, he makes those forbidding signs. I imagine, one night as he works late, the tendril of a grapevine creeping in his window and, when his back is turned, gently nudging itself around him. "No Touching!" he admonishes. But, with a clutch and a snatch, the vine retracts, and he finds himself hurtling through the night sky above a North Florida state park. "Do Not Swing From Vines!" he shrieks. And with that the vine drops him into the vortex of a limpid spring. "No Swimming!" he sputters as the dark, icy water closes over his head. As he sinks, pale-colored fish swim up and cock their eyes at him. "Do Not Feed The Fish!" he squeaks. But slowly and precisely, the fish angle up, move in, and then, all over, he feels the pick-pick-pick of those prickly lips. **15**

Vocabulary

focal (1)	exophthalmic (5)
gorge (1)	prohibitions (14)
reverence (1)	skulking (14)
geologic (1)	furtively (14)
remnants (1)	tendril (15)
chasm (1)	retracts (15)
unobtrusive (2)	vortex (15)
anemones (4)	limpid (15)

Understanding What You Have Read

Check the correct answer in the blank provided.

1. What is the first example of a sign the author gives?

   _____ **(a).** "Do Not Feed the Fish or Birds."

   _____ **(b).** "Do Not Throw Food Or Trash In Gorge."

   _____ **(c).** "No Trespassing."

   _____ **(d).** "No Swinging From Vines In Trees."

2. What did the writer try to do in the Los Angeles bus station?

   _____ **(a).** Feed some homeless people.

   _____ **(b).** Walk behind the cashier's window.

   _____ **(c).** Drop a gum wrapper on the floor.

   _____ **(d).** Wash his feet in the restroom sink.

3. What happened when the author tried to place some bread crumbs in a restaurant fish tank?

   _____ **(a).** He noticed a sign stating, "Use Only Cracker Crumbs to Feed Fish."

   _____ **(b).** Some children wanted to do the same.

   _____ **(c).** A fish bit him.

   _____ **(d).** He saw a sign stating, "Do Not Feed The Fish."

4. Does the author approve or disapprove of signs prohibiting certain actions?

   _____ **(a).** He approves.

   _____ **(b).** He disapproves.

   _____ **(c).** He wishes they were not necessary.

   _____ **(d).** He thinks they will lead to political dictatorship.

5. The author imagines that the one writing the signs is

   _____ **(a).** an editor at the Chicago Tribune.

   _____ **(b).** a little old lady from Boston.

   _____ **(c).** a schoolteacher who hates children.

   _____ **(d).** a sour little man skulking around in public places.

Thinking About What You Have Read

1. The major question on the writer's mind is, "Who makes up all those signs that tell us what we must not do?" Why do you think this question intrigues him? Does it intrigue you? Why or why not?

2. Do you agree that human beings have a deep urge to break rules? What other rules do you see people breaking?

3. What penalty do you suggest for graffiti writers? ("Graffiti Forbidden" does not seem to work.)

4. Think of another possible imaginative creature whom you might describe as the sign creator. What kind of person would he or she be? Describe him or her as vividly as the author described his creature.

5. Do you believe it is necessary to have signs forbidding certain behaviors in public places? Why or why not?

Writing Assignments

1. Write an essay on the importance of keeping public places clean. Use examples to support your point.

2. Write an essay about the way nature and beautiful monuments are destroyed by people. Illustrate your essay with examples.

Long Live High School Rebels

Thomas French

The essay that follows encourages high school students to think for themselves and disobey rules imposed only to keep them quiet and passive. This position is quite different from that of contemporary articles attacking high school students for laziness, irresponsibility, the way they speak, or the way they dress. What is your own opinion? Are high school students stifled by their principals and teachers? As you read, notice the author's use of examples to support his argument. Are his examples convincing?

Ten years ago I was in high school. It was the most absurd and savage place I have ever been.   **1**

To listen to the morning announcement, you'd have thought the most pressing crisis in the world was our student body's lack of school spirit. Seniors were grabbing freshmen, dragging them into the bathrooms and dunking their heads in the toilets—a ritual called "flushing." Basketball players were treated like royalty; smart kids were treated like peasants. And the administrators worshipped the word "immature." Inevitably, they pronounced it "imma-tour." Inevitably, they used it to describe us.   **2**

The principal and his assistants told us to act like adults, but they treated us like children. Stupid children. They told us what we could wear, when we could move, how close we could stand to our girlfriends, how fast we could walk to lunch and what topics were forbidden to write about in our school newspaper.   **3**

When I went out for the tennis team, I remember, the coach told me to cut my hair. It was down to my shoulders and looked terrible, but I loved it. I asked the coach what was the point. Just do it, he said.   **4**

If we were taught anything, it was that high school is not about learning but about keeping quiet. The easiest way to graduate was to do what you were told, all of what you were told, and nothing but what you were told. Most of us did just that. I smiled at the principal, stayed out of trouble, avoided writing articles critical of administration, asked only a few smart-alecky questions and cut my hair as ordered. I was so embarrassed afterwards that I wore a blue ski cap all day every day for weeks.   **5**

I admit to some lingering bitterness over the whole affair. I'd still like to know, for one thing, what the length of my hair had to do with my forehand. Maybe that's why, to this day, I almost always root for high school students when they clash intelligently with administrators. High school needs a good dose of dissension. If you've been there in recent years, and I have because I work with student newspapers around Pinellas County, you'd know it needs dissension more than ever.   **6**

A reminder of this came with the news that one day last month an assistant principal at St. Petersburg High was rummaging through a student's car in a school parking lot. When the assistant principal found three empty wine-cooler bottles and what was suspected to be some spiked eggnog inside the car, the student was suspended for five days.   **7**

Though the student has argued that the search was an unconstitutional violation of his rights, the incident should not have come as any huge surprise. High school officials around this county have been searching through   **8** kids' cars and lockers for some time. One day a couple of years ago, a teacher tells me, officials at Lakewood High allowed police to search for drugs with dogs. At the time, students were gathered at an assembly on God and patriotism.

Searches tell students plainly enough what administrators think of **9** them. But in this county, such incidents are only part of a larger tradition of control. Some memorable moments over the years:

- In 1983, a group of boys at Lakewood High decided it was unfair that they weren't allowed to wear shorts to school but that girls were allowed to wear miniskirts. The rationale for the rule was that shorts—but not miniskirts—were too "distracting." To make fun of the rule, the boys began wearing miniskirts to school.

  Administrators laughed at first, but once the rebellion began attracting publicity, the principal suspended the ringleader. When dozens of students staged further protest in front of the school and refused to go to class, the principal suspended 37 of them, too. Later, although close to 1,400 signatures were gathered on a petition against the rule, the Pinellas County School Board bore down and decided to ban shorts from all middle and high schools. Miniskirts, however, were still allowed.

  "We need to set a moral standard for our children," explained board member Gerald Castellanos.
- Last year, William Grey, the principal of St. Petersburg High, suspended a ninth-grader who dyed her hair purple. "I just don't think school is the place for multi-colored heads," Grey said. He did acknowledge that he allowed students to dye their hair green for special events—the school's colors are green and white—but he insisted that was different because it was "promoting school spirit."
- Earlier this year at Pinellas Park High, two of the school's top students—they're number one and two in their class academically—were criticized by the principal when they wrote articles in the student newspaper pointing out that many of the school's students are sexually active and do not use birth control. I was working with the staff that year, and I know the two students wrote the articles in an effort to prevent teen-age pregnancies. But the principal called their work irresponsible—he disagreed with their methodology—and told the newspaper staff it should write more "positive" articles.
- This fall, says a teacher at Pinellas Park, the administration cracked down on cafeteria infractions by warning that anyone caught leaving a lunch tray on a table would be suspended.
- Last year, 16-year-old Manny Sferios and a group of other students from public and private high schools put together an underground magazine called Not For Profit and distributed several issues to students around the county. The magazine ridiculed apartheid, protested the proliferation of nuclear weapons and tried to prod students into thinking about something more than their next pair of designer jeans.

Not For Profit also contained a variety of swear words and ridiculed the **10** small-mindedness of many school officials, and when administrators saw it, they began confiscating copies from kids and warning that those caught with the publication risked suspension.

Though the officials said their main objection to *Not For Profit* was its **11** language, the magazine's activist stance also came under fire. Gerald Castellanos, the school board member, said he did not believe students were sophisticated enough to put together such a magazine.

"I sincerely sense the hand of some very anti-American, anti-free enter- **12** prise types in here," he said. "And I don't believe they're students."

Castellanos' attitude was not surprising. Too often the people who run **13** our high schools and sit on our school boards are not prepared to accept or deal with students who think for themselves and stand up for themselves. It would mean a loss of some control, increased resistance to petty rules and a slew of hard questions for those official who'd rather present a "positive image" than openly confront the real problems in our schools.

There are plenty of real problems that need confronting. Alcohol. Drugs. **14** Broken families. Teen-age pregnancies. Not to mention what's happening in some of our classrooms.

While working on an article published earlier this year, I sat in a **15** couple of classes at St. Petersburg High—the school run by William Grey, the principal who took a stand on purple hair—and what I saw were rows and rows of kids who were bored beyond description. They were trading jokes while the teachers tried to speak. They were literally falling asleep at their desks. One boy who had no interest in the subject matter—it was American history, by the way—was allowed to get up and leave. Another sat in his seat, strumming his finger across his lips, making baby noises.

Dealing with apathy as deep as this is challenge enough for anyone. **16** It requires more teachers, more money, inspiration, real change—all of which are hard to come by. Throw that in with the other problems in our high schools, and the task becomes monumental.

I'm not saying that administrators aren't trying to cope with that task. **17** I know they are. But frequently they waste time and distance themselves from students by exerting their authority in other ways. Make sure the kids don't wear shorts. See to it they put away their lunch trays. Bring in the dogs every once in a while and let them sniff around the lockers. In the face of everything else, keep the school quiet. It's a way that adults tell themselves they're in charge. It's a way they tell themselves they're making a difference.

In the meantime, the ideas that our high schools should promote— **18** freedom of thought and expression, for one—get shoved aside. And the students whom we should be encouraging—the ones who have the brains and spirit to start their own magazine, to protest silly rules, to ask what the color of one's hair has to do with an education—are lectured, suspended and told to get back in line.

Kids know it stinks. Once in a while, they find the guts to step forward **19** and say so, even if it means getting in trouble. I think they should do it more often. Because if there's anything I regret about my own days in high school, it's that more of us didn't fight against the absurdity with every ounce of adolescent ingenuity and irreverence we had.

We should have commandeered the p.a. system one morning and read **20** aloud from Thoreau's *Civil Disobedience*. We should have boycotted the food in the cafeteria for a solid week. We should have sent a note home to the principal's parents informing them he was suspended until he grew up. We should have boned up on our rights in law library and published what we found in the school paper. And every time an adult said "immatour," we should have pulled kazoos out of our pockets and blown on them to our heart's content.

Vocabulary

inevitably (2)   confiscating (10)
dissension (6)   apathy (16)
methodology (9)   ingenuity (19)
apartheid (9)   irreverence (19)
proliferation (9)   commandeered (20)

Understanding What You Have Read

Check the correct answer in the blank provided.

1. Ten years ago, when the author was in high school, he found it
   _____ **(a).** a place where students learned about true democracy.
   _____ **(b).** the most absurd and savage place he had ever been.
   _____ **(c).** a campus with a modern building and good gym equipment.
   _____ **(d).** an ideal spot to find your future wife.

2. The author objects to the fact that in his high school, the principal and assistants
   _____ **(a).** cared only about getting salary raises for themselves.
   _____ **(b).** would not allow students to have a senior prom.
   _____ **(c).** told the students to act like adults but treated them like children.
   _____ **(d).** expected too much from students who had not yet reached the age of 20.

3. When the boys at Lakewood High were not allowed to wear shorts to school while the girls could wear miniskirts, they
   _____ **(a).** wrote to the local newspaper about how unfair the rule was.
   _____ **(b).** staged a walkout and would not attend school for a week.
   _____ **(c).** filled the principal's office with barrels of popcorn.
   _____ **(d).** wore miniskirts to school.

4. Which of the following examples is not listed as an infraction in this essay?
   _____ **(a).** Dyeing one's hair purple.
   _____ **(b).** Locking the principal in his office.
   _____ **(c).** Writing in the school paper that students were sexually active.
   _____ **(d).** Putting together an underground magazine.

5. One of the great challenges of dealing with high school students is fighting their
   _____ **(a).** apathy.
   _____ **(b).** rudeness.
   _____ **(c).** stupidity.
   _____ **(d).** bad language.

Thinking About What You Have Read

1. The author states (paragraphs 19, 20) that he regrets that more students in his day did not fight against the absurdity of high school discipline with all of the "adolescent ingenuity and irreverence" they had. Do you agree with his attitude? Give reasons for your answer.

2. What makes the author's task difficult as he sticks up for the rights of high school students? Do you think he manages to overcome the difficulty?

3. How would you counter the argument that high school students should rebel against all of the "absurd" regulations, such as dress codes and restrictions against freedom of speech?

4. Looking back on your own high school experience, how would you judge your high school principals or your teachers? What attitudes did they have toward you and the other students? Were you subjected to the kinds of regulations described in French's article?

5. Does French present both sides of the question? Why or why not? Do his examples strengthen his point of view? Why or why not?

Writing Assignments

1. Do you agree with French? Write an essay in which you support or oppose his point of view, using convincing examples of your own.

2. Write about your high school experience, indicating whether or not it encouraged you to think on your own. Use examples that prove your point.

Explaining a Process

How I Was Bathed

Michael Ondaatje

This description of a process is a delightful peek into the life of the narrator. It captivates us because all of us have memories of special moments and people stored in our brains. We remember Grandpa taking us for ice cream, a teacher scolding us in front of the class, a scout hike up some glacier, or a quarrel with our best friend. This particular memory describes the process of being bathed at the age of five. Notice how the steps are described clearly and in logical order.

1   We are having a formal dinner. String hoppers, meat curry, egg rulang, papadams, potato curry. Alice's date chutney, seeni sambol, mallung and brinjals and iced water. All the dishes are on the table and a good part of the meal is spent passing them around to each other. It is my favourite meal—anything that has string hoppers and egg rulang I eat with a lascivious hunger. For dessert there is buffalo curd and jaggery sauce—a sweet honey made from the coconut, like maple syrup but with a smoky taste.

2   In this formal setting Gillian begins to describe to everyone present how I used to be bathed when I was five. She had heard the story in detail from Yasmine Gooneratne, who was a prefect with her at Bishop's College for Girls. I listen intently, making sure I get a good portion of the egg rulang.

3   The first school I went to was a girls' school in Colombo which accepted young boys of five or six for a couple of years. The nurse or ayah in charge of our cleanliness was a small, muscular and vicious woman named Maratina. I roamed with my pack of school friends, usually filthy from morning to night, and every second evening we were given a bath. The bathroom was a sparse empty stone room with open drains in the floor and a tap to one side. We were marched in by Maratina and ordered to strip. She collected our clothes, threw them out of the room, and locked the door. The eight of us were herded terrified into one corner.

4   Maratina filled a bucket with water and flung the contents towards our cowering screaming bodies. Another bucket was filled and hurled towards us hard as a police hose. Then she strode forward, grabbed a child by the hair, pulled him over to the centre, scrubbed him violently with carbolic soap and threw him towards the opposite side of the room. She plucked another and repeated the soaping. Totally in control of the squirming bodies she eventually scrubbed us all, then returned to the bucket and thrashed water over our soapy nakedness. Bleary-eyed, our bodies tingling and reeling, our hair curved back from the force of the throw, we stood there shining. She approached with a towel, dried us fast and brutally, and threw us out one by one to get into our sarongs and go to bed.

5   The guests, the children, everyone is laughing and Gillian is no doubt exaggerating Yasmine's account in her usual style, her long arms miming the capture and scrub of five-year-olds. I am dreaming and wondering why this was never to be traumatically remembered. It is the kind of event that should have surfaced as the first chapter of an anguished autobiographical novel. I am thinking also of Yasmine Gooneratne, now teaching at a university in Australia, whom I met just last year at an International Writers' Conference in New Dehli. We talked then mostly about Gillian who had

also been at university with her. Why did *she* not tell me the story—this demure woman in a sari who was once "bath prefect" at Bishop's College Girl's School, who officiated over the cleansing of my lean five-year-old nakedness?

Vocabulary

lascivious (1)	sarongs (4)
prefect (2)	miming (5)
sparse (3)	traumatically (5)
cowering (4)	demure (5)
carbolic (4)	sari (5)

Understanding What You Have Read

Check the correct answer in the blank provided.

1. According to certain details provided, where would you guess the narrative takes place?

_____ **(a).** Africa.

_____ **(b).** Russia.

_____ **(c).** China.

_____ **(d).** India.

2. Who is in charge of the boys' cleanliness?

_____ **(a).** The cook, Alice.

_____ **(b).** The author's older sister.

_____ **(c).** The nurse, Maratina.

_____ **(d).** Yasmine.

3. What is the first step in the bath process?

_____ **(a).** To have the boys pick out some clean clothes.

_____ **(b).** To have the boys strip.

_____ **(c).** To recite a patriotic verse.

_____ **(d).** To have each boy pick out a towel.

4. After the boys are brutally towel dried, what are they ordered to do?

_____ **(a).** Say their prayers.

_____ **(b).** Write letters to their parents.

_____ **(c).** Read a book.

_____ **(d).** Get into their sarongs and go to bed.

5. How do the guests react to Gillian's exaggerated account of the bath?

_____ **(a).** They are bored.

_____ **(b).** They laugh.

_____ **(c).** They feel embarrassed.

_____ **(d).** They are relieved that those days are over.

Thinking About What You Have Read

1. The author wonders why the brutal bathing process never traumatized his life. In your view, why didn't it?

2. Why are the boys so terrified when they are herded into one corner to be bathed? Would you have been terrified at that age? Why or why not?

3. Does Maratina strike you as an evil woman? Why does she terrify the boys?

4. After Gillian has described the bath routine, the guests laugh in response. Do you consider the description humorous? If yes, what are the humorous details?

5. List the separate steps involved in the process of bathing the boys in order.

Writing Assignments

1. Write about some routine process you remember from your childhood. Break it down into separate, clearly listed steps.

2. Write an essay about the process of getting up every morning. Describe each major step clearly and in the order in which it occurs.

Research Can Beat Making a Frustrating Call to Tech Support

Bill Husted

Many of us either own a computer or use computers in our daily lives. And most of us, at one time or another, have had trouble with them. When computers go bad, the cause is often in the software rather than the hardware. But finding and fixing the problem usually requires a frustrating call to technical support. However, as the writer tells us, tech support today is not what it used to be. Often you can't get a live person to talk to, and if you're lucky enough to reach someone, you probably waited forever. The writer, a computer advice columnist, outlines a typical problem, shows us a side of technical support many of us unfortunately know, then takes us through a series of steps we can follow to help ourselves.

1 If you've dealt with a computer manufacturer's technical support lately you may have ended up feeling like you just made an emergency landing in China and were met by hostile troops.

2 That's why when computer makers moan and groan about slow sales, they don't get much sympathy from me. Obviously there are exceptions, but generally there's an arrogance toward the customer that has been slowly building over the past few years.

3 From what I hear from my readers, my friends and from my own experience, things have reached the level where a pleasant technical support experience is a shock. Personally, I haven't had many shocks lately.

4 Last weekend I had my own computer problems when a printer I own didn't have a driver (a small program that lets the computer and printer communicate) that worked with a test version of Windows. To be fair to the manufacturer, the printer is a couple of years old and the version of Windows (Windows XP) is still being tested.

5 But without that driver, I won't be able to use a perfectly good printer that works great with Windows ME, the version of Windows on the market now.

6 I didn't expect miracles—considering the age of my computer and the fact that Windows XP won't be on the market until fall, I simply wanted to know if the printer company would eventually release a driver for it. So I sent in an email but didn't tell the company I write about computers. (After all, if I did that, I might get special treatment and wouldn't be able to judge how good the customer service is for you.)

7 A day after sending in my question to the manufacturer, I got an answer that didn't waste many words: "Sorry, but it is not available."

8 Well, I knew that. After all, that's what I wrote to tell them. What I wanted to know, and what I asked, was: Will it be available later? And it would have been nice to get some advice on ways that I could make things work without the driver.

9 So I had to help myself. By trial and error, I installed drivers for the company's other printer models and found one that worked. That's something the company could have recommended. A novice user probably wouldn't think to try that. As a customer, you have a right to expect some help when you're faced with a problem that will force you to shell out hundreds of dollars.

10 The temptation is to simply shrug and move on. But I'm here today to suggest two things. One, when you get bad customer service, register your

complaint with the company. Maybe some genius will finally make a connection between the crummy service and falling sales. Two, until that magic day happens, learn to get help on your own.

Here's a battle plan for what to do when your company lets you down. **11**

First, check the company's Web site. I did that with my printer problem. **12** While the information on the page didn't solve my own problem, there was an impressive amount of canned help. In many cases, you'll be able to solve your problem that way.

Next, do a general Web search. I had another problem recently when **13** my computer reported an error loading a specific file. I simply entered the name of that file in a Web browser. (In this case I used Altavista at www.altavista.com). That search provided me with a list of Web pages that mentioned the file. I found at least two sites that provided specific information that fixed the problem.

If those two steps don't work, check out the newsgroups. These are **14** special-purpose areas devoted to a specific topic—usually a narrow one.

Odds are that your computer or printer or other accessory will have a **15** newsgroup devoted to it. Members of newsgroup post questions, and usually there are plenty of people willing to provide answers. (Like in other parts of life some of the answers will be right, some will be wrong.) You can reach newsgroups through your Web browser. If you use Internet Explorer, look under the Tools menu for "mail and news." Or you can get a program specifically designed to browse and search the news groups. Check out the selection at www.tucows.com.

Finally, know when to give up. If you're not especially knowledgeable **16** about computers, seek out the paid help of a computer technician. It's possible for an amateur to actually create larger problems trying to fix a small one.

Atlanta Constitution, April 22, 2001

Vocabulary

novice (9)

Understanding What You Have Read

Check the correct answer in the blank provided.

1. How, according to the author, are you likely to feel after calling technical support?

   _____ **(a).** Good.

   _____ **(b).** Satisfied.

   _____ **(c).** That you were met by hostile troops.

   _____ **(d).** That you were saved in the nick of time.

2. For what software problem did the author seek help from technical support ?

   _____ **(a).** Incompatibility with word processing programs.

   _____ **(b).** An outmoded operating system.

   _____ **(c).** A printer driver.

   _____ **(d).** A telecommunications program.

3. What unhelpful message did the writer receive from technical support in reply to his query?

_____ (a). We'll contact you immediately with additional help.

_____ (b). Technical support is not available unless you pay for it.

_____ (c). Go away, there's nothing we can do to help.

_____ (d). Sorry, but it is not available.

4. On what does the author blame sagging sales of computers?

_____ (a). Crummy service.

_____ (b). Overly rapid expansion.

_____ (c). The boom and bust cycle of the economy.

_____ (d). The Intel Pentium 4 chip.

5. About homemade fixes, the author says:

_____ (a). Amateurs can always perform them.

_____ (b). Professional technicians are always necessary.

_____ (c). An amateur can create a bigger problem by trying to fix a small one.

_____ (d). Amateurs should never tried to fix computer problems.

Thinking About What You Have Read

1. What figure of speech does the author use to open his article? How effective do you think this opening is?

2. The author writes an advice column intended for general readers. What obvious steps does he take to make his technical discussion understandable to amateurs?

3. What are some of the transitions the author uses to make the sequence of steps in his process clear?

4. What is the purpose of the skimpy paragraph 11?

5. The author spends considerable time explaining his technical dilemma with the printer driver. What purpose is served by this explanation?

Writing Assignments

1. Write a paragraph about any problem or issue you've ever had with a computer.

2. Write a paragraph on the usefulness of computers.

Defining

Bullying Broadly Defined

John Leo

Ever since the terrible 1999 massacre at Columbine High School in Littleton, Colorado, and the subsequent school murders that followed, pressure has been building on the authorities to do something. A closer look at the shooters in these incidents have revealed one common trait: All felt alienated and had reported being bullied. With something to sink their teeth into, the authorities moved to stomp out bullying. National panels were formed to study the problem and to propose remedies. But, as this writer asks, what exactly is bullying? Is calling someone a jerk bullying? Rather than being a simple and easy to define word, "bullying" turns out to be more complicated than it at first looks.

1 Now we have a big national study on bullying, and the problem with it is right there in the first paragraph: Bullying behavior may be "verbal (e.g., name-calling, threats), physical (e.g., hitting) or psychological (e.g., rumors, shunning-exclusion)."

2 Uh-oh. The study may or may not have put bullying on the map as a major national issue. But it rather clearly used a dubious tactic: taking a lot of harmless and minor things ordinary children do and turning them into examples of bullying. Calling somebody a jerk and spreading rumors counted as bullying in the study. Repeated teasing counted, too. You achieved bully status if you didn't let the class creep into your game of catch, or if you just stayed away from people you didn't like (shunning, exclusion).

3 With a definition like that, the total number of children involved in either bullying or being bullied themselves ought to be around 100 percent. But no, the bullying study says only 29.9 percent of the students studied reported frequent or moderate involvement—and that total was arrived at by lumping bullies and their victims together in the statistics.

4 The low numbers and highly debatable definitions undercut the study's conclusion that bullying is "a serious problem for U.S. youth." Of the 29.9 percent figure, 13 percent were bullies, 10.6 percent were targets of bullying, and 6.3 percent were both perpetrators and victims. The study, done by the National Institute of Child Health and Human Development, is based on 15,686 questionnaires filled out by students in grades 6 through 10 in public and private schools around the country.

5 We have seen this statistical blending of serious and trivial incidents before. The American Association of University Women produced a 1993 report showing that 80 percent of American students have been sexually harassed, including a hard-to-believe 76 percent of all boys. The AAUW got the numbers up that high by including glances, gestures, gossip and naughty jokes. The elastic definition encouraged schools and courts to view many previously uncontroversial kinds of expression as sexual harassment. Before long, schools were making solemn lists of harassing behaviors that included winking and calling someone "honey."

6 Another set of broad definitions appeared when zero-tolerance policies descended on the schools. Anti-drug rules were extended to cover aspirin. Anti-weapons regulations covered a rubber knife used in a school play. Just two months ago a third-grader in Monroe, Louisiana., was suspended for

drawing a picture of G.I. Joe. Now the anti-bullying movement is poised to provide a third source of dubious hyper-regulation of the young. One anti-bullying specialist says "hard looks" and "stare-downs"—everyday activities for millions of hormone-driven adolescent boys—should be punishable offenses under student codes.

This has all the makings of an anti-bullying crusade, with many of the same wretched excesses of the zero-tolerance and anti-harassment campaigns. Serious bullying can be ugly. Parents and schools should stop it and punish offenders. And schools should do whatever they can to create a culture of civility and tolerance. But rumors and dirty looks and getting along with horrible classmates are all part of growing up. So are the teenage tendencies to form cliques and snub people now and then. Adults shouldn't faint when they see this behavior, or try to turn it into quasi-criminal activity.   **7**

Another pitfall: In focusing on gossip, rumors and verbal offenses, the crusade has the obvious potential to infringe free speech at schools. Will comments like "I think Catholicism is wrong" or "I think homosexuality is a sin" be turned into anti-bullying offenses? The crusade could also demonize those who bully instead of helping them change. Some of the anti-bully literature circulating in Europe is hateful stuff. One screed calls "the serial bully" glib, shallow, evasive, incapable of intimacy, and a practiced liar who "displays a seemingly limitless demonic energy." Yet a lot of the academic literature reports that bullies often aren't very psychologically different from their victims. And the national study says a fifth of bullying victims are bullies themselves.   **8**

The example of Europe's more advanced anti-bullying crusade should make Americans cautious. The European campaign has expanded from schools into the adult world and the workplace. Several nations are considering anti-bullying laws, including Britain. Definitions are expanding, too. A proposed anti-bullying law in Portugal would make it illegal to harass workers by giving them tasks for which they are overqualified. Deliberately giving employees erroneous information would also count as bullying.   **9**

Ireland's anti-bullying task force came up with a scarily vague definition of bullying: "repeated inappropriate behavior, direct or indirect" that could "reasonably be regarded as undermining the individual's right to dignity at work." Imagine what the American litigation industry could do with wording like that. It's time to stop and ask, Where is our anti-bullying campaign going?   **10**

Vocabulary

bullying (1)	poised (6)
verbal (1)	dubious (6)
physical (1)	hyper (6)
psychological (1)	crusade (6)
shunning (1)	civility (7)
exclusion (1)	cliques (7)
dubious (2)	quasi (7)
moderate (3)	infringe (8)
debatable (4)	demonize (8)
questionnaires (4)	screed (8)
trivial (5)	evasive (8)
harassed (5)	litigation (10)
uncontroversial (5)	

Understanding What You Have Read

Check the correct answer in the blank provided.

1. What motivated the author to write this essay?
   _____ **(a).** He himself was bullied in his youth.
   _____ **(b).** He wanted to define the word "bullying."
   _____ **(c).** A national study on bullying had just come out.
   _____ **(d).** The author's editor assigned the essay.

2. The author objects to
   _____ **(a).** taking harmless things children do and calling those actions bullying.
   _____ **(b).** keeping the class creep out of the game of catch.
   _____ **(c).** army sargents who bully enlisted soldiers.
   _____ **(d).** the American Constitution and its Bill of Rights

3. As another example of blending serious and trivial incidents, the author cites a report
   _____ **(a).** picking on homeless people who beg in the streets.
   _____ **(b).** trying to keep foreigners out of our country.
   _____ **(c).** rebelling against college teachers.
   _____ **(d).** stating that 80% of Americans students have been sexually harassed.

4. According to the author, a third-grader in Monroe, Louisiana, was suspended for
   _____ **(a).** using foul language at recess.
   _____ **(b).** pulling a knife on a fellow student.
   _____ **(c).** drawing a picture of G.I. Joe.
   _____ **(d).** using aspirin on campus.

5. The author suggests that an anti-bullying crusade could
   _____ **(a).** save our country from destruction by young people.
   _____ **(b).** limit free speech at schools.
   _____ **(c).** give Britain, Portugal, and Ireland too much power.
   _____ **(d).** create more bullies than ever.

Thinking About What You Have Read

1. What worries the author about the current definition of "bullying"? Do you agree with his concern? Why or why not?

2. What do you consider real bullying? Give your best definition and provide an example.

3. The author believes that "serious bullying" can be ugly and he believes that parents and schools should stop it and punish offenders. What measures do you think parents and schools

should take to stop bullying? Offer some specific strategies that might work.

4. What is your view of the sexual harassment regulations currently used in places of employment? What are their merits if any? What are their faults if any?

5. Do you consider the statement "homosexuality is a sin" an instance of bullying or do you consider it exercising your freedom of speech? Try to answer this question using your reason rather than your emotions.

Writing Assignments

1. Write an essay in which you describe an instance of bullying you either experienced or observed. Be sure to offer your opinion of this situation.

2. Write an essay in which you define a bully. Begin with a dictionary definition and support your definition with appropriate facts, examples, opinions, and anything else that will strengthen your definition.

"Both" or "Other"?
It's Not as Clear
as Black and White

Pamela Swanigan

This newspaper article uses definition as an organizing strategy, even though it begins on a different note—as a locker room interview following an NBA basketball game. The writer soon finds herself being pulled into a discussion of her racial heritage and ends up acknowledging that she belongs to the category of "other." The rest of the article tells what it feels like to be an interracial "other," neither black nor white but somewhere in between. Out of her discussion comes a definition of "other," the racial category that appears on many official forms. Note how the writer defines "other," even though she does so without using many of the techniques taught in the unit on defining a term (Unit 12).

1   I don't make a habit of arguing with semi-naked men who are taller sitting down than I am standing up, and I didn't go to the Chicago Bulls' exhibition game in Toronto last fall intending to do anything but watch the game and perhaps get a story for the newspaper I work for.

2   In talking with Bulls forward Horace Grant, the subject of my biracial heritage came up. When he asked me whether I consider myself black or white, I found myself having a very familiar debate in strange territory. As the daughter of a light-skinned black man and a white woman, I have been asked that question more often than I care to remember. After almost 29 years of experimenting with variations of the word "both," I have found that although this statement of fact is sometimes accepted in Canada, where I now live, most Americans I encounter reject it out of hand.

3   Horace Grant, a gentle and humorous man, proved remarkably stubborn in insisting that I couldn't say I was both, that I had to say one or the other (in his opinion, black, since that's what my birth certificate says—though my skin is actually white). But since "both" is the biological and cultural truth, I stuck to it until Michael Jordan gave me a better answer.

4   In the locker room after the game, after Grant, Bulls guard Scottie Pippen and I had been discussing the issue for several minutes, Jordan put his hands on my shoulders and said, "I'll tell you what you are. You're 'Other.'"

5   Jordan shrugged away my automatic protest and said matter-of-factly, "You can't put half a check mark in 'black' and half a check mark in 'white,' You have to check 'Other'—that means you're black and white."

6   I doubt he heard that equation as he spoke it, and certainly he didn't mean it as symbolically as I have since taken it.

7   But he was right. I am "Other" to a lot of people: To those who can't function unless they can apply their cultural assumptions; to those who see me as some sort of neutral point to be lobbied to one side or the other; to those who simply hate the other race too much to accept their co-existence in one person.

8   I am even "Other" to my step-grandmother, who once wrote to me, "Birds of a different feather may sit on the same branch but should not mate."

9   And yes, I'm "Other" to the people who make forms and created the category of "Other" instead of "Both" or "Mixed" or "Race Irrelevant."

10   Contrary to popular opinion, I do not have a choice of race; I have what I was given, which is the genes, traits and prejudices of both. As a child of the East Oakland, Calif., streets, I developed a lot of anger toward whites.

As a member of white society, I have absorbed some stereotypes of black people. I have been called a nigger and a honky; for anyone who's curious, they both hurt, equally.

Like most people, I crave a sense of belonging, but I can only make the most of brief episodes of affinity before my "Otherness" drives me back into internal exile. There are many glib conclusions and sweeping judgments about racial issues; there are few easy answers. Maybe they could start by changing the question. Until they do, I'll give the answer Jordan gave me, in its logical inversion: I'm black and white—that means I'm "Other." **11**

Vocabulary

affinity (11)
inversion (11)

Understanding What You Have Read

Check the correct answer in the blank provided.

1. Where does the article open?
   _____ **(a)**. New York.
   _____ **(b)**. Kingston, Jamaica.
   _____ **(c)**. Toronto.
   _____ **(d)**. Los Angeles.

2. Which NBA player kept pressing the author to declare her race?
   _____ **(a)**. Horace Grant.
   _____ **(b)**. Michael Jordan.
   _____ **(c)**. David Robinson.
   _____ **(d)**. Charles Barkley.

3. Which nationality rejects the author's identification of herself as "both"?
   _____ **(a)**. Canadian.
   _____ **(b)**. Finnish.
   _____ **(c)**. English.
   _____ **(d)**. American.

4. Which NBA player classified the writer's race as "other"?
   _____ **(a)**. Michael Jordan.
   _____ **(b)**. Scottie Pippen.
   _____ **(c)**. David Robinson.
   _____ **(d)**. Horace Grant.

5. How does the writer describe her complexion?
   _____ **(a)**. Brown.
   _____ **(b)**. Sepia.
   _____ **(c)**. White.
   _____ **(d)**. Black.

Thinking About What You Have Read

1. Nowhere does the writer declare her intention to define, yet we are not surprised when she attempts a definition. How does she prepare us for the purpose of her article?

2. The author says that Canadians are willing to accept her calling herself "both" but that most Americans are not. Why? How do you explain the unwillingness of most Americans to accept "both" as her racial designation?

3. What technique does the author use in defining her racial heritage?

4. The author says she can "only make the most of brief episodes of affinity." What are "brief episodes of affinity"? Give an example.

5. Why do official forms generally ask for racial information about people? What purpose do you think such information serves?

Writing Assignments

1. Define yourself in an essay.

2. Write an essay on interracial relations, using yourself and your friends as examples.

Classifying

Wait Divisions

Tom Bodett

From the very beginning, the author makes it clear that this is an informal classification with made-up categories of his own invention. His aim is to entertain, and his down-to-earth vocabulary and chatty sentences add to the folksiness of the piece. Notice how early he tells us of his intent to classify. Notice also that his categories are based on a single principle that he closely follows from beginning to end. As you read, try to find the writer's classifying principle.

1   I read somewhere that we spend a full third of our lives waiting. I've also read where we spend a third of our lives sleeping, a third working, and a third at our leisure. Now either somebody's lying, or we're spending all our leisure time waiting to go to work or sleep. That can't be true or league softball and Winnebagos never would have caught on.

2   So where are we doing all of this waiting and what does it mean to an impatient society like ours? Could this unseen waiting be the source of all our problems? A shrinking economy? The staggering deficit? Declining mental health and moral apathy? Probably not, but let's take a look at some of the more classic "waits" anyway.

3   The very purest form of waiting is what we'll call the *Watched-Pot Wait.* This type of wait is without a doubt the most annoying of all. Take filling up the kitchen sink. There is absolutely nothing you can do while this is going on but keep both eyes glued to the sink until it's full. If you try to cram in some extracurricular activity, you're asking for it. So you stand there, your hands on the faucets, and wait. A temporary suspension of duties. During these waits it's common for your eyes to lapse out of focus. The brain disengages from the body and wanders around the imagination in search of distraction. It finds none and springs back into action only when the water runs over the edge of the counter and onto your socks.

4   The phrase "A watched pot never boils" comes of this experience. Pots don't care whether they are watched or not; the problem is that nobody has ever seen a pot actually come to a boil. While they are waiting, their brains turn off.

5   Other forms of the Watched-Pot Wait would include waiting for your drier to quit at the laundromat, waiting for your toast to pop out of the toaster, or waiting for a decent idea to come to mind at a typewriter. What they all have in common is that they render the waiter helpless and mindless.

6   A cousin to the Watched-Pot Wait is the *Forced Wait.* Not for the weak of will, this one requires a bit of discipline. The classic Forced Wait is starting your car in the winter and letting it slowly idle up to temperature before engaging the clutch. This is every bit as uninteresting as watching a pot, but with one big difference. You have a choice. There is nothing keeping you from racing to work behind a stone-cold engine save the thought of the early demise of several thousand dollars' worth of equipment you haven't paid for yet. Thoughts like that will help you get through a Forced Wait.

7   Properly preparing packaged soup mixes also requires a Forced Wait. Directions are very specific on these mixes. "Bring three cups water to boil, add mix, simmer three minutes, remove from heat, let stand five minutes." I have my doubts that anyone has ever actually done this. I'm fairly spineless

when it comes to instant soups and usually just boil the bejeezus out of them until the noodles sink. Some things just aren't worth a Forced Wait.

All in all Forced Waiting requires a lot of a thing called *patience,* which is a virtue. Once we get into virtues I'm out of my element, and can't expound on the virtues of virtue, or even lie about them. So let's move on to some of the more far-reaching varieties of waiting. **8**

The *Payday Wait* is certainly a leader in the long-term anticipation field. The problem with waits that last more than a few minutes so that you have to actually do other things in the meantime. Like go to work. By far the most aggravating feature of the Payday Wait is that even though you must keep functioning in the interludes, there is less and less you are able to do as the big day draws near. For some of us the last few days are best spent alone in a dark room for fear we'll accidentally do something that costs money. With the Payday Wait comes a certain amount of hope that we'll make it, and faith that everything will be all right once we do. **9**

With the introduction of faith and hope, I've ushered in the most potent wait class of all, the *Lucky-Break Wait,* or the *Wait for One's Ship to Come In.* This type of wait is unusual in that it is for the most part voluntary. Unlike the Forced Wait, which is also voluntary, waiting for your lucky break does not necessarily mean that it will happen. **10**

Turning one's life into a waiting game of these proportions requires gobs of the aforementioned faith and hope, and is strictly for the optimists among us. For these people life is the thing that happens to them while they're waiting for something to happen to them. On the surface it seems as ridiculous as following the directions on soup mixes, but the Lucky-Break Wait performs an outstanding service to those who take it upon themselves to do it. As long as one doesn't come to rely on it, wishing for a few good things to happen never hurt anybody. **11**

In the end it is obvious that we certainly do spend a good deal of our time waiting. The person who said we do it a third of the time may have been going easy on us. It makes a guy wonder how anything at all gets done around here. But things do get done, people grow old, and time boils on whether you watch it or not. **12**

The next time you're standing at the sink waiting for it to fill while cooking soup mix that you'll have to eat until payday or until a large bag of cash falls out of the sky, don't despair. You're probably just as busy as the next guy. **13**

Vocabulary

apathy (2)   expound (8)
extracurricular (3) interludes (9)
demise (6)

Understanding What You Have Read

Check the correct answer in the blank provided.

1. Why is the "Watched Pot Wait" so annoying?

    _____ **(a).** Because it is long.

    _____ **(b).** Because it is too steamy.

    _____ **(c).** Because you have to do it every day.

    _____ **(d).** Because there is absolutely nothing to do while it is going on.

2. What is an example of the classic "Forced Wait?"

_____ **(a)**. Waiting for your car to warm up.

_____ **(b)**. Waiting for the train.

_____ **(c)**. Waiting to use the bathroom.

_____ **(d)**. Waiting in line at a grocery store.

3. What kind of wait is a leader in the long-term anticipation field?

_____ **(a)**. The Watched-Pot Wait.

_____ **(b)**. The Payday Wait.

_____ **(c)**. The Lucky-Break Wait.

_____ **(d)**. The Forced Wait.

4. What virtue does forced waiting require?

_____ **(a)**. Luck.

_____ **(b)**. Love.

_____ **(c)**. Laziness.

_____ **(d)**. Patience.

5. According to the author, how much of our lives do we spend waiting?

_____ **(a)**. A third.

_____ **(b)**. A quarter.

_____ **(c)**. A half.

_____ **(d)**. A fifth.

Thinking About What You Have Read

1. On what single principle is the author's wait classification based?

2. What example from campus life can you give of the "Forced Wait"?

3. What other principle can you think of that might be used to classify wait periods?

4. The author says that as the "Payday Wait" draws near, there is less and less we are able to do. Why?

5. How does the author end his essay? What makes this ending so effective?

Writing Assignments

1. Write an essay that uses an organizing principle to classify the different kinds of waiting students must do.

2. Write an essay classifying any common student activity or task.

The Plot Against People

Russell Baker

This humorous essay is a tongue-in-cheek informal classification of inanimate objects. Baker tells us at the outset the basis of his classification and then pretends to quote the findings of science to back up his observations. Notice that once he has begun his classification, he sticks to it and does not waver or stray from his purpose. Pay attention to the transitions he uses as he moves from one category to another.

1   Inanimate objects are classified into three major categories—those that don't work, those that break down and those that get lost.

2   The goal of all inanimate objects is to resist man and ultimately to defeat him, and the three major classifications are based on the method each object uses to achieve its purpose. As a general rule, any object capable of breaking down at the moment when it is most needed will do so. The automobile is typical of the category.

3   With the cunning typical of its breed, the automobile never breaks down while entering a filling station with a large staff of idle mechanics. It waits until it reaches a downtown intersection in the middle of the rush hour, or until it is fully loaded with family and luggage on the Ohio Turnpike.

4   Thus it creates maximum misery, inconvenience, frustration and irritability among its human cargo, thereby reducing its owner's life span.

5   Washing machines, garbage disposals, lawn mowers, light bulbs, automatic laundry dryers, water pipes, furnaces, electrical fuses, television tubes, hose nozzles, tape recorders, slide projectors—all are in league with the automobile to take their turn at breaking down whenever life threatens to flow smoothly for their human enemies.

6   Many inanimate objects, of course, find it extremely difficult to break down. Pliers, for example, and gloves and keys are almost totally incapable of breaking down. Therefore, they have had to evolve a different technique for resisting man.

7   They get lost. Science has still not solved the mystery of how they do it, and no man has ever caught one of them in the act of getting lost. The most plausible theory is that they have developed a secret method of locomotion which they are able to conceal the instant a human eye falls upon them.

8   It is not uncommon for a pair of pliers to climb all the way from the cellar to the attic in its single-minded determination to raise its owner's blood pressure. Keys have been known to burrow three feet under mattresses. Women's purses, despite their great weight, frequently travel through six or seven rooms to find hiding space under a couch.

9   Scientists have been struck by the fact that things that break down virtually never get lost, while things that get lost hardly ever break down.

10   A furnace, for example, will invariably break down at the depth of the first winter cold wave, but it will never get lost. A woman's purse, which after all does have some inherent capacity for breaking down, hardly ever does; it almost invariably chooses to get lost.

11   Some persons believe this constitutes evidence that inanimate objects are not entirely hostile to man, and that a negotiated peace is possible. After all, they point out, a furnace could infuriate a man even more thoroughly by getting lost than by breaking down, just as a glove could upset him far more by breaking down than by getting lost.

12   Not everyone agrees, however, that this indicates a conciliatory attitude among inanimate objects. Many say it merely proves that furnaces, gloves and pliers are incredibly stupid.

The third class of objects—those that don't work—is the most curious **13** of all. These include such objects as barometers, car clocks, cigarette lighters, flashlights and toy-train locomotives. It is inaccurate, of course, to say that they never work. They work once, usually for the first few hours after being brought home, and then quit. Thereafter, they never work again.

In fact, it is widely assumed that they are built for the purpose of not **14** working. Some people have reached advanced ages without ever seeing some of these objects—barometers, for example—in working order.

Science is utterly baffled by the entire category. There are many the- **15** ories about it. The most interesting holds that the things that don't work have attained the highest state possible for an inanimate object, the estate to which things that break down and things that get lost can still only aspire.

They have truly defeated man by conditioning him never to expect any- **16** thing of them, and in return they have given man the only peace he receives from inanimate society. He does not expect his barometer to work, his electric locomotive to run, his cigarette lighter to light or his flashlight to illuminate, and when they don't, it does not raise his blood pressure.

He cannot attain that peace with furnaces and keys and cars and **17** women's purses as long as he demands that they work for their keep.

Vocabulary

inanimate (1)   inherent (10)
plausible (7)   conciliatory (12)
virtually (9)

Understanding What You Have Read

Check the correct answer in the blank provided.

1. What three basic categories does this essay propose for inanimate objects?
    _____ (a). Those that are solid, those that are liquid, and those that are gaseous.
    _____ (b). Those that don't work, those that break down, and those that get lost.
    _____ (c). Those we own, those we steal, and those we borrow.
    _____ (d). Those that are male, those that are female, and those that are neither.

2. According to the author, what is the goal of all inanimate objects?
    _____ (a). To resist and defeat man.
    _____ (b). To work for man and please him.
    _____ (c). To make man's life longer.
    _____ (d). To tempt man to stray.

3. What are keys especially prone to do?
    _____ (a). Misfit.
    _____ (b). Jiggle in one's pocket.

_____ **(c).** Stick in keyholes.

_____ **(d).** Get lost.

4. What fact are scientists particularly struck by?

_____ **(a).** That some objects never break down.

_____ **(b).** That objects that break down never get lost.

_____ **(c).** That objects are highly dependable.

_____ **(d).** That objects have vibrations.

5. What particular object does the author single out as hardly ever working?

_____ **(a).** A barometer.

_____ **(b).** A bicycle.

_____ **(c).** An ax.

_____ **(d).** A spoon.

Thinking About What You Have Read

1. How does the author achieve humor in this essay?

2. To support his classification of inanimate objects, what other strategy does Baker draw on extensively?

3. Where is the thesis statement of this essay? Why do you think the author chose to place it in this particular spot?

4. Read the thesis statement again. What is odd about the author's discussion of the categories, given this particular thesis statement?

5. Is this classification of objects complete? How do you know? Does its completeness matter? Why or why not?

Writing Assignments

1. Write an essay classifying animals or pets.

2. Write an essay to entertain, using the classification strategy.

Comparing and Contrasting

Doctor-as-God Is Dead, or Dying

Ellen Goodman

Some comparison/contrasts are indirect and seem to emerge from an essay almost as an afterthought. For example, in this essay the writer presents an anecdote about a friend's discovery of a new kind of doctor; the discussion leads naturally to a comparison/contrast between doctors, new and old. Look for the transitions that guide you to the comparison/contrast as well as for the examples Goodman uses to clarify what the new doctors believe and how they think.

1   My friend went to the doctor's office expecting to find God. The doctors whom she knew always played God, except on Wednesday afternoon, when they played golf.

2   But what she discovered was that Doctor-God-Sir, the professional keeper of the Temple o¡f the body, was not available. Instead, a new doctor sat down before her, opened up her chart, met her eyes sincerely and asked her to think of him as her "junior partner in health care."

3   This somewhat abrupt transfer from God to the junior partner had a startling effect on my friend's blood pressure. But she had discovered the latest trend of the medical profession: God is dead, or at least dying out.

4   The whole history of Doctor-as-God began way back when medicine men were merely priests. Eventually they got academic degrees and demanded a promotion, although there were some who thought that God was a little high.

5   Medicine still remained a profound mystery to the laity. Such is the way with all religions. It was conducted in Latin or Medicalese, which was Greek to the average person. The patient-supplicant was required to have faith, hope and a little something to put on the plate when it was passed.

6   We were expected to submit to such rituals as the knife and to such magic as pills. Few of us ever saw the appendix that was removed or understood how antibiotics work. But we took penicillin as a kind of oral penance for illness: four times a day for ten days, and bow to the east three times.

7   Somewhere along the way in this skeptical secular era the medical laity became less worshipful. The best and brightest of the young apprentices were also less willing to pretend omniscience.

8   And so we have now entered the era of the junior partner in health care.

9   What are the characteristics of a junior partner? First of all, an aura of humility. You can tell a junior partner by precisely how many times he or she uses the expression "We really don't know. . . ." Junior partners believe in sharing—especially in sharing doubts.

10   You can also identify junior partners by their passion for education. This friend called her J.P. recently when a bee sting had blown her arm up to the size of a large thigh. "What do I do?" she asked. He answered, "First let me tell you something about bee stings."

11   All junior partners have been educated by the full-disclosure, informed-consent school of medicine. Gods give out proclamations; J.P.s give odds. The odds that you will get better, the odds that you will get worse. Along with every prescription comes a description of side effects. If just one

Manchurian lost an ear lobe or a belly button from this cream, you will hear about it.

Consider the true story of a woman who discussed the possibility of **12** surgery with her J.P. After listening to his explanations she tried to recap the pros and cons. "So," she said, "the worst that can happen. . . ." "Oh, no," he interrupted. "The worst that can happen is that you'll die from the anesthesia." After peeling her off the floor he admitted that this possibility was fairly remote—one in 30,000. This is called overinformed consent.

The most basic thing to remember for your next encounter with a J.P. **13** is that he or she will not tell you what to do. Gods give commandments, but J.P.s only lay out options. It is up to you, the Senior Partner, to take responsibility for your health decisions. (This fact is on a poster in the J.P.s waiting room, near stacks of pamphlets on fiber in the diet.)

It is still possible, of course, to find God. But he is likely to be (1) he, **14** (2) older or (3) a specialist in heart or brain surgery. The life-and-death stuff still seems to fall into the hands of you-know-Who.

Should we be surprised by the takeover of the junior partners? After all, **15** isn't this what we all wanted? We wanted doctors to stop treating us like children. We wanted them to talk to us, tell us the whole story. We wanted them to stop acting like gods. We wanted them to admit their fallibility.

Isn't that right? Absolutely. Positively. I swear to God. **16**

Vocabulary

laity (5)   omniscience (7)
skeptical (7)   fallibility (15)
secular (7)

Understanding What You Have Read

Check the correct answer in the blank provided.

1. With what other profession was early medicine identified?

    _____ **(a).** Law.

    _____ **(b).** Farming.

    _____ **(c).** Clerical copying.

    _____ **(d).** Priests.

2. What name does the author call the new kind of doctor?

    _____ **(a).** The new god.

    _____ **(b).** The junior partner.

    _____ **(c).** The magistrate.

    _____ **(d).** The pope.

3. What phrase is the new doctor fond of muttering?

    _____ **(a).** We really don't know . . .

    _____ **(b).** It's up to you . . .

    _____ **(c).** You should stop smoking . . .

    _____ **(d).** Walking is good for you . . .

4. What do the new doctors have a passion for?

_____ **(a).** Tennis.

_____ **(b).** Golf.

_____ **(c).** Political parties.

_____ **(d).** Education.

5. According to the author, what did we say we wanted from our doctors?

_____ **(a).** That they stop playing so much golf.

_____ **(b).** That they stop treating us like children.

_____ **(c).** That they be religious.

_____ **(d).** That they charge less.

Thinking About What You Have Read

1. The author expands on the characteristics of the new doctor. By implication, what are the characteristics of the old doctor?

2. The author says that the old doctor is likely to be a male. What effect has the increased number of women in medicine had in bringing about the new type of doctor?

3. What pattern of comparison/contrast is used in this essay? Point to specific paragraphs to back up your answer.

4. What transitions does this writer use in this comparison/contrast?

5. Which of the two types of doctors would you rather have? Why?

Writing Assignments

1. Write a comparison/contrast of any two medical people you know—doctors, nurses, dentists, medical receptionists.

2. Write an essay about your doctor.

They Stole Our Childhood

Lee Goldberg

Some comparison/contrasts are more complex than others. This one, for example, compares a generation of kids, as the writer sees them, and the media's image of those kids, especially as seen on television. What generation is he talking about? Kids who grew up in the seventies or eighties? What's different between kids today and those described by the author? What does the title mean? Who stole the writer's childhood? What is so special about the kids portrayed in the television programs mentioned by the author?

We're the wonderful generation. 1

We are the kids who were "so adult" when our divorced par- 2
ents readjusted to the rigors of being suddenly single. We are the
kids who discovered sex so early in our lives and were such overachievers
in school.

We are looked on by our elders with admiration and awe. And yet, if 3
you wipe away the surface gloss, you will find that we are actually victims,
casualties of our parents' need for us to grow up fast. That which we are
praised for is our biggest problem.

Day-to-day family life for us was a contradiction between what we saw 4
on the *Brady Bunch* and *Courtship of Eddie's Father* and what we were actually living. We were supposed to be thinking about the big dance, playing
baseball, getting new handlebars on our bikes, gossiping about our favorite
TV stars and, when our parents weren't around, dressing up in their clothes
and looking at ourselves in the mirror.

Instead we found ourselves not only dressing up in their clothes, but 5
adopting their state of mind as well. We worried about whether mom would
receive her child-support check, whether our parent's date for tonight would
become a breakfast guest tomorrow, whether our little sister would ever
remember what it was like to have two parents under one roof.

Our parents were always so proud of our capacity to make it on our own, 6
to "be adult." Parents were thinking of us less like children and more like
peers. Suddenly we kids weren't being treated like kids anymore.

Part of being adult was not indulging the child in us that hungered for 7
affection. Our generation, it seems, turned to sex for the affection we
lacked at home. As we saw it, needing a hug wasn't very adult. Sleeping
with someone was. It was an acceptable way to ask for the physical affir-
mation of self-worth that we weren't getting from our parents, who we saw
doing little hugging and a lot of sleeping around.

We found that spending more time at school or work was a welcome 8
alternative to going home in the afternoons. The media had taught us that
coming home from school meant milk and cookies, TV and playing with
friends, mom or a babysitter in the kitchen and dad back from work at 6.
Suddenly, going home meant confronting dad's new girlfriend, mom's unpaid
bills or playing parent to our younger siblings and our parents, too.

It's no wonder so many of us, barely into our 20s, feel as though we've 9
already been married and raised children. In divorce, parents seem to
become teen-agers, and the kids become the adults. Many of our younger
brothers and sisters see us more as their parents than their real parents.
As our parents pursued careers and re-entered the dating scene, we children coped by forming our own little mini-families, with the older kids par-
enting for the younger siblings. It was common for single mothers to joke
about how their eldest son played doting father, checking out her dates and

offering sage advice. Or for parents to find their younger kids wouldn't accept candy from them unless an older sister OK'd it first.

Our parents expected us to understand their problems and frustra-   **10** tions, to grasp the complex machinations of divorce proceedings and the emotional hazards they faced by dating again. More than understanding, they even solicited our advice and guidance in these delicate matters. Our parents sometimes pressured us into becoming participants in their divorce proceedings, encouraging us to take sides. We found ourselves having to withdraw from them just to protect ourselves from the potential pain that could be caused by mixed parental loyalties in the midst of court-room warfare.

We were rewarded with approval: "my kids are so grown-up," "my kids   **11** can handle things," "my kids coped so well," "my kids can make it on their own," "my kids are so together." What we missed was a chance to be child-ish, immature and unafraid to admit we didn't have it all together.

We pay the price when we need parents to turn to and don't have   **12** them—as we toil with our first serious relationships and when our long-sup-pressed childish side rears its playful head.

Divorce didn't just split up our parents. It stole our childhood.   **13**

Our parents are paying, too. They ache for the closeness with us they   **14** never had and may never get. They try to grasp memories of our childhood and come up nearly empty. They find themselves separated from their chil-dren and wonder how the gap appeared. Some wake up to realize that they know their gas-station attendant better than their children.

The cure is not to curb divorce. We can start by realizing that this gen-   **15** eration, which may have it together intellectually, paid with its adolescence. What needs rethinking are the attitudes and expectations of parents. Kids who are mature are fine. Kids who are "so adult" need help.

Vocabulary

peers (6)	machinations (10)
indulging (7)	solicited (10)
affirmation (7)	long-suppressed (12)
siblings (9)	

Understanding What You Have Read

Check the correct answer in the blank provided.

1. How, according to the author, was his generation looked on by their elders?

   _____ **(a).** With horror.

   _____ **(b).** With anger.

   _____ **(c).** With pity.

   _____ **(d).** With admiration and awe.

2. What two television programs contradicted the day-to-day family life of the author's generation?

   _____ **(a).** *The Addams Family* and *The Munsters.*

   _____ **(b).** *The Brady Bunch* and *Courtship of Eddie's Father.*

   _____ **(c).** *Star Trek* and *Lost in Space.*

   _____ **(d).** *Maude* and *Growing Pains.*

3. How did parents treat the author's generation?

   _____ **(a).** Like peers.

   _____ **(b).** Like children.

   _____ **(c).** Like scolding babysitters.

   _____ **(d).** Like jailers.

4. What does the author say his generation missed?

   _____ **(a).** Television.

   _____ **(b).** Outdoor sports.

   _____ **(c).** Participation in group activities.

   _____ **(d).** The chance to be childish.

5. What does the author claim his parents ache for?

   _____ **(a).** Closeness with their children.

   _____ **(b).** Money.

   _____ **(c).** Promotion at work.

   _____ **(d).** Responsibility.

Thinking About What You Have Read

1. What paragraph can you point to that suggests a comparison/contrast will be drawn in this essay? What sentence states the purpose of this piece?

2. The writer begins by saying, "We're the wonderful generation." How do you think he means us to read that sentence?

3. What is the basis of the contrast drawn in paragraphs 3 and 4? Sum it up in one sentence.

4. How would you characterize the writer's tone? If he were talking to you face to face on this topic, how do you think he would sound?

5. The writer says the cure is not to curb divorce. What do you think the cure is?

Writing Assignments

1. Write an essay comparing and contrasting the portrayal of family life on television and how it really is.

2. Compare and contrast your family with another family you know well.

Arguing

Tune In to TV, Tune Out to Language

Jack Smith

This essay from a weekly newspaper column presents an informal argument on the damage done by television viewing to the ability to read and write well. Note that the writer's dual purpose—to persuade and to entertain—is responsible for his light treatment of a serious subject. As you read, try to find the single sentence that sums up the writer's position. Ask yourself what combination of reasons and evidence the writer presents to support his opinion. Finally, determine whether he persuaded you to his point of view.

A recent nationwide survey shows that children 10 to 14 think television influences them to have sex before marriage, to regard money as the main goal in life, and to make them disrespectful of their parents. **1**

It is thought-provoking to hear from children what everybody else already knows—that television is bad for you. **2**

Movies on television such as "Indecent Proposal," in which multimillionaire Robert Redford offers a young married woman $1 million to spend one night with him (and she does), tend to support such conclusions. **3**

I think television is not only corrupting our moral behavior, but also degrading our language. It is shocking that shows that have more obscene language than a Marine Corps barracks are hailed. **4**

I have no doubt television is partly to blame for the plethora of teen pregnancies. If Michael Douglas and Sharon Stone can do it on the screen outside marriage, why not us? **5**

But I am against censorship. TV movies are gamy because people like them that way. As I have often admitted, I myself like a good sexy movie, though I've had it with screen violence. **6**

I certainly wouldn't like to see TV go back to the morality of the Hays Office, when a sexual encounter was suggested by wind blowing the curtains, but a little restraint wouldn't hurt. **7**

The damage goes deeper than sexual morality. It's my opinion that TV movies are damaging our language. People used to read. Now they watch TV. If we learn the language by hearing it, and not by reading it, the language will suffer. **8**

The Times itself, which should be a model of literacy, suffers from this fact. Although newspaper reporters are of necessity more literate than the average plumber, the younger ones may be losing their fine-tuning because of their addiction to television. **9**

Hardly a day goes by that one can't find a misused homophone in the paper. A homophone is a word that sounds like another but is spelled differently and has a different meaning. *Plane* and *plain,* for example. Or *hair* and *hare.* Or *gnu* and *new.* **10**

No one is likely to write *gnu* when he means *new.* or *hare* when he means *hair.* But the homophone error is so common that even more unlikely examples of it may be found. **11**

Recently, a local newspaper (not *The Times*) wrote in a headline that a certain *heir* (not *air*) apparent was giving up the *thrown.* **12**

There is only one explanation for this kind of mistake. When the language is learned by television, one never sees a word spelled. **13**

Most of these errors are so outrageous that you can hardly believe **14** they got past a proofreader. But the old-fashioned proofreader, who wore an eyeshade, chewed tobacco and was armed with a stubby pencil, is no more. Those old curmudgeons may have been grumpy and cynical, but they "gnu" the language. It isn't that we don't have proofreaders today, but they probably aren't grumpy enough.

The Times is about to publish a new stylebook—a manual to guide writ- **15** ers in the use of the language. It will be a miracle of research and judgment. It will advise reporters that 18-year-old girls are not *girls,* but *women;* that the F in *French fries* is capitalized; and that *graffiti* is both singular and plural. It also advises that *forgo* and *forego* are not the same.

However, it does not furnish a list of homophones. As I say, there are **16** hundreds and a mere list would not fix them in a reporter's mind. One must learn which is which by visual experience. By reading.

I used to be a great reader. I read *War and Peace* when I worked on the **17** night desk of the *Honolulu Advertiser.* I read *Les Miserables* in high school.

I have read hundreds of books. But today I am lucky if I read one a **18** month. I am a couch potato.

That is a phrase brought into the language by television. It means a **19** person who is so addicted to the tube he sits there on his couch, like a potato, mindlessly watching TV, commercials and all.

I am also given to "channel surfing," which means using your hand **20** monitor to search through the channels for something sexy or violent, or maybe the latest on O.J. Simpson.

I'm not saying television is all bad. For example, "The Three Tenors" **21** was great. I like old movies, even when sex is suggested by wind blowing the curtains. I love football and tennis.

However, I learned words by reading, so I know the difference between **22** *hare* and *hair* and between *hoarse* and *horse.* And I haven't given up.

Some day, I swear it, I'm going to read the Bible, top to bottom, find **23** out what it's all about.

Vocabulary

plethora (5)   curmudgeons (14)
gamy (6)

Understanding What You Have Read

Check the correct answer in the blank provided.

1. Who were the subjects of the nationwide survey about television?

    _____ **(a).** Everyone.

    _____ **(b).** Women only.

    _____ **(c).** Men over 50.

    _____ **(d).** Children between 10 and 14.

2. What does the author say television is partly to blame for?

    _____ **(a).** The plethora of teen pregnancies.

    _____ **(b).** Low boy scout membership.

    _____ **(c).** The decline of Little League.

    _____ **(d).** Drive-by shootings.

3. What misused word type does the author blame on television viewing?

    _____ **(a).** Nouns.

    _____ **(b).** Verbs.

    _____ **(c).** Interjections.

    _____ **(d).** Homophones.

4. Which one of the novels listed below does the author claim to have read?

    _____ **(a).** *Moby Dick.*

    _____ **(b).** *War and Peace.*

    _____ **(c).** *Gone With the Wind.*

    _____ **(d).** *Ben Hur.*

5. What does the author call himself?

    _____ **(a).** A fool.

    _____ **(b).** A couch potato.

    _____ **(c).** A dedicated reader.

    _____ **(d).** A curmudgeon.

Thinking About What You Have Read

1. What is the author's thesis statement? What about its phrasing might your teacher find objectionable?

2. What evidence does the author offer in support of his thesis statement? What is your opinion of his evidence?

3. This is an informal argument rather than a strictly formal one. If this were intended as a formal argument, how would you evaluate its effectiveness and the quality of its evidence and logic?

4. What effect, if any, do you think television has had on your own reading and writing skills?

5. What is the primary example cited by the author in his argument on the effects of television on reading? Why do you think he chose to focus on this one example? How would you rate this example as evidence?

Writing Assignments

1. Using yourself as your main example, write an essay arguing that television has had a negative effect on reading and writing skills.

2. Write an argument about the good aspects of television.

If I Were a Carpenter

John Balzar

One of the oddities of the education revolution and its prime goal of giving everyone a college education has been a decline in what used to be called vocational tech careers. Going begging are jobs in such practical and necessary occupations as electrician, plumber, and carpenter. Yet, as the author tells us, these skills are in such short supply and in such high demand that they offer extraordinary advantages to those who practice them. The sticking point seems to be that many see these jobs as having low status compared to the white-collar work that college graduates do, often for lower pay. And this snobbery is costing us dearly in valuable crafts workers.

 Make $75,000 a year! Challenging and satisfying work. Be your own **1** boss. Choose whom you want to do business with. Pick your own hours. Let your creative side show through.

If there were such a job listing, you'd think Americans would be tram- **2** pling over each other for the chance.

But actually, it's the other way around. Work like this goes begging for **3** the lack of good people to do it.

Craftsmen who hang a door, install a stove, rewire a circuit box, build **4** a counter top, sheetrock a bathroom, and thatch a Tiki hut are in high demand.

How can this be? **5**

Well, I've been asking that very question as I try to transform the well- **6** worn 47-year-old house we just purchased into a home.

I think blame rests with America's misguided tunnel vision about career **7** values. A generation ago, vocational education earned a bad rap in public schools. Based not on aptitude but on ethnicity or socioeconomic upbring- ing, students were directed either into college prep programs or vocational ed. Surely, this did many children wrong. But instead of fixing the system, educators began pushing everyone into college prep programs. By social consensus we agreed that college was the path to satisfaction, money and, most important, status.

In a recent essay in this paper, Drew Limsky of City University of New **8** York summed up this view. College, he suggested, is "the difference between a white collar and a job at Burger King." That is silly. I personally know at least 10 PhD marine biologists, not one of whom makes $30,000 a year. The *Washington Monthly* recently ran a long, first-person account titled, "Why a PhD is a fast ticket to the unemployment line." The parents of these deadend intellectuals are no doubt proud and still have their "my child is an honors student" bumper stickers.

But more than a few PhDs are wondering about their career choices. **9** Not to mention the many college grads in the same straits, backstabbing each other for footholds in the dreary world of mid-management.

Meanwhile, the social status we confer on craftsmen has not risen to **10** match the importance of their work.

Stories in newspapers describe programs that train juvenile delinquents **11** and ex-cons how to build and fix things around the home. The successful among these students soon will realize that the joke is on society.

When you call for help, they'll respond at their leisure. If they approve **12** of you, they may squeeze in time for your job. They may or may not feel obliged to meet the schedule they promised. They may disappear for days at a time. But if they do a sound job, in the end you'll call them back and recommend them to your neighbors. And if they do a really creative job, you'll do anything to keep them happy and working.

After finally locating a craftsman/contractor worthy of the title, I found **13** myself driving three hours to watch him race his sprint car. I never felt the need to prove my loyalty to my dentist or doctor. But a top-flight craftsman cannot be shown too much respect. And I confess, when he smashed his race car into the wall and flipped, my concern for his welfare was mixed with worry about my half-completed kitchen.

A dear friend of mine has a 20-year relationship with his contrac- **14** tor/handyman and calls him a more important person to the family than even the woman who provides at-home child care. That's because my friend knows that he can replace a child care worker.

A colleague recalled one day when he sneaked away midweek and went **15** surfing at the beach. The lineup was full of adults. "They said they were contractors, plumbers and tile layers," this colleague recalled. "No work was getting done that day, not when the swell was up."

"Personally, I'd never go back," a former corporate vice president told **16** me. After forty years climbing the career ladder, he was laid off. Now he's a handyman. "I'm not responsible for anyone but myself. This work provides instant gratification. You please a customer, and they tell you so. You rarely hear that in the corporate world. Plus, I can pick the people I work for. For most of my life I couldn't do that."

Vocational education may be the wrong thing to call it. Handyman may **17** not be enough of a title. But in this era of fleeting careers, there is something venerable and solid about putting a chisel to wood and getting the cabinet door to close as sweetly as a vault—especially if it gets you to the beach on those good days.

Vocabulary

circuit (4)	obliged (12)
sheetrock (4)	instant (16)
vocational (7)	gratification (16)
ethnicity (7)	corporate (16)
socioeconomic (7)	fleeting (17)
consensus (7)	venerable (17)
marine (8)	vault (17)
craftsmen (10)	

Understanding What You Have Read

1. Which of the following items was NOT mentioned in the author's imaginary job listing?

_____ (a). Make $75,000 a year.

_____ (b). Challenging and satisfying work.

_____ (c). Let your creative side show through.

_____ (d). Work for someone you don't like.

2. According to the author, one reason why craftsmen are not held in high esteem is
   _____ **(a).** America's misguided tunnel vision about career values.
   _____ **(b).** that everything today is done by computer.
   _____ **(c).** the movie industry's constant emphasis on adventure rather than work.
   _____ **(d).** that the country needs more people with PhDs.

3. At one point, the author calls the world of mid-management
   _____ **(a).** exciting.
   _____ **(b).** stressful.
   _____ **(c).** dreary.
   _____ **(d).** dangerous.

4. According to the author, a top-flight craftsman
   _____ **(a).** should be encouraged to finish college.
   _____ **(b).** cannot be shown too much respect.
   _____ **(c).** must be paid as much as a doctor.
   _____ **(d).** does not exist in our country.

5. A former corporate vice president said the following about being a handyman:
   _____ **(a).** "It is grueling work, and I hate it."
   _____ **(b).** "My family makes me do all of their repairs."
   _____ **(c).** "I plan to go back to the corporate world as soon as possible."
   _____ **(d).** "This work provides instant gratification."

Thinking About What You Have Read

1. How important is job satisfaction in your view? Is it more important than making good money to provide your family with the niceties of life?

2. What is your personal attitude toward craftsmen? How important are they to the well being of our society?

3. What is your view of a two-tiered educational system—that is, testing students to see whether they should go on to college or settle for a vocational job? What might be the advantages or disadvantages of such a system?

4. What experience have you had with people who were profoundly unhappy with their jobs? Cite examples and suggest what might be done to improve the situation.

5. What, if anything, can a college education provide to both the white collar person and the craftsman?

Writing Assignments

1. Write an essay describing what for you would be an ideal lifework Your topic sentence should state why the work would appeal to you. For instance, you might write, "The work of a forest ranger appeals to me because it would allow me to work among the splendors of nature."

2. Write an essay in which you either attack or defend a two-tiered educational system that would test students early on in order to prepare them for a vocational school or for the university, depending on their test results.

Credits

TEXT CREDITS

Russell Baker, "The Plot Against People" from *The New York Times* (January 1, 1968). Copyright © 1968 by The New York Times Company. Reprinted with the permission of *The New York Times*.

John Balzar, "If I Were a Carpenter" from *The Los Angeles Times* (July 25, 2001). Copyright © 2001 by Times Mirror Company. Reprinted with the permission of the Los Angeles Times Syndicate.

Tom Bodett, "Wait Divisions" from *Small Comforts: More Comments and Comic Pieces*. Copyright © 1987 by Tom Bodell. Reprinted with the permission of Perseus Books Publishers, a member of Perseus Books, L.L.C.

Bart Edelman, "Black Cadillac" from *Under Damaris' Dress*. Copyright © 1996 by Bart Edelman. Reprinted with the permission of Lightning Publications.

Thomas French, "Long Live High School Rebels" from *St. Petersburg Times* (November 25, 1986). Copyright © 1986. Reprinted with the permission of *St. Petersburg Times*.

Lee Goldberg, "They Stole Our Childhood" from *Newsweek* (March 31, 1983). Copyright © 1983 by Lee Goldberg. Reprinted by permission of the author.

Ellen Goodman, "Doctor-as-God Is Dead, or Dying" from *The Washington Post* (1998). Copyright © 1998 by The Boston Globe Newspaper Co./Washington Post Writers Group. Reprinted with permission.

Bill Husted, "Research Can Beat Making a Frustrating Call to Tech Support" from *The Atlantic Constitution* (April 22, 2001). Copyright © 2001. Reprinted with the permission of the Copyright Clearance Center.

Francisco Jiminez, "The Circuit" from *The Circuit: Stories from the Life of a Migrant Child*. Copyright © 1997 by Francisco Jimenez. Reprinted with the permission of The University of New Mexico Press.

John Leo, "Bullying Broadly Defined" from *The Washington Times* (May 2001): A17. Copyright © 2001. Reprinted with the permission of United Media.

Patsy Neal, "My Grandmother, The Bag Lady" from *Newsweek* (February 11, 1985). Copyright © 1985 by Patsy Neal. Reprinted with the permission of the author.

Joseph T. O'Connor, "A View from Mount Ritter" from *Newsweek* (May 25, 1998). Copyright © 1998 by Newsweek, Inc. Reprinted with the permission of *Newsweek*. All rights reserved.

Michael Ondaatje, "How I Was Bathed" from *Running in the Family*. Copyright © 1982 by Michael Ondaatje. Reprinted with the permission of W. W. Norton & Company, Inc.

PHOTO CREDITS

Index